EUROPEAN BUSINESS

SECOND EDITION

Neil Harris

MACMILLAN
Business

First edition 1996
Reprinted twice
Second edition 1999

First published by
MACMILLAN PRESS LTD
Houndmills, Basingstoke, Hampshire RG21 6XS
and London
Companies and representatives throughout the world

ISBN 0–333–75407–7

A catalogue record for this book is available from the British Library.

10   9   8   7   6   5   4   3   2
08   07   06   05   04   03   02   01   00

Copy-edited and typeset by Povey–Edmondson
Tavistock and Rochdale, England

Printed and bound in Great Britain by
Antony Rowe Ltd, Chippenham, Wiltshire

Contents

List of figures

▌List of tables

■List of abbreviations

AIM	Alternative Investment Market
APEC	Asia Pacific Economic Cooperation
ASEAN	Association of South East Asian Nations
ATM	Automated Telling Machine
BAT	Best Available Techniques/Technology
BPR	Business Process Re-engineering
BENELUX	Belgium, the Netherlands and Luxembourg
CAD	Computer Aided Design
CAM	Computer Aided Manufacture
CAP	Common Agricultural Policy
CD-ROM	Compact Disk: Read Only Memory
CEEC	Central and Eastern European Countries
CET	Common External Tariff
CIS	Commonwealth of Independent States
CIT	Communication and Information Technologies
COMECON	Council for Mutual Economic Assistance
COREPER	Committee of Permanent Representatives
CSFP	Common Security and Foreign Policy
DM	Deutschemark
DTB	Deutsche Terminbörse
EAGGF	European Agricultural Guidance and Guarantee Fund
EAP	Environmental Action Programme
EASDAQ	European Association of Securities Dealers Automated Quotations
EBRD	European Bank for Reconstruction and Development
EC	European Community
ECB	European Central Bank
EC6	The 6 founding members of the European Union (see also EEC)
EC12	The 12 EC members before Austria, Finland and Sweden joined the EU
ECOFIN	The Council of Economics and Finance Ministers
ECSC	European Coal and Steel Community
ECU	European Currency Unit
EEA	European Economic Area

EEC	European Economic Community (see also EC6)
EFTA	European Free Trade Association
EIA	Environmental Impact Analysis/Assessment
EIB	European Investment Bank
EIF	European Investment Fund
EMCF	European Monetary Cooperation Fund
EMEA	European–Mediterranean Economic Area
EMI	European Monetary Institute
EMS	European Monetary System
EMU	Economic and Monetary Union
ERDF	European Regional Development Fund
ERM	Exchange Rate Mechanism
ESC	Economic and Social Committee
ESCB	European System of Central Banks
ESF	European Social Fund
EU	European Union
EU12	The 12 members of the European Union before 1994 when Austria, Finland and Sweden joined
EU15	The present 15 members of the EU
EURATOM	European Atomic Energy Community
EUROSTAT	Statistical Office of the European Communities
EURO X Club	EU countries qualifying for membership of the single currency
FDI	Foreign Direct Investment
FEOGA	French initials for EAGGF above
FF	French Franc
Forex	Foreign Exchange
FMS	Flexible Management Systems
FN	Front National
FSM	Financial Support Mechanisms
FYROM	Former Yugoslav Republic of Macedonia
GATT	General Agreement of Tariffs and Trade
GDP	Gross Domestic Product
GDR	German Democratic Republic (former East Germany)
GFR	German Federal Republic (former West Germany)
G7	The Group of Seven Industrialised Nations
G8	G7 plus new member Russia
G24	see OECD
HRM	Human Resource Management
IBRD	International Bank for Reconstruction and Development (also known as the World Bank)
IGC	Inter-Governmental Conference
ILO	International Labour Office
IMF	International Monetary Fund
JIT	Just in Time
LDC	Lesser Developed Country

LIBOR	London Inter-Bank Offered Rate
LIFFE	London International Financial Futures and Options Exchange
MBO	Management Buy-Out
MEP	Member of the European Parliament
MNE	Multinational Enterprise
MRP	Materials Requirement Planning
MRP II	Manufacturing Resource Planning
NAFTA	North American Free Trade Association
NASDAQ	National Association of Securities Dealers Automated Quotations
NATO	North Atlantic Treaty Organisation
NIC	Newly Industrialised Country
NTB	Non-Tariff Barrier
OCA	Optimum Currency Area
OECD	Organisation for Economic Cooperation and Development (see also G24)
PAYG	Pay As You Go
PC	Personal Computer
PCA	Partnership and Cooperation Agreements
PEST	Political, Economic, Social, Technological
PESTLE	Political, Economic, Social, Technological, Legal, Ethical/ Environmental
PIA	Product Impact Assessment
PR China	People's Republic of China
PRP	Performance Related Pay
PTAS	Pesetas
QMV	Qualified Majority Voting
RES	Renewable Energy Sources
R&D	Research and Development
ROMP	Radical Office Mobility Programme
SEA	Single European Act
SEC	Single European Currency
SF	Swiss Francs
SLD	Democratic Left Alliance (Polish political party)
SLIM	Simpler Legislation for the Single Market
SME	Small and Medium Sized Enterprise
SWOT	Strengths, Weaknesses, Opportunities, Threats
TQM	Total Quality Management
USSR	Union of Soviet Socialist Republics (also called the Soviet Union)
VAT	Value Added Tax
VER	Voluntary Export Restraint
WEU	Western European Union
WTO	World Trade Organisation

CHAPTER 1

The European business environment

■ 1.1 Introduction

This chapter explores what is meant by the term European business and what constitutes the environment in which it currently operates. This includes an analysis of the economic, political, legal, cultural and other factors which determine this environment. The recent economic performance of different European Union countries is reviewed and compared with that of the EU's main competitors, the US and Japan, to determine the relative strengths and weaknesses of the EU as it moves to a single currency. Finally, international organisations which have a major influence on EU countries are examined. This covers bodies such as the IMF, the World Bank, G8 and the World Trade Organisation. The financial crisis of the Southeast Asian economies, and its impact on the EU, is examined as a case study.

■ 1.2 What is European business?

European business is a generic term which describes a very wide variety of agricultural, industrial and service activities undertaken by a large number of different organisations across the continent of Europe. Examples of European business might include:

- privatised telecommunications companies such as Germany's Deutsche Telekom and Italy's Telecom Italia;
- a French recording company based in a converted barn in Normandy, France;
- a farm in Eastern England, highly mechanised and engaged in agribusiness;
- a transnational organisation such as the German car producer Volkswagen, with factories in Germany (VW and Audi), Spain (Seat), the Czech Republic (Skoda) and the UK (Bentley);
- US and Japanese banks in the City of London or Frankfurt or Zurich, which operate worldwide 24 hours a day;
- stock markets in Prague, Moscow or Brussels;
- an extended family who live in Crete, farm olives and vines and own a small fishing boat;
- major international brewers like Carlsberg of Denmark, or the clothing manufacturer Benetton of Italy;

1

- a football club such as England's Manchester United, floated in 1991 and now with a market capitalisation of £625m, following the takeover bid by BSkyB;
- the Airbus consortium currently owned by British, German, French and Spanish businesses but soon to be launched as a joint stock company.

A European business may be run by one person or it may be a small private company. Alternatively it may be a large organisation employing thousands of people, with assets worth hundreds of millions of euros and based in many different European countries. The US company International Business Machines (IBM) is such an organisation; so a European business doesn't even have to be European owned. A European business may be publicly quoted on the stock markets of Europe. Examples of this include the Netherlands bank ABN-Amro Holdings, the German chemicals company BASF, the Spanish electrical and electronics company Acerinorox, and the paper and packaging company Smurfit (Jefferson) of Ireland. Or it may be large and powerful and yet a private company, such as the Dutch-owned retail chain C&A, or the British Virgin Group. Finally a European business may be state-owned, such as the non-privatised businesses still remaining in Central and Eastern European countries (CEEC), for example the largely Russian state-owned monopoly gas supplier Gazprom, or major Western European businesses such as the French bank Crédit Lyonnais, or Air France or the Spanish airline Iberia.

Against this disparate background a number of common threads may nonetheless be drawn. European businesses are important as creators of wealth and employment. Economic theory identifies profit maximisation as the prime objective of private sector organisations. If this is achieved then all other issues such as minimising production costs and most efficient use of resources will follow automatically. In reality, however, profit maximisation is not the only motive. When there is a downturn in the business or economic cycle, as in the early 1990s, the desire of non-state-subsidised businesses merely to survive may override this. At other times businesses may merely act as profit satisficers, with their managers being content with achieving an adequate return on capital invested by shareholders rather than seeking to maximise returns. Subsidised businesses may be content to make losses safe in the knowledge that the government will bale them out. This is one strong argument for privatising such industries.

■ 1.3 The European business environment

European business environment refers to the conditions within which European businesses operate. Typically it involves a number of different interacting forces which shape the environment, and thus how a business formulates its long-term strategy, its tactics and its daily operations within this environment. These factors may include political, economic, social, cultural, religious and linguistic forces. Figure 1.1 illustrates them.

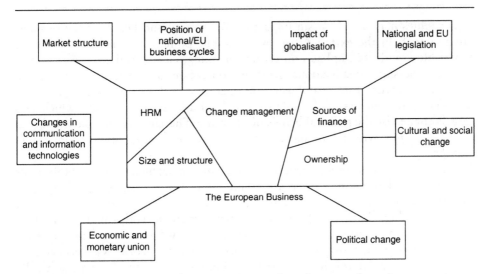

Figure 1.1   The European business: internal and external environments

The strength of each of these, and their interaction with the others, will vary between countries. Consequently the behaviour of European businesses will similarly need to vary in response to these forces. The individual characteristics of each business, such as who owns it, its ability to manage change and its human resource management (HRM) policies will, in turn, make its precise response distinctive to it alone.

One tool which can be used to appraise a business's environment is a PEST analysis or a PESTLE analysis where:

P   Political factors influencing a business environment
E   Economic factors
S   Sociological influences
T   Technological influences
L   Legal factors
E   Environmental/ethical issues

This framework is used below to analyse the European business environment.

■ Political

The political beliefs of governments and the policies they implement to pursue them have a major impact on the European business environment. This is both in their own right and also through other policies, such as economic ones – hence the re-emergence of political economy in recent years. Additionally, other political philosophies may also have an impact on EU society and hence on the business environment. In the extreme case the economic policies pursued by the former Soviet bloc, with its emphasis on central planning, clearly had a massive impact on the ownership, organisational structure, operations and lack of profitability of government-owned European businesses operating in this area. Similarly, the UK Thatcher governments of the 1980s created a business environment which was largely shaped by the political beliefs of Margaret Thatcher and her close political advisers – and which has subsequently influenced many other countries in Europe.

In times of high unemployment or other economic problems Europe sadly seeks scapegoats and sometimes these are ethnic minorities – even though frequently undertaking jobs in which the indigenous population is not interested. In the past this would have been the Jews; in Germany more recently migrant Turkish workers have been attacked, in France North Africans have become the focus for hostilities, while the most extreme case since the Second World War has been the 'ethnic cleansing' of Muslims by Serbs in Bosnia, which the EU so shamefully failed to address.

Often persecution is on a small albeit organised scale, for example the neo-Nazis of Eastern Germany and links with extremist soccer supporters in other countries. Extremism also breeds political parties who seek to legitimise their racism. In France the neo-fascist Front National (FN), led by Jean-Marie Le Pen, is a classic example, albeit at the local government/regional level, of politicised racism. In the southern French town of Vitrolles, for example, power was gained on a policy of law and order, lower taxes and an active policy against immigrants. The local police force has been increased from 35 to 70 and dressed in black uniforms (the traditional fascist garb), while in February 1998 the Front National-dominated local council awarded a gift of FF 800 to every child born in the town of French or EU parents in support of its policy of 'national preference'. Courts later declared this to be illegal. Support for the FN has also recently grown among younger middle-class French who compete with North African immigrants for jobs in an area of high unemployment.

Apart from the moral aspect of racial and religious discrimination, a policy such as that outlined above clearly impedes the effective working of the single market with its promotion of free movement of labour and equal opportunities for all. And although southern France is largely, although not exclusively, dependent on tourism and agriculture, political extremism may hinder potential investors who fear future problems which will affect profitability. This in turn will continue the economic problems of which neo-fascism is a symptom.

As another example of the political impact on the European business environment, before the Italian elections of 1996 Umberto Bossi, the leader of the Liga Nord, caused considerable anger by his assertion that he wanted to make prosperous industrially-based Northern Italy a separate country called Padania. This was to be formed by secession from the rest of Italy of Lombardy, Tuscany and Piedmont and would contain Italy's most important industries, its best agricultural land, most of its financial wealth and such leading cities as

Venice, Turin, Milan and Bologna. Bossi used Northern Italian resentment of rule from Rome and union with the poor, agricultural and crime-ridden Southern Italy as a means to build his power-base. If achieved this would have broken up modern Italy which was finally united in 1870 under the leadership of Giuseppe Garibaldi – hence it would have been a violation of the Italian federal constitution. In the election Bossi secured many less votes than he had hoped for and, realistically, the threat has receded.

■ Economic

The economic policies pursued by EU governments clearly have a significant influence on the environment within which European businesses operate.

Since the signing of the Treaty of Maastricht was completed in 1993 EU economic policy has largely focused on the adoption of a single European currency (SEC) – formerly called the European currency unit (ecu) but now known as the euro – as part of the moves to Economic and Monetary Union (EMU). The commitment by EU governments to meet the Maastricht convergence criteria (see Chapter 3), as a precondition for acceptance to the first wave of membership of the single European currency, has obliged them to demonstrate fiscal restraint to meet the criteria relating to budget deficit (not to exceed 3 per cent of the country's gross domestic product or GDP) and national debt (not to exceed 60 per cent of GDP). The purpose of the convergence criteria, as their name suggests, is to converge potential members' economies to broadly similar levels in terms of the rate of inflation, the level of long-run interest rates, the stability of their exchange rates and, as noted, government debt.

Also implicit in this is the ability of countries to converge to a common position in their business cycles – in practice to converge their business cycles with that of Germany's as the leading EU economy. Figure 1.2 shows the position of various EU business cycles from 1985–99, the growing convergence of the French and German cycles and the divergence of the UK cycle from these. These are measured by the extent to which a country's actual gross domestic product (GDP) exceeds or falls short of its potential GDP – known as the output gap. When actual GDP falls short of potential GDP the negative gap indicates that the economy is in recession. The change in the negative output gap shows if the economy is recovering from recession (the negative value lessens) or getting worse (the negative value becomes greater).

Through convergence, when the single currency comes fully into use in 2002, and the politically independent European Central Bank (ECB) controls monetary policy (particularly the use of interest rates, and possibly the use of a money supply target such as is used by the Bundesbank and as was used by the UK government in the early 1980s), it will, as far as possible, be appropriate to the economic situation of all countries in the single currency zone or euro-zone – or Euroland as it is now being called. Otherwise if, for example, the EU experiences rising inflation the ECB, which is situated in Frankfurt, will raise interest rates to

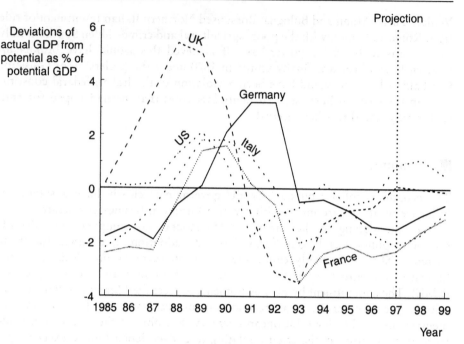

Data from OECD, *Economic Outlook*, December 1997, no. 62. Copyright OECD, 1997.

Figure 1.2   EU business cycles, 1985–99

make borrowing more expensive and hence reduce consumer demand and investment by European businesses. Yet some EU countries, which may not be experiencing these inflationary pressures, or not to the same extent, will still be forced, in the single currency zone, to accept the same interest rates. In the worst scenario, without convergence, a country experiencing recession could still be forced to raise its interest rates at a time when it needed to lower them to promote economic growth.

In practice the problems of non-convergence were demonstrated in the early 1990s when Germany raised its interest rates to counter inflationary pressures. These had resulted from borrowing to fund major expenditure in Eastern Germany to redevelop the infrastructure and productive capacity after the collapse of the communist regime of the former East Germany or German Democratic Republic (GDR). Through the need to keep the value of their currencies stable against the deutschemark, to converge their inflation rates to that of Germany's, other EU countries were, therefore, also forced to raise their interest rates at a time when their economies were in recession and they needed to lower them. Had they not done so speculators, attracted by higher returns in Germany and its superior economic track record, would have moved their funds from France, Italy and so on to Germany. This would have caused the franc and the lira to fall in value against the deutschemark and would have defeated the exchange rate mechanism (ERM) objective of exchange rate stability. Indeed, EU currency crises in 1991, 1993 and 1995 clearly demonstrate the massive impact of the large-scale movement of such speculative funds.

When the single currency is fully in operation, then, as governments meet the Maastricht government debt criteria, they will not willingly raise taxes or cut spending since the Stability and Growth Pact (see Chapter 3) will require them to maintain these criteria. So fiscal policy is likely increasingly to be minimised as an effective policy instrument for controlling EU economies. Longer term there is also the probability of common taxation policies and rates, even though the Commission argues this is not on the current economic agenda. Further, countries will not be able to use their exchange rates as a policy instrument to competitively devalue, that is lower the exchange rate to make exports cheaper – so more are sold – and imports dearer – so less are bought (subject to the elasticities of demand for exports and imports) – to gain a foreign trade advantage and help their balance of payments. This policy option is currently removed by the convergence criterion for exchange rate stability when the SEC comes into operation, by the absence of exchange rates between EU countries which have adopted it.

Therefore monetary policy – the use of interest rates set by the ECB – is the only instrument remaining. If the rate set is adverse to some regions of the EU, then they will have to make adjustments through the labour markets which, currently, are not flexible. In the US if there is high unemployment in, say, Oregon, then people will move to California or New York State looking for work. In the EU labour market flexibility, although technically feasible as one of the four freedoms of the Single European Act 1987, in practice happens only very limitedly. This is partly because some labour markets are rigid through government intervention and restrictions (see Chapter 4), and partly through language and cultural differences. Without labour market flexibility economic adjustments will have to occur through changes in the level of employment. Additionally, large-scale transfers of funds to depressed regions will be required under regional policy.

The purpose of this analysis is to show that, in the 1990s, governments have therefore been constrained in terms of their ability to influence their economies, with a resultant impact on European businesses. The above has clearly had implications for European businesses in that unemployment has been high through the mid to late 1990s in most EU countries (see Chapter 1.7). Partly this has been aggravated by the lack of flexibility in EU labour markets and partly, as discussed above, by the constrained ability to use fiscal policy and devaluation of the exchange rate to boost aggregate demand in economies. Consequently, consumer demand has been low, harming sales, profitability, investment and the ability of European businesses to compete effectively on a global basis.

Also, long-term unemployment can be psychologically adverse for those experiencing it. Furthermore, it is disruptive for society as a whole, breeding in some cases political extremism which, as discussed above, easily degenerates into racism against migrant workers undertaking poorly paid menial jobs in which the indigenous population is not interested. The EU's economic performance is discussed more fully later in this chapter.

■ Sociological

This is examined in three broad areas: culture, language and religion.

□ 1 Culture

The fact is that the British have a totally private sense of distance. This is most visibly seen in the shared pretence that Britain is a lonely island in the middle of an empty green sea. Oh yes, I know you are all aware, in an abstract sort of way, that there is a substantial landmass called Europe near by and that from time to time it is necessary to go over there to give old Jerry a drubbing or have a holiday on the Med, but it's not near by in any meaningful sense in the way that, say, Disney World is. If your concept of world geography was shaped entirely by what you read in the papers and saw on television, you would have no choice but to conclude that America must be about where Ireland is, that France and Germany lie roughly alongside the Azores, that Australia occupies a hot zone somewhere in the region of the Middle East, and that pretty much all other sovereign states are either mythical (viz., Burundi, El Salvador, Mongolia and Bhutan) or can only be reached by spaceship.

(Bill Bryson, *Notes from a Small Island*, p. 32. London, Black Swan Books, 1996)

Culture has been described as 'the way we do things round here'. In this sense it may be viewed as the inherent values, attitudes, social conventions and mores of a nation. In most cases these are transmitted from one generation to another, usually through the family. Increasingly, however, culture is modified by education, the media and peer influences as the pace of change accelerates in modern society. In particular Marshall MacLuhan's 1960s concept of the world shrinking to a 'global village' is increasingly true as a result of cheap international travel, the consequent tendency of many to holiday abroad and the advent of satellite television, computer games and the Internet. This is creating, to some extent, elements of a common American-influenced culture throughout many parts of the world, even in ideological opponents such as the People's Republic of China and Iran.

Nonetheless cultural differences contribute to the diversity of the people who live in Europe and hence are an enriching experience. Cultural differences can also create barriers, however, which in turn have significant implications for European businesses since, if they are to succeed in other than their domestic market, these differences must be taken into account. Among examples of cultural differences are:

The business organisation   In Germany businesses are rigid in their approach and expect everything to done through proper bureaucratic channels with full technical detail provided. In contrast, British firms involved in collaborative ventures, or who have opened subsidiary companies in Germany, are more casual and relaxed enabling them to be more flexible when sudden response is needed to market change. This difference in operational philosophy can cause problems.

Class is also a major factor in determining social attitudes in the business environment, particularly in the UK but also in France and Italy. In contrast, in less class-divisive societies such as Denmark, Sweden and Norway attitudes may be quite different; people such as senior managers' secretaries are regarded as important people in the organisation, whereas in the previously mentioned countries this would not be so to the same extent.

Business attitudes to delivery dates are also important. European businesses operating in Germany soon find that when they promise a delivery date for a new product consumers expect it in the shops on that day, not several weeks later. Firms who have failed to observe this simple rule have found themselves bombarded with telephone calls, letters and faxes soon after. In contrast, in Spain and Greece attitudes are much more casual in this respect.

Personal appearance and behaviour   The French place much emphasis on establishing personal contact in business dealings and expect the people they deal with to have style. The Spanish believe in the importance of being smartly but conservatively dressed and demonstrating worldly knowledge, for example of good cuisine and wine; these are important issues when dining out, attending trade delegation receptions and so on, where business contacts are made. Scandinavians in contrast are much more casual in their dress.

American-owned European businesses are now encouraging staff to move from suits for men and white blouse, black skirt and high heels for women to more casual clothes at least one day per week and increasingly all week. This is perceived to create a more relaxed and efficient working environment, although jeans and T-shirt still tend not to be generally acceptable. Other attitudes and behaviours vary considerably between different EU races. Examples include:

1. the amount of personal body space races give each other: Northern Europeans value personal space more than Southern Europeans – so they will step back if someone stands too close to them;
2. attitudes to clock-watching at meetings: this is acceptable in Germany and the UK but not in Greece or Spain, for example, where it insults other attenders by implying a desire to escape their company;
3. the use of titles in the business organisation: this is most important to the Swedes and Germans (and to Japanese), to a lesser extent to the French but not to the British;

4. the hidden agenda: small talk is important to some races in terms of setting the scene before business is transacted. Other races such as the Finns are very direct and prefer to go straight to the issue of the meeting rather than 'wasting time' with trivia first. This is to some extent typical of all the Scandinavian countries and also the Protestant countries of the EU whose nationals tend to be direct and to mean what they say. In contrast, Latin races like small talk, subtleties, and not saying what they mean directly by words but rather by implication;

5. relations with the opposite sex: in France it is always acceptable to flirt with members of the opposite sex since this makes life interesting. In the UK and even more so in the US this would be regarded as politically incorrect at least, or sexual harassment at worst.

Cultural training programmes   These differences have implications for the training policies adopted by companies; some European businesses are now adopting recruitment policies where new employees are expected not only to have fluency in more than one language, but also to demonstrate some cross-cultural knowledge. Specialist firms offer cultural training programmes for executives who will be working in particular countries to help them integrate more effectively. In essence any firm needs, therefore, to take cultural differences into account in public relations, in advertising and in its daily running. If it can undertake this cultural analysis and adjust its resulting marketing strategy successfully it can increase sales.

What is crucial to European businesses in the final analysis is that they do not stereotype a nation through the perceived characteristics of some of its population – as the case study opposite does.

☐ 2 Language

In the EU there are currently 13 EU official languages and another 35 territorial minority languages, which include Basque, Breton, Catalan, Cornish, Frisian, Galician, Letzeburgesh, Irish Gaelic, Occitan, Slovene and Welsh. Language above all else defines a group of people as distinct from all others in Europe, since it also implies culture, inherited knowledge and beliefs and terms of reference and thought specific to that group alone. In that sense there is therefore an overlap with the above.

French and Flemish speakers may both be Belgian but they perceive themselves as two distinct groups. The creation of the Czech and Slovak republics; the autonomy granted to the Basque, Catalan and Galician regions of Spain; the linguistic divisions of Switzerland; the referendum decision by Scotland to have its own government with tax varying powers and by Wales to have its own regional assembly – all create market differences. Greek opposition to the use of the name Macedonia by the Former Yugoslav Republic of Macedonia (FYROM) arose from its jealousy over a quintessentially Greek name associated with Alexander the Great, the pre-Christian general. In all these cases and more the divisions are partly linguistic, partly cultural; but firms ignore them at their peril. For example,

CASE STUDY   Differing EU Perceptions of Each Other

- France and Britain are fundamentally different countries with quite separate working practices, according to a joint research report by INSEE, the French statistical institute, and the UK's Office for National Statistics, published in *Social Trends*, January 1998. Both nations have similarly-sized and aging populations and gross domestic product. In the workplace, however, the British are likely to work longer hours, or at the weekend, with British males in full-time employment working the longest hours per week in the EU, at 45.8 hours, compared with a French figure of 40.6 hours. The British are also less likely to strike, less likely to live in local authority-provided housing, and receive less generous social security payments. Tourism is skewed with the British visiting France 6.3 million times in 1996, compared with French visits to the UK of 1.7 million. British visitors to France spend five times as much money as French visitors to the UK. 56 per cent of British think learning a foreign language is important compared with 87 per cent of French.

- A survey by Sofres pollsters, published in *Le Monde* in November 1997, exploring the two nations' attitudes to each other, found that while more than 50 per cent of French citizens had a 'largely favourable' view of the British, only 35 per cent of British felt the same way about the French, while 20 per cent declared 'antipathy' towards them. Over 33 per cent of the 1000 British respondents described the French as 'arrogant', 25 per cent described them as 'cold and distant', while 10 per cent said they were 'greedy and hypocritical'. Less than 8 per cent of British considered the French 'resourceful, amusing or courageous', while only 7 per cent regarded honesty as a French trait. The best aspect of French life was identified by the British as the French sense of knowing how to enjoy life, while the French regarded the best aspects of British life as the monarchy, pubs and afternoon tea.

- Germans view the British as polite, conservative and chaotic while the British perceive Germans as aggressive and humourless people who seek to dominate hotel poolside sunbeds with their beach towels, according to a report in the February 1998 edition of *Psychologie Heute* (*Psychology Today*). After more than 50 years, the Second World War is still a major theme in the UK in films, TV and the press with Germans being presented as aggressive, reinforcing this national stereotyping.

- The above report also discusses a project which has been started by Stefan Schmid, of Regensburg University, to prepare German exchange students for living in Britain. He concludes that British managers only give direct orders occasionally and use elaborate courtesy to convey what they want done, causing Germans not to understand what is required of them. He also notes that the British quickly switch to the use of first names but this is politeness not real interest – whereas Germans often mistake it for friendship. Handshakes are a normal greeting in Germany whereas this is exceptional in the UK. Also the dress code at work in the UK, although unstated, is often strict.

- German academics perceive student exchanges to be the most effective way of breaking down cultural stereotyping. The Goethe Institute commissioned a survey of 1300 British school students aged 14–16 years, divided into four groups according to the closeness of their contact with Germany and the German language. Those who had not been to Germany perceived them as arrogant and nationalistic, whereas those who had been saw Germans as friendly, polite and hardworking.

the people from the Basque province of Spain regard themselves first as Basques and secondly as Spanish. Their language, very different from Castilian Spanish, gives them this separate identity.

The ability of business persons to be bilingual or multilingual is of major importance in breaking down barriers for several reasons:

1. It enables a trader to speak to potential partners in their own language, which creates an excellent impression.
2. In negotiations it precludes the opportunity for potential customers to discuss issues in front of the exporter's group without the latter understanding.
3. It gives competitive advantage over those who cannot speak the language.

One aspect of global communications which has caused concern in recent years is the widespread adoption of English and American English vocabulary into other languages through the impact of computing terminology, the Internet, American films and satellite-TV programmes. European countries such as France, Germany, Spain and Russia have all become worried that the purity of their languages are being diluted by the widespread importing of English and American English.

CASE STUDY   Maintaining the Purity of the French Language?

In France, in 1996, *Le Figaro* newspaper argued that American English and English words which are now part of the French language should be given a French spelling to counter the spread of the so-called Franglais. Words which would be converted include Le parking (le parquingue); Le pull-over (le pule-au-vers); Le baby-boomer (le bébébumère); Le football (le fûtbol); Le sandwich (le sandouiche) and Le shampoo (le champ-oü). In contrast English (both from the US and the UK) is probably the fastest changing language in the world and readily borrows from other languages without problem. *Le Figaro*'s response fails to recognise the impact of global communications; 94 per cent of French students now choose English as their second or third language, at the expense of Spanish, German and Italian.

☐ 3 Religion

In the traditional Catholic countries of Europe, particularly Eire, Italy, Poland and Spain, the impact of formal organised religion on society and hence business is very important. Past controls on the sale of contraceptives in Eire is one such example. In Poland the Catholic church has a vital role to play in the political scene with all parties having a commitment to Christian values in their policies. In Southern Italy the church has traditionally been a focal point for opposition to the Mafia, which has helped stifle economic reform in traditionally agrarian areas and has also syphoned off large amounts of funding from the European Agricultural Guidance and Guarantee Fund (EAGGF or FEOGA to use its French initials), which administers the Common Agricultural Policy (see Chapter 2.5: The work of the Court of Auditors). Although the Catholic church has now been disestablished in Spain it still plays an enormous role in the culture of society.

Although in Northern Europe the Protestant churches do not generally have the same influence or tradition as the Catholic church in Southern Europe, still their influence does exist and businesses should be sensitive to them and to the European nationals who make up their congregations. A Benetton advertisement of a catholic priest and a nun kissing was found to be offensive by many in non-Catholic countries as well as in the Catholic states. Similarly in 1998 Volkswagen (VW) cars had to withdraw a series of billboard advertisements from France after the threat of being sued for FF3.3m by the Roman Catholic Church to compensate for damages suffered by Christians. The series of advertisements, promoting a new model of the VW Golf, compared it to a religious revelation – 'After he saw the new Golf [Saint] Francis [of Assisi] was converted', as the headline above reads – and showed Jesus Christ recommending it to his disciples at the Last Supper shortly before being crucified. Following the legal threat VW declared 'we have no disrespect for the fundamental values of society nor for the beliefs of the faithful. We decided to retract the posters immediately to show our respect for the faith and the feelings expressed by certain believers.' VW also made a substantial donation to a charity chosen by the Catholic church.

Businesses must also bear in mind that increasingly the EU is becoming a society of many faiths. Certainly the large number of Jews resident in Europe has always been obvious. Now however many Muslims have entered EU countries and their religious and moral susceptibilities must also be heeded as much as any other religion.

■ Technological

Clearly technology has had a major impact on the European business environment, particularly information technology. This is discussed in various sections of this book but its impact is so pervasive as to be hard to imagine life without it. This ranges from autopilots on aeroplanes to computer-controlled traffic management systems in our cities; from computer-controlled robots on factory assembly lines to screen trading in stock and foreign exchange markets; from the growth of consumer purchases via the Internet to the use of e-mail rather than conventional letters or faxes. Crucial to this is the concept of information both as an output and as an input. In this sense Bill Gates of Microsoft has argued that the Internet will in effect act as a market-maker, bringing together buyers and sellers with minimum friction – and not just for goods and services but also in the labour market. In practice the perfectly competitive market with its assumption of perfect knowledge will come nearer.

In 1994 the EU set up a first policy framework for the EU information society. This proposed initiatives to regulate the information society: it sought to bring together all those involved in creating networks, applying information technology and establishing the basic services; and it sought to raise public awareness about information technology. Most of these have now been implemented or are in the process of being implemented. In December 1997 the Commission published a Green Paper on the convergence of telecommunications, the media and information technologies, including the speed of such convergence and its impact on the single market. It also proposed a directive to provide significant protection for intellectual property particularly on-line services, the Internet, CD-ROMs, and digitisation – in other words to provide a level playing field as with other single market legislation. All of this has significant implications for European businesses by shaping the environment within which they operate.

■ Legal

Inevitably legal systems can differ significantly from European country to country both in terms of their content and how they are interpreted. At the one extreme in Russia, transformation has required work, in the 1990s, to develop a legal system to come to terms with the concepts of private property (particularly ownership of land) and the legal existence of private and public limited companies with the ability to hire and dismiss labour, enter into contracts, buy, own and sell assets and so forth. At the other extreme, in the EU, Union legislation applies to all member countries and is establishing elements of a common legal framework for all, even though individual countries still, of course, have their own laws. It is based on the key treaties – the Treaty of Rome 1957, the Single European Act 1987, the Treaty of Maastricht 1993, and the most recent Treaty of Amsterdam 1998; the regulations, directives and so on passed by the Council and the Commission (see Chapter 2); and case law through the interpretations of the European Court of Justice. All of these will directly affect European businesses.

EU law is based on the codified law model (either Napoleonic or developed individually) because this is the legal system used by the original EC6, although it has had to adapt as new countries have brought in new legal systems, for example the UK. As such, these differences impact upon the rights and obligations of individuals and businesses as legal identities (known as substantive law), the drafting of laws, the structure of courts in the different countries and the precise meaning of legal terminology in different languages. The main influences of a country's legal system on a business are through their impact on the business's marketing mix and the laws affecting competition. For the EU most legal systems are based on civil law, that is detailed rules and regulations which are strictly interpreted. In the UK, in contrast, the legal system is based on common law which is determined by past precedent and is more flexible in its interpretation.

In terms of marketing a product EU countries tend to be more regulated than say CEEC because the latter are only now experiencing western marketing methods. For example tobacco companies advertising their products have found significant differences within Europe regarding legal constraints. In Greece, Denmark and the UK attitudes to tobacco advertising have been quite liberal, although in late 1997 the UK government imposed tighter controls on tobacco advertising, with the exception of Formula 1 racing in case the UK Grand Prix was transferred to the Far East where tobacco sponsorship is permitted. This is more in line with most other countries where there is a desire to ban tobacco advertising completely. In CEEC, where heavy tobacco consumption is more common, legislation is much more lax.

Regarding competition national governments pass legislation to ensure that private monopolies or cartels do not prevent other firms from entering markets. Nonetheless, this has not stopped governments from operating state monopolies nor subsidising them heavily. The French government's constant subsidies to the ailing bank Crédit Lyonnais is an example of this. Overarching this is EU competition policy developed largely in the Treaty of Rome which all of the 15 EU countries (EU15) must enforce through their courts.

In essence, then, the implications of this are that different EU countries operate legal systems with different philosophical foundations and, hence, since legal systems are nationally based, the same issue may be treated in different ways in different states. At times, of course, legal systems are used to national advantage against other EU members. If political union does come about in time then moves towards one legal system, shared by all nations, will have to be implemented. In the meantime current EU legislation provides an overarching framework which seeks to ensure some consistency in areas such as competition policy, environmental issues and so forth.

■ Environmental and ethical issues

These are also discussed in detail elsewhere in this book so are not explored in depth here. However, it should be noted that in terms of environmental issues the impact of global warming is already having an effect on the operations of European businesses, partly in response to consumer pressures and partly because of the actions of the EU. For example the Community's Fifth Action Programme, intended to provide guidelines for member states, argued that environmental costs be included in the prices of goods and services – the so-called 'green' levy – to reflect the principle of 'the polluter pays'. However, the Commission insists that these should not be used as an unofficial tariff barrier against the products of other countries in the single market.

In terms of ethical issues this is not yet a major item on the EU agenda, with other areas taking precedence. However, the issue of corporate governance is likely to assume greater importance in future particularly with issues such as the directors of privatised companies and, in the UK, demutualised building societies awarding themselves substantial pay increases and share bonuses, in Germany concerns over opaque accounting systems, and in France problems of cross-shareholdings. Again these are discussed more fully elsewhere in this text.

■ 1.4 The changing political and economic face of Europe

The map of Europe changed more in the early 1990s than at any other time since the late 1940s, essentially due to the collapse of communism in Central and Eastern Europe and the breakup of Yugoslavia and Czechoslovakia.

If a map of Europe were to be examined in 1988 it would show the 12 members of the EC (known as the EC12 for short), consisting of Belgium (B), Denmark (DK) France (F), Germany (D), Greece (GK), Ireland (IRL), Italy (I), Luxembourg (L), the Netherlands (NL), Portugal (P), Spain (E), and the UK (UK). (The EU abbreviation for each country is shown in brackets after its name in the previous sentence; hence D represents Deutschland, the German name for Germany, and E España, the Spanish name for Spain.)

The CEEC (Central and Eastern European Countries) were dominated by the might of the Union of Soviet Socialist Republics (USSR). In 1988 this included the now independent Baltic republics of Estonia, Latvia and Lithuania. Additionally Czechoslovakia and Yugoslavia were countries united politically even if not in other ways. In contrast there were two Germanies, East Germany or the German Democratic Republic (GDR), and West Germany or the German Federal Republic (GFR).

In contrast Figure 1.4, the current European map, shows that the EC12 has now become the 15 members of the European Union (EU15) including the new members Austria (A), Finland (SF for Suomi Finland) and Sweden (S) who joined in 1994. The USSR has been replaced by a number of independent countries, some of which are linked together under the banner of the Commonwealth of Independent States (CIS). Czechoslovakia has split into the Czech Republic and Slovakia, while Yugoslavia has fragmented into Serbia, Croatia, Bosnia-Herzegovina, Slovenia, the former Yugoslav Republic of Macedonia (FYROM) and Montenegro. Serbia and Montenegro together still retain the name of Yugoslavia. The GDR, flourishing and seemingly the most powerful of the CEEC, both economically and militarily in 1988, became the five Länder (provinces) of Eastern Germany.

Such changes have also been accompanied in CEEC by the movement from centrally-planned to market economies. These are explored in some depth in Chapter 5. What is clear, however, is that these changes have posed considerable adjustment problems for the businesses of Western Europe and Scandinavia, but also considerable opportunities.

Key:
B   Belgium
L   Luxembourg
NL   Netherlands
Switz   Switzerland
UK   United Kingdom

Shaded area denotes the EC 12

Figure 1.3   Map of Europe, 1988

What Figure 1.4 does not show is how the centre of political and economic power has shifted eastward within Europe. With the capital of West Germany in Bonn, the Bonn–Paris axis was the most important alliance underpinning the European Community. With the shifting of the German capital back to Berlin and the development of the market economies of Central and Eastern Europe, the focus of power has now shifted eastward. Current applications for European Union membership by the Czech Republic, Estonia, Hungary, Poland and Slovenia reinforce this.

Most importantly, of course, the fundamental difference of the 1990s has been the economic, political and military reunification of the continent of Europe after divisions dating from 1945. The collapse of communism, the 1991 ending of

Key:

A	Austria
B	Belgium
Czech Rep.	Czech Republic
FYROM	Former Yugoslav Republic of Macedonia
L	Luxembourg
NL	Netherlands
Switz	Switzerland
UK	United Kingdom

Shaded area denotes the EU 15

Figure 1.4   Map of Europe, 1998

COMECON (the Council for Mutual Economic Assistance – the Soviet-led trading bloc for Central and Eastern Europe), and the demise of the Warsaw Pact (the military alliance of the USSR and Central and Eastern European countries established to counter NATO), the CEEC applications for EU membership and the eastward expansion of NATO (the North Atlantic Treaty Organisation) to include countries of Central and Eastern Europe all mean that Europe has the first real chance to unite for nearly 60 years. The eastwards expansion of NATO runs parallel with the eastwards expansion of the European Union. Poland, Hungary and the Czech Republic hope to become members soon while the US president also signed a formal Charter of Partnership with the Baltic

Republics of Estonia, Latvia and Lithuania in January 1998 laying the basis for their potential future membership of NATO.

■ 1.5 The main economic groupings within Europe

■ The European Union (EU)

Founded as the European Economic Community (EEC) under the Treaty of Rome, which was signed in March 1957 and came into force in January 1958, it consisted originally of Belgium, the Netherlands and Luxembourg (a customs union known as Benelux), France, West Germany and Italy. In July 1967, as a consequence of the Merger treaty signed in April 1965, the EEC, the ECSC (European Coal and Steel Community, created by the Treaty of Paris 1951 which entered into force in 1952), and Euratom (the European Atomic Energy Community also founded by the Treaty of Rome 1958) collectively became the European Community (EC). This name was used until November 1993.

In 1973 Denmark, Eire and the UK joined the EC; Norway voted in a national referendum not to take up its negotiated membership and so stayed outside. In 1981 Greece joined the EC. In 1982 the people of Greenland, who had joined the EC in 1973 as a part of Denmark, voted to leave. This came into effect in 1985 with Greenland being given the status of an associated overseas territory. In 1986 Spain and Portugal became the eleventh and twelfth members. The reunification of Germany in 1991 brought the former German Democratic Republic (GDR) or East Germany into the EC.

In November 1993 Germany became the last nation to ratify the Treaty on Union (also known as the Treaty on European Union or, more commonly, the Treaty of Maastricht, after the Dutch town where it was negotiated in December 1991), and the European Community consequently became known as the European Union. The Treaty of Amsterdam, agreed at the EU summit of July 1997 and ratified in 1998, further extended Maastricht albeit not to the extent originally intended. In March 1994 Austria, Finland and Sweden successfully negotiated membership of the EU and joined on 1 January 1995, taking it to 15 countries. Again, in a national referendum, the people of Norway voted not to join the EU after the Norwegian government had successfully renegotiated admission.

This process of enlargement is ongoing, however. As part of Agenda 2000, the EU's vision of how it will develop as it enters the twenty-first century, six countries were authorised by the Luxembourg summit of December 1997 to begin negotiations for full membership of the EU. These are the Czech Republic, Estonia, Hungary, Poland, Slovenia and Cyprus. Additionally, five other states have been told their applications will be considered later. These are Bulgaria,

Latvia, Lithuania, Romania and Slovakia. Turkey has also applied for EU membership for a number of years, but without success as yet.

■ The European Free Trade Association (EFTA)

With the accession of the three new members to the EU in January 1995 EFTA was decimated. It now consists of Iceland, Liechtenstein, Norway and Switzerland and is a free trade association. Its membership had contracted previously when the UK and Ireland left it to join the European Community in 1973 and when Portugal followed in 1986.

Initially established in 1960 to provide a forum for Western European countries which were not EC members, EFTA sought only to remove tariffs on trade in industrial products between its members. It never required its members to charge common import duties on goods from outside EFTA, in contrast to the EU which had required its members to do precisely this (known as the Common External Tariff). It also had a very small bureaucracy to administer its affairs, again unlike the EU. In recent years EFTA has largely been regarded as a half-way house for potential EU membership, a function it has now largely fulfilled.

■ The European Economic Area (EEA)

Signed in October 1991 the agreement to create the EEA originally proposed to encompass the 12 nations of the European Union and the then 7 countries of EFTA. However, a Swiss referendum voted against membership and so the EEA covers the remaining 18 countries. Its aim was to create the world's largest common market, with a total population of 380 million consumers.

The EEA extends to all its member countries the four freedoms offered by the EU's internal market, that is, the freedom of movement for goods, services, capital and labour. This includes such measures as removal of the technical barriers to trade in goods, simplification although not full removal of border controls between the EU and EFTA, the ability of service sector organisations to trade throughout the EEA on the basis of a licence granted in one country, and cooperation over such policy issues as mergers, state aid, company law, consumer protection, the environment and social policy. The EEA came into force on 1 January 1994. Since 1995 there has been a reinforcing of political dialogue between the two sides.

There is a clear logic for the creation of the EEA in that 58 per cent of EFTA exports are to EU countries and 26 per cent of EU exports are to EFTA.

■ The Commonwealth of Independent States (CIS)

When Boris Yeltsin announced the formal dissolution of the Union of Soviet Socialist Republics (USSR) in 1991, following the defeat of the August 1991 coup and Mikhail Gorbachev's fall from power, as many problems were created as had just been ended. The economic and political interdependence which had existed between the 15 members of the former Soviet Union could not be suddenly set aside. The continuing presence of Soviet troops and Russian populations in all these countries, the dependence on each other for markets for exports and sources for imports, the continuing use of the rouble to finance trade, and a host of other factors meant that the countries were still locked together by fact if not by name.

Although the Baltic republics soon sought and achieved complete independence, to the extent that Estonia is hoping to join the EU within five years, the other 12 countries saw advantages economically and strategically in maintaining cooperative links. Hence the CIS was created as a loose economic and trading bloc with countries maintaining their independence yet benefitting from the advantages of continued cooperation.

Some countries such as Belarus (formerly Byelorussia), Georgia and Kazakhstan, although seeking economic independence and even establishing their own currencies (the quaintly named zaichik or bunny in the case of Belarus), soon realised that they were not strong enough to maintain political and economic independence in the long run. Hence Belarus rejoined the Russia Federation in 1995. To a Russia with some of the older generation, nationalists and unreformed communists still shocked by the loss of an empire and superpower status, such desires are welcome. Indeed Russia has actively sought to make the CIS a much tighter organisation with it exerting much greater control over its former Soviet neighbours. Since Russia is itself also a federation of states it sought to exercise control over its constituents as shown by its 1994 abortive invasion of Chechnya. The latter has now been granted semi-autonomy.

The Ukraine, another CIS member, is viewed by the EU and other western nations as the second most important nation after Russia economically. As Table 1.1 shows it has by far the largest population of former Soviet Union members apart from that of Russia. Its surrender of the former Soviet nuclear weapons it held won it financial aid from the West in the mid-1990s, while further funding has been obtained from such bodies as the IMF and EBRD since then. It has been seen as a useful counterweight to over-dependence on Russia, particularly through the uncertainty arising from Boris Yeltsin's policies and health. Economically the Ukraine has made progress with stabilising its economy. Since 1994 the rate of contraction of annual output has slowed from −19 per cent in 1994 to only −5 per cent in 1997, while inflation has fallen from 400 per cent to just over 12 per cent during the same period. However, structural reforms have continued to be slow, especially privatisation, which hinders future economic recovery.

■ 1.6 EU economic performance

This section briefly reviews the performance of selected EU economies in the context of important economic variables such as inflation, unemployment, economic growth and so on. To avoid swamping the reader with large amounts of data or large numbers of graphs, the information is provided usually for the

EU15, two individual EU countries, and the US and Japan for comparison. The individual EU countries vary from figure to figure, partly to examine interesting data variations and partly to give the reader a perspective of the whole EU rather than just the leading nations.

As discussed previously it is important to provide the US and Japanese data since, although this book focuses on European business, it can only do so in the context of the global economy. As such the EU must constantly monitor and evaluate its performance against its great competitors (see Table 1.2). In ten years' time such countries as the Peoples' Republic of China (PR China), Brazil and Argentina and India will also need to be included in comparisons, such is their economic growth.

Table 1.1   The members of the CIS

COUNTRY	CAPITAL	POPULATION (millions)
Armenia	Yerevan	3.3
Azerbaijan	Baku	7.03
Belarus	Minsk	10.26
Georgia	Tbilsi	5.45
Kazakhstan	Alma Ata	17
Kyrgyzstan	Bishkek	4.3
Moldova	Chisinau	4.34
Russia	Moscow	147.4
Tajikstan	Dushanbe	5.36
Turkmenistan	Ashkhabad	3.6
Ukraine	Kiev	51.7
Uzbekistan	Tashkent	19.91

Table 1.2   The EU and its main competitors

European Union (EU)	Consists of the EU15 with a membership of 370 million consumers. Its ultimate aim is economic and monetary, and political union.
North American Free Trade Association (NAFTA)	This is an agreement liberalising trade between the US, Canada and Mexico. It has 370m consumers and a combined GDP of US $7 trillion. It is a common market with no desire for economic or political union. Chile is now seeking to join.
The Asia Pacific Economic Cooperation (APEC)	This seeks to be a Pacific Basin NAFTA, aiming to achieve trade liberalisation through the creation of a common market.

■ Unemployment rates

Figure 1.5 gives unemployment rates for the EU15, Germany and the UK for 1985 to 1999. It is important to note how EU unemployment has remained at around 11 per cent for most of the 1990s, demonstrating structural economic problems in a number of EU countries including France, Italy and Spain. Germany has also contributed to the high EU figure with the rise in its unemployment in the 1990s partly reflecting the absorption of former East Germany and the shedding of labour by businesses following the large-scale privatisation programme effected by the government-created agency, the Treuhand. The unemployment is also a consequence of Germany struggling to achieve the Maastricht debt criteria and hence having to curtail government expenditure rather than undertake a Keynesian-type programme of macroeconomic expansion.

It is worth comparing these graphs with the unemployment rates of the UK and especially the US, which clearly demonstrates the benefits these countries argue are obtained from more flexible labour markets (see Chapter 4). Japan has very low unemployment rates, with the slight rise in the forecast figures in the late 1990s partly being due to the Southeast Asian economic crisis of 1997–98.

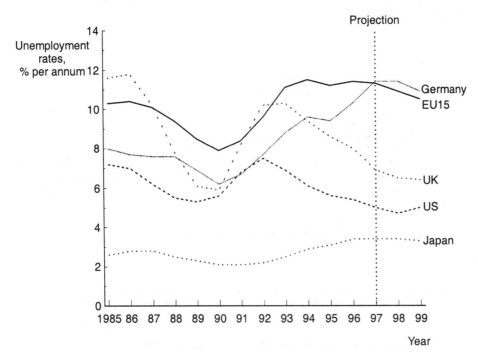

Data from OECD, *Economic Outlook*, December 1997, no. 62. Copyright OECD, 1997.

Figure 1.5   Unemployment rates, 1985–99: selected EU countries and competitors

However, although changing slowly, Japanese business culture still largely expects to provide jobs for life. Japan's high employment figures are also helped by high investment rates, close financing links between businesses and banks (often parts of the same conglomerate), and a long-term perspective rather than the short-term profitability focus of western businesses.

■ Consumer price indices

Figure 1.6 gives consumer price indices which measure inflation in retail prices. The figures show the percentage change from the previous period. The high EU inflation rate until the early 1990s is, in part, distorted by the very high Greek inflation rate, its index increasing by over 300 per cent between 1985–95. Broadly for the EU, and for Austria and the Netherlands, one can see a pattern of low inflation in the late 1980s, rising in the early 1990s consequent on a peak in the business cycle, and then declining from the mid-1990s. This latter decline strongly

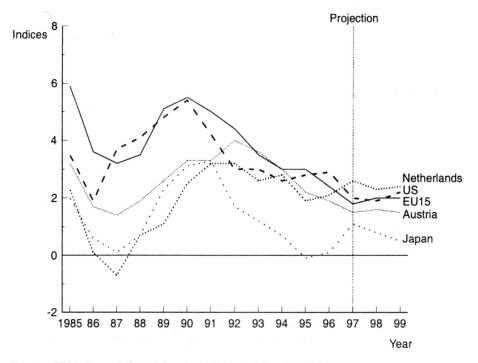

Data from OECD, *Economic Outlook*, December 1997, no. 62. Copyright OECD, 1997.

Figure 1.6   Consumer price indices, 1985–99: selected EU countries and competitors

reflects the linking by EU members of their currencies to the deutschemark, the low inflation currency, and hence pursuing fiscal and monetary policies appropriate to maintaining these exchange rates. The French government's policy of 'Le franc fort', where its interest rates were kept high to maintain the exchange rate parity of the French franc against the deutschemark, and hence to squeeze inflation out of the system by deterring consumer and investment demands when economic recession argued interest rates needed to be lowered, demonstrates this. Linked to this was the issue that, to be a founder member of the single currency, EU countries had to meet the Maastricht criterion on inflation, which requires a country's inflation rate to be no more than 1.5 per cent above the average for the three EU members with the lowest rates during the previous year. The fact that 11 EU countries have met the convergence criteria demonstrates their success in lowering inflation.

The US has also achieved low inflation, considerably due to the expertise of the Federal Reserve Bank, while Japan consistently achieves very low inflation rates over the whole period. Indeed it is fair to say that inflation is declining globally after the excesses of the 1970s and early 1980s, although, regrettably, there is not the space here to explore the reasons for this.

■ Annual growth rates

Figure 1.7 gives real gross domestic product (GDP) annual growth rates for the EU, Sweden and Ireland, with comparisons against the US and Japan. As will be recalled from Figure 1.2 modern economies exhibit cyclical tendencies of approximately 5 years between each peak or trough – these are known as business cycles or economic cycles. For the EU, it will be recalled, the economy peaked in the late 1980s/1990, dipped in the early 1990s and has shown a more steady recovery in the late 1990s, partly helped by large privatisation programmes. What is really interesting is the substantial growth exhibited by Ireland. Helped by major EU regional funding, a liberal corporate tax regime, cheaper labour and large-scale foreign direct investment it has exhibited growth rates in the late 1990s consistent with those of South East Asia – hence its nickname of the 'Celtic tiger economy'. Sweden, which undertook a major paradigm shift in the early 1990s when its welfare state became so resource-consuming as to be unsustainable, has generally been much nearer to the EU average.

US economic growth endorses other aspects of its successful economic performance in the middle to late 1990s, while Japan has, with the exceptional year, been much less successful. Partly this has been through the high value of the yen for much of the decade deterring exports, while the need to deregulate its economy and open it more to foreign imports has caused problems. Japan has also suffered from cheaper labour costs and hence stronger competition from other parts of South East Asia in its export markets. These reasons explain, in part, why it has undertaken heavy foreign direct investment in the EU.

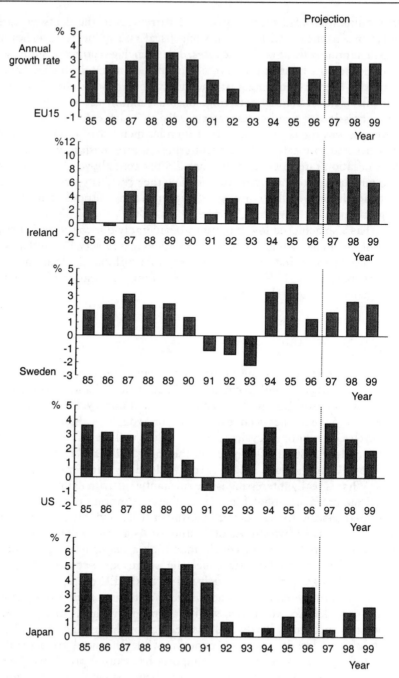

Data from OECD, *Economic Outlook*, December 1997, no. 62. Copyright OECD, 1997.

Figure 1.7   Annual growth rates 1985–99: selected EU countries and competitors

■ Short-run interest rates

Figure 1.8 shows nominal short-run interest rates. These are interesting to view because movements in these both reflect a government's monetary policy and contribute to movements in exchange rates. The reader might like to match interest rates against consumer price indices in Figure 1.6.

S/he will observe that, broadly speaking, there is a downward trend in nominal short-run interest rates through most of the 1990s. The upsurge in German interest rates in the early 1990s was a consequence of inflationary pressures through German reunification. However, since then the movement of rates has been downwards. UK rates dropped sharply after the UK left the exchange rate mechanism (ERM) in 1992, but it has struggled to bring inflation down to continental European levels since it relied on depreciating sterling to offset the effects of inflation rather than being tougher on the causes of inflation. The granting of independence to the Bank of England in 1997 and its resultant ability to pursue a politically independent monetary policy, as well as the need to prepare for possible membership of the single currency after 2002, suggest that, in future,

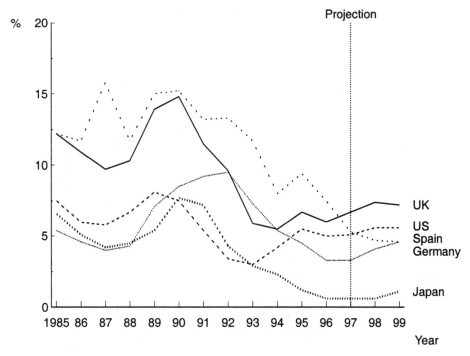

Data from OECD, *Economic Outlook*, December 1997, no. 62. Copyright OECD, 1997.

Figure 1.8 **Short-run interest rates, 1985–99: selected EU countries and competitors**

the UK will adopt a more vigorously anti-inflationary monetary policy. Spanish rates have fallen since 1993 reflecting its efforts to meet the convergence criteria and qualify for the single currency.

Like all other variables, Japanese interest rates are low compared with other countries' rates. US rates were forecast to rise during the late 1990s as the Federal Reserve continued to pursue a pragmatic macroeconomic management policy, essentially to avoid the risks of the American economy overheating; however, in September 1998 the Federal Reserve reduced them. This was to boost consumer demand and business investment in the light of the threatened recession arising from the South East Asian crisis, as well as to stimulate global liquidity.

The Organisation for Economic Cooperation and Development (OECD) and Eurostat (the statistical service of the EU) both provide data for long-run interest rates as well. These reflect, in part, expectations of future rates and are based on government 10-year bond rates. The interested reader may wish to examine these.

■ Current account balances

These consist of the visible balance (goods exported minus goods imported) plus the invisible balance (services exported minus services imported) on a country's balance of payments accounts. Figure 1.9 shows these. In practice they only present half the picture since capital flows are of major importance to many

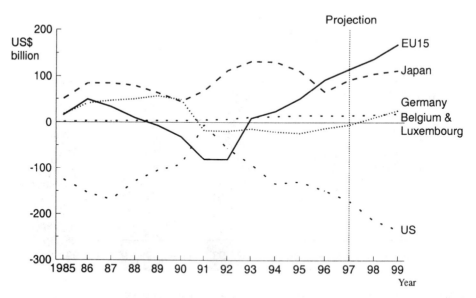

Data from OECD, *Economic Outlook*, December 1997, no. 62. Copyright OECD, 1997.

Figure 1.9   Current account balances, 1985–99; selected EU countries and competitors

countries and so a country's capital account may well offset any current account deficit. Nonetheless the current account is worth examining because of its relationship with a country's exchange rates as well as being a reflection of that country's competitiveness and hence its economic base. So Japan has experienced a substantial surplus throughout the whole period whereas the US has had a current account deficit through the same period. Clearly Japan's surplus has significantly been the US's deficit, although more recently PR China has also been a major source of the US deficit. Germany's deficit of the mid- to early 1990s has been partly through German reunification although increasing imports also reflect declining German competitiveness through high domestic labour costs. It is worth noting that Germany is the EU's primary exporter of manufactured goods. The UK also consistently runs a large current account deficit which contributes to the EU deficit, although its capital account offsets its visible deficit.

■ Gross domestic product (GDP)

This consists of the output of goods and services produced in a country or group of countries. It does not matter who owns the producing plant (for example, Japanese) so long as the goods are produced in the country – so foreign direct investment can have major implications for a country's GDP. Figure 1.10 gives the increase in real GDP for the 'Big 3' for 1994–97, measured in ECU billions. The

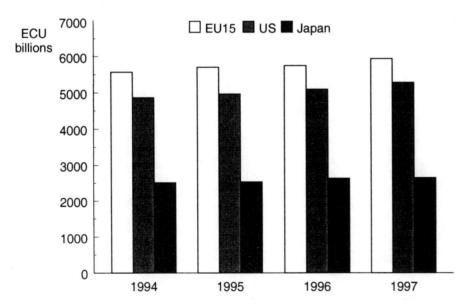

Source: © Eurostat. *Eurostatistics: Data for Short-term Economic Analysis* (May 1998).

Figure 1.10 Gross domestic product, 1994–97: the EU, the US and Japan

EU shows growth of 6.98 per cent between 1994-97, the US 8.76 per cent, and Japan lies in third position with 6.40 per cent.

■ Effective exchange rates

Measured as effective exchange rates Figure 1.11 shows the movement of EU currencies, where 1991 = 100. Each year shows the average of daily rates. The effective exchange is a rate measured not against one other currency such as the US$ but against all other main currencies and expressed as an index number. The more it falls below 100 the more the currency loses its value when traded against other currencies. Whereas an exchange rate against one other currency may reflect developments in that economy, this rate gives a more balanced view since it is measured against many currencies. What Figure 1.11 demonstrates is the strength of the deutschemark and its leading position in the EU during the 1990s. The French franc, linked to the deutschemark by French economic policies, also exhibits similar tendencies. In contrast sterling, the Spanish peseta and the Italian lira, all consistently below 100 for most of the period, reflect weak economic policies in terms of combatting inflation and problems in controlling government expenditure (and in the case of Italy collecting sufficient of the revenue owed it). It can be seen why Germany was concerned about admitting

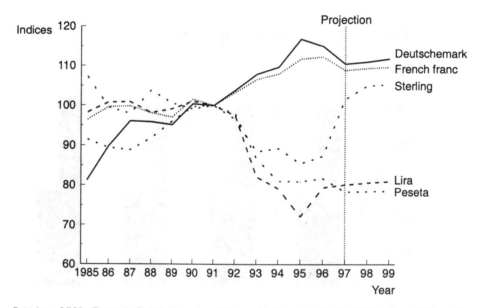

Data from OECD, *Economic Outlook*, December 1997, no. 62. Copyright OECD, 1997. Indices: 1991 = 100; average of daily rates.

Figure 1.11 Effective exchange rates, 1985–99: selected EU countries

Italy and Spain to the first wave of membership of the single currency. The UK solved this problem by refusing to join anyway.

■ **EU trade flows between the three major trading blocs**

Figure 1.12 shows exports and imports, measured in ECU millions, between the EU and its two major competitors for the year 1996. As can be seen the US is the major market for EU exports, which also takes nearly the same amount of US exports. In contrast, trade with Japan shows a significant surplus in favour of the latter. This is partly because Japan operates extensive non-tariff barriers to exclude foreign goods. Also as a cultural issue Japanese consumers do favour domestically produced goods over foreign goods.

The other main export markets for the EU are the Mediterranean Basin countries, to whom the EU exported ECU 72 739m worth of goods and services in 1996 (and imported goods and services worth ECU 49 518m), and the newly industrialised countries of Hong Kong, Singapore, South Korea and Taiwan to whom the EU exported ECU 53 962m of goods and services (and imported ECU 40 486m).

■ 1.7 Transnational and inward investment

Direct investment abroad is important since the dividends and interest payments from direct investment can be a significant source of income to a country

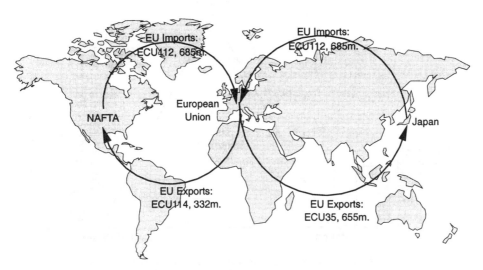

Source: © Eurostat. *Eurostatistics: Data for Short-term Economic Analysis* (May 1998).

Figure 1.12 Trade flows between the three major trading blocs, 1996

offsetting in part, at least, any deficit in its visible trade in goods. Figure 1.13 shows direct investment abroad for 1996. The EU was the world's main exporter of capital, with direct investment totalling $153 812m. The four largest investors were the UK, Germany and France, as shown in Figure 1.13, and then the Netherlands with $21 399m. All other EU countries fall far short of this.

US foreign direct investment only totals 57 per cent of the EU's direct investment but, of course, far exceeds any other individual country the next nearest being the UK. Japan lags far behind and is actually below the levels of Germany and France. During the years 1993–96, US foreign direct investment grew by 52 per cent, and Japanese by 71 per cent. Within the EU Germany's direct investment increased by 73 per cent, the UK's by 65 per cent and France's by 26 per cent.

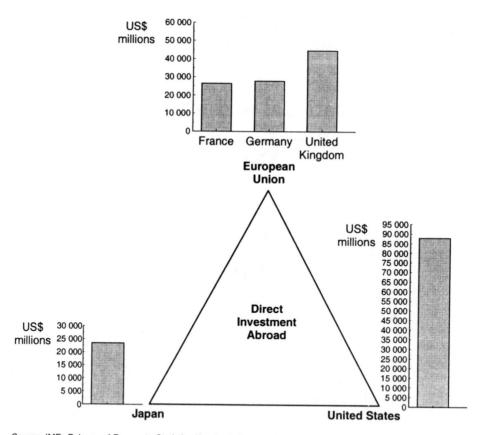

Source: IMF, *Balance of Payments Statistics Yearbook*, Part 2, World and Regional Tables, 1997.

Figure 1.13 **Direct investment abroad, 1996 (US$ millions)**

reduce trade barriers by use of the 'most favoured nation' clause, which said that any benefits one country gave to another must also be given to all other GATT members.

Following the signing in April 1994 by delegates of over 120 countries of the final Act of the Uruguay Round, GATT was replaced by a new body, the World Trade Organisation (WTO). The WTO's prime function is to act as watchdog for the multilateral free trade agreement created by the Uruguay Round of GATT talks.

US opposition to the Peoples' Republic of China (PR China) has prevented the world's largest nation in terms of population, and one of its fastest growing economically, from joining the WTO. This is mainly because its economic reforms still barely reach the minimum required threshold for membership. For example, to liberalise it needs to reduce import duties (often unpublicised and variable in amount), remove subsidies on agricultural exports, cut subsidies to loss-making industries, open its markets in banking, finance and telecommunications to foreign businesses, and improve laws covering intellectual property – especially computer software and music CDs. There are also non-tariff barriers to foreign exports to China such as logistical barriers in getting goods to customers once they enter docks' warehouses after being unloaded. The EU also suffers significantly from these tariff and non-tariff barriers. China's big fear which inhibits it from removing subsidies is that this will generate high unemployment, social unrest and a political crisis. Arguments that China should be allowed in also neglect the fact that the WTO is still establishing its position – accepting such a severe violator of free trade could undermine this.

■ The Group of Eight nations (G8)

The G8 nations are the leading industrial countries of the world and consist of Canada, France, Germany, Italy, Japan, the United States, the UK and, most recently, Russia. The June 1997 meeting, in Denver, Colorado, was the first attended by Russia as a fully accredited member except in economic affairs. Japan has a veto over this, because of the former Japanese-owned Kurile Islands occupied by Russia since the Second World War. The G8 nations' economies have a major impact on each other and on the rest of the world, and consequently their leaders and finance ministers meet at an annual summit to discuss world economic issues.

In the past their meetings have emphasised macroeconomic policies to be pursued; the most famous meeting of G7 (as G8 were then called), in 1987, produced the Louvre Accord. This attempted to stabilise domestic price levels and exchange rates, specifically of the US dollar against the yen and the deutschemark, and reduce large trade surpluses (of Japan and Germany) and deficits (specifically of the US). However, the hype of their meetings has not always matched with the reality of the outcomes. The 1997 summit was largely dominated by the US telling the other countries how to get their economies working as well as the US economy does – when often it has been the other way round!

■ The Organisation for Economic Cooperation and Development (OECD)

This body owes its origins to the Organisation for European Economic Cooperation (OEEC), which was created in 1948 on the prompting of US Secretary of State George Marshall. Its purpose was to enable Western European countries to operate a common programme for postwar reconstruction. When the US provided substantial financial aid to support this cooperation (known as the European Recovery Program or Marshall Plan) the OEEC was the vehicle through which this money was distributed. The Marshall Plan had a large multiplier effect on European economies which laid the basis for rapid postwar economic recovery to occur. In 1961, with the US and Canada as members, the OEEC became the OECD.

Based in Paris, the OECD is an intergovernmental forecasting and coordinating organisation. It has 24 members and hence is also known as the Group of 24 or G24. It consists of the EU15 members, other Western European nations, the US, Canada, Japan, Australia and New Zealand. It therefore retains a strong European bias. Member nations' foreign and finance ministers meet every spring before the annual G8 summit to discuss the state of the world economy. Its importance is that it undertakes impartial surveys of member countries' economies, which may contradict more partisan forecasts by a member government's own forecasters, and offers policy advice based on these. It also addresses key global issues such unemployment; its forecasts are published in its twice yearly *Economic Outlook*.

■ 1.9 Case study: the collapse of the Asian tiger economies – implications for the European Union

■ The origins of the crisis

In 1997 the 'tiger economies' of South East Asia, which had symbolised economic success and efficient production methods during the 1980s and 1990s, were afflicted by economic crisis. Suddenly, issues which had been overlooked, or accepted as part of the way 'they did things over there' revealed a crisis of bad debt with collapsing currency values, recklessly extravagant lending causing bank failures, sharply weakened consumer confidence and substantially weakened stock markets, corruption, undue favouring of family and bad management, often concealed by the network of inter-company alliances and local partnerships.

Asian currencies – for example the Thai baht – had been pegged to the US dollar or to a basket of currencies. Governments intervened to prevent their real exchange rates rising by selling their currencies to buy mainly dollars and by keeping interest rates low – they could then maintain their nominal exchange rates, and their competitiveness. To finance the foreign currency purchases governments borrowed or created extra domestic currency which, in turn, built up large foreign exchange reserves for them. The increased liquidity from borrowing or creating extra domestic currency was then channelled into the property or stock markets. Since exchange rates were fixed, South East Asian companies and banks borrowed cheap dollars and yen but did not hedge, that is insure themselves against exchange rate fluctuations. For example the Thai private sector incurred short-term debts totalling $50 billion.

As Asian economies boomed so imports increased, inflation rose and real exchange rates appreciated causing exports to lessen and trade deficits to increase, and stock and property markets – especially speculative office building – to reach unrealistic and unsustainable heights financed substantially by foreign bank lending. In these circumstances foreign investors ceased their capital inflows or began withdrawing money. In spite of attempts by Malaysia and Thailand to defend their exchange rates by using much of their foreign exchange reserves, exchange rates fell causing Asian borrowers to bear the costs of the fall in the value of their currencies. For example, by December 1997 the South Korean currency, the won, had lost half its value against the US dollar during the year. The stock markets of South East Asia also fell heavily, including Japan, whose banking system has lent heavily to South Korea, Hong Kong, and the London market, especially those banks with heavy exposure to Asia. As discussed above, Thailand, South Korea and Indonesia have had to borrow heavily from the IMF to bail themselves out.

■ The effect on the EU

As has often been said the world is now a global market which means that the crisis has had an impact on the EU, although, at the time of writing, not too severe. Indeed Jacques Santer argued that Asian problems would have only a marginal effect on the EU. In practice this impact has included:

- A contraction of export markets for EU goods which in turn feeds through to a reduction in employment and investment in the manufacturing sector (or an opportunity cost in terms of lost potential growth). Hans Teitmeyer, Bundesbank President, has argued that there will be tougher competition ahead since Asian purchasing power has fallen with German exports of capital goods to South East Asia particularly likely to be hit. However, exports to South East Asia account for only 15 per cent of EU exports – for Japan the figure is 40 per cent.
- An impact on pension funds, especially for the UK – at the beginning of 1998 6 per cent (£34 billion) of funds were tied up in the Far East. The crisis also prompted financial institutions to reduce their shareholdings in UK companies quoted on the stock market which had exposure to Asia – as traders or investors.
- Foreign direct investment from South East Asian countries to the EU faces a significant risk of either delay or cancellation. For example, Hyundai Semiconductors of South Korea deferred investment in its £1.25 billion semiconductor plant in Fife, Scotland.

- Tourists coming to Europe have reduced significantly in numbers while sales in the more expensive department stores in Paris, London, Brussels and so on have been hit – as have duty-free sales at major European airports. However, conversely, cheaper vacations have emerged for EU citizens wishing to take their holidays in the Far East.
- Imported goods from South East Asia should help EU countries' balance of payments positions since the falling value of South East Asian currencies makes them cheaper to buy. In practice these lower prices have not fed through to customers in shops as retailers have taken higher mark-ups rather than pass the benefits to customers.
- Loss of revenue in higher education as South East Asian students can no longer afford to study overseas in the EU – with the resultant loss of revenue to universities and colleges. This has also hit the US and Australia.

■ The position of EU banks

EU banks have been major losers in the Asian financial crisis due to lending too much money at a time when there were warning signs that the bubble was about to burst. The major EU lenders to South East Asian countries have been Germany ($105bn); the UK ($74bn); France ($58bn); Belgium ($24bn); Italy ($17bn); and the Netherlands ($8.3bn). In total, EU banks have loaned over $300bn to South East Asia. (in contrast US banks are owed only $32bn). Of the individual banks France's Crédit Lyonnais is the most exposed (over $30bn), while in Germany the major culprits have been Deutsche Bank, Commerzbank, Dresdner Bank, Bayerische Landesbank and Westdeutsche Landesbank. In some cases up to 50 per cent of their equity capital is at risk.

For the UK the most exposed banks are HSBC and Standard Chartered. To enable debts to be repaid the banks are having to extend loans as the only alternative is to write off the debts, something they were forced to do with bad loans to Latin America in the late 1970s. There has also been criticism of EU banks lending to South East Asia at a time when US banks were pulling out. The impact of this is that some banks will inevitably need government support while domestic lending and growth will be inhibited by the bad South East Asian lending.

The ways in which the IMF and the World Bank have sought to bail out South Korea, Thailand, Malaysia and Indonesia have been discussed previously in this chapter.

■ Review questions

1. Why has the concept of the global economy become so significant in recent years? Why can't European businesses just concentrate on EU markets and not worry about the rest of the world?
2. Discuss why cultural differences are of major importance to businesses seeking custom in other EU markets than their own.
3. What are the implications for European businesses of the proposed growth of the EU to 21 members in the next five years?

4. What is the purpose of the G7 and G8 meetings? Using your library as an information source, discuss what happened at the most recent G8 meetings.
5. Using the data provided in section 1.6, and any other sources you wish, summarise the main trends in EU economic performance in the 1990s. Why should Germany be concerned about its high levels of unemployment?

■ Bibliography

Eurostat. Office for Official Publications of the European Communities (Luxembourg) *Eurostatistics: Data for Short-Term Economic Analysis* (May 1998).

Gilligan, C. and Hird, M., *International Marketing: Strategy and Management* (London: Routledge, 1986).

IMF, *Balance of Payments Statistics Yearbook*, Part 2, World and Regional Tables, 1997.

Nugent, N. and O'Donnell, R. (eds), *The European Business Environment* (Basingstoke: Macmillan, 1994).

OECD, *Economic Outlook*, no. 62, December 1997 (Paris: OECD).

Salvatore, D., *International Economics*, 5th edn (New Jersey, USA: Prentice Hall, 1995).

Also:

The Economist
The European
The Financial Times
The Times
IMF website   http://www.imf.org/
World Bank website   http://www.worldbank.org/

CHAPTER 2

The organisation of the European Union

◾ 2.1 Introduction

This chapter explores briefly the origins of the European Union (EU) and how it has developed from the founding discussions of the early 1950s to its present position as one of the world's major trading groups. The main EU decision-making organisations, which impact on European businesses by the policies they develop, will also be discussed.

◾ 2.2 The origins of the European Economic Community

Following the ending of the Second World War in Europe in May 1945, the continent was very different to that which had gone to war in September 1939. Militarily the might of the German Third Reich had collapsed with Germany and the rest of Europe effectively partitioned in two, the eastern half occupied by the Soviet Army and the western half by US, British and French troops. This military division was also to herald an economic division in Europe between command and market-based economies which was to last until 1990.

Economically, the situation in Europe was even worse. Large amounts of infrastructure had been destroyed. Road and rail links, factories, housing, power-generating plant and ports were largely unusable. For many people there was no work to earn the money to live. Food was in short supply and many faced starvation. This created a refugee problem on a scale only seen recently in Africa and the former Yugoslavia. It was from this wholesale desolation and destruction that the idea of European cooperation was to arise, like a phoenix, if the wars of the past were to be avoided in the future. Previous attempts by Napoleon and more recently by Hitler to unite Europe by force had failed. This time economic cooperation would be the key. Furthermore, Europe's position as the most powerful continent in the world had been usurped by the emergence of two superpowers, the United States of America (USA) and the Union of Soviet

Socialist Republics (USSR). If Europe was to survive in the postwar world its countries would have to work together.

The role of France was crucial since it often proved to be the driving force in this process of cooperation. France had been invaded by Germany during the Franco-Prussian war of 1871 and during the First and Second World Wars. After 1945 successive French governments were therefore motivated by the need to tie Germany closer to France and to the rest of Western Europe and hence avoid any future intra-European conflict. The victorious allies had also learned from the experience at the end of the First World War when they had imposed very harsh reparation payments on Germany. These, coupled with the economic depression of 1929–32, had created the conditions which permitted the development of political extremism of the left and right and the rise to power in Germany of Adolf Hitler and the National Socialist (Nazi) Party, conditions which led to the Second World War. In other European countries the same conditions also created political extremism, permitting, for example, the rise of Mussolini in Italy and Franco in Spain.

The first post-Second World War real call for a united states of Europe was made by British statesman Winston Churchill in September 1946. However, British foreign policy was driven by its empire and by its perceived special relationship with the US. Britain therefore had only limited commitment to European cooperation at this decisive time. The ultimate effect of this was that Europe subsequently moved along a route committed to closer economic and political union and the creation of supranational bodies rather than evolving as a free trade area with only loose links between members, and national governments remaining supreme. This latter approach was therefore under-represented in subsequent debates over the future of Western Europe.

■ 2.3 Towards the Treaty of Rome

Postwar developments in Europe focused in two directions. Firstly there was on-going cooperation with the United States of America as Europe continued to look across the Atlantic for support and leadership in the face of the threat from the Soviet Union.

■ Transatlantic cooperation

The founding of the OEEC in 1948 has already been discussed in Chapter 1. The military pact known as the North Atlantic Treaty Organisation (NATO) was formed in 1949 by the US, Canada and most of Western Europe. This provided security guarantees between its members for the defence of Western Europe against the threat of the armies of the USSR and Central and Eastern Europe (who later formed the Warsaw Pact military alliance in opposition to NATO).

■ Developments within Western Europe

□ 1 Benelux

The second direction for postwar Western European development was to look inwards to Europe itself, including countries which might otherwise wish to retain economic and political neutrality such as Sweden and Switzerland. The first evidence of this was the creation of the Benelux customs union in 1947. This was an economic grouping by which trade between Belgium, the Netherlands and Luxembourg was made completely free and a common tariff was imposed against non-member countries.

□ 2 The Council of Europe

This was followed in 1949 by the formation of the Council of Europe. Its aims were to encourage greater cooperation between member governments, to support parliamentary democracy, to promote economic and social progress, and to support human rights. To that extent it has proved to be successful. It was never intended to promote federalism nor the creation of supranational organisations. Although its membership overlaps with it the Council of Europe is not a part of the European Union. Its most notable achievement has been to promote the European Convention for the Protection of Human Rights and Fundamental Freedoms which was adopted in November 1950 by the Council's original members. Currently it has 39 members, including the EU15 (the 15 members of the European Union). Most recent joining members have been Russia, Bosnia-Herzegovina and Belarus.

□ 3 The Western European Union

Separate from NATO but with many of the same European members, the Western European Union (WEU) was formed in 1954. Its aim was to strengthen security arrangements between Britain, France and Benelux and to bring West Germany and Italy into this military fold. It also gave a more unified European voice in NATO debates. By its constitution NATO is precluded from fighting outside Europe and so it was the WEU which represented Western European countries, as part of the coalition forces, in the Gulf War against Iraq in 1992. Already a Eurocorps is being formed of French, German, Spanish and Belgian troops which will eventually exceed the size of UK ground forces. This or the WEU may well be the basis of any future united European Union defence force.

In October 1994 associate membership was extended to countries of the former Warsaw Pact such as Estonia, Romania, Bulgaria, Hungary and the Czech Republic. Associate membership has also been extended to some neutral countries. The Treaty of Amsterdam 1998 promised closer ties between the WEU and the EU as a compromise to the original proposal of integrating the WEU into the EU.

□ 4 The European Coal and Steel Community 1952

The most important move towards greater European cooperation, however, was the 1950 Schuman Plan, developed by French Foreign Minister Robert Schuman with Jean Monnet, who was responsible for the French industrial modernisation plan. The aims of the Schuman Plan were to reintegrate West Germany fully into Western Europe, including encouraging her to take a share in the defence of Western Europe against the threat posed by the Soviet Union. France in particular felt a need to influence the strategic West German coal and steel industries which provided inputs for West German armaments producers such as Krupps. However, the steel industry was in crisis with overproduction creating the risk of cartels and price fixing. The Schuman Plan therefore proposed a pooling of French and West German coal and steel production, controlled by a common High Authority. This was intended not only to exercise control over any West German rearmament but also to promote joint prosperity and lay the basis for establishing an economic community.

The outcome of the Schuman Plan was the creation under the Treaty of Paris, which was signed in April 1951 and came into force in July 1952, of the European Coal and Steel Community (ECSC). Its signatories France, West Germany, Italy and Benelux agreed, crucially for future developments, that the High Authority's decisions would be binding on all members; in other words a supranational authority was established which overrode national government decisions in this field. A Council of Ministers was created to enable national governments to express their opinions, while a (non-elected) Parliamentary Assembly and a Court of Justice were also established. These remain the basis of European Union institutions to the present day.

It has been argued that four principles arising from the Schuman Plan still underpin the European Union today (Noel, 1993). Firstly, institutions (such as the High Authority or the European Parliament) are superior to national conflict; secondly, Community institutions are independent of national interest; thirdly, cooperation exists between Community institutions; and fourthly there shall be equality between states, regardless of size of country.

■ 2.4 The Treaty of Rome to the Treaty of Amsterdam

■ The Treaty of Rome 1958

The creation of the ECSC was so important because it laid the basis for the subsequent developments towards the present-day European Union. This first manifested itself in a conference of ECSC foreign ministers at Messina, Italy, in June 1955, with the objective of creating a united Europe. The ministers' aim was to promote further economic growth and social cohesion for their member countries. This might be encouraged and shared by all in a single or common market which would offer European industry and agriculture major opportunities to enter large new markets without restriction and so increase production and profits. For consumers a single market should offer greater choice and cheaper goods. Most importantly, however, it would build deeper political cooperation between its members.

A committee headed by Belgian Foreign Minister Paul-Henri Spaak was formed to investigate this further and in 1956 submitted its report. Negotiations between the six ECSC members, based on this, led to the creation of two further communities, the European Economic Community (EEC) and the European Atomic Community (Euratom). The Treaty of Rome which brought these into existence was signed in March 1957 and became operative in January 1958. The main function of Euratom was to promote nuclear industries in the six member states. The role of the EEC was to create a single market with freedom of movement for goods, services, capital and labour.

For the EEC the Treaty of Rome sought to implement what may be termed both internal and external measures. The internal measures required EEC members to remove all tariffs and quotas levied against each other enabling businesses to access each other's markets; to end all restrictions on services supplied between the six members; and to remove all non-tariff barriers to trade between EEC members. This would control cartels and restrictions on competition by dominant firms, and also allow freedom of movement for the labour force and capital between member states.

The external measures required under the Treaty of Rome were the introduction of the Common Commercial Policy whereby each country levied a common external tariff against imports from non-member countries; and the introduction of common policies for agriculture (the Common Agricultural Policy), transport (the Common Transport Policy), energy (the Common Energy Policy), and also the establishment of the European Social Fund and the European Investment Bank.

■ The Merger Treaty 1967

A problem with having three separate communities was that institutions were duplicated. For example each of the three communities had its own commission. Under the Merger Treaty, signed in 1965, the three commissions were merged into one body. Also a single Council of Ministers was established as the supreme body for decision-making. From its implementation on 1 July 1967 the three separate communities became known as the European Community.

■ 'Eurosclerosis': the failures of the late 1970s and early 1980s

After the rapid EC economic growth of the late 1950s and 1960s, and the expansion of EC membership in 1973, the mid-1970s saw economic growth and progress towards further EC development begin to slow in spite of the Tindemans Report of 1976.

Named after the then Belgian Prime Minister, this was a response to the EC summits of 1972 and 1974 which declared the objective of achieving European union by 1980. It proposed the introduction of European Monetary Union (including a common currency), social and regional policies to reduce inequalities, reform of EC institutions to provide them with the power to implement common policies, and measures to protect the rights of EC citizens. The time span was, of course, unrealistic and the plan was not implemented.

The plan was also hampered by the continuing effects of the 1973 oil crisis which had seen the price of crude oil rise by 400 per cent. This had contributed to economic recession, hitting European businesses heavily and causing EC members to look inwards at their own national problems instead of outwards at the EC as a whole. It was reinforced by the further spread of subsidies and other protectionist policies to maintain industries which otherwise would not survive. The impetus for progress to further reform therefore abated, creating a period of lethargy within the European Community in the late 1970s and early 1980s which became known as 'Eurosclerosis'. The lack of EC progress was further aggravated by the 100 per cent oil price increase of 1979 which contributed to the global economic recession of the early 1980s.

The Tindemans Report is important for two reasons, nonetheless. Firstly it demonstrated that, although the momentum had slowed, the will for further economic and political union still existed. Secondly it argued that, for these proposals to be implemented, there was effectively a need for a two-speed EC. The core of strongest countries would move rapidly towards greater integration while the others would follow behind in the slow lane. In the light of the current debate about a two-speed or even multi-speed European Union it is interesting that this proposal was surfacing two decades ago.

■ The Single European Act 1987

The European Commission's White Paper on the internal market, drawn up under the guidance of Lord Cockfield, identified a comprehensive programme of some 300 measures to be implemented to complete the single or internal market. This was by the removal of internal barriers to free trade including physical, technical and fiscal restrictions on trade in goods and services, and was to be achieved by 31 December 1992.

On the basis of the Cockfield Report, the Single European Act came into force in July 1987. It was a major step forward in the development of the EC by moving it towards the completion of the Single European Market. It also speeded up decision-making through the extension of qualified majority voting (QMV) and laid the basis for the subsequent Treaty on European Union. The terms of the Single European Act, its impact on European businesses and associated policies are discussed more fully in Chapter 3.

■ The Treaty on European Union (the Treaty of Maastricht) 1993

The intention of the Treaty of Maastricht was to build on the previous achievements of the EC by identifying a number of aims which it sought to achieve. These included:

   (i)   to promote balanced and sustainable economic and social progress through 'the creation of an area without internal frontiers, through strengthening economic and social cohesion and through establishing economic and monetary union';
   (ii)   to develop 'a common foreign and security policy', and eventually 'a common defence policy';
   (iii)   to strengthen the protection of the rights and interests of EU nationals through introducing EU citizenship;
   (iv)   to develop close cooperation on home affairs and justice.

Specifically the Treaty identified three main elements or pillars:

- The European Community (relating to aims (i) and (iii) above).
- Foreign policy (aim (ii) above).
- Interior policy (aim (iv) above).

European businesses were affected by Maastricht in a number of areas:

- Firstly, by 1999 at latest a single currency was to be introduced by countries able to meet the Maastricht convergence criteria (see Chapter 3). The single currency would reinforce the 1992 implementation of the single market by encouraging further trade growth between EU members. An independent European Central Bank was also to be established with responsibility for issuing the single currency and determining EU monetary policy. This independence was to be from both national government influences and the influence of EU bodies such as the Commission and the Council. It would thus be able to pursue its statutory obligation of achieving price stability without these trying to influence its monetary policy to suit short term political objectives. The first meeting of the six-member executive board of the ECB was held on 2 June 1998.
- EU citizenship reinforced the single market by giving citizens the right to 'move and reside freely within the territory of the member states' and covered the rights to live, work and vote. Also businesses could recruit from anywhere in the EU for skilled staff.
- Finance covered a number of areas including the responsibility of the Commission to ensure that new expenditure proposals were within existing financial limits, that the Commission be accountable to the parliament for this and that national governments addressed EC fraud as effectively as national fraud. This is important since fraud incurs unnecessary expenditure which ultimately reflects in the taxes paid by consumers and businesses. Additionally many businesses, especially agricultural, are themselves guilty of fraud through claims on the Common Agricultural Policy.
- A social chapter was proposed as part of the Treaty of Maastricht but, because the UK refused to accept this, it formed a separate agreement or protocol outside of the treaty. The development of social policy and its implications for European business is discussed in detail in Chapter 4.
- To permit greater competitiveness of EU industry, measures would be supported provided they did not distort competition. These sought to speed adjustment to structural change, to promote an environment encouraging initiative, especially among small and medium-

sized enterprises (SMEs), to encourage business cooperation and to promote better exploitation of innovation and R&D (research and development).

- New initiatives affecting European business included the Cohesion Fund to provide financial support for poorer regions of the EU (Greece, Ireland, Portugal and Spain) in the financing of transport networks and environmental projects. This was to offset any widening of regional wealth disparities as a result of the single market. The Committee of the Regions was created and was to be consulted on EU policy affecting the regions. It was anticipated that both of these would have a major impact on regional business activity. Trans-European Networks were emphasised to further facilitate the integration of the single market by improving road, rail and inland waterway networks, telecommunications networks and energy infrastructure.
- A number of other issues were also addressed at Maastricht. Subsidiarity, covered by a.3b (a denotes 'article') of the Treaty of Maastricht, sought to offset criticisms of unnecessary centralist bureaucracy interfering in the lives of ordinary people, for example legislation on the level of noise from lawnmowers. Subsidiarity means that the power to legislate and make regulations should be devolved to the lowest level possible eg national or even regional governments, unless it is absolutely necessary for the EU to take decisions.
- New powers were granted to the European parliament regarding joint decision-making and scrutiny of the Commission. These are discussed more fully below in section 2.5.
- Regarding a common foreign and security policy, the aim was to promote greater cooperation between member states in the above areas and possibly the development, in time, of a common defence policy. As part of this it was proposed that the WEU be strengthened and EU non-members invited to join.
- For justice and home affairs there was an attempt to develop a common policy for issues such as immigration, political asylum, international crime, especially narcotics, and terrorism. Linked to this was the creation of Europol, the European police network, since crime does not restrict itself to national boundaries.
- Other initiatives related to promoting greater cultural cooperation between the EU and other European states, to improving public access to EU information and to extending the use of majority voting in the Council of Ministers.

☐ Conclusions

The Treaty on European Union was a major point in the development of the European Community with very many initiatives impacting directly and indirectly on European businesses. It introduced a wide range of new measures which all worked towards greater economic integration. These ranged most obviously from the proposed single currency to initiatives such as the Cohesion Fund and the Social Policy which sought to spread the wealth from the single market among all EU members, states, businesses and individuals. Many of these issues are addressed elsewhere in this book. Most fundamentally it should be noted that the title of the Treaty itself states quite explicitly what its overarching objective was – European Union. Maastricht is an important step down the path to a United States of Europe; Table 2.1 shows these stages.

■ The Treaty of Amsterdam 1998

If Maastricht was a major development in the integration of the EU then the Amsterdam Summit of June 1997, whose outcomes are implemented as the Treaty of Amsterdam 1998, was a major disappointment. Indeed Jacques Santer, talking of the summit, stated 'I don't hide the deficiencies, the weaknesses, the gaps . . . I would have liked it to have been more adventurous in one or two areas.' The main reason for this lack of ambition was the anxiety not to disturb progress to monetary union.

Much of the debate at Amsterdam focused on French and German perceptions of future EU integration. Germany stressed the need for national budgetary discipline in the moves to a single currency and after. Hence the proposed Stability and Growth Pact, established by the Dublin Summit of December 1996,

Table 2.1   Stages in the development to economic union

TRADING ARRANGEMENT	CHARACTERISTICS
Trade Agreement	Gives trade preference to member countries, in the form of lower import tariffs on certain goods, in contrast to non-members who pay full tariffs. May be intended to promote trade or be politically motivated, e.g. US's most favoured nation status granted to Russia and PR China, or to countries meeting certain human rights requirements.
Free Trade Area	Removes totally tariffs between signatories to encourage free trade in goods. Members may levy their own tariffs against non-free trade area members. There are no political intentions. EFTA and NAFTA are examples of free trade areas.
Customs Union	Tariff and quota barriers between members are removed. Members levy a common external tariff (CET) against non-members (known in the EU as the Common Commercial Tariff), i.e. each country charges the same import duties. The proceeds of the CET are distributed among members. The EC was at this stage in the early 1980s.
Common Market	As well as the characteristics of a customs union there is free movement of capital and labour within a common market. Non-tariff barriers – e.g. customs controls and import/export documentation – need to be standardised or removed. Also common policies on the environment, social/working conditions, transport etc. need to be developed. The EU was at this stage in 1995.
Economic Union	Here there is complete economic and monetary integration: e.g. single currency; single central bank; common fiscal and monetary policy. Increasing political union is likely to develop with this leading to loss of economic and political independence. Core EU countries will largely be at this stage by 2002.

on German insistence, placed great emphasis on fining countries who failed to meet the convergence criteria after the single currency is implemented (see Chapter 3). Additionally, the role of the European Central Bank (ECB) was always seen by Germany as politically independent of national governments with the remit of maintaining a rigorous stance against inflation – as the Bundesbank has done.

French concerns, however, were that national sovereignty must not be ceded to central bank bureaucrats. For example, if fines were to be levied on countries failing to maintain the convergence criteria, these must be imposed by national governments. They also believed that more emphasis needed to be placed on jobs creation. They argued, therefore, that there was need for some form of European political control or economic government to offset the power of the ECB.

The final compromise to this dispute was an addition to the Stability and Growth Pact with EU leaders broadly stating a commitment to employment and agreeing a need to coordinate further their macroeconomic policies. The European Investment Bank was also recommended to broaden its remit by investing in small and medium-sized health care, high-tech and environmental projects rather than just large businesses. However, in the spirit of German fiscal discipline, no new money was made available to promote job creation!

One of Amsterdam's key tasks was to restructure EU organisations, designed for the EC6, to enable them to cope with the influx of six additional members in the early part of the next decade, and five more subsequently (an EU26). It had been proposed to streamline decision-making to ensure that the newcomers do not cause a logjam in the Commission and in the EU decision-making machinery. For example, reducing the opportunities for countries to use the national veto was one option. In practice, after two years of negotiations, the summit was unable to come up with any agreement on the future size of the European Commission (except the stopgap that the five countries with two commissioners should each surrender one to the five new Eastern European members) nor on how, in the Council of Ministers, votes might be reweighted. Nor was qualified majority voting (QMV) extended. Indeed France, Germany and Italy have called for a further treaty to address these issues before new members are admitted.

With the ending of UK objections to the social chapter this was incorporated into the Treaty of Amsterdam and so become part of the EU's basic constitution.

The Amsterdam summit also accepted a 'flexibility' system which, in theory, permits a multispeed EU in limited areas. Under this, actions can be initiated by majority voting and not directly subject to any veto provided they do not interfere with the single market and other practices already in existence. This is particularly relevant in the moves by most members to greater economic integration and the advent of new members in due course. However, incorporated into this is what is known as the Luxembourg compromise which allows a state to block a decision on the grounds of supreme national interest. Of course how this latter concept is defined, and by whom, will determine how effective this compromise really is if a nation did try to block a majority vote on a crucial issue. In practice, however, it does seem to water down very substantially the flexibility proposals.

In spite of proposals that the WEU, the European wing of NATO, be incorporated into the EU the final agreement was merely the compromise of a promise for closer ties between the WEU and the EU. This particularly satisfied the UK which was concerned about marginalising the US from the defence of Europe.

The Schengen Agreement, signed in 1990 by France, Germany and Benelux to guarantee all travellers the freedom to cross internal borders without the need for passports, was, until Amsterdam, a private treaty between the signatories. It has now become a common EU policy. (Ireland and the UK have full exemptions and Denmark a partial opt-out on this.) However, this may be storing up further problems since the influx of illegal immigrants into the EU, especially through Italy's relatively unprotected borders, causes concern to all members.

Other issues covered by Amsterdam were a human-rights charter to stop any form of discrimination – by sex, race, religion, age, sexual orientation or disability; the option of imposing sanctions on member states for human-rights abuses, including the death penalty, by suspending the voting rights of persistent violators; civilian judicial cooperation and harmonisation of divorce laws to become common EU policies; the right of citizens to have access to the documents of the Council of Ministers unless three countries oppose this – hence promoting transparency; the EU being given a legal personality to permit it to negotiate as one; and the Secretary-General of the Council of Ministers being empowered, in future, formally to represent the EU in foreign policy decision-making.

■ 2.5 The main EU organisations: decision-making in the EU

Decision-making in the European Union is a complex process involving a number of different organisations which, to a greater or lesser extent, interact on each other. The decisions they make have a major impact on European businesses and so are explored here in some detail to give the reader an understanding of how the processes work.

■ The Council

This may be distinguished as two separate groups:

□ 1 The Council of Ministers

The most powerful policy-making body of the EU, this is composed of 15 member states whose representatives make all major decisions. It varies in membership depending on what is being discussed. For example, if economic policy is being discussed then it will consist of finance ministers; if the Common Agricultural

politically-integrated EU it would, as the only democratically body, need to play a central and major role.

CASE STUDY   The European Parliament at Work

In March 1998 the European Parliament was debating how to reduce deaths on EU roads – currently 45 000 p.a., with one-third under the age of 24. Drink-driving is believed to be responsible for 20 per cent of these. Parliament wants to reduce fatalities to 25 000 p.a. by 2010 through tougher drink driving laws (a blood alcohol limit of 0.5mg/litre), harmonising speed limits and designing and producing safer cars. The accident death rate in the EU varies from six per 100 000 of the population (Sweden and the UK), to 21 per 100 000 for Greece and 29 per 100 000 for Portugal. The European Commission estimate that the total economic costs of this carnage (police and emergency services; medical expenses; lost economic output of the dead) to be ECU 45 billion p.a. – equal to just under 1 per cent of EU GDP. Others estimate the costs could be as high as ECU 100bn with an extra ECU 62bn from costing the pain and grief of losing loved ones. Whereas Parliament has argued for EU-wide standards, Transport Commissioner Neil Kinnock has said it is up to individual nations to implement these measures.

■ EU legislation: understanding the jargon

Under the terms of the Treaty of Maastricht the decisions listed in Table 2.2 may be issued by the Council of Ministers itself or in conjunction with the European Parliament, or by the European Commission.

■ The Court of Justice

Based in Luxembourg, the Court of Justice is a permanent institution which has been described as the most supranational of the EU's bodies. It consists of 15 judges, one nominated by each state. They are assisted by six Advocates General whose functions are to sum up in public the cases which are before the judges and also to give their expert legal opinion before the judges make their decisions.

One main responsibility of the Court of Justice is to ensure that legislation which is passed by EU institutions is compatible with EU treaties. An issue may be brought before the Court by an EU institution or a national government or a private citizen. For example, the European Commission may take to the Court a government which has failed to implement directives concerning the purity of drinking water and sewage disposal. Similarly, a member government which feels that another EU government is illegally subsidising an industry may appeal to the Court of Justice for that subsidisation to be stopped.

The Court's other main responsibility is to give its opinion, if asked by a national court, on how to interpret correctly the provisions of EU treaties, or indeed whether they are valid. In these circumstances, it usually favours an

Table 2.2   Types of EU decision

TYPE OF LEGISLATION	MEANING
Directive	This is binding on all member states to which it is addressed regarding the outcomes to be fulfilled. However, the organisation and how these might be fulfilled are left to individual governments, e.g. by national laws and decrees.
Regulation	This is mandatory for all member states in its totality. A regulation takes precedent over national law.
Decision	This may apply to a government, or an EU business or to an EU citizen. It is mandatory for the party to whom it is addressed.
Recommendation	This is not binding.
Opinion	This is not binding.

interpretation which promotes further integration of the Union and increases the authority of its institutions. The Court's decisions are taken in secret by simple majority and no dissenting opinion is published. This reinforces its independent authority and its role as the Community watchdog. The major criticism is the slowness of decision-making. In mid-1994 there were 386 cases awaiting the judges' verdicts, of which 142 had been tabled since 1 January 1994.

In 1989 an additional court was established, known as the Court of First Instance, to take some of the workload experienced by the European Court of Justice. Its backlog of cases to be heard is 789, of which 192 have been tabled since 1 January 1994.

■ The Court of Auditors

This is an independent body which scrutinises the financial operations of the European Union. As part of its work it publishes an annual report which identifies areas of malpractice and where EU funds are misappropriated. However, it has limited powers and can only refer financial irregularities, even criminal ones, to the appropriate authorities, who are usually the member states themselves. This poses real problems since much of the fraud and malpractice is at national level.

■ Other institutions

□ 1 ECOFIN

This is the Council of Economics and Finance Ministers which has been responsible for the overall running of the EMS; their remit covers all matters economic and financial within the EU. They provide an overview and initiate policies which the Commission will draft and, once approved, implement.

With the development of the Euro X Club the UK, particularly, has expressed concern that the latter will usurp the role of ECOFIN, of which the UK is a member – whereas in not participating in the first wave of the single currency it is only an observer at meetings of the Euro X Club.

CASE STUDY Combatting Fraud in Agriculture

The 1997 annual report of the European Court of Auditors identifed the extent of fraud within the EU by refusing, for the third year in a row, to pass the EU's annual budget. It estimates that $6.63 billion of the annual $83 billion budget (5.5 per cent) cannot be accounted for while potential revenues are being lost because of the differences in how countries collect value added tax (VAT) and customs duties (on imports from outside the EU).

Since the CAP is the biggest area of expenditure within the EU's budget then, not surprisingly, this demonstrates the greatest scope for fraud and malpractice. One area of particular concern (apart from the moral and health issues from aiding it) is the EU's tobacco industry, mainly based in Greece and heavily subsidised, yet the source of a multi-million dollar scandal in 1993. Other areas of concern include overpayment of ECU 3 billion ($2.7 billion) in 1995–96 to cereal farmers for the low market prices of cereals at a time when, in practice, they rose steeply, and overpayment to German farmers in the wake of German reunification.

The EU is handicapped by a statute of limitation preventing cases being prosecuted beyond three years, which enables large numbers of culprits to escape all legal action. Further, there is a need to change attitudes at national government level since countries such as Italy and Greece regard fraud as an essential part of the regional economy, while France regards the CAP and other regional aid schemes as means to support rural economies. Also, as noted above, the Court of Auditors may do no more than refer 'irregularities' to national governments who are often the guilty parties.

Attempts by the Commission, operational from 1998, to address these problems include tightening the criteria for grant eligibility, improving standards for financial control and making it easier to recover misspent funds. The concern of MEPs, however, is that the Commission too willingly accepts corruption as something inevitable which can be lived with. For example, according to a November 1997 report by Spanish Socialist MEP Joan Colom I Naval certain companies in the EU are mass-producing synthetic trees, vines and olives to enable farmers to defraud the Common Agricultural Policy. These are then 'planted' by farmers to secure subsidies and other payments from Brussels. According to the MEP some companies supplying these plastic plants guarantee them to be undetectable when compared with the real thing. They can then be moved to other sites as necessary to secure further funding.

☐ 2 The Economic and Social Committee (ESC)

This represents a cross-section of economic and social interests in the EU, including employers, workers and special interest groups such as small and medium-sized enterprises (SMEs). It must be consulted by the Council of Ministers and the Commission before decisions relating to its areas of responsibility can be undertaken.

☐ 3 The Committee of the Regions

This was established under the Treaty of Maastricht to enable local authorities and regions to have an input into EU policies directly affecting them. It has an advisory assembly of 222 directly elected members including mayors, city councillors etc and meets in Brussels for five plenary sessions per year. It must be consulted about regional issues such as public health, education, culture, European transport and economic and social cohesion. More recently it has been criticised for croneyism.

☐ 4 The European Investment Bank (EIB)

The EIB, whose members are the EU15, raises funds on the world's capital markets and loans them long-term to companies and governments to finance projects, particularly where one country alone cannot provide them. Particular emphasis is placed on projects through individual loans, upwards of ECU 25m and up to 50 per cent of the project cost, which will promote the objectives of the European Union regarding economic integration and economic and social cohesion. Regional development is seen as crucial to promoting economic growth with over half the EU's population living in areas where there is slow economic development or where there are problems in converting from declining industries or agriculture. Examples of EIB lending include infrastructure projects such as telecommunications, the environment, transport and energy, and to promote the international competitiveness of industry. From 1992–96 the EIB loaned approximately ECU 180 billion; in 1996 the UK received ECU 2.4bn out of EIB total lending of ECU 23bn.

The EIB also lends externally and, for the period 1997–2000, is providing funding of over ECU 7 billion, focusing particularly on South Africa, the Caribbean and the Pacific; the Mediterranean region; Central and Eastern Europe; and Asia and Latin America.

As a consequence of the 1993 Edinburgh Summit the European Investment Fund (EIF) was established with a subscribed capital of ECU 2 billion. Its function is to guarantee projects especially to help more funds to be channelled to small and medium-sized enterprises (SMEs).

■ 2.6 Widening and deepening the EU: the way forward

■ Widening

The Union's environment is changing fast, both internally and externally. It must set about adapting, developing and reforming itself. Enlargement repre-

sents an historic turning point for Europe, an opportunity which it must seize for the sake of its security, its economy, its culture and its status in the world.
(Jacques Santer, Commission President, introducing the launch of Agenda 2000 on 16 July 1997)

The EU grew in membership from the initial six countries in 1958 to 15 in 1995. In 1998 the Council agreed that six new applicants could take part in the next round of EU membership – Cyprus, the Czech Republic, Estonia, Hungary, Poland and Slovenia. If successful they will join the EU in about 2002, adding 60 million extra people to the EU's population. Additionally, five other countries may be considered for EU membership in the future although they are not yet ready. These are Bulgaria, Latvia, Lithuania, Romania and Slovakia and their cases will be reviewed annually. However, Jacques Santer has argued that to integrate these five would cost in the region of £50 billion.

Malta has decided not to seek membership while Turkey, a key member of NATO, has been applying for 30 years without success. This process of enlarging the EU is known as widening and, currently, is based on the Agenda 2000 programme of Jacques Santer. It contrasts with the deepening process – as the moves towards greater EU integration through economic and monetary union are known – which is also being embarked on by 11 EU qualifying countries at the same time, and is discussed in Chapter 3.

To be eligible for EU membership a state has to be European, a functioning democracy, have a functioning market economy and be able fully to integrate into the EU after a short adjustment period; that is be able to assume the responsibilities of monetary union, the single market and adopt the main body of EU law.

For the Central and Eastern European countries (CEEC) the need for EU membership is both economic and political. Economically it will bring access to EU regional funds including those for agriculture. These will be crucial to assist in the long-term process of economic modernisation, although the EU will not be able to provide the total amount of financing they require. It will also give full access to EU markets, which is crucial to underpin economic development in the period following economic restructuring. CEEC are also conscious of the inherent instability of Russia, aggravated by the unpredictability of President Yeltsin and the failure of economic reforms to take off fully, causing considerable poverty and hardship to remain nearly a decade after the fall of communism. Consequently they wish to tie themselves to Western Europe as closely as possible, as demonstrated by applications also to join NATO.

The proposed membership of Cyprus seems bizarre given that it was invaded by Turkey in 1974 and is currently partitioned into two sectors. Indeed France was, for some time, opposed to allowing its application to proceed. The northern part of Cyprus is the Turkish Republic of Northern Cyprus which is recognised only by Turkey. If Cyprus were admitted then the EU argued that first there would have to be some progress towards peace on the island, and secondly the Turkish Cypriots would have to be consulted at some time. This has now taken place.

Turkey, a strategically important country during the cold war with the former USSR, and potentially strategic now in acting as a barrier to the spread of fundamental Islam, has been unsuccessful in its applications over many years for a number of reasons. It has a history of repression of dissidents – especially Kurds – which is disliked by parliamentary democracies. It is also economically a long way behind the EU and there is concern in Brussels that large amounts of subsidies would be required under the Common Agricultural Policy, European Regional Development Fund and the Cohesion Fund. Also, Turkey straddles Europe and Asia and so is felt not to be truly European. Turkey, a secular muslim state, has accused the EU of wanting only a christian European Union. Indeed Turkey is now begining to refocus its attention away from the EU and looking to develop closer links with its Asian neighbours.

All the prospective members above do have association agreements with the EU at present, which is a useful way to establish economic links before a country is ready for full membership. For the countries who are further away from being ready for EU membership the EU has negotiated trade and cooperation agreements. It is fairly obvious that there are real gains to applicants if their membership applications succeed, but what does the EU gain from enlargement?

Firstly, increased membership will bring a bigger single market, new consumers hungry for the latest goods and services, for some time at least cheaper labour giving the EU a competitive edge and, arising from this, greater economic growth and prosperity. As importantly, however, it will tie these countries into the framework of a democratic market-oriented Western Europe and guarantee political stability on the borders of the existing EU – although the membership of the new countries will bring new boundaries and new potential problems. If one considers that for four of the six applicants the period 1989–2002 could see them move from being either members of the Soviet Union (Estonia) or the Soviet bloc (Czech Republic, Hungary, Poland) to full members of the EU, the scale of this transition is amazing.

The other main area of importance to the EU is the southern shore of the Mediterranean. In October 1994 it was proposed to create a Euro-Mediterranean Economic Area (EMEA), consisting of North Africa (that is, Algeria, Libya, Morocco and Tunisia); the Arab Near East (that is, Egypt, Jordan, Lebanon and Syria); and Israel. This would create free trade agreements, provide economic aid for the North African and Near East countries and markets for EU goods, and hopefully encourage political stability and security. It would be financed by direct aid of ECU 5.16bn during 1995–2000. In reality the different cultures, religions and some countries' reputations for political extremism mean that any parallels with economic links with CEEC are not very appropriate, and these countries are unlikely to be candidates for EU membership in the foreseeable future.

■ Financing the widening

The Agenda 2000 programme seeks to integrate the new applicants into the EU while radically restructuring EU spending to limit the costs of absorbing them.

Attention has focused particularly on the two main expenditure items: the Common Agricultural Policy, which absorbs roughly 45 per cent of the EU's annual £60 billion budget (at its peak in the 1970s it accounted for 68 per cent of the budget), and regional aid which takes about 35 per cent. The overall aim of the reform programme, due to take effect from 2000, is to keep total spending below 1.27 per cent of EU GDP.

The difficulty of reforming the EU budget is that the major donors all complain about what they have to give while the major recipients will not surrender any of their income. Germany, the major donor, has argued that it will not give more, particularly as it is still financing the restructuring of Eastern Germany; the Netherlands complain they give more per capita than any other country; while the UK, the eleventh poorest EU member, is the third largest donor, paying the EU a net £1.6bn p.a. The UK refuses to surrender the budgetary concessions secured by Margaret Thatcher in the mid-1980s, while the major recipients of CAP funding and regional aid (which often cover the same regions) – such as Ireland, Greece, Spain and Portugal – have flatly declined to receive less money from the EU. Additionally, the ability to finance the widening is based on the Commission's projection of 2.5 per cent p.a. economic growth by the EU15 until 2006, and more than 4 per cent p.a. by the new applicants – which some view as optimistic.

☐ 1 Regional funding

The regional aid programme was reformed in 1989 to bring upward harmonisation of living standards within the EU. Under Agenda 2000 the European Commission is seeking to provide ECU 218bn (£142bn) of structural funds for the period 2000–06. The aim of Agenda 2000 is to target funds on the least developed regions of the EU, reducing the seven existing objectives to three. This will reduce the coverage of the regions eligible for support from 51 per cent to 35–40 per cent of the EU's population and hence allow for the demands which will be imposed by the entry of the six new applicants for EU membership. The poorer regions of the EU will have to get used to much less aid if enlargement is to take place. Additionally, competitiveness and job creation are most strongly emphasised, the rules favouring the most successful programmes, with more autonomy also being granted to member states to determine their expenditure priorities.

ECU 145bn (£94bn) of the EU's current regional funding will go to the underdeveloped Objective 1 regions for such infrastructure projects as road-building. Regions receiving this funding must have per capita GDP of less than 75 per cent of the EU average. After 2000 this will cover only 20 per cent of the population compared with 25 per cent now as some of the poorer regions are excluded – however they will receive transitional aid up to 2006.

For Objective 2 regions – those in structural crisis affected by rural and industrial decline – economic aid to support economic and social conversion is available. It covers industrial, urban, rural and fisheries areas and accounts for 18 per cent of the EU population (reduced from 26 per cent). Yet this is a limited reform since a safety net provided will limit the cuts to each state to one third, and there will be 4 years of transition aid. Unemployment will be used as a criterion of eligibility for the first time. This will hit the UK which has lower unemployment compared with other EU countries. As illustration of the impact of the proposed cuts, for the UK this will exclude such areas as the Scottish Highlands and Islands region and Northern Ireland.

Objective 3's purposes are to support EU-wide training, education and employment initiatives and support European Social Fund (ESF) activities (see Chapter 4). These ESF activities relate to: promoting active labour markets to combat unemployment; combatting social exclusion; promoting life long training and education to encourage labour flexibility; anticipating economic and social change; and ensuring equal opportunities for men and women.

☐ 2 The Common Agricultural Policy (CAP)

Since its creation in the 1950s, the CAP has worked on the principles of subsidising agricultural production to boost output and maintaining high prices for foodstuffs (and hence satisfactory incomes for farmers) by buying and storing what was not bought at these prices. In theory this store would be released onto the market in times of shortage. Imports of food were taxed to raise their prices to those of EU-produced food. This was to benefit the farmers of the original EC6 but, as other countries joined, the costs of the CAP have risen higher and higher. In practice the CAP has led to overproduction and misallocation of resources.

Attempts to reform it by paying farmers set-aside money not to produce crops, imposing milk quotas and reducing subsidies have had some effect in reducing the beef mountains and milk lakes of earlier days, but the political power of the farming lobbies in EU countries – most memorably shown by French farmers blockading roads and throwing produce into the sea – has always inhibited major reform. So EU consumers have always paid higher than free market prices as the penalty for having the CAP. In 1998 the National Consumer Council estimated the cost of the CAP to the average UK family of four to be £980 p.a. With the six new EU entrants, who have large agricultural sectors – especially Poland – the cost of financing the existing CAP will be unsustainable.

The current reform, which has been described as evolutionary rather than revolutionary, therefore has a two-fold aim of reducing guaranteed produce prices to nearer free market levels, and reducing subsidies paid to farmers for crops grown. Additionally, set-aside payments would also be terminated. Concerning the reduction of guaranteed prices, those for beef would be cut by 30 per cent between 2000 and 2002; cereal prices by 20 per cent in 2000; and dairy prices by 15 per cent between 2000–04. This in turn will lower other prices, for example cheaper poultry through falling grain prices. It is estimated that this bill could thus be reduced by £1bn a year, saving every EU family £80 per year.

The timidity of the reform programme is shown by the fact that farmers will be compensated for about 50 per cent of the lost cereal revenues and 80 per cent of beef revenues by being given cash grants transferred directly from taxpayer to farmer. However, this direct aid will be gradually reduced for farmers earning more than £65 000 a year. Also national governments will be able to prioritise grant allocation to favour the environment and preservation of the countryside. More money will also be provided by national governments and the EU to encourage early retirement. However, no time limit has been given for ending these grants, while it is likely that these proposals will be reduced in the negotiations leading to the next budget.

■ The deepening of the EU

The process of EU integration – known as deepening of the EU – is discussed in various sections of this book. This section seeks briefly to draw together some of the strands.

The moves to a single currency discussed in Chapter 3, with one central EU bank and coordinated monetary policy, demonstrate that even more than its commitment to widening, the EU is committed to moving towards greater economic and monetary integration. This in turn underpins the development of the single market and lays the basis for subsequent political union.

As the Treaty of Amsterdam shows, there is the basis for a flexible or multispeed model of the EU consisting of several concentric rings – an inner core of single currency members; an outer core of the four EU countries not expected to participate initially in the euro-zone; the six countries negotiating to join the EU in 2002; and the hopefuls waiting to be allowed to negotiate membership sometime in the middle future. In practice this is already starting through the very nature of the single currency. However, this would essentially be a transitional process with the final goal being full integration for all EU members. What is now clear is that the single currency will act as a catalyst to accelerate deepening for countries outside the euro-zone/Euroland which will soon realise that they cannot afford to be excluded from it. The UK has always preferred a broad-based shallow EU where no further deepening occurs, countries retain national sovereignty and relations between EU members are essentially based on free trade through the single market. Clearly that time has passed.

It is unusual for a group of nations to seek firstly monetary union and then political union subsequently – although this is not spoken aloud within the EU for general consumption – yet. What has never been sustained long-term is the one without the other. Assuming then that political union will occur in time the debate will focus on the institutional structure and the extent to which democratic accountability can be in-built. At present the Council of Ministers' approach, where major decision-making is retained by nation states, is clearly the preferred model – hence the reluctance of the Council to surrender more powers to the European Parliament. However, as the EU moves to greater deepening or integration, it will have to consider whether this is still a feasible model. If the intention of the EU is to create a United States of Europe, based on the United States of America, then clearly substantial power must be vested in the democratically elected European Parliament rather than unelected bureaucrats. A prime minister or president or whatever s/he is called can then be chosen from the majority party as with national governments now. Whether the Council of Ministers becomes an upper house – like the Senate in the US – or whether some alternative is devised will depend on future negotiations. Power over EU-wide policies – economic policy, foreign policy, defence and so on – would be vested in this centre.

This would then leave national governments with reduced powers and functioning as regional assemblies – as do state governments in the US. They might have control over local education, sales-tax-varying powers, and perhaps some local income-tax-raising powers. However, they would clearly operate within the constraints of the EU government. This, at present, would be asking a very great deal from London, Berlin, Paris and others, but it is the logical final outcome.

■ 2.7 The impact of EU policy on business organisations

To be successful in the modern European business environment it is essential that managers have a clear understanding of the decision-making processes in the EU and especially how economic and social policies are formulated. Chapter 1 set the context for EU policy-making and this chapter has attempted to demonstrate its functioning and the dynamic nature of EU development. The policies implemented by the EU in turn have a major impact not just on the business environment but also on how the business may function within that environment. The advent of the single market in 1992 and the wave of privatisations by national governments in response to this and to meeting the Maastricht criteria have affected businesses in all countries significantly. For example this is shown by the spate of mergers within the EU. Most importantly, of course, are the moves to the single currency which, at the time of writing, many businesses still seem relatively unprepared for.

Environmental policy, which is discussed in Chapter 11, is another example of the effect of the EU. Environmental policies introduced in the next 10 years in response to global warming will have a major impact on firms' production methods, production costs and on the very goods and services which they produce. Most importantly, however, is the pace of change which is accelerating as technology changes and new competitors enter the market, giving businesses shorter lead times in which to make decisions. The EU has sought to develop communication and information technology strategies which will lay a framework to ensure that no areas of the EU are excluded and that, as far as possible, it is able to compete effectively against the US and Japan.

As discussed in Chapter 3, the playing field is no longer European but global. The ability of EU firms to remain competitive, through initiatives such as the Single European Act and a single currency, will be tested most strongly by the new players of the Pacific Rim – countries such as South Korea, China, Malaysia and Indonesia who will recover from the 1997–98 crisis. The effectiveness of EU competition policy, discussed in Chapter 4, to promote competitive global players, the so-called Euro-champions, will be most tested in this context.

Against this there is the debate over EU social policy, also discussed in Chapter 4. Whether this will raise production costs and make EU firms less competitive, or whether it will create a skilled workforce able to meet the challenges of the twenty-first century, remains to be seen. Whatever the outcome it will be largely due to the impact of EU policies on European businesses. Numerous other examples of the effects of EU policies could be quoted; its contributions to the European Bank for Reconstruction and Development (EBRD), with the opportunities the CEEC offer to EU producers and the promotion of trans-European networks all impacting significantly on European businesses.

Hence European businesses need to be proactive to change, not reactive. This may mean increasing production to achieve economies of scale, diversifying into new products, undertaking foreign direct investment, merging with other EU firms (with all the implications for competition policy) or raising finance from new sources. In the end the EU can create the business environment and even give financial support – but it is for businesses themselves to seize the opportunities which have been created for them.

■ Review questions

1. To what extent did the people drafting the Treaty of Rome have European union as one of their objectives?
2. Discuss critically the moves towards greater European integration in the period since 1987.
3. What impact was the Treaty of Maastricht intended to have on European business?
4. Why did the Treaty of Amsterdam not achieve what it set out to do?
5. What are the arguments for:

   a. Maintaining the present nature of the EU where power rests largely with member states.
   b. Moving to a federal model where most power passes to the centre (EU institutions) as with the US, and European nations become equivalent to American states.

■ Bibliography

European Documentation (Luxembourg: Commission of the European Communities).

Noel, E., *Working Together – The Institutions of the European Community*. European Documentation (Luxembourg: Office for Official Publications of the European Communities, 1993).

Swann, D., *The Economics of the Common Market*, 8th edn (Harmondsworth: Penguin Books, 1993).

Also:

The Economist
The European
The Financial Times
The Times
The European Commission website   http://www.cec.org.uk
EU General Report website   http://europa.eu.int/abc/doc/off/index-en.htm
European Investment Bank website   http://www.eib.org/over.htm

CHAPTER 3

From Single Market to Single Currency

■ 3.1 Introduction

In this chapter the introduction of the single market will be considered, including its rationale, how successful its implementation has been so far, and its impact on European businesses.

The single or internal market has also provided the motivation for another EU policy which will be examined here, the EU's economic and monetary policy. If the EU is to compete successfully in global markets there is a clear need for a single currency, just as the US and Japan each have a single currency. This must include one central bank, common monetary policy and, in time, common fiscal policies.

■ 3.2 The Single Market

■ The Treaty of Rome

The origins of the single market, an example of a common market as defined in Table 2.1, are to be found in the Treaty of Rome. Articles 3 and 9 required, by 31 December 1969:

1. 'the implementation of a common customs tariff and a common commercial policy towards third countries';
2. 'the abolition as between member states of obstacles to freedom of movement for persons, services and capital.' Article 9 adds to this '. . . which shall cover all trade in goods';
3. 'the establishment of a system ensuring that competition in the common market is not distorted';
4. 'the creation of a European Social Fund in order to improve the possibilities of employment for workers and to contribute to the raising of their standard of living'.

It also required the coordination of economic policies to remedy disequilibria in the balance of payments.

The removal of tariffs and quotas was achieved by 1968. The other articles have now been implemented to a considerable extent although 2 and 3 above need continual attention as new obstacles to the free movement of goods and services develop and businesses seek to gain competitive advantage by undermining competition. The importance of these aims can be seen by the fact that one integrated market was a clear objective of the founders of the EEC from its inception.

■ The 1980s revival

After the stagnation of the late 1970s and early 1980s aggravated by economic recession and high inflation, when little was achieved, January 1985 saw the new president of the European Commission, Jacques Delors, introduce the proposals for the internal market (known as the 1992 initiative) to the European Parliament on behalf of the national Heads of State. This was followed by the publication of the white paper known as the Cockfield Report, finally ratified by member states as the Single European Act.

The problems which the EC faced, as Delors soon realised, were that not only had all the original non-tariff barriers (NTBs) not been eliminated, but that new ones had come into being during the intervening years. VAT differences between member states, differences in environmental laws, subsidies, exchange controls, different technical standards, as well as the doubling in size of the EC, all meant that much still had to be done to create a single market.

Among the controls needing to be removed were physical controls over cross-border movement by people and goods, differing health requirements for livestock and foodstuffs, differing technical standards for the same goods manufactured in different countries (for example, televisions – technical barriers), and non-recognition of other countries' educational and professional qualifications. Additionally there were fiscal barriers in existence inhibiting trade such as differential VAT rates between countries. Earlier attempts at harmonising standards had clearly failed so there was a need for concerted action to move things forward.

There were a number of reasons why action towards a single market had to be a priority:

1. To complete the still unachieved objectives defined by the Treaty of Rome.
2. If the EC were to compete successfully against the US and Japan one unified EC market was needed rather than 12 fragmented national markets. This would enable the growth of Euro-champions, European firms capable of competing on equal terms with American and Japanese multinationals. It would be addressed in terms of such issues as R&D, product quality, competitiveness, productivity, labour relations, innovative ideas for products and cost and hence price.
3. European consumers would benefit as a result of firms achieving economies of scale through a larger market, rationalisation of production in two or three centres instead of in each EC country (as Dutch giant Phillips was able to do), standardised products instead of a separate one for each national market, and producers able to pass these lower costs on as lower prices.
4. A single market would involve freedom of movement for all factors of production, reducing the differentials between countries on factor returns such as interest rates

and rents. Most importantly it would facilitate freedom of movement for EC citizens, for business travel, vacations and for migration of labour to new jobs.
5. Following the introduction of the European Monetary System in 1979 a single market was an essential prerequisite to further movement towards Economic and Monetary Union (EMU) and a single currency, and, ultimately, political union.

■ The Single European Act 1987

This Act was passed as a consequence of the European Commission's white paper *Completing the Internal Market*, drawn up under the chairmanship of Lord Cockfield, one of the two British Commissioners (and hence also known as the Cockfield Report). Noted for its thoroughness, the white paper identified a comprehensive programme of 282 measures to be implemented to complete the single or internal market and the timetable to achieve this. The Single Market Programme included an examination of how the internal barriers to free trade might be removed and the consequences of these. Such barriers included physical, technical and fiscal restrictions on trade in goods and services. The deadline for completion of the single market was to be 31 December 1992.

Allied to this was an emphasis on the need for the Commission to introduce other measures to complement the single market initiative, in areas such as regional and social policy. It stressed the need for three areas in particular:

1. Ensuring economic cohesion between the EC 12 was maintained – due to the risk of poorer regions suffering at the expense of richer ones.
2. To create a competitive economy free from cartels, monopolistic abuse of power and government favouring of national companies.
3. The role of the EC in implementing community law – and its precedence over national law in achieving these objectives.

It was realised from the beginning that the white paper would inevitably have a major impact both on European businesses and on national economies if its aims and objectives were achieved. However, the exact effect was not quantified at the time – that was left retrospectively to the Cecchini Report.

On the basis of the Cockfield Report the Single European Act was endorsed by the European Council in December 1985, signed by all member states in February 1986 and entered into force in July 1987. The Act was a major step forward in the development of the then EC. It amended the Treaty of Rome 1958, its first major reform in nearly thirty years. Its aims were:

1. Moving the EC forward towards the achievement of the single market by the end of 1992. Most fundamentally it sought to introduce the 'Four Freedoms'; that is, freedom of movement for goods, services, capital (money) and labour within the internal market. To achieve these a wide range of barriers had to be addressed, including those affecting food, labour, capital, public procurement, services (including financial), transport and broadcasting. These were identified by the Single European Act.
2. Speeding up decision-making through the extension of majority voting by qualified majority voting (QMV) for measures concerning the establishment and operation of

the single market. This was to accelerate the legislative process by preventing any one country (usually the UK) blocking reform for all.
3. Development of the cooperation procedure giving the European parliament a greater input to the legislative process, through consultation with the Commission and the Council (of Ministers).
4. Modifications to the Treaty of Rome regarding economic and social cohesion, the environment and so on. For example, it was thought that the impact of the single market would accentuate the economic and social differences between the EC core and its periphery (Greece, Ireland, Southern Italy, Spain and Portugal). Consequently it was decided to target the periphery with more funds to redress any worsening of this imbalance, and to encourage more EC businesses to locate in peripheral regions or at least to stay there if already so located.

The Single European Act was also an important building block for the subsequent Treaty of Maastricht.

■ The Cecchini Report: the cost of non-Europe (1989)

This was drafted by a group of economists and consultants under the chairmanship of Paulo Cecchini. The report, so named because of the opportunity costs to the EC if a single market were not fully implemented, identified physical (e.g. customs control and paperwork), technical (e.g. differing national product standards) and fiscal (e.g. different rates of VAT and excise duties) barriers which needed to be removed to create a single market. It also sought to estimate the gains from removing barriers directly affecting intra-EC trade, hence enabling firms to enter EC markets other than their own, and therefore derive the benefits from unrestricted EC-wide competition.

The process of benefits from the single market was identified as:

- removal of non-tariff barriers leads to
- fall in production costs – which leads to
- fall in prices through greater competition – which leads to
- increased demand – which leads to
- increased output – which leads to
- better resource exploitation – which leads to
- increasing economies of scale and global competition

Summarising the findings of the Cecchini Report, the following were identified as immediate and medium to long-term:

☐ 1 Real and potential gains

1. The total gain to the EC from completion of the single or internal market would be ECU 216 billion at 1988 prices. This was equivalent to approximately 4.5 per cent of EC GDP.
2. The medium-term creation of between 1.8m to 5m new jobs, depending on macro-economic policies.
3. A medium-term reduction in consumer prices of an average 6.1 per cent.
4. A medium-term growth of EC trade with other countries of 1 per cent of EC GDP (the external balance).

☐ 2 Real and potential savings

1. ECU 12.5bn to 23bn from abolishing border controls and procedures.
2. Removing public procurement and hence opening domestic markets to competition from other EC countries: ECU 17.5bn.
3. Cost savings from enabling manufacturers to achieve economies of scale from increased market size which are not yet obtained: 2 per cent of GDP.
4. Medium-term economies in public sector costs of 2.2 per cent of GDP.

☐ 3 How accurate was the Cecchini Report?

- A survey of 3500 business executives, conducted by the EU in November 1997, found that the benefits of the single market are being felt across European businesses. Most restrictions on trade have been eliminated and competition is more intense causing lower prices, improved quality and variety of products manufactured.
- Margaret Beckett, then the British Minister for Trade and Industry, appeared before the House of Commons in February 1998 during the UK's presidency of the EU to stress the former's commitment to making EU industry and its environment more competitive. This, she said, would enable more jobs to be created and living standards to be raised. She argued that research indicated that the single market had already created 900 000 new jobs, increased EU GDP by between 1.1 to 1.5 per cent, and lowered inflation by 1 per cent.
- In essence, however, the benefits of the single market have never fully emerged. In the 1980s the Single Market programme became bogged down in a detailed programme of harmonisation measures. 1992 which was meant to deliver the internal market did not achieve this, partly because EU consumers and most businesses have not acted as if the single market existed. This was exacerbated by the economic recession of the early 1990s while the continued existence of exchange rates has acted as a quasi-tariff inhibiting single market trade.

■ The current position

The main objective of the European Union regarding the internal market is to ensure it is working effectively by 1 January 1999, when the single currency is introduced. This has involved:

(i) **Making single market rules more efficient and effective** – reinforced by the 1996 SLIM (simpler legislation for the internal market) initiative which, as its name suggests, seeks to simplify EU legislation. Proposals from the 1985 white paper remaining to be implemented include a European company statute, legislation relating to takeovers, and eliminating double taxation of companies, that is when taxes have to be paid in two EU countries. This last issue is being tackled through a directive, proposed in March 1998, which will seek to eliminate taxes being paid at the source of payments of interest and royalties between associated companies in different EU countries. These will be paid only where the company receiving the funds is located. It is proposed that this will apply to companies with cross-share holdings of at least 25 per cent.

(ii) **Eliminating remaining barriers to the completion of the internal market** – the Commission has created networks for improving cooperation between member governments. One problem is that different member states apply EU laws in different ways. This can serve as barriers to trade since companies are uncertain as to the legal frameworks within which they operate; they are then discouraged from exploiting the internal market.

CASE STUDY   Breaching the Rules of the Single Market

The European Court of Justice strongly criticised the French government in November 1997 following actions by the Commission, Spain and the UK to take it to the Court. The Court ruled that for years the French government had 'manifestly and persistently abstained' from taking action against French farmers for disrupting movements of fruit and vegetables from Spain – a breach of single market rules. The Commission was particularly annoyed by the failure of the French police to take action against the Coordination Rurale, the organisation of militant farmers which organised attacks on trucks bringing Spanish agricultural produce into France between 1993–95. France was ordered to pay costs – however, the ruling also opens the possibility of the French government being sued for damages in UK and Spanish courts. In the case of the UK the concern was over the economic impact of the 1996 French truckers' strike – after 18 months the French government had only settled a small percentage of compensation claims.

Following from this the Commission proposed a regulation whereby member states with serious road blockages inhibiting the free movement of goods, such as through strike action, must remedy this.

The Commission also publishes a single market scoreboard which monitors the progress made by EU members towards completion of the market. In May 1998, this scoreboard indicated that 18 per cent of measures still had not yet been implemented by all the EU15, albeit a substantial reduction from the figure of 35 per cent when the Single Market Action Plan was implemented in June 1997. Belgium was the worst country still having to implement 7.1 per cent of the 1368 directives involved, compared with the best country, Finland, which had only 1.2 per cent outstanding. The UK still had 3.8 per cent of the directives to be implemented. The deadline for completion by all countries is 1 January 1999.

The European Commission pursues infringement procedures against member states for failing fully to implement directives related to the single market. Members are brought before the European Court of Justice. In 1998 these proceedings related to public procurement directives (the UK, Austria, Germany, Portugal, Greece and Spain are the main culprits); the freedom to provide services and freedom to establish businesses in other countries (Belgium, Italy and France); barriers to trade (France, Belgium, Italy and Greece) and freedom of services linked to recognition of qualifications (Greece and France).

The scoreboard also monitors the time it takes a country to respond to EU notices issued under the infringement proceedings; that is, when a country has action taken against it for failing fully to implement a directive – Austria has the best record with 37 days, while Portugal has the worst with 237 days.

(iii) **Removing obstacles which might inhibit the integration of the market** – or more accurately a series of sub-markets for different goods and services which, in total, comprise the internal market. For example, in November 1997 the informal Internal Market Council, established to monitor progress to the completion of the internal market, agreed a mechanism to ensure transparency (openness so that citizens can clearly see how and why EU decisions are made) for information services. Its purpose is to make sure that the internal market for communication and information services does not become fragmented and that new national regulations do not appear which could promote a divided market by favouring domestic suppliers.

At the same time the Internal Market Council agreed to legal protection for biotechnological inventions. In other words national rules for patenting biological inventions will be harmonised, but the patenting of discoveries such as substances already present in nature – say from particular plants – will not be permitted. The cloning of human beings will also be prohibited under this legislation.

It should be remembered that harmonisation of rules and regulations is not always necessary. Where rules are not harmonised at EU level the principle of mutual recognition applies; that is, countries must recognise each other's rules and regulations (this dates back to the 1979 Cassis de Dijon case when the European Court ruled that goods legally made and marketed by one member state must be able to be sold in any other EU country). The Commission is also concerned with the number of technical rules which countries are introducing at national level; these are creating new barriers to completion. In 1997 doubts were raised 240 times about their compatibility with the single market.

(iv) **Maximising the benefits of the single market to ensure that all EU citizens benefit from it** – for example, the Schengen Agreement guarantees all travellers freedom to travel across internal EU borders without the need for passports (although they are still needed for identification), and for passengers arriving on flights from signatory states. Similarly, legislation such as the directives relating to working time, works councils and sexual discrimination have helped to improve citizens' working conditions. Consumer protection and the settlement of consumer disputes have also improved; a new proposed directive is intending to give consumers the right to a refund or replacement merchandise if a fault appears within one year of delivery. If a fault occurs in the second year the consumer can have it repaired free or at a reduced price.

The Internal Market Council has been responsible for proposing many directives to complete the single market. These have included:

- A directive to enable lawyers to practice fully in a member state other than the one where they gained their professional qualification.
- A directive relating to food irradiation and covering general provisions relating to treatment, approval and compulsory labelling.
- A directive on the legal protection of designs. This approximates national provisions of design law which most affect the workings of the internal market.

- A directive relating to intellectual property. Its aim is to harmonise rules concerning the reproduction of materials, communicating information to the public, and its distribution. This proposed directive is aimed at the growth of such media as CD-ROMs, the Internet, digital reproduction and other electronic systems.

■ Conclusions

The EU has made very substantial progress towards completing the internal market. This has mainly been through economic motives as a means to promote economic efficiency and thus enable European businesses to compete more effectively. It is also an essential prerequisite to Economic and Monetary Union, particularly the introduction of the single currency which, in turn, should enable the internal market to function better. Additionally, the EU is working actively to put in place a regulatory framework for new communication and information technologies and negotiating with six potential members of the EU, which will enlarge the single market. However, it should also be remembered that there is an underlying political agenda, namely that the above are means to pursue the political integration of the EU through an economic route. In extremis this could lead to the creation of a United States of Europe.

■ 3.3 Economic and Monetary Union

■ What is Economic and Monetary Union (EMU)?

Monetary union is the process whereby the exchange rates of a group of members are irrevocably fixed, or replaced by a single common currency. It also implies the existence of one monetary authority with responsibility for, *inter alia*, the growth of money supply, interest rate policy (an average appropriate rate for the whole EU will be determined by the European Central Bank – see below), exchange rate policy and control of foreign currency reserves.

Economic union implies a single market free of barriers to trade in goods and services, or capital and labour movements; the ability of firms to compete freely through a competition policy implemented throughout the market to strengthen its operation; a social policy to demonstrate the benefits of the single market to consumers; the coordination of macroeconomic policy (particularly the alignment of inflation rates); and harmonisation of fiscal policy, including common taxation rates through the union and significant fiscal transfers from wealthier to poorer regions. Their purpose is to promote structural change and regional development.

Although the EU is not yet committed to introducing common fiscal policies, nonetheless harmonisation of tax rates must inevitably come as part of economic integration. In October 1997, the Commission proposed measures to achieve greater coordination between member states on tax policy and to cut tax competition which is widely perceived to distort the free working of the single market. With differing tax rates some governments experience serious losses of tax revenue, and also there is a growing tendency to shift the burden of taxation onto labour to offset taxation on more mobile factors such as capital. The proposals cover a draft code of conduct on business taxation, principles for the taxation of income from capital, abolishing cross-border withholding taxes and royalty payments, and indirect taxation. They seek to recognise the principle of subsidiarity yet also strike a balance between different member states' interests.

■ Optimum currency areas: the theory underpinning EMU

The theory of optimum currency areas, developed by R. Mundell in 1961 and R. McKinnon in 1963, is the model for the European Monetary System (EMS) which has provided the framework for the moves to Economic and Monetary Union (EMU). It relates to a group of nations with currencies linked through permanently fixed exchange rates – stage 3 of the EMS; or, in extremis, a single currency – and what makes this an optimum arrangement. Simply, the currencies of the optimum currency area (OCA) can then float jointly against those of non-members. This removes exchange rate uncertainty for intra-OCA trading and hence should promote intra-OCA price stability, production (since businesses will view the OCA as a single market offering opportunities to achieve scale economies), trade and investment. With permanently fixed exchange rates there is less need for official intervention in the Forex (foreign exchange) markets and, if a single currency is adopted, exchange conversion costs are eliminated. Also, businesses no longer have to hedge against potential exchange rate variations through forward currency contracts. A single currency also removes risks that permanently fixed exchange rates may in fact diverge through speculative funds (so-called 'hot money') moving from financial centre to centre and thus destabilising the rates – since global speculative funds far exceed the official reserves of central banks.

The downside of an OCA is that individual members cannot pursue independent economic policies to promote macroeconomic stabilisation and growth since this would destabilise the fixed exchange rates. Where there are major economic differences between, say, a depressed region and a high-growth region, the former is unable to pursue an expansionary fiscal and monetary policy while, simultaneously, the latter pursues deflationary policies. To some extent this problem may be offset by the movement of capital and labour (the aim of the four freedoms of the single market) from the depressed regions to the prosperous ones. The returns to labour and capital will then rise in the depressed region (where the supply of factors is reduced) and fall in the prosperous region receiving the influx of factors. More likely, however, the central authorities controlling the OCA (the European Commission) will have to transfer funds from prosperous to depressed regions – which is the purpose of the European Regional Development Fund (ERDF), the Cohesion Fund and the Common Agricultural Policy (CAP).

■ Why is Economic and Monetary Union important to the EU?

With the advent of the single market on 1 January 1993 the EU was able to compete on more equal terms with the US and Japan, both unified markets without internal barriers. The disadvantage that the EU still faces is the use of many currencies instead of one. As the theory of optimum currency areas demonstrates, this poses major economic and business barriers in terms of:

- exchange costs incurred whenever an intra-EU trade transaction is undertaken;
- possible deterrence of internal trade by the uncertainty and potential costs of actual or potential exchange rate movements, which is aggravated by potential speculative behaviour;
- lack of a unified monetary and fiscal policy inhibits greater economic convergence and cohesion between different countries, including lower interest rates; and
- adverse effects on resource allocation, particularly capital movements, of differences in the economic stability and performance of different EU countries.

Additionally, economic and monetary union is a co-requisite of political union. In some federal nations, such as the US and Switzerland, political union has preceded a single currency and economic and monetary union. In the case of the EU the aim is to use EMU as a vehicle to promote subsequent political union.

■ 3.4 The development of EMU

■ The first steps

The Treaty of Rome, as originally written (that is, before subsequent amendments by the Single European Act and so on), did not seek Economic and Monetary Union. This was because under the Bretton Woods system of managed exchange rates currency stability was assumed to be the norm. However, (article) a.103–109 did address such objectives for members as balance of payments equilibrium and full employment and coordination of economic policies.

By the late 1960s, with the European Community well-established and tariff and quota barriers to the single market largely removed, thoughts turned to the possibility of a single currency and economic and monetary union. This would reinforce the progress made with the single market and also the political aspirations of the EC6 regarding future developments of the EC. However, there were differences of opinion as to the path to be followed to achieve this, particularly over whether economies should converge their economic performance before fixing exchange rates irrevocably (the current Maastricht model), or whether exchange rates should first be fixed and countries allowed subsequently to converge through the exchange rate discipline that would follow (as discussed above). This led in 1970 to the establishment of the Werner Committee to resolve these problems.

This committee proposed European Monetary Union (also known as EMU) by 1980. It included a number of stages which have also appeared in the more recently proposed Economic and Monetary Union (EMU) as discussed below. Among these were fixed parities for EC currencies with narrow margins of fluctuation (known as the snake in the tunnel), an EC currency subsequently, and an EC central banking system. However, the failure of the Smithsonian Agreement, the resort to floating by a number of snake members, and the 1973 oil price increase of 400 per cent ended any hope of EMU for the foreseeable future. This included an unsuccessful attempt by Commission President Roy Jenkins to resurrect it in 1977.

■ The European Monetary System (EMS)

□ 1 Why was the EMS established?

The EMS was established in March 1979 as a consequence of the EC's desire to promote greater economic integration of the EC12 and the coordination of economic policies, both internal (through the control of inflation) and external (through the development of a system of stable exchange rates).

Greater economic integration was important because of the increased regional disparities caused by the lower per capita income of the three new members, Greece, Portugal and Spain. Inflation was the major economic problem of the 1970s (just as long-term unemployment is in the 1990s), necessitating a coordinated approach to overcome it. Additionally, the desire to return to the stability of a Bretton Woods-type exchange rate system, and the need for such stability if members' economic policies were to be coordinated and intra-EU trade were to grow, prompted the development of the EMS.

□ 2 The main components of the EMS

At its founding the EMS consisted of four main components:

1. The European Currency Unit (ECU)
2. The Exchange Rate Mechanism (ERM)
3. The Financial Support Mechanisms (FSM)
4. The European Monetary Cooperation Fund (EMCF)

The European Currency Unit   The ECU was typically described as a basket of all EU currencies, the amount of each weighted according to its country's share of EU GDP, external trade and so on. The precise mix of the ECU varied every five years to reflect changes in these variables after consultation with the member states. However, its composition has been constant since 1 November 1993 and it will be replaced by the euro from January 1999.

The main advantage of the ECU was that it spread the risks of individual EU currencies changing in value; for example if the deutschemark rose in value and the peseta fell the value of the ECU would change less than either currency individually, since the opposite movements in part cancelled each other out. The ECU's main functions were as a denominator for the EU – the EU budget was denominated in ECU; it served as a major component of the ERM, indicating when a currency diverged from its central rate; and it was used as a means of settlement within the EU, for example in payment of set-aside to farmers or grants to peripheral regions.

The Exchange Rate Mechanism   The ERM has been the central element of the European Monetary System. It is a system of pegged exchange rates with each member currency linked to others' currencies and hence to the ECU at a central rate or parity. When the ERM was initiated each currency was allowed to fluctuate by $+/-2.25$ per cent against its central rate. New currencies likely to have initial adjustment difficulties due, for example, to speculative pressures were permitted to join with $+/-6$ per cent bands. This applied at various times to Italy, Spain, Portugal and the UK. Since August 1993, when currencies suffered severe speculative attacks, the bands have technically been $+/-15$ per cent, although in practice they operated within very narrow bands again once confidence was regained.

Financial support mechanisms   These are financial facilities to assist central banks when they need to intervene in the forex markets to support their currency if is falling in value or if encountering balance of payments difficulties. There are a variety of short, medium and long-term facilities ranging from a maximum of three months for the short term, to five years for the long term.

The European Monetary Cooperation Fund   This was a central fund into which central banks pooled 20 per cent of their gold and foreign exchange reserves. In return they received ECUs which were then used to settle payments between members. The EMCF ran the EMS on a day-to-day basis in conjunction with the central banks, whose governors were on its board, until its functions were taken over by the European Monetary Institute on 1 January 1994.

■ The ERM's track record

In the early years of the ERM (1979–83) there were a series of exchange rate adjustments aggravated by the lack of appropriate domestic economic policy by governments to support stable exchange rates. The years 1983–87 saw growing stability with the deutschemark emerging as the cornerstone of the ERM which was being described effectively as a deutschemark zone. This was reinforced by the French decision to link the franc to the deutschemark (Le franc fort) after 1987 through the use of monetary policy (high interest rates) to control inflation and maintain a high exchange rate rather than making economic growth the primary objective (before 1987, due to the existence of exchange controls, France had relied primarily on fiscal policy to control inflation).

The convergence of member countries' inflation to the German level, which subsequently ensued, was achieved by other ERM governments also taking internal action to control inflation, particularly through monetary policy. Furthermore, since being in the ERM, governments could not allow exchange rates to fall to offset the effects of high inflation; inflationary wage claims were therefore met by deflationary policies, especially monetary, causing increasing unemployment. This convergence of other countries' inflation rates to the German level resulted in much greater real exchange rate stability. From 1987 to 1992, reinforced by the increasing coordination of interest rate changes among the ERM members exchange rates remained stable despite the abolition of capital exchange controls, emphasising the central role of the Bundesbank and creating an impression of non-moveable exchange rates. It was this stability which reinforced the concept of movement to a single currency.

Exchange controls are important regarding the EMS since the 1988 EC directive requiring their abolition freed capital flows. This enabled such funds to move from international financial centre to centre to take advantage of interest rate differentials. This can be very destabilising to exchange rates, as the ERM crises of September 1992, August 1993 and March 1995 proved. Capital movements also impact on a nation's monetary policy since, for countries within the ERM, high interest rates are needed to keep their currencies closely linked to the value of the deutschemark. Yet this then dictates domestic economic policy and adversely affects economic growth.

After 1992 real doubts were cast on the future viability of the ERM. The crisis of 16 September 1992 (Black Wednesday), when sterling and the lira left the ERM, shook it to its foundations. This was attributable to a considerable extent to the effects of German reunification, with a Bundesbank policy of high interest rates to offset the inflationary effects of a large budget deficit, making the DM even stronger against other currencies. With sterling and the lira overvalued in the ERM in relation to their countries' economic conditions, speculators sold these in exchange for DM. The inability of these countries' central banks to stop speculative selling in spite of their large-scale buying of their currencies and raising interest rates forced sterling and the lira to leave the ERM.

In August 1993 the ERM came under renewed speculative selling and the franc, one of its cornerstones, barely managed to avoid devaluation. The cost of this, achieved by a high interest rate policy, was a French economy which took longer than most to recover from the recession of the early 1990s and even now has significant economic problems, as demonstrated by President Chirac's attempts to combat high unemployment. Worst of all, the ERM bands were widened from +/−2.25% to +/−15%, making the ERM a system of managed floating exchange rates in all but name. However, retention of the name was important since stable exchange rates are one of the Maastricht convergence criteria on the route to a single currency. Also, subsequently, the remaining ERM members effectively operated within the old +/−2.25 per cent bands, even though the technical limits are still +/−15 per cent.

The March 1995 ERM crisis, due to further speculative selling aimed as much against the French franc as any currency, weakened the viability of the ERM still further. This was due as much to the strength of the deutschemark as to the weaknesses of other currencies. Since 1995 there have been no further exchange rate crises and ERM countries are now working towards the single currency as is discussed below. The major concern of the core countries, France and Germany, has been the problems of high unemployment which are discussed elsewhere.

■ 3.5 The Delors Report 1989

This originated in the June 1988 European Council meeting in Hanover which appointed a committee of experts, chaired by Jacques Delors, then European Commission President, to determine how to complete economic and monetary union. Their report was made to the June 1989 Madrid Summit of the European Council, where it was decided to begin the first stage towards EMU on 1 July 1990 and to prepare for an Intergovernmental Conference (IGC) on EMU to be held in Maastricht, the Netherlands, in December 1991. As can be seen in Table 3.1 the Delors Report identified three stages in the transition to economic and monetary union.

Stage 1 would see a convergence of members' economic indicators to a common level, the creation of a single market and all EC currencies to have joined the ERM. Stage 2, which was less well-defined, would see a transition to EMU with the newly emergent European System of Central Banks (ESCB) taking considerable macroeconomic responsibilities in terms of coordinating national policies, although national governments would still retain final responsibility during this period. By stage 3 the ESCB would assume still greater responsibility for monetary policy with internal exchange rates being totally fixed and subsequently and rapidly replaced by a single currency. The ESCB would also control foreign exchange reserves.

This required a very substantial surrender of national autonomy, and the UK and Denmark among the EC12 refused to agree to this without a referendum. Stage 1 was targeted to begin in July 1990, and stage 2 was to begin on 1 January 1994. The ESCB was to assume a major role through its committee of central bank governors. This included ensuring that national monetary policies were executed in accordance with general monetary directives for the EC as a whole; replacing the EMCF (part of the EMS) and using members' pooled foreign exchange reserves to intervene in the Forex markets to defend currencies under speculative attack; irrevocably locking exchange rate fluctuations within the ERM; and establishing the basics for a structured EC wide monetary and banking system. Stage 3 was to begin on or after 1 July 1998.

As Table 3.1 shows, the key issue regarding the Delors Report was that every EU member would join the ERM at Stage 1 and hence, at Stage 3, the proposed single currency – there would be no need to prove that one was economically worthy to join as has been the case with Maastricht. Monetary and fiscal policy

Table 3.1   The Delors Report 1989

THE DELORS REPORT JUNE 1989: STAGES TO EMU

Stage One: Convergence of Members' Economic Indicators
1. End all physical/technical/fiscal barriers by end 1992.
2. Strengthen competition policy and reduce state aid to industry.
3. Reform structural funds.
4. Closer coordination of economic and monetary policies.
5. Deregulate financial markets; establish a single financial area.
6. Free intra-EC movement of capital.
7. All currencies to join ERM.
8. Removal of restrictions to private use of the ECU.

Stage Two: Transition
1. Revision of existing institutions.
2. Establishment of new institutions, including European System of Central Banks (ESCB).
3. Substantial transfer of economic power from national governments to ESCB – including coordination of independent monetary policies through collective decision-making (although ultimate macroeconomic responsibility to remain with national governments).

Stage Three: Completion
1. Further strengthening of structural and regional policies to ease transition.
2. Move to irrevocably fixed exchange rates.
3. Binding constraints on national budget deficits imposed by ESCB.
4. EC to act as a single entity in international economic and monetary cooperation.
5. Formulation and implementation of monetary policy by ESCB (in liaison with national ministers).
6. ESCB to control all foreign exchange reserves in the EC.
7. ESCB to determine each country's exchange rate against each other, and Forex market interventions.
8. Introduction of a single currency.

(especially constraints on national budget deficits) would be determined through qualified majority voting by the national representatives on the ESCB. Hence under the Delors Plan economic convergence by member countries will be continued at stage 2 through the dominant ESCB.

■ 3.6 The Treaty of Maastricht 1993

The Delors Report was the basis for discussions on Economic and Monetary Union at the Inter-Governmental Conference at Maastricht in 1991, from which emerged the programme identified in Table 3.2. It can be seen that the stages to

EMU, defined by the Treaty of Maastricht, rely heavily, although not exclusively, on the Delors Report.

A crucial difference between the two is that under the terms of Maastricht countries have been obliged to demonstrate their economic worthiness to join the single currency by their ability to meet the Maastricht convergence criteria (see Table 3.3). There is not automatic membership for everyone. This was a requirement of Germany's to ensure that the hard (that is, inflation-resistant) deutschemark was not replaced by a weaker more inflation-prone euro (or ecu as it then still was), thus undermining Germany's strong stance against inflation over the postwar period.

Also, the role of the Frankfurt-based European Monetary Institute (EMI) was to coordinate but not control national monetary policies in preparation for the functioning of the politically independent European Central Bank, which has now replaced it. Hence its power was much less than that envisaged for the ESCB under Delors. For example, to intervene in the foreign exchange market to defend ERM currencies it needed the permission of its constituent members – the Delors' ESCB would have had the right to intervene automatically. Indeed member countries were not obliged to transfer foreign exchange reserves to the EMI whereas they were to the proposed Delors' ESCB. The EMI's members were governors of the national central banks and the EMI cooperated with them and established a framework for the operation of the Maastricht-type ESCB (European System of Central Banks), which includes the European Central Bank.

Table 3.2   The Treaty of Maastricht: stages to EMU

THE TREATY OF MAASTRICHT DECEMBER 1991: STAGES TO EMU

Stage One: 1 July 1990–End 1993
1. Completion of the Single European Market by 1 January 1993.
2. Unification of financial markets.
3. All ERM members to enter normal bands (usually taken to be +/−2.25 per cent).

Stage Two: 1 January 1994–1999
1. Member countries to seek to avoid excessive budget deficits.
2. Creation of an autonomous European Monetary Institute (EMI) to be replaced subsequently by the European System of Central Banks (ESCB) which includes the European Central Bank.
3. EMI to acquire foreign exchange reserves of the ERM, held by the EMCF.
4. Governments to move towards making their central banks independent.
5. Governments to converge their main economic indicators (see below).
6. Member countries' currencies to enter narrow bands (+/−1 per cent).

Stage Three: 1999–2003
1. All members' currencies to be irrevocably fixed.
2. European Central Bank (ECB) to be able to issue a single currency.

The European System of Central Banks will consist of the European Central Bank (based in Frankfurt) and modelled on the US Federal Reserve Bank, and the EU15's own central banks. The first president of the ECB will be Wim Duisenberg, who initially was to be in power for an eight-year term; however, Jean-Claude Trichet of France is meant to be taking over after four years to appease French expectations that a Frenchman must be the head of all major international financial organisations. Its main area of responsibility is price stability (a.105). The EU and national governments will be required to consult with it on any areas within its realms of competence. Ultimately it will have sole responsibility for note issue in the EU. By stage 3 it will also have authority to adjust the central parity rate of the euro *vis-à-vis* other currencies, for example the yen or US dollar.

■ The Maastricht convergence criteria

The convergence criteria were identified in stage 2 (5) of Table 3.2 above, and are shown in Table 3.3 below. These must be achieved by member countries before being able to move to stage 3 and the single currency.

The Maastricht convergence criteria are important because without convergence by single currency countries to common levels for the main economic indicators, there would be significant difficulties once EMU had occurred – as would have resulted had the Delors Plan been implemented. For example, differences in inflation rates of different countries would mean that those countries with higher inflation would have less-competitive businesses. As discussed in Chapter 1, when economically separate, countries outside the ERM – particularly the UK – have allowed their nominal exchange rates to depreciate to offset their higher inflation and thus make their exports more

Table 3.3   The Maastricht convergence criteria

THE MAASTRICHT CONVERGENCE CRITERIA

---

1. **Inflation:** to be no higher than 1.5 per cent above the average for the three EU members with the lowest rates during the previous year.
2. **Long-Run Interest Rates:** to be no higher than 2 per cent above the three EU countries with the lowest rates during the previous year.
3. **Exchange Rate:** the exchange rate to have been in the normal band of the ERM (usually taken to be +/−2.25 per cent) for two years without devaluing.
4. **Budget Deficit:** the country's budget deficit should not exceed 3 per cent of its gross domestic product (GDP).
5. **National Debt:** should not exceed 60 per cent of GDP.

Note:
(i)   Inflation is measured by each country's retail price index or equivalent.
(ii) Long-run interest rates are determined by interest rates on government securities or 'gilts'

competitive. With fixed exchange rates or a single currency, that is an Optimum Currency Area, this is not feasible. Consequently, with less-competitive exports unemployment will rise and businesses in the high-inflation countries will fail. This dilemma can only be resolved when real wages fall to make labour a more attractive resource economically and hence production costs fall.

Similarly, with high inflation, long-run interest rates are also likely to be high. This will raise the cost of financing a government's budget deficit and national debt (items 4 and 5 of the convergence criteria) and also deter consumer expenditure and business investment in new capital, communication and information technologies, and so on. This again will harm the economic development of the country *vis-à-vis* converged members of the EMU; it will also harm low-inflation countries since there can only be one level of interest rates in EMU, determined by the European Central Bank. Consequently, high-inflation countries will have to use the only remaining weapon, namely fiscal policy. However, as noted before, probable harmonisation of tax rates and the need to maintain the public debt requirements of the convergence criteria mean that although this can be tightened there is a limit to how much this is politically acceptable. Also it cannot be loosened beyond the Maastricht criteria. This leaves deflation and unemployment, perhaps offset by fiscal transfers through regional policy, as the only remaining alternative.

When the first edition of this book was written no EU country had met all the Maastricht criteria in 1994, and only three, France, Luxembourg and the UK, had met four of them. At the other extreme Italy and Spain did not meet any of the criteria. Perhaps this was not surprising as the EU12 were still recovering from recession with the attendant impact on government expenditure (on social security for the unemployed, for example). Also, the 1993 and 1995 exchange rate instabilities explain why the exchange rate criterion was not met. In March 1998 11 EU countries qualified for membership of the single currency.

■ 3.7 The costs and benefits of the single currency

EMU offers countries a number of benefits and costs which are briefly reviewed in this section.

■ Benefits

1. Reinforcement of the single market (with its advantages to European businesses) by permitting all transactions in one currency – more than 60 per cent of EU countries' trade is with each other. This will promote competition within the EU and globally and enable European consumers and businesses to compare costs of goods and services produced in different countries without the distortions of exchange rate movements (transparency).

2. Wage rates will also move more to common levels through arbitrage – however, this is unlikely to promote greater movement of labour due to language, cultural and housing differences between different EU countries, particularly when economic shocks affect one part of the EU.
3. A larger and more liquid capital market, trading euro-denominated corporate bonds, will be created replacing inefficient domestic capital markets, especially banking systems, and promoting easier investment across the EU. In contrast, unstable national exchange rates discourage investment because the fluctuations often overshoot or undershoot their real values. A single currency may also attract more inward foreign direct investment.
4. Removal of exchange rate movements causing risks and uncertainties for European businesses.
5. Coordinated economic and monetary policy creating greater downward convergence of key economic variables such as inflation and consequently promoting greater economic growth.
6. Removal of exchange rate instability enables resources to be allocated more efficiently within the Union.
7. Unemployment should fall due to structural and regional changes (assisted by funds transferred to the poorer regions, such as the 1993 Cohesion Fund).
8. Greater competition arising from a single currency offers better choice, lower prices and better quality.
9. Reduced costs of travel and tourism – both major employers.

■ Costs

1. To promote economic union large-scale fiscal transfers will be needed from richer to poorer areas.
2. Eleven of the EU15 have achieved the convergence criteria and will adopt the single currency. This could lead to a two-speed EU, with the inner core of euro users – the so-called Euroland – and the outer core of the UK, Denmark, Sweden and probably Greece.
3. Citizens and their central banks may resent the loss of sovereignty and the inability to pursue their own economic policies. Instead the restrictions of other countries' policies, especially Germany's, will have to be accepted. Particularly, countries will be unable to use monetary policy (because interest rates will be determined by the ECB) while fiscal policy options will be limited by the need to maintain the Maastricht public debt criteria once in the single currency, enforced by the Stability and Growth Pact (see below). As noted elsewhere exchange rate adjustments can also no longer be used so any economic adjustments will have to be through adjusting output and employment, including wage cuts where necessary.
4. Any significant economic divergences between EU regions in the single currency zone will have to be met by transfers of funds. Yet the major EU donor countries are reluctant to contribute more, while the major recipient countries are unwilling to give up any EU funds. Additionally, newcomers from Central and Eastern Europe will expect substantial financial aid when they join – hence the need to reform the costly Common Agricultural Policy.
5. Also aggregate demand or supply-side shocks which are asymmetrical, that is peculiar to some countries but not others, cannot be offset by exchange rate adjustments as would be the case without EMU.

Cost number 3 above is the main concern of UK eurosceptics to membership of the single currency.

■ 3.8 The current progress to EMU

EU members are required by the Treaty of Maastricht to coordinate their macroeconomic policies within the Council of Ministers. The framework within which these policies are established is determined by the European Council.

■ The Stability and Growth Pact

In December 1996 the Dublin Summit of the European Council established a set of rules relating to currencies and budgetary discipline for countries inside and outside the single currency area – or euro zone. At this meeting two separate schools of thought developed.

On the German side there were demands for strict enforcement of the 3 per cent (of GDP) numerical target relating to budget deficits, with automatic fines for euro-zone countries exceeding this, and monitored by the independent European Central Bank. Essentially this was to stop countries relaxing their tough fiscal stances once they had secured euro-zone membership. In other words once a country had met the Maastricht convergence criteria it had to maintain these over time. This was to ensure that the euro remained a hard currency, as opposed to an inflation-prone soft one such as sterling in the past, an issue very important to Germans giving up their deutschemark, since the German central bank, the Bundesbank, had always maintained a rigorous stand against inflation.

On the other side was France which argued that, although fines were acceptable, the discretion to impose these must be retained by euro-zone member countries' government ministers to maintain national sovereignty.

The final outcome was the approval of a growth and stability pact. The growth aspect of this was a recognition of the severe problems faced particularly by France and Germany in terms of high unemployment for the reasons discussed in Chapter 1. The pact stipulated that:

1. Fines will be levied on a country which exceeds the convergence criterion requiring its budget deficit to be less than 3 per cent of the country's GDP. These fines will vary on a sliding scale from 0.2 to 0.5 per cent of the offending country's GDP. Whether these will actually be levied or whether they are merely intended to be a deterrent to warn potential offenders (because of the political implications of a country actually being fined by the ECB) remains to be seen.
2. Member states (of the euro-zone) which experience a fall in GDP of at least 2 per cent p.a. will automatically qualify for 'exceptional status'. A country experiencing a fall in GDP of 0.75 per cent or less can argue to the Council of Ministers that they are a special case.

The other area where Germany and France were in disagreement was over France's demand, supported by Italy, for a 'Stability Council' made up of ministers from EMU countries and intended as a political counterbalance to the ECB. Its argument was that national governments needed to be able to influence the running of the euro-zone rather than all decisions being made by technocrats – that is, the bureaucracy of the ECB. The majority of EU countries, including Germany and the UK, felt there was no need for such a body.

■ ERM 2

At the Dublin summit attention was also given to those countries remaining outside the euro-zone, that is, the periphery countries (or, as Brussels calls them, the 'pre-ins'). It was argued by ministers that there was a need for a 'hub and spokes' ERM, built around the euro and providing currency discipline between core or euro-zone members and the rest or periphery countries. Under ERM 2, due to come into operation in January 1999, the aim will be to create a stability zone by periphery countries linking their currencies to the euro.

ERM 2 will have three key characteristics. Firstly it will offer flexibility. Each periphery country will choose a central rate for its currency against the euro, after consultation with the ECB and the euro-zone members, and determined by its chances of joining the euro-zone. The fluctuation band will be relatively wide although a country can choose a narrower band if it wishes. Secondly, although periphery countries will be expected to join it will not be compulsory. The ECB and euro-zone countries will intervene in the foreign exchange markets to support the central exchange rate if it comes under speculative pressure but they may suspend this if there is a threat to price stability. (For example, if sterling came under pressure the ECB would have to use euros to buy pounds to maintain the central rate; however, supplying large amounts of euros to the Forex market can create inflationary pressures.) Thirdly, the principle of ministerial surveillance, whereby countries' economic programmes are scrutinised to ensure they stay within the convergence criteria, will apply both to euro-zone and ERM 2 countries alike. Hence countries whose currencies fluctuate wildly, for example, will not be permitted to join the single currency.

The UK has stated that it will not join ERM 2 but nonetheless is likely to try to maintain a stable exchange rate against the euro (shadow the euro) in the same way that in the late 1980s, before it joined the ERM, it shadowed the deutsche-mark.

■ The Euro X club

Initially dubbed the Euro X committee because of uncertainty over the number of countries who would qualify for single currency membership, this body was established at the insistence of France and Germany to coordinate policy in the euro-zone, especially during the period 1999–2002, from when exchange rates are fixed until when the euro enters circulation, and monitor economic, budgetary, exchange rate and other economic indicators' performance. Perceived as an

EU equivalent to G8 it is likely to be an important new centre of power and decision-making, although its founders insist that it will not infringe on the work of the European Central Bank or on Ecofin, the EU's economic and financial law-making body.

In a compromise solution to a dispute between France and the UK over the latter's right to attend Euro X meetings, it was agreed that the single currency countries would meet informally on issues specific to them while the other four EU members will be able to join them for matters of common interest.

■ Achieving the criteria for the single currency

As noted previously, Germany's concern has always been that there should be a hard rather than a soft euro – in other words that, as with the deutschemark, the authorities should exercise tight control over inflation and government debt. This would also reflect in a stable exchange rate against the US dollar, the Japanese yen, and so on – hence its demand for a stability pact to enforce monetary and fiscal discipline on member countries after the creation of the euro. This also explains its concerns over allowing Italy into the first wave of membership, because of its poor record of control over inflation and public debt. Indeed the OECD forecasts Italy as having public debt of 117.5 per cent of GDP in 1999 (against a 60 per cent maximum), and Belgium as having 118.7 per cent.

Nonetheless when it came to meeting the public debt criteria Germany and France were as glad as Italy to engage in what is known as creative accounting. Italy tried the tactic of selling gold to the Bank of Italy, levying capital gains tax on the sales and using this revenue to cut its 1997 budget deficit. However, the Commission blocked this. It has also levied a one-off 'euro tax'. Similarly, Germany sought to raise the value of its gold reserves but this proposal was subsequently blocked. France imposed a 'euro-tax' surcharge of 15 per cent on large corporations (to fall to 10 per cent after 1998) to raise an extra FF22bn tax revenue on corporate profits. It also sharply raised the long-term corporate capital gains tax from 19 per cent to 41.6 per cent, and cut defence spending by FF10bn.

The budgetary deficits of these countries were exacerbated by high unemployment which caused heavy spending on unemployment benefits while losing potential income tax and VAT revenues from people who could have been working and spending. In Germany, tax revenues have also been harmed by tax concessions given to companies to improve their international competitiveness and by individuals on the highest income-tax rates using the many loopholes to reduce their tax liabilities. These have caused the loss of much potential revenue.

Revenues from partially privatising such organisations as France Telecom and Deutsche Telekom helped provide much needed revenues while Germany also resorted to East German debt rescheduling (that is, delaying payments to help reduce government expenditure), by an interest rate swap between the government and the banks, and by excluding hospital debt. Stronger than expected German economic growth, creating more jobs, has also helped.

■ The qualifying countries

On 25 March 1998, an historic day in the history of the EU, the European Commission formally recommended that 11 countries should adopt a single currency from 1999. Formal confirmation by the European Council followed in May 1998. The single currency area will consist of 300m people and will be responsible for 18.6 per cent of world trade and 19.4 per cent of world GDP. However two countries, Belgium and Italy, were criticised in its convergence report by the European Monetary Institute for their failure to sufficiently reduce their public debt from 120 per cent of GDP to the Maastricht agreed target of 60 per cent.

Denmark, Greece, Sweden and UK are not part of the single currency zone. However, in mid-March 1998 Greece announced its intention of still qualifying for this exclusive club in 2002 by joining the Exchange Rate Mechanism for the first time since its creation in 1979, after a 14 per cent devaluation of the drachma against the ECU. This is a further step in the reformist economic policies adopted by the Greek government. Nonetheless it still needs vigorously to pursue liberalisation policies since over 50 per cent of the economy is in the public sector, agriculture provides employment for 27 per cent of the population (and hence is heavily dependent of the CAP), the social security system needs reform and the labour market is one of the most rigid in Europe.

■ The timetable to the single currency

This is set out in Table 3.4 overleaf.

■ The UK opt-out

From May 1998 emphasis will be placed on establishing bilateral exchange rates between the participating countries in the euro-zone to minimise exchange rate fluctuations during the period until when exchange rates are irrevocably fixed on 1 January 1999 and a single monetary policy operates across the euro-zone.

The UK has opted out of the Treaty of Maastricht regarding stage 3, enabling it to make a separate decision as to whether to accept the single currency and ECB or not. In October 1997 the UK's Chancellor of the Exchequer, Gordon Brown, announced the Labour government's principled support for the single currency but argued that the UK was not yet ready to join. However, the government has suggested that membership after 2002 (the date of the next UK general election) is a distinct possibility. Five reasons were advanced as to why the UK was not yet ready. These were:

1. There is not yet sustainable convergence between the UK economy and the economies of the countries adopting monetary union.
2. Countries accepting monetary union need to be even more flexible to cope with unexpected internal or external shocks affecting their economies, for example the 1970s oil crises and German reunification. The UK still suffers from long-run unemployment and a persistent lack of skills in its labour force which inhibits this flexibility.
3. The effect on investment – although single currency membership should create conditions for higher/more productive investment, there are dangers in entering without proper preparations. The UK has a record of macroeconomic instability which partly explains its past poor investment performance – hence the need for convergence before it joins.
4. The biggest impact of the single currency will be on the UK's financial services industry. There will be a need for all banks to adapt their procedures for the new currency – including from payments and settlements systems to ATMs. This will take time.
5. Until the UK converges its economic cycle with that of continental Europe membership of the single currency could affect UK economic stability – hence the need for a period of time to achieve stability and low inflation to achieve sustainable convergence.

Denmark is also allowed to hold a national referendum before moving to stage 3.

Table 3.4   Timetable for progress towards the single currency

DATE	WHAT WILL HAPPEN
March 1998	Decision as to which countries qualify to join the single currency.
During 1998	Creation of the European Central Bank. Production of euro banknotes and coins begins. Adoption of secondary legislation needed to implement the single currency.
1 January 1999	Exchange rates of participating countries fixed. Legislation defining legal status of the euro comes into effect. The single monetary policy of participating countries defined and executed in euros. ESCB begins foreign exchange operations in euros. Participating governments, Commission and EIB begin issuing debt (borrowing) in euros
1 January 1999–1 January 2002 (at latest)	Financial services sector switches to the euro. Commission assists participating states to change over to euros.
By 1 January 2002 (at latest)	Euro banknotes and coins start circulating. Change to the euro in public administration by all member states.
1 July 2002	Last date to cancel legal status of national banknotes and coins.

■ 3.9 The way forward

As the EU widens, with the probable addition of six new members after 2002, the euro-zone will subsequently become bigger and the euro more influential globally – in time supplementing the US dollar as a global trading currency and as a reserve currency for many states. There has already been a significant pooling of authority by the member states as various stages in EU integration have been passed – the Single European Act; the Treaty of Maastricht; and the moves to meet the Maastricht convergence criteria. As the single currency is adopted and further harmonisation is implemented, both through new members joining and through further deepening such as fiscal integration, moves towards a federal EU – even a United States of Europe in time – will require further surrender of national sovereignty.

There has also been much debate about the emergence of a multi-speed EU with a core of euro-using countries and a periphery of countries not wishing to join or not able to. Then on the fringes will be the countries waiting to join the EU. In practice, with 11 and possibly 12 of the EU15 joining the euro-zone in 2002, the periphery is suddenly reduced to a few outsiders who are likely to be anxious to join. Certainly it seems probable that the UK will join after 2002 subject to a favourable national referendum.

Yet many European citizens are concerned about the fact that the EU is largely governed by unelected bureaucrats – the so-called 'democratic deficit'. Attempts to delegate responsibility away from Brussels down to the level most appropriate to exercise it – subsidiarity, to use more Eurospeak – have worked to some extent yet still many people perceive the EU to be centralised without the safety checks of being accountable to the electorate. Moreover, attempts to introduce transparency, whereby people can see clearly how decisions are made, have not always succeeded. To address the issue of the democratic deficit greater authority will have to pass to the European parliament which, as the only elected EU body, should be the final arbiter of EU legislation. This will require a considerable surrender of power by the Commission and, more importantly, the Council of Ministers, which is the forum where individual EU nations express their policies and national interests. It has been a hard battle to make any gains in this respect yet, until nation states are prepared to surrender power to the European Parliament, then the concerns of ordinary citizens and of businesses will remain.

■ The effect of the euro on European businesses

One issue of concern, highlighted in a survey of 485 multinationals in 21 countries published in late 1997 by Price Waterhouse, was their failure to assess the impact of EMU. It found that under half had attempted to assess the impact on their business of the euro, and, even those who had given thought were thinking operationally rather than strategically, that is short-term not long-term. This applied to the senior management of companies.

Firms facing the advent of the euro need to think carefully about the strategic opportunities it affords. In particular there is the ability to exploit cross-border opportunities by developing new products which can be sold across the internal market, to develop new and more effective distribution channels – including securing marketing synergies, to form new strategic alliances and seek acquisitions, particularly as a result of price transparency. This may involve internal restructuring including centralising operations to serve the internal market better. Companies also need to consult and cooperate with other businesses through the supply chain to ensure they best meet consumer needs. Already in mid-1998 major multinationals have said that they will favour suppliers, including those outside the euro zone, who are prepared to trade in the euro. This puts pressure on firms further down the supply chain to behave similarly.

In practice, therefore, the effect of the euro will be to make European businesses more competitive, particularly as pricing becomes keener across the internal market as a consequence of transparency, that is, price variations can no longer be concealed behind exchange rates. Indeed, even firms in countries not joining the first wave of single currency membership are likely to be under pressure to display prices in euros once consumers gain familiarity with the new currency. Businesses will have to quote, invoice and market in euros.

European businesses must hope, however, that lost revenue from lower prices will be offset by lower costs arising from greater operating efficiencies – especially simplification and standardisation – and economies of scale. Transaction costs will be lower, while the threat of currency fluctuations will be removed. The internal market is, therefore, likely to see the reduction of fragmentation and the development of standardised products which can be packaged and marketed across Euroland in broadly the same way.

On the operational side there will be significant costs for banks, public authorities and businesses during the transition period associated with adapting accounting, IT and other systems for the new currency – from converting slot machines and supermarket tills to invoicing and keeping financial records in the new currency. Consumers will soon want to pay bills in euros, for example. This is particularly a problem since the new currency will run in parallel with the existing ones during the transition period, although the December 1995 Madrid meeting of the European Council said this should not exceed six months. The Commission has also made recommendations regarding the dual display of prices in shops, for example, during this transition period. Add this to the year-2000 problem for computers – the so-called millennium bug – and European businesses face a difficult time.

Financial services providers face a particularly challenging time. Apart from a major loss of revenue due to the removal of many exchange rates and hence foreign exchange transactions, they must also adjust to all records being in euros with the implications for their computer software. Customers will want to change to euro-denominated bank accounts, cheques and credit cards. The Commission has defined rules for banks arguing that converting cash and bank accounts into euros should be free of charge, to prevent the advent of the euro forcing up prices.

Banks also face new opportunities with euro-based products for saving, investing and lending – such as the euro-mortgage.

However, the EU also has a further role to play in completing the single market and the benefits of the single currency – for example by pushing hard for a single tax structure across all member countries.

■ Review questions

1. What do you understand by the term 'single market'? Why did moves towards a single market stagnate in the 1960s and 1970s?
2. Discuss why the single market had to be implemented in 1992 as the next logical step in the development of the EU.
3. Compare the Delors and Maastricht approaches to Economic and Monetary Union. Do you think the Delors approach would have worked had it been implemented?
4. You are required to give a 15-minute speech to your local chamber of commerce on the advantages and disadvantages of membership of the single currency to local businesses. Draft a plan of the main issues you will need to cover.
5. 'Economic and Monetary Union is merely a further step on the way to a United States of Europe'.

   (a) Do you think this is true? Explain your answer.
   (b) What would be the advantages and disadvantages of an EU political union?

■ Bibliography

Addison, J. and Siebert, W. S., *Labour Markets in Europe: Issues of Harmonisation and Regulation* (London: The Dryden Press, 1997).

Cecchini, P., *The European Challenge 1992: The Benefits of a Single Market* (Aldershot: Wildwood House, 1988).

Commission of the European Communities, 'The Economics of 1992', *European Economy*, no. 35 (Luxembourg: Office for Official Publications of the European Communities, 1988).

El-Agraa, A. M., *The European Union: History, Institutions, Economics and Politics*, 5th edn (Hemel Hempstead: Prentice Hall Europe, 1998).

Handy, C., *The Empty Raincoat: Making Sense of Modern Business* (London: Arrow Books, 1994).

Hitiris, T., *European Union Economics*, 4th edn (Hemel Hempstead: Harvester Wheatsheaf, 1998).

Swann, D., *The Economics of the Common Market*, 8th edn (Harmondsworth: Penguin Books, 1993).

CHAPTER 4

Creating a level playing field: EU competition and social policies

■ 4.1 Introduction

Chapter 3 examined the moves towards the creation of a single market and how and why a single currency is needed to permit this market to function most effectively. This chapter examines EU competition policy and EU social policy and explores why these have had to be promoted alongside the development of the single market. If businesses are to take advantage of access to other EU markets previously denied them, and hence achieve the benefits of economies of scale especially lower production costs, they must be able to compete freely. EU competition policy seeks to ensure that, as far as possible, restrictions to competition are not employed by firms.

The gains of the single market also need to be demonstrated to the citizens of the EU and social policy is one way of ensuring that, as far as possible, all share the wealth that the single market generates. This is particularly important as employment patterns change due to the replacement of labour by technology, the rise of new cheap producers in the Pacific Rim countries, and the increased importance of women in the labour market. Because of this the concept of a lifelong job, or even full-time work, has disappeared for many.

■ 4.2 Competition policy

■ What is competition?

Competition may be defined as a market situation where firms bid for customers without restriction and hence for the resources to satisfy their demand. The more successfully a firm competes the stronger its claim for resources. By competing against each other businesses are able to exploit cost and hence price differences, product design, quality of goods or services, marketing campaigns and so on. Also, in a competitive market new businesses are not discouraged from entering by barriers such as capital costs, brand loyalty or the operation of cartels. Nor are firms prevented from leaving by exit barriers such as the difficulty of selling specialised plant or the operation of cartels.

Mergers between previously competing firms, acquisitions by some firms of others or other collaborative agreements may, of course, frustrate competitive behaviour. This may lead to a business securing a dominant or even monopolistic position in an industry, which it may then exploit to prevent competition. Agreements between firms to control price, output and so on, known as cartels, may also stifle competition. Finally, governments may favour local firms over other EU firms by allocating construction and other contracts to the former and so deliberately excluding the latter. This again inhibits competition. If therefore competition is to exist these activities must be moderated.

■ Market structures and competitive forces

Economic theory distinguishes four main types of market structure: perfect competition, monopolistic competition, oligopoly and monopoly. The extent to which competition exists, and hence the extent to which legislation in needed, will vary according to the market structure in which businesses operate.

At the one extreme is the largely theoretical model of perfect competition which is useful for providing a template against which to judge less-competitive markets. The best example of this, in the context of European business, is the foreign exchange (Forex) market for buying and selling foreign currencies. This, as near as possible, meets such characteristics as perfect knowledge, a very large number of buyers and sellers, no transport costs and low entry barriers. Also, although currencies obviously differ – for example, the lira and the drachma – units of the same currency are homogeneous.

At the other extreme is the monopolistic market where either one business, or a group acting as one, exercises very substantial or total control over market supply. Various examples will have been met in different chapters of this book. A monopoly may be a limited company or it may be a public sector company such as the state-controlled suppliers of voice telephony services prior to the liberalisation of the EU telecommunications market in 1998. Deutsche Telekom and France Telecom were examples of this. Impossibly high entry barriers existed through government control of the businesses and a refusal to grant licenses to other potential suppliers. With state-owned monopolies in particular, X-inefficiencies can be a serious problem where the business's actual costs of producing substantially exceed its theoretically achievable operating costs. This has frequently been the situation with EU state monopolies and is one reason for the wave of privatisation across the EU in recent years.

Monopolies have a tendency to be higher cost and less innovative than perfectly competitive firms because they are shielded from the forces of competition. They may also employ product differentiation and generate brand loyalty through advertising to create higher entry barriers. However, in the context of the single market and the need to be able to compete against US and Japanese suppliers, monopolies have the potential to be global players through their sheer size. This enables them to obtain economies of scale and/or scope which may be passed on as lower product prices. These are likely to be lower than those of the perfectly competitive firm. It is the attractiveness of this which was distinguished by the Cecchini Report as one important benefit of the single market. Monopolists also have the opportunity to run big R&D programmes to develop new products.

Monopolies are clearly one area which EU competition policy has to address. Experience shows that where state monopolies have been privatised, the transitional adjustment has often proved to be very painful, particularly for the large amount of labour being shed in significant delayering programmes. Furthermore, creating a private monopoly instead of a state owned one doesn't necessarily guarantee an increase in competitiveness since the nature of the market structure has not changed, merely the ownership of the business. The 1894 Sherman Anti-Trust Laws, which are the basis of US legislation, require monopolies to be broken up with the constituent elements required to compete against each other. As will be seen this is not the EU model.

Between the two extremes lie the market structures of oligopoly and monopolistic competition. The latter does not pose any real threat to consumer interests by its very nature. Because entry and exit barriers are low the number of businesses is very large and, since the size of any one business precludes it from gaining a dominant position, then product differentiation through branding and advertising pose minimal problems. Competition through price and the quality of product and service are likely to be more important. A patisserie in Boulogne or a cafe in Vienna would be an example of this market structure.

Where the EU has experienced problems is in terms of oligopolistic market structures. Since such a market typically has only a small number of large suppliers then there is a real danger of oligopolistic businesses colluding. This will lead to price fixing, market sharing, the imposition of high entry barriers against newcomers such as loyalty rebates to faithful customers, and other measures aimed at ensuring that competition is restricted. Consumers suffer by having to pay higher prices than would be so if competition were able to function, and they experience less choice.

Previous theory to explain how such firms behaved relied on the Sweezy kinked demand curve. This has now been criticised as unrealistic and leaving unresolved more problems that it solves. More recently, therefore, game theory has been used as the theoretical model to explain oligopolistic market behaviour. The interested reader who wishes to pursue this further is referred to any of the standard economics texts available.

■ Why does competition matter?

Competition, even though not perfect, offers significant advantages to both consumers and producers. For consumers these advantages are: lower prices; greater choice between suppliers and their output; continuously improving quality and a growing range of products being offered; and firms being more responsive to consumer needs and demands, that is increased consumer sovereignty. For producers the gains are pressure to contain costs (through economies of scale) and offer lower prices (known as technical efficiency); greater efficiency in organisation and operation, frequently through technological change; an incentive to innovate through R&D and hence to resist competition from other suppliers (known as dynamic efficiency); and an incentive to grow and expand into new markets.

For the economy as a whole the benefits arising from competition are a more efficient utilisation of scarce resources – although this may be inhibited by external costs arising from production which are born by society rather than the business, for example pollution; the avoidance of monopolies; and the ability to reach a higher level of GDP.

■ The significance of competition to the EU

EU legislation has placed substantial emphasis on the role of competition in its single market and industrial policies. This is because EU economies are market-based as opposed to centrally-planned. As discussed in Chapter 6, businesses have a variety of motives for operating. Serving the consumer, although important, may not be central to the business's activities. Different stakeholders have different priorities, and maximising shareholders' dividends and directors' salaries and bonuses may take precedence over lower prices and quality for customers. Consequently a firm's long-run strategy may actually be to minimise the number of competitors it faces and hence to secure a dominant market position. This may be through merger or takeover; alternatively it may be through other restrictive practices. In either case, once it has obtained dominant position then there is an incentive to raise entry barriers, increase prices and so forth in order to maintain this position.

The purpose of the Single European Act was to remove national market barriers to enable all firms in the then EC12 to compete in the one market. There would be little benefit in removing non-tariff barriers (NTBs) if firms then faced additional NTBs due to cartels, restrictive practices or other anti-competitive activities. Additionally, through policies favouring their own nationals, governments may give only contracts to these rather than to businesses from other member states of the EU.

The EU has therefore pursued a policy of seeking to encourage competition by creating an environment and common framework, supported by EU law, where firms might operate without facing unfair restrictive practices such as those outlined above. This seeks to eliminate trade distortions, ensure more effective resource allocation and, where this does not exist, introduce remedies to ensure that it does. This has been effected through legislation which is discussed below. In particular this has sought to ensure that barriers to trade do not exist, that changes in the structure of EU industry are accounted for by EU legislation and that modifications to regional aid can be reconciled with EU competition policy. This is important since a business located in a depressed region may receive state aid which will give it an unfair advantage over other businesses not in receipt of such funds.

Member states do have their own national legislation to preserve competition, for example, the UK has the Monopolies and Mergers Commission and the Office of Fair Trading. However, it is the European Commission which polices the single market to ensure that consumers derive its benefits. The European Court of Justice exercises legal supervision of the Commission's actions while the Court of First Instance handles actions brought against the institutions of the EU.

■ 4.3 EU legislation

■ The Treaty of Rome

Articles 85 to 94 of the Treaty of Rome define rules governing competition in the EU, although these have subsequently been modified by the Single European Act. Several main areas may be distinguished:

☐ 1 Restrictive practices (a.85)

This article (denoted a.) seeks to maintain competition in the EU by preventing the issue of anti-competitive behaviour by two or more businesses in restraint of trade. Restrictive practices include:

1. **Market sharing**: for example, each company in a producers' agreement is allocated a share of the EU market – or national firms are each allocated their domestic market with a guarantee that firms from other EU countries will not compete there. Where market share is less than 5 per cent the EU does not regard this as restricting competition.
2. **Price fixing**: whereby all businesses charge the same or very similar prices for their products.
3. **Production quotas**: each business agrees to produce a specific amount – if a cartel (a formal agreement between a few large producers) has been established, any firm which exceeds its limit may be punished by other cartel members, for example by a fine or having its production quota reduced the next year.

These practices are regarded as restrictive by the EU whether the agreement is horizontal (that is between firms supplying the same goods or services onto the market) or vertical (for example an agreement between a manufacturer and its supplier of components, or its distributor). If the business's turnover is less than ECU 200m then a.85 will not apply.

The restrictions of a.85 apply also to cross-border trade unless the benefits can be demonstrated to exceed the disadvantages. These benefits include that consumers gain from the restrictive practice, and that the restriction improves production, distribution or economic progress. These may be granted to an individual firm or on a group basis relating to issues such as patent licensing, and R&D agreements. Where a restrictive practice is found to exist then it is declared null and void and a fine of up to ECU 1 million or 10 per cent of annual turnover of the businesses restricting trade, may be levied.

CASE STUDY   Price Fixing Steel Producers' Cartel

The European Commission levied fines totalling ECU 27.38m on six steel producing companies which were convicted of taking part in a cartel to fix prices in 1998. The companies involved were Acerinox SA (Spain); ALZ NV (Belgium); Acciai Speciali Terni SpA (Italy); Avesta Sheffield AB (Sweden and UK); Krupp Thyssen Nirosta GmbH (Germany) and Usinor SA (France). They all decided to levy an 'alloy surcharge' at the same time on their stainless steel flat products resulting in what was almost a doubling of stainless steel prices between January 1994 and March 1995. This was contrary to EU law, a.85 of the Treaty of Rome.

☐ 2 Dominant positions (a.86)

This article prohibits businesses in a dominant position, that is with significant market power, including monopolies, from exercising their powers in restraint of competition and affecting inter-state trade. The factors determining whether a business is in a dominant position include:

1. its market share (greater than 40 per cent implies dominance);
2. that the dominant position is in a significant area (however defined) of the EU;
3. that it is abusing its dominant position through unfairly high prices;
4. that it is employing price discrimination, that is charging different customers different prices for the same good or service;
5. the use of loyalty rebates; and
6. refusing to sell to a customer without legitimate reason.

Another example of the abuse of dominant position relates to the sale of World Cup tickets in France. In early 1998 the French organisers of the Summer 1998 World Cup were ordered by the European Commission to make more tickets available to foreign supporters. The French authorities had allocated 60 per cent of tickets to France and 40 per cent to the rest of the world. The Commission ruled that this was discriminatory against non-French citizens and in breach of EU monopoly rules (a.86). It also expressed concerns that the French telephone and Internet World Cup ticket ordering services could only be reached with difficulty from outside France. Also any tickets purchased had to be sent to French postal addresses! The organisers were given two weeks to respond or the Commission would start proceedings which would lead to heavy fines of 10 per cent of the total revenue of the competition. The French authorities' defence was that the ticket allocations had been fixed by Fifa, the world soccer body and they rejected the Commission's assertion that all 110 000 unsold tickets should go to foreign fans, offering only 50 000 to other national federations.

CASE STUDY   Volkswagen Fixing Car Prices

As an illustration of the above, under EU rules if a person buys a car in another country than his/her place of residence they must register the car in their home country and pay the VAT there. In 1994, taking advantage of the fall in value of the lira against the deutschemark and the Austrian schilling, German and Austrian citizens tried to buy Volkswagen (VW) cars in Italy. However, once Italian sales staff discovered where the potential customers lived they refused to sell them the cars, on the insistence of VW. Indeed VW threatened to withhold supplies from the dealers if they violated this rule.

In January 1998 the European Commission therefore imposed a record fine of £65m (ECU 100m) on VW. The Commission has been trying to force car makers to allow consumers the best deals by buying cars across national borders – this is to meet the requirement for a single European car market. Even in the region of the Franco-Spanish border, where sales have boomed, customers have often encountered problems when revealing where they live. However, manufacturers have argued that price differences for the same car in different countries are due to a number of factors including different local taxes and exchange rate movements rather than price discrimination.

Using index numbers to compare the pre-tax retail price for a 1997 VW Golf across the EU, where the Netherlands is lowest in price at 100, most countries' Golf prices are no more than 8 per cent higher (Austria 100.1; Sweden 102.6; Italy 106.7; Belgium 108.8). The next highest is Ireland (114.3) while the highest is the UK with 130.9, that is over 30 per cent dearer than a similar VW Golf in the Netherlands. Partly this is due to the rising value of sterling which problem membership of the single currency would address.

For the Commission this action was the latest in a series of moves against what are perceived to be illegal restrictive practices by sporting bodies such as Uefa – the European Football Association – and FIA – the motor racing authority which runs Formula 1. In 1996 the European Court's Bosman decision gave freedom for soccer players to move without a transfer fee at the end of their contract with a club. Karel van Miert, EU Competition Commissioner, wants to test against EU trading laws how sporting bodies determine their laws. In particular he argues that the Formula 1 system is an illegal monopoly since it recognises only one motor sport body per country and has a stranglehold on Formula 1 events and where they are held.

The counter-argument from Formula 1 supremo Bernie Ecclestone is that the alternative would be chaos. There must be a central global authority to regulate events and determine where revenues from tv screenings are allocated.

☐ 3 State aid (a.92 to 94)

These articles are concerned with governments favouring their own national businesses over those of other EU countries through the use of grants, tax allowances, tax holidays and so on. Under a.92, all state aid to businesses which affects trade by distorting competition between member states is illegal. Examples of state aid include government grants, low or zero interest loans, tax concessions and state acquisition of shares in a business.

There are, however, exceptions to this including *inter alia*:

- aid to promote improvements of a social character to assist individual consumers;
- aid to promote economic development in areas with high unemployment or where living standards are exceptionally low (including Greece, N. Ireland, parts of Italy, Spain and French overseas territories);
- aid to promote a project of common EU interest;
- aid to the former German Democratic Republic (now Eastern Germany);
- aid to disaster areas; and
- sectoral aid to assist in the restructuring of an industrial sector in structural decline, for example textiles and shipbuilding.

If a new aid scheme is to be introduced by a member government then the Commission must be given ample advance warning of it. The Commission is also responsible for constantly reviewing existing proposals. Recent attempts have been made to introduce transparency, that is, to make policy predictable by laying down ground rules so that governments may anticipate a likely Commission response before they give state aid.

The Commission has also introduced the concept of 'one time, last time' meaning that aid for restructuring an industry or rescue aid should only be granted once – unless in exceptional circumstances; although the position regarding the aviation industry is not so clear because of its psychological and economic importance to a nation (see below). Currently however EU control over state aid to national carriers is becoming tougher. Decisions as to the economic legitimacy of state aid are made by the Commission on the 'market investor principle', that is, would a rational investor get a reasonable return on the investment undertaken. If not then the state finance is regarded as aid, not as an economic investment.

In practice the majority of state aid is approved by the Commission so long as it meets any of the following:

- is the project financed by the aid for the benefit of the EU as a whole?
- is the project entirely dependent on aid being available? or
- is the type and amount of aid suitable for what is trying to be achieved?

Generally, for aid to be acceptable to the Commission it needs to relate to regional or sectoral projects.

◼ Public procurement

Public procurement is the situation whereby national or regional EU governments or other public bodies offer contracts for public works by tender. Those businesses which are interested offer, within a specified time scale, price quotations for completing the work by a specified time; to avoid collusion between competing firms these bids must be in secret. For example, the construction of the second Severn Bridge linking England to Wales was bid for by tender and the contract awarded to a French civil engineering firm. The steel was provided by a sub-contracted Italian firm, while much of the labour and other materials were provided by sub-contracted UK firms.

CASE STUDY   British Government Aid to British Aerospace and Ford Cars

For example, the British Government gave substantial financial aid to two companies in February 1998. British Aerospace (BAe) received £123m to help the development and production of a new aircraft – the A340-500/600 – by Airbus Industrie, in which British Aerospace has a 20 per cent share. This funding will help secure 2000 jobs which are dependent on the production of this new aircraft. BAe will pay back the funding in the form of a levy on future sales.

A further £43m was provided to ensure the production in the UK of the new Jaguar car at Halewood, Merseyside and safeguard 2900 jobs – with the hope of an additional 500 being created. The money is part of a £300m package agreed with Ford, who own Jaguar, to finance work on the new X400 'baby' saloon. The money has been provided to bridge the gap between the cost of producing it in the UK and cheaper production costs elsewhere.

Although this may seem at first to contradict a.92–94 of the Treaty of Rome this is not in fact the case. The BAe financing can be justified on the grounds that it is 'aid to promote a project of common EU interest'. The latter can be justified on the grounds that it is 'aid to promote economic development in areas with high unemployment' – which Merseyside certainly is.

The awarding of a public contract can have a significant impact on the economy and the firm securing it in terms of the creation of extra jobs, helping firms which are short of work, promoting R&D by the successful firm(s) and the multiplier effects of the investment on the regional or national economy. Indeed in 1998 public procurement was worth ECU 720bn (£477bn) or 11 per cent of EU GDP. Hence there has often been a tendency for public authorities to advertise such works nationally rather than across the EU and to award the contracts to national firms – which is clearly in contravention of the spirit of the single market and the legislation of the Single European Act 1987. The effect of such national bias has been to maintain the fragmented nature of what should be one internal market in public procurements. It has also prevented the full achievement of five benefits arising from the liberalisation of public procurement identified by the 1989 Cecchini Report. These were cost savings from buying from the cheapest source (the static trade effect); competitive pressures from rival firms tendering for contracts reducing prices (the dynamic trade effect); the ability to achieve scale economies arisng from a completed internal market (the restructuring effect); greater incentives for businesses to become more innovative and invest more to compete more strongly and hence secure contracts; and the fact that private sector buyers will benefit from cheaper prices by firms supplying to the public sector.

In 1998, to make public procurements more open and transparent the Commission proposed amendments to the EU's public procurement directives. The aims were to consolidate existing directives, promote a 'competitive dialogue' procedure to ease contact between buyers and suppliers and encourage the use of electronic procurement systems. Other measures sought to improve the implement of public procurement procedures and disseminate more effectively public procurement opportunities.

☐ 4 Regulation EC 4064/89

This was introduced to prevent the creation and enlargement of dominant market positions by European businesses. With effect from September 1990:

- Where two or more firms proposing to merge have a worldwide turnover exceeding ECU 5 billion, then prior clearance is needed from the European Commission.
- For a merger with a worldwide turnover of less than ECU 5 billion, or a larger one where each business has at least two-thirds of its EU turnover in one EU state, application must be made to the state's monopolies and mergers authority, rather than to the European Commission. However, the Commission may intervene if invited to do so by the national authority.
- Large companies which are incorporated *outside the EU* but which have a turnover of at least ECU 250m in the EU are also subject to these regulations, if a merger between them will impact on competition *within the EU* (author's emphasis).

In March 1998 these merger rules were extended and simplified by a number of amendments to ease the burden on merging companies. They now also relate to all 'full-function joint ventures' which stand alone and which meet the turnover threshold, such as the Atlas joint venture between France Telecom and Deutsche Telekom – joint ventures not previously subject to legally binding deadlines. Investigations of these will now be governed by the same strict deadlines which apply to mergers, giving them greater legal certainty, whereas in the past they have had to wait a long time for a Commission response.

Also procedures have been changed to make it easier to notify the European Commission of mergers and to avoid companies which are proposing to merge from having to notify individually each different national authority. To qualify for clearance from Brussels:

- The merging companies must have a combined aggregate world-wide turnover exceeding ECU 2.5b (£1.66bn).
- In each of at least three member states the combined turnover of all the companies concerned must exceed ECU 100m.
- In each of these three countries the total turnover of at least two of the companies concerned must exceed ECU 25m.
- The aggregate EU-wide turnover of each of at least two of the undertakings concerned must exceed ECU 100m.

Banking, finance and insurance have their own rules. Companies which do not agree with the fines levied on them in cases violating the above principles may appeal to the European Court of Justice. In recent years further developments in EU competition policy have relied largely on case law from the European Court of Justice.

■ 4.4 The development of mergers

As implied above, a business may grow in a number of ways. Most commonly in the early years this will be organically; that is, ploughing back earned profits and, where necessary, supplementing them with bank loans or by issuing new shares. As the business continues to grow it is likely to do so by other strategies including acquisitions or take-overs and mergers. Figure 4.1 illustrates possible routes. Before these are examined, however, the distinction between take-overs/acquisitions and mergers should be clarified.

(i) **An acquisition** occurs when one firm (the predator) secures control of another (the victim) by gaining a majority of its voting shares, that is 51 per cent. It does this by offering to shareholders of the victim company an attractive price for their shares, or a swop of its shares for theirs, to tempt the shareholders to part with them. It then has the power to ensure its strategies are implemented in the newly merged company. If the victim is willing to be taken over (known as a friendly takeover) this is usually because it is encountering difficulties and sees the loss of control as the best way to preserve jobs or brand names. Its directors may also gain financially.

If the takeover is hostile, however, then the victim company may seek a 'white knight'. This is another company who will make a counter-bid for the victim company and is one with whom the directors of the victim company better feel they will be able to work. Victim company shareholders must then choose between the offer of the predator and that of the white knight.

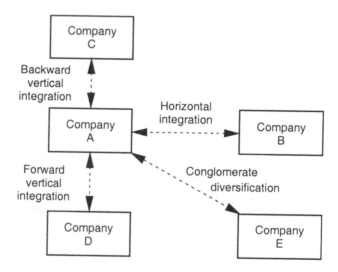

Figure 4.1   **Integration and Diversification**

In both friendly and hostile mergers the decisions of institutional investors such as banks and insurance companies will be of major influence since they may well hold a significant proportion of the shares. There is of course the probability that jobs will go at all levels in the victim company and indeed its very identity may disappear, whichever takeover occurs. Alternatively the two companies may still offer their own product ranges if these are regarded as naturally complementary.

(ii) **A merger** occurs when two companies willingly join together to form a new business. In this case they will again be looking for synergy gains. These arise from two companies sharing common tasks and the implication is that the gains from forming one new business are greater than for the two businesses operating separately. One aspect of this is economies of scale which is reducing unit costs the higher the level of output. Since the new merged organisation is going to be larger than each of the two separate ones then the opportunities for achieving economies of scale will inevitably be greater. This applies to horizontal mergers. There may also be economies of scale in terms of access to financial resources and in terms of marketing and these will apply whether the company has integrated horizontally or vertically. Of course, if this raises the risk of anti-competitive practices then the proposed merger will be investigated by the European Commission.

Whether a merger or a takeover occurs these may be in a number of directions:

1. *Horizontal integration* – when one business acquires another engaged in the same activities; for example VW's acquisition of Bentley car production.
2. *Forward vertical integration* – when a firm acquires another further down the production line towards the consumer; probably the best example is a car manufacturer setting up its dealerships.
3. *Backward vertical integration* – when a firm acquires another further up the production line towards the raw materials stage; for example the British firm De La Rue, the world's largest printer of banknotes, sought to take over Portals, a firm which makes banknote paper.
4. *Conglomerate diversification* – when a firm diversifies into totally unrelated activities; for example the Swiss watch company Swatch which in conjunction with Mercedes-Benz proposed making the Swatchmobile, a new small car.

EU mergers grew in the late 1980s corresponding with the upturn in domestic business cycles. Between 1985 and 1990 total mergers and acquisitions of majority holdings rose from 227 (in 1985) to 1384 (in 1989–90). However, this number fell away in the early 1990s, due to the impact of the European recession and the loss of business confidence. In the mid-1990s there has again been major growth in EU merger activity, with particular areas of activity being financial services, pharmaceuticals and automobiles; so that in 1997 there were 2444 cross-border takeovers worth a total of $157bn.

Research by the European Commission has suggested that the main reasons for EU mergers generally have been:

1. the desire to strengthen market position;
2. expansion;
3. complementarity to achieve the benefits of synergy;
4. diversification;
5. restructuring;
6. research & development, production and marketing; and
7. cooperation.

Restructuring relates to reduction in X-inefficiencies. These exist when the actual costs of producing a level of output are higher than the potential costs; this means that production is not cost-effective enough. A merger or takeover will force the new management to look again at all aspects of production to achieve cost-savings.

CASE STUDY   Boeing–McDonnell Douglas Merger: Meeting the Objections of the EU

In December 1996 these two American companies announced a £14bn proposed merger to create the world's biggest aircraft manufacturer, with 200 000 employees. Boeing is the world's largest commercial aircraft manufacturer with a 60 per cent share of the global market, while McDonnell Douglas is the leading manufacturer of military aircraft as well as manufacturing commercial aircraft. (The merger was the latest in a wave of mergers by US aerospace companies since a 1993 declaration by the US government that there were too many American companies and that mergers were needed to maintain competitiveness and drive down costs; between 1993–96 the 15 main companies merged into three.) For Boeing, Airbus, the EU commerical aircraft manufacturing consortium, was perceived as a growing threat to market-share having been brought to maturity, it argued, by generous EU subsidies.

In July 1997 the US Federal Trade Commission (FTC) unconditionally approved the merger. However, the European Commission objected on the grounds that (i) it was a breach of competition rules and would stifle competition in the aerospace industry – the merged company would have a 70 per cent share of worldwide sales of commercial planes; and (ii) the military activities of McDonnell Douglas attracted huge subsidies from the US Department of Defence. Karel van Miert, the Competition Commissioner, threatened the companies with fines of up to 10 per cent of the turnover of the merged company, and confiscation of new Boeing aircraft delivered to European customers, if the merger took place. The justification for this was that the Commission has authority to police the terms of an all-American business deal with global (and hence EU) implications.

Finally, after threats by President Clinton of appeals to the WTO or retaliatory sanctions, the Commission agreed to the merger. Boeing had already offered to report regularly on any cross-subsidies from McDonnell Douglas's military business to its own civil aircraft manufacturing and to licence to other manufacturers (that is, Airbus) any know-how gained from military contracts if used in civil aircraft manufacturing. Following negotiations with the EU it was agreed that (a) Boeing would drop its controversial exclusive supplier contracts with three US airlines and would not conclude any new exclusive aircraft supply contracts with airlines before 2007; (b) it also agreed not to enforce its exclusivity clauses in its existing contracts with Continental, Delta and American Airlines; (c) Boeing would not use its position regarding current McDonnell Douglas customers as a lever to obtain competitive advantage in the sales of new aircraft; and (d) McDonnell Douglas' commercial aircraft division will be kept separate for 10 years.

Obviously all gains should be demonstrated in the form of higher profits, otherwise the merger or takeover has been of no use. The union of the two businesses may lead to greater industry concentration, that is less firms controlling a greater market-share. The customary measure used is the concentration ratio. So the n-firm concentration ratio (denoted CRn) is the percentage share of the market held by the n largest firms. Often n is taken to be 3 or 5. So if CR3 for the EU pharmaceutical industry were to be 60 per cent, this would mean that the top 3 firms control 60 per cent of the market. If the concentration ratio is too high then the risks of concentration are those defined by oligopolistic markets, that is entry barriers, the ability to influence prices, advertising and branding to create separate identities for similar goods, and the risk of collusion, perhaps even leading to cartels.

Underlying these reasons for mergers have been the near completion of the single market offering further opportunities for businesses and the moves to a single currency. Other factors have been rising corporate profitability as EU economies have generally exhibited economic growth, and a need to increase in size to cope with global competition. Koutsoyiannis (1987) has argued that there are two main reasons for mergers and takeovers – to achieve economies of scale and rationalisation. Economies of scale will reduce unit costs, increase profits and hence increase returns to shareholders either as dividends or increased share prices. With rationalisation, as well as using existing resources more efficiently, post-merger rationalisation and reductions in costs are also available.

In practice most mergers achieve only minimal cost reductions if indeed any. This is because either firms which have merged do not rationalise sufficiently and hence fail to exploit potential economies of scale or experience diseconomies of scale due to lack of control or lack of knowledge of the new business by its managers. Moreover, although an increase in profitability might be expected to be the outcome of a merger or takeover, in reality this does not happen. Rather, what does happen is that the stock market value of the new company increases compared with that of the pre-merger individual companies and so the shareholders benefit.

Research by the London Business School has found that 75 per cent of British-based acquisitions and mergers fail to reach their financial targets, while 50 per cent never recover the premium they had to pay above the market price of the shares to effect the merger or acquisition. LBS's researchers also argue, in contradiction of the previous paragraph, that lower productivity post-merger, coupled with lost investor confidence and defecting customers, actually lower the share price of the merged or acquired company. In other words most mergers are not worth the effort. Anderson Consulting confirm this arguing that mergers have only a 50 per cent chance of success.

It must also be remembered that many attempts to merge actually fail. British Telecom's proposed acquisition of American long-distance carrier MCI failed when it was gazumped by American company Worldcom, while SmithKline Beecham and Glaxo Wellcome failed because of personality clashes between senior executives. French retailer Promodes was unable to merge with its rival,

Casino, while it also failed in its attempts to unite with supermarket group Rallye . . . the list is substantial.

On the other hand there is a need for EU industries to be competitive in the global marketplace. This is not to advocate that restricting competition is the way to achieve this but rather that collusive behaviour is often a consequence of large firms dominating an industry. The problem is to encourage collaboration while discouraging collusion. Hence there is a need for Euro-champions, that is firms who can compete globally with other major international producers in the US, Japan and so on.

CASE STUDY   Mergers in European Banking

The following two cases are interesting examples relating to the above.

- Germany's second largest retail bank was created in 1998 through a complex merger deal between Hypo-Bank and Vereinsbank, the fourth and fifth largest banks in a very overbanked economy which has 36 000 public, cooperative and commercial banks fighting for market position. The major rationale for the merger, creating a new bank with combined assets of DM 743m, is to reduce costs with an anticipation that at least 7000 jobs will go from a total staff of 40 000. The two branch networks will be combined over a period of four years at a cost of DM1.4bn and estimated savings of DM1bn p.a. will be generated. The merger took place in two stages, the first involving a share exchange and the second a submission of proposals to all shareholders for approval.
- Also, at the end of 1997, the Union Bank of Switzerland and the Swiss Bank Corporation announced a $59bn merger deal. To be known as the United Bank of Switzerland, it has assets of nearly $600bn and is expected to cut its workforce worldwide from 56 000 to 43 000. A one off restructuring charge of SF7bn will be incurred during 1998, it was announced, but by 2002 the new merged business should generate a return on equity of between 15–20 per cent p.a. compared with a current return of 13–17 per cent p.a. The deal will be financed by a share swop. The merger is part of an on-going wave of financial consolidation with Switzerland described as one of the most over-banked markets in the world.

■ 4.5 How effective has EU competition policy been?

Although competition policy has demonstrated some successes it has also exhibited some problems:

1. Often the Commission puts expediency before principles in evaluating governments' provision of state aid to failing industry, for example, French finance for Crédit Lyonnais. The Commission is often too willing to support such financing rather than keeping to the principles of competition policy. Its counter-argument is that since unemployment has clearly been identified as the economic and social problem of the 1990s it would be at times be unsound to stop aid at the risk of creating still greater unemployment.

2. EU competition policy often overlaps with other policies such as the Common Agricultural Policy and regional policy. Regional aid providing state aid to depressed regions may, if persisted with long enough, give unfair advantage to local businesses and hence violate competition policy, especially a.92–94.

3. The European Commission's own procedures often fail. These include the time taken to investigate initially, delays in submitting relevant documentation about offending businesses to the courts in time, and failure to provide documentation in all the official languages.

   The Commission has been seeking to redress this by resolving more cases. In 1997 it handled 1338 new competition policy cases compared with 1246 in 1996. In 1997 it resolved 1165 cases compared with 1061 in 1996.

4. Regarding a.85, restrictive practices are often difficult to prove, for example if they are spoken or implied. Hence it is only by observing the outcome of such implicit agreements that the Commission can undertake action – and this takes time. In the same way the growth of other invisible barriers to competition which are not defined in existing competition policy mean that new practices may be employed which are beyond the scope of the Commission. The failsafes against this are that the Commission regularly reviews existing legislation – as demonstrated by the extension of Regulation EC 4063/89 to include 'full-function joint ventures', that the Court of Justice extends and develops competition policy through case law, and the fact that there are also national government competition policies which may be implemented. These vary significantly, however, and in the case of Italy, for example, were exceedingly weak until the pressure of EU competition policy forced it to take action to put its own house in order.

5. Regarding a.86 there is the converse problem that EU competition policy may deter a merger which would otherwise be beneficial to the EU and hence to its ability to compete globally. Certainly the merger between cross-channel ferry companies P&O and Stena, initiated in response to loss of traffic to the channel tunnel, was delayed for most of 1997 because of the European Commission. They had serious concerns about the new merged company having 40 per cent of the market and the risk of it being cross-subsidised by their other activities.

   The £17bn proposed merger between Reed Elsevier, the Anglo-Dutch information and publishing group, and Wolters Kluwer of the Netherlands was cancelled in March 1998 due to fears that the European Commission might demand large-scale disposal of some of their business activities in order for them to secure regulatory approval. The Commission had received complaints from rival companies about the proposed company's potential dominance of the tax and legal publications business. The Commission denied that they had made unreasonable demands but subsequently argued that the merger would be 'several times larger than any other publisher of professional information in the EU' and 'could prevent a competitive situation in the supply of legal, fiscal, and scientific information in the EU with a significant impact on the terms and prices at which this information is made available to users and consumers.'

   The need for Euro-champions requires size yet the prevention of mergers will deny this or require the firms to achieve size through organic growth which may not be feasible. Also, once shares have been exchanged between two businesses it is very difficult to enforce a demerger.

■ 4.6 EU competitiveness

The ability of EU businesses to compete effectively in the global economy is crucial to long-term economic growth for EU economies. This applies whether the business supplies goods or services although, in this section, we will assume goods production. The competitiveness of EU businesses depends on many factors some of which are within their control and some of which are not.

External factors which are beyond a business's control include:

- The domestic inflation rate and its relationship to other countries' inflation rates – the higher this is the less competitive will goods be in overseas markets.
- The real exchange rate – the higher the value of a currency in relation to other currencies the more expensive will exports be, making them harder to sell, while imports will be cheaper, encouraging more to be bought in the domestic economy.
- The economic growth rate of the country/countries where the business is resident.
- Economic policies pursued by a government to ensure a stable economic environment.
- The power of trade unions and their ability to secure high wage rates, bonuses, a shorter working week and so on – especially where these are negotiated nationally. These will all push up production costs.
- The economic condition of the main export markets – the extent to which they operate protective barriers; the state of domestic suppliers in the foreign market, and so on. Southeast Asia, for example, currently does not have the ability to buy EU goods as much as before; Japan has traditionally operated all sorts of tariff and non-tariff barriers to prevent EU exports gaining access; CEEC businesses are still updating their capital stock and production methods hence offering valuable exporting opportunities to European businesses.
- The extent to which the EU, the national government or other public bodies provide guidance and support for businesses.
- The corporate governance system (see Chapter 11).
- The extent to which national governments can attract foreign direct investment – which will create competitive new European businesses, albeit that they will compete head-on with existing European businesses. This will depend on financial support, the tax regime (for example, the UK has been criticised for favouring a dividend culture rather than one which re-invests profits), the extent to which bureaucracy helps or hinders business enterprise, and so on.
- The quality and extent of education provision, particularly further and higher education, and apprenticeships – albeit that this is a long-term link.

Internal factors influencing a business's competitiveness include:

- Its Research & Development (R&D) record.
- Its costs in producing the goods and hence the final price charged.
- This in turn will depend on production methods and management practices – for example, does the firm seek to produce most efficiently with minimum wastage, for example, by using total quality management methods (see Chapter 9); are its markets big enough to secure economies of scale?
- The productivity record of the business, that is output per employee.
- Its record in terms of investment in new capital equipment.
- The quality of the goods it produces and their reputation for quality – including their innovativeness.
- The design characteristics of the products.
- How punctual delivery dates are.
- The quality and extent of after-sales service, for example is a two-year guarantee offered as standard with no quibbling if a customer returns a good?
- The types of goods European businesses produce. Nearly half of EU exports are concentrated in sectors where demand is only moderate – such as machinery, paper

products, plastic products, rubber and tobacco; or weak – such as metals and metal products, textiles, leather and minerals. In practice there needs to be much greater concentration of industrial sectors offering high economic growth – such as IT equipment and software; electronics – TVs, audio equipment, microwave ovens and so on; chemicals, and precision and optical instruments.

Competitiveness may be measured by a number of indicators. These include a country's trade balance (the more it is in deficit the less competitive it is); the share of world trade in relative terms; and the level of investment undertaken – including inward investment. There are two main reports published which measure national competitiveness – the International Institute of Management Development (IMD), a Swiss-based think tank, and the World Economic Forum. These two organisations use different measures but in essence each tries to gauge countries' overall economic performance by compiling a performance index. This includes a range of indicators such as progress in achieving economic growth, trade, investment, taxes, employment, education and science and technology. For the IMD there are 233 such measures.

For 1997 the league was headed, for the sixth year, by the US and followed by Singapore and Hong Kong. Japan slipped to eleventh following the impact of attempts to make the Japanese economy more open and transparent (having been top in 1991). The UK lay twelfth and Germany fourteenth. In terms of internationalisation the UK came sixth due its attractiveness resulting from competitive labour costs, and seventh for finance because of the continuing strength of the City of London as a financial centre. Where the UK particularly lags behind some of its fellow EU members is in terms of its poor productivity. Many businesses have poor productivity records which seriously harm their competitiveness.

■ 4.7 Social policy

■ Why does the EU have a social policy?

European social policy owes its origins to the EC's founding Treaties of Paris and Rome in the 1950s. However, these treaties and the subsequent policies arising from them achieved less than was desired. The growth of the EU is therefore, in part, a history of the development of social policy which, in turn, is an on-going attempt to improve the living and working conditions of its citizens. This has been partially on moral grounds as an obligation of democratic governments to improve the living and working conditions of their electorates. Additionally, there are economic and social arguments. Viewing the population as a factor of production, then to make labour as efficient as possible it needs to be provided with good living and working conditions, training to improve existing working skills or acquire new ones, and support when not in the working population, that is when young or old. Most importantly Europe in the 1950s and beyond has tried to build a better world for its citizens. It may not always have succeeded but this is the development of social policy in the EU.

Having argued that, it was not until the 1980s, and particularly as a consequence of the Single European Act, that social policy assumed a central role within the EC and consequently began to impact upon European business. In this context it is now seen also as a means to improve the quality of the products which the EU labour force produces through the improved quality of the working environment, and as a means to match competition from the Pacific Rim and developing economies, through creating an educated, skilled and flexible work-force. As the nature of work and of business organisations changes and national labour markets become harmonised across the EU, so social policy must adapt to meet the needs of the twenty-first century.

The major stages in the development of EU social policy are briefly discussed below.

■ The early stages

Postwar Western European social policy was born with the Treaty of Paris which was signed in April 1951 and came into force in July 1952, creating the European Coal and Steel Community. Among its initial objectives was the social one of improving the working conditions and living standards of coal and steel industry employees by means of increased output. It also offered scope to rehouse and retrain those who sought to leave the industry, an important issue later when production over-capacity occurred.

The creation, by the Treaty of Rome, of Euratom, the European Atomic Energy Community, and the EEC, the European Economic Community, built on this. In the preamble and a.117–22 emphasis was placed on the EC6 promoting improved and harmonised living and working standards (a.117), while a.118 emphasised specific social factors relating to employment, labour law, vocational training, social security, the right of association, collective bargaining and so on. Article 119 stressed the importance of equal pay for equal work for men and women. Some articles were binding on all members while others were not. The assumption of the Treaty was that these changes would occur naturally. Partly this would be through implementation by individual members, for example by coordinating national social security systems to assist migrant workers (a.51) in order to improve mobility of labour among the member countries, and partly as an inevitable consequence of the common market generating the wealth to finance these.

The Treaty of Rome also created the European Social Fund (ESF) (a.123), which sought to increase the geographical and occupational mobility of the workforce and thus increase employment prospects and hence living standards. Particular emphasis was placed on retraining and resettlement of unemployed workers and job-creation schemes. Handicapped by limited funds in its early years, the ESF went through a number of reforms in 1971, 1977, 1983 and 1988.

Currently the ESF is being thoroughly reformed again to enable it to function effectively by providing funding to underpin member states' Employment Action Plans. Its aim will be to support 'the adaption and modernisation of education, training and employment policies and systems across the EU'. It will implement policies to combat unemployment, promote social inclusion, develop lifelong education and training systems to promote employability, anticipate and promote economic and social change, and improve womens' involvement in the labour market. This will be done by promoting framework agreements between employers' and employees' organisations rather than through centrally directed legislation. The ESF will ensue that all the EU15 participate to a minimum extent in all these areas while allowing members to choose their own priorities for ESF funding.

The late 1970s and early 1980s, the so-called period of Eurosclerosis when progress stagnated, is discussed elsewhere. It was only with the accession of Jacques Delors to the presidency of the European Commission and the Single European Act that a major revival in EU social policy occurred.

■ The Single European Act (SEA) 1987

By the mid-1980s social policy was in need of resuscitation. It was also seen as a natural concomitant of the economic reform presaged by the forthcoming internal or single market. There were a number of concerns which related to the need for EC citizens to see clearly and share the benefits of the internal market, the need to promote greater freedom of movement for, *inter alia*, labour, and a need to combat social dumping. One aspect of social dumping was the worry that workers would migrate in large numbers from countries with low social welfare provisions to those with the highest. Another aspect was that firms would locate plant in countries with the lowest social welfare standards since this would reduce firms' fixed costs and make production cheaper. One way advanced to minimise social dumping is by the process of upward harmonisation of social standards; that is, raising social welfare provisions of all EU countries to those with the highest standards.

The SEA addressed social issues in a number of ways aimed at promoting economic and social cohesion. The Treaty of Rome had discussed the free movement of labour within the then EEC but due to different tax and benefit systems among the members this had not been fully achieved. The SEA therefore modified the Treaty of Rome (new a.118A and a.118B) regarding social policy, with the introduction of qualified majority voting (QMV) making it possible to bypass countries such as the UK which sought to block legislation.

Emphasis was placed on health and safety provisions for workers (one of the less contentious issues) and promoting social dialogue to improve industrial relations (known as co-determination – that is, the right of workers to be consulted, express their views and to have an input to management decisions). The SEA also introduced into the Treaty of Rome the need for the ESF to work more closely with the European Regional Development Fund (ERDF) and the European Agricultural Guidance and Guarantee Fund (EAGGF) guidance section to enable structural funds to be coordinated and targeted better.

■ 4.8 The Social Charter 1989

The Community Charter of Fundamental Social Rights of Workers, to give it its full name, was developed out of a concern by the main institutions of the EC that the implementation of the internal market would lead to the reduction of social rights. This would be caused by business needs for greater cost-efficiencies created through competition once the single market was complete. It also recognised that increased competition from the low-cost Pacific Rim producers would further impact on EC producers and hence social welfare provisions. The Social Charter therefore established a list of minimum conditions which all countries should implement (upward harmonisation) to ensure that social dumping did not occur. Table 4.1 identifies these 12 points.

The Social Charter was to clearly demonstrate to all citizens that social policy was being developed in conjunction with, and as a sharing of, the benefits of the development of the Single European Market. However, although approved by 11 EC countries at the Strasbourg summit of December 1989, the UK felt unable to accept its provisions since this contradicted its own beliefs in free labour markets untrammelled by government (or EC) intervention. This prompted then Prime Minister Margaret Thatcher's comment that the EC was introducing into the UK 'socialism by the back door'. The UK's argument was that the costs of the Social Charter are imposed on European businesses causing their costs to rise, raising the product's price and reducing sales as EU firms become less competitive. The counter-argument is that raising the working and living conditions of labour enable better quality and more output to be produced. Also the EU cannot compete with the Pacific Rim countries on cost grounds alone – unless everyone accepts large cuts in living standards which is politically unacceptable.

The Social Charter was not legally binding. However, the directives and regulations arising from this were based on the Treaty of Rome, as amended by the Single European Act, to both of which the UK is a signatory. Hence, when adopted by the Council of Ministers the UK was obliged to implement these. Because of UK opposition to social policy the Social Charter, originally intended to be a chapter of the Treaty of Maastricht (the Social Chapter) was therefore excluded from it and instead appended as a separate agreement between the 11, that is excluding the UK (as is stated in the preceding protocol). This meant that when a proposal was made which the UK could not accept the other EU members opted into the Social Chapter. One of the new UK government's first actions after the May 1997 elections was to announce its intention of accepting the social chapter.

Decisions can be reached by qualified majority voting for a number of areas such as health and safety, equal working opportunities, and working conditions.

Table 4.1   The 12 rights of the Social Charter 1989

THE 12 RIGHTS OF THE SOCIAL CHARTER

1. **Freedom of Movement:** the right of citizens of any EU country to work anywhere in the EU and on equal terms of employment with nationals of the country where the work is.

2. **Employment and Remuneration:** the right to employment and to receive a fair wage (however defined) for that work.

3. **Improved Living and Working Conditions:** with emphasis on upward harmonisation, e.g. introduction of maximum permitted hours of working week; rights to annual paid leave; and the extension of this to all modes of employment including, in recognition of changing labour markets, part-time and fixed contract workers.

4. **Adequate Social Protection:** this guarantees all EU workers a minimum wage (although not the same one) regardless of status, and social assistance for citizens excluded from the labour market or who lack adequate subsistence.

5. **Freedom of Association:** any worker or employer may belong to any trade union or professional organisation of his or her choice. This also recognises, implicitly, freedom to bargain and conclude collective agreements and, if necessary, collective action including strikes.

6. **Vocational Training:** recognising the changing nature of the labour market and the end of jobs for life, every worker shall have the right to vocational training. This should be provided by the public sector, companies and trade unions and other workers' organisations.

7. **Equal Treatment for Men and Women:** specifically equal pay for equal work. The careful reader will note that a.119 of the Treaty of Rome also stressed this same point. The fact that it had to be addressed again after 30 years shows how little progress has been made on this issue.

8. **Worker Information, Consultation and Participation:** this refers to the rights of workers to be informed and consulted and even have the right to participate in management decisions of the business they work for, where these affect working conditions and job security. The recent introduction of European Works Councils is a consequence of this.

9. **Health and Safety at Work:** every worker has the right to satisfactory health and safety conditions at work. Emphasis is placed on upward harmonisation of these conditions.

10. **Protection of Children and Adolescents:** among other things this gives school leavers the right to two years vocational training, defines 16 as the minimum working age and guarantees fair wages for those who do work.

11. **The Rights of the Elderly:** this guarantees the right to a pension for those who have retired to permit decent living standards. If s/he does not have a pension then minimum social protection and medical assistance is to be provided.

12. **Disabled Persons:** are to be entitled to training and occupational and social integration and rehabilitation.

Other areas such as social security and the collective bargaining rights of employers and employees require unanimous voting.

■ 4.9 The changing nature of work

The EU designated 1996 as 'the year of lifelong learning' in recognition that EU citizens can no longer assume that they have a job for life and hence will need continuously to update their knowledge and skills. Fifty years ago a young person leaving school might have safely assumed that, had he or she wished, they could have stayed with the same employer, and quite possibly in the same job, for the rest of their working life – although the woman probably would have had to give up work for perhaps 10–15 years to bring up children, assuming she married and worked after marriage. As such there would be no particular pressures to gain new qualifications later in one's life.

Work has now changed. In the UK the average length of stay with an employer is eight years – in the US it is less. The expectation of a job for life has gone and with it the assumption that no new training is necessary once one has qualified initially. In the last 20 years many people have faced redundancy or enforced early retirement – blue collar (manual) workers particularly in the 1970s and early 1980s, and white collar (clerical) workers in the late 1980s and early 1990s. For manual workers this has been caused by automation of assembly lines, the decline or loss of overseas markets and of traditional industries such as steel, coal, shipbuilding and so on to Japan and developing nations in the Far East; increased import-penetration by foreign suppliers – especially Japan but increasingly now the People's Republic of China; and a fundamental shift of economies from manufacturing to services creating structural/regional unemployment. In the UK there was also a loss of trade union powers inhibiting the unions' ability to fight for their members, while privatisation of state-owned utilities – a policy now pursued vigorously in the remainder of the EU – also meant substantial labour reductions as businesses were forced to maximise profits to satisfy their owners, the shareholders, rather than rely on state-provided subsidies.

For white-collar workers, the buzzwords of some influential US management gurus of the 1980s were downsizing and delayering – taking out whole levels of middle management from business organisations to cut costs, leaving those remaining to undertake their own work and, to some extent, that of those who had left. Clearly this is an effective way to save costs but also it creates considerable pressures on those remaining, creating stress through work overload. At times this is exhibited by working very long hours in order to be seen to do so by one's line manager. IBM was a classic example of a company, under considerable pressure to stem large losses caused by the success of IBM PC clones, which undertook a major restructuring and delayering programme. More recently research has shown that firms which heavily delayered have suffered reduced profitability compared with those who downsized to a lesser extent. This is because shedding middle managers loses the company valuable experienced staff, creates fear in those remaining that they could be next, and creates new corporate structures which take time to adjust to.

This strategy of downsizing has been summarised by Charles Handy as:

$$\text{Competitiveness} = \tfrac{1}{2} \times 2 \times 3 = P$$

where $\tfrac{1}{2}$ = half the people are employed in an organisation; 2 = they are paid twice as much as previously; 3 = they are expected to produce three times as much as previously; and P = profit/productivity.

Other characteristics of the new labour market include the tendency of firms to out-source; that is, to contract out to agencies work previously undertaken in-house. This may range from cleaning and catering to information technology services, marketing and human resource functions. For the international car industry this has included major components. Part-time staff are increasingly being preferred to full-time staff and in many cases this tends to be women rather than men. Research for the UK's Department of Education and Employment forecast that for the decade 1996–2006, of 770 000 new jobs created in the UK 725 000 would be part-time. In the UK, where the growth of part-time work has been especially prevalent, the economy has been jokingly referred to as a McJobs economy – taken to the extreme everyone will have a McDonalds type low-paid part-time series of jobs. Women are perceived by employers as more flexible and adaptable workers, often they are seen as more suitable than men in growth areas such as retailing (supermarkets and so on) and office work, while they may prefer to work part-time to fit in with the schooling of small children (in the above forecast for 1996–2006 two-thirds of the new jobs are forecast to be taken by women). Since women are still under-represented in senior management positions (although this is now changing rapidly), and earn on average only 70 per cent of what men earn for the same jobs – an issue the EU has supposedly been trying to address since the Treaty of Rome – they are cheaper to employ. In all these cases the aim is to reduce costs.

■ The flexible firm

A model developed by J. Atkinson in the mid-1980s to explore the emergence of the flexible firm distinguished between core and peripheral workers. Core workers are employed full-time and, as the name suggests, are core to the operations of the business. They may have managerial or creative functions, for example working for graphic designers, and will have guaranteed employment, the ability to train and develop, good facilities and salary, and so on. However, as core workers they must be flexible – for example working in a team looking at a marketing project – and capable of working by themselves. Also they will be expected to acquire expertise in different areas as their work demands.

In contrast peripheral workers will undertake work less essential to the business and consequently their financial remuneration and job security will be less. Their skills will be more generalised and they will work on short-term contracts, undertake job-sharing and part-time work, or be youth trainees on apprentice-ships or similar. These people will be particularly vulnerable when the firm needs to reduce costs because of the nature of their employment contracts. They will also have less opportunities for staff development.

There is a third group, furthest from the centre of the business, who consist of self-employed workers, sub-contracted staff and agency temporary staff. These undertake the out-sourced work discussed above.

Atkinson's model has subsequently been criticised for several reasons. It has been argued that, in practice, firms have not deliberately pursued flexibility. Rather the influx of Japanese foreign direct investment (FDI) into the UK has forced firms to respond to and adopt Japanese production methods – so-called Japanisation. Firms such as Honda, Nissan and Sony expect their employees, represented by one union, to demonstrate flexibility in moving from one job to another. This is increasingly being adopted by other firms.

■ How the EU is responding to the changing nature of work

Handy's perception of the near future (already the present for some) for many workers is one where people will undertake a portfolio of activities because of the lack of a guarantee of long-term full-time work. These might include several part-time jobs, possibly a retirement pension for people forced to take early retirement; some voluntary work – for example, helping an animal-rescue organisation; hobbies – for example, playing in a local orchestra; and other unpaid activities such as DIY, rather than paying someone else to do the work. He also argues that people will dip in and out of work during their lives and will have to accept that there are periods of unemployment. Clearly they will need the skills to cope with this changing pattern of work.

As noted earlier the EU has recognised the rapidly changing nature of society and of work, for example the impact of Communication and Information Technologies (CIT) on both. As such it has sought to promote the concept of lifelong learning, supporting education and training policies linked more specifically to employment policies, for example through the ESF. These strategies are overarching across the EU and are intended to supplement and support national initiatives, rather than replace them. The 1998 European Social Policy initiative is intended particularly to improve the prospects for employment through focusing on wider economic and strategic issues, like CIT. For example the EU has an unemployment rate of 12 per cent (compared with the US rate of 5 per cent) and since 1980 has created 4 million new jobs compared with 25 million in the US. France insisted on an employment chapter in the Treaty of Amsterdam which emphasises the serious concerns governments have for this.

■ The Anglo-Saxon and continental models of the labour market

There has been much debate in recent years as to which model is more effective for promoting economic growth and, particularly, creating jobs. The Anglo-

Saxon model, as the French have dubbed it and as practised in the UK and US, seeks to remove restrictions on the employment of labour including institutional, legal and fiscal. Liberalisation and deregulation of markets, it is argued, involves reducing excess trade union powers through legislation and the removal of subsidies to staple industries where union power was strongest (perceived as an example of market failure), or their privatisation; reducing the costs of hiring labour such as payroll taxes and redundancy payments; making labour easier to hire and dismiss, including using short-term contracts; promoting education and training to provide the workforce with new skills; and in the case of the last UK Conservative government refusing to endorse social policies such as a maximum working week and a minimum wage.

In other words the government should create the conditions for labour markets to work freely but should not interfere with them except to protect the really weak and disadvantaged. Additionally it should also raise labour productivity by investment in developing skills, infrastructure and research and development – as the UN's International Labour Office (ILO) has argued. Also the UK's falling unemployment rate in the early to mid-1990s was helped by 600 000 people leaving the workforce – becoming economically inactive. Yet this stores up real problems for the shrinking workforce having to finance them and their pensions.

In contrast the continental European or social market model regulates labour markets. It relies on direct government intervention through the use of subsidies to inefficient industries to maintain employment (inhibiting the effective functioning of the market as an allocator of resources including capital); use of public procurement policies to favour local industries for the same reasons; imposing high financial costs on employers, for example employment taxes whenever a new employee is recruited and requiring high redundancy payments on dismissal; a large public sector; and heavy regulation of companies. As such, the creation of new jobs is difficult as is any change generally. For example, in 1996 in Germany approximately one-third of its economic output was needed to finance the welfare state, and for every deutschemark paid to an employee by a business another 80 pfennigs had to be paid for welfare costs.

International bodies, such as the OECD and the IMF, have urged the EU to deregulate their labour markets and the EU is trying to act as a catalyst to promote this. The Commission's green paper of November 1993, entitled *European Social Policy: Options for the Union* and authored by Commissioner for Social Policy Padraig Flynn, sought to promote debate about the social issues facing the EU during the remainder of this decade and into the twenty-first century. The Luxembourg job summit of November 1997 took this further, albeit limitedly, by agreeing that member states should create more flexible labour markets, reduce the burden on employers and employees (since taxes can act as a disincentive to work), promote businesses and enhance training of the labour force. All of the EU15 are to submit national action plans to Brussels for peer review once a year to prompt recalcitrant members to comply. The 1997 summit also stressed the importance of employers' organisations and unions working together as social partners to modernise work patterns. Indeed this typifies the EU approach and is very much based on the German philosophy of industrial relations.

However, changing national cultures is difficult and takes time – particularly in countries like Germany, France, Italy and Greece with entrenched perceptions – as the example below demonstrates.

■ 4.10 EU social policy: the way forward

The period since the Single European Act 1986 has seen fundamental advances in EU social policy in parallel with the implementation and management of the internal market. A number of directives and draft collective agreements between the EU's social partners – that is, employers and trade union bodies (and subsequently ratified under the Social Chapter) – have become law in recent years which seek to improve workers' rights. These include:

1. **Posted workers**: this relates to minimum pay and conditions for workers from one member state working in another, particularly to prevent posted workers being employed for lower wages than domestic workers (a form of social dumping). It also covers holiday leave and social security rules to ensure that employers of posted workers have the same obligations to fulfil.
2. **Acquired rights**: this seeks to protect employees' rights by guaranteeing them protection and consultation in the event of the transfer of the business or parts of it to a different owner. Its intention was to develop the original 1977 directive on workers rights and the right to continuing employment when an enterprise is transferred to a different owner. However, confusion was thrown on this in March 1997 when the European Court of Justice ruled that it does not automatically apply when a service changes from one contractor to another.
3. **Uniform parental leave**: under this both parents are entitled to three months' parental leave after the birth or adoption of a child, and the right to return to work after at the same pay scale.
4. **Creation of works councils**: this requires companies employing more than 1000 people, or more than 100 in two European countries, to establish a worker-representative committee. The idea is to give workers much greater consultation in the running of their business. It is currently proposed to extend this to all but the smallest firms
5. **Part-time workers**: part-time workers employed for more than eight hours per week have been conferred with the same rights pro rata under this directive as full-time workers, including pay and holidays. Of particular importance is the right of part-time workers to belong to company pension schemes and for employers to contribute to these. It is proposed that long-term part-time workers be entitled to pursue these back to 1977, which would impose very high costs retrospectively on employers who have used the same part-time staff for a long period of time.
6. **Maximum working week**: taking force in late 1996 this is intended to limit the maximum working week to 48 hours, an important point in the light of working hours rising across the EU in the 1980s, in the case of the UK back to the level of the 1950s. In practice opposition to this directive has caused it to be diluted to incorporate the provision '. . . unless they wish to [work more than 48 hours].'

7. **Sexual harassment at work**: under this the burden of proof is shifted to the employer, who is required to prove that there has been no discrimination once a plaintiff provides sufficient evidence to demonstrate that there is a case to answer.

In spite of the above progress, there are areas where social policy has not yet been effectively implemented. For example, upward harmonisation of social conditions (raising every country's to the level of the highest) has not occurred, undoubtedly aggravated by the early 1990s economic recession. Having said that, some economists argue that this is essentially a political justification and that if a standard social policy is imposed on all countries it will be necessary to provide them with substantial regional subsidies to offset the costs of this.

CASE STUDY   The 35-hour Working Week

By July 2000 France will have fully implemented a new law requiring every employer to cut working hours per employee to 35 without any reduction in pay. Anyone working more than 39 hours per week will, from 1998, face a tax surcharge. The aim of this is to combat the very high French unemployment. The French Government argues it will create 540 000 new jobs as companies are forced to take on new workers to offset the shorter working hours; however businesses say it will increase costs, affect productivity and cause job losses, not create more jobs. The French government hope to offset this by offering businesses up to FF13 000 for every job created under the new legislation.

Currently the average French person works 1645 hours per year compared with a British worker's 1732 hours and an American worker's 1951 hours per year. The French also work less hours than Germany or Japan. A French worker costs one-third more to employ than a British worker, yet takes home lower net pay after social costs and taxation.

The maximum working week directive has been watered down, which defeats its purpose to some extent. Debate on the introduction of a minimum wage across the EU has provoked a range of views, many of which are hostile to the concept through its impact on EU competitiveness. Included in this debate, of course, is what is meant by a fair wage, since a fair wage in Germany would be a high wage in Greece or Portugal. The current position of the Commission is that a minimum wage is an issue for individual members, not the EU. In practice, with the introduction of the minimum wage in the UK, every EU member will have some form of minimum wage. Other causes for social policy not progressing as fast as was initially intended include the slowness and inflexibility of the EU bureaucracy in introducing directives, the reluctance of some national governments through fear of loss of sovereignty, and the cost of implementation.

The rising cost of social welfare provision in the EU, contributed to by an aging population, further exacerbates these problems. This can be met so long as the EU can achieve increasing prosperity financed through greater output and sales. If this is not achieved then declining social cohesion is the risk. This debate, which also challenges the countries of Central and Eastern Europe, is likely to dominate EU thinking in the foreseeable future.

■ Review questions

1. Why has an EU competition policy been an essential part of the moves to a single market?
2. 'State aid, such has been provided to support the growth of Airbus Industrie, is essential to promote Euro-champions able to compete globally, and should be used much more.' Discuss
3. If mergers rarely achieve their declared objectives, why then are so many mergers occurring in the EU?
4. Discuss the economic and social problems likely to be encountered in the EU by the movement away from a job for life.
5. Compare and contrast the advantages and the disadvantages of the Anglo-Saxon and the Continental models of the labour market.

■ Bibliography

Atkinson, J., 'Manpower Strategies for Flexible Organisations', *Personnel Management*, vol. 16, no. 8, 1984.

Addison, J. T. and Siebert, W. S., *Labour Markets in Europe: Issues of Harmonisation and Regulation* (London: The Dryden Press, 1997).

El-Agraa, A. M., *The European Union: History, Institutions, Economics and Politics*, 5th edn (Hemel Hempstead: Prentice Hall Europe, 1998).

Handy, C., *The Empty Raincoat: Making Sense of Modern Business* (London: Arrow Books, 1994).

Hitiris, T., *European Union Economics*, 4th edn (Hemel Hempstead: Harvester Wheatsheaf, 1998).

Koutsoyiannis, A., *Modern Microeconomics*, 2nd edn (Basingstoke: Macmillan, 1987).

Swann, D., *The Economics of the Common Market*, 8th edn (Harmondsworth: Penguin Books, 1993).

Thornton, B., 'The Human Impact of Organisational Change' in Harris, Neil, *Change and the Modern Business* (Basingstoke: Macmillan, 1997).

Also:

The Economist
The European
The Financial Times
The Times
The European Commission website   http://www.cec.org.uk
EU General Report website   http://europa.eu.int/abc/doc/off/index-en.htm

CHAPTER 5

Central and Eastern Europe: economies in transition

■ 5.1 Introduction

The period since 1989 has seen fundamental changes in Central and Eastern Europe and the former Soviet Union, changes which have revolutionised the economic, political, legal and social systems of these countries. This chapter looks particularly at the economic developments and their impact on the operation of business. It examines why command economies failed; how reform processes have taken place, particularly privatisation; the problems experienced in the transition from command to market economies; and the current position of the transition economies at the beginning of the new millennium. The chapter concludes with an analysis of the work of the European Bank for Reconstruction and Development (EBRD). The role of Western European businesses in contributing to this economic development is explored in Chapter 10.

■ 5.2 The role of the state in European economies

An economic system concerns itself with the means of production, distribution and exchange of goods and services, both for now and the future. Since economic resources are scarce, correct choices have to be made to enable these to be used with optimum efficiency. How different systems make these choices may depend on the historical evolution of the country, or on some political ideology adopted by its ruling government or perhaps its imposition by force. All three of these have applied in Europe in the twentieth century.

For some countries in Western Europe, such as the UK, France, Benelux and the Scandinavian countries, historical evolution has seen the emergence of parliamentary democracies, with or without monarchies, and market economies. At different times the balance of resource ownership may shift between the public and private sectors or back again. Much of Western Europe in the post-Second World War period favoured state ownership of assets, and governments nationalised staple industries such as coal, steel and the utilities. France undertook a series of nationalisations in the early 1980s to rescue major firms encountering economic difficulties. Since the late 1980s, however, Western European opinion has shifted the other way and large-scale privatisation programmes have been undertaken, partly to reduce government debt and to generate revenues to meet the Maastricht debt criteria. In the late 1980s and 1990s this has been mirrored by the privatisation programmes of the former communist countries of Central and Eastern Europe (CEEC) and the former USSR.

For Western Europe this has coincided with a re-evaluation of the role of the state in macroeconomic management and a growing conclusion that the state can be most effective when it manages the economy, creating optimal conditions in which businesses can function rather than being a major player in the economy, that is owning and controlling large amounts of resources. The argument is, therefore, that large-scale state ownership and consequent borrowing has been harmful to the private sector through crowding out, the inefficient use of subsidies and over-regulation – although some EU countries are finding it harder than others to move far down this path. It also follows the turning away from demand management through Keynesian budget deficit policies to greater concentration on supply-side policies, monetary policy and, particularly with the UK, exchange-rate management, although it is not, of course, applicable to ERM members.

In the CEEC between 1945–90, state ownership extended to control of all assets in their economies – the centrally planned or command economy. In the case of Russia in 1917, inspired by the writings of Karl Marx, this policy was adopted by Vladimir Lenin and the Bolshevik party. It was maintained by subsequent leaders until the limited reforms of Mikhail Gorbachev in the late 1980s with his policies of *glasnost* (openness) and *perestroika* (restructuring of the economy). Here all assets were owned by the state and even labour was controlled by the government to the extent of determining where people might work and in what jobs. However, this was not just a consequence of central planning but also of the police state introduced by Josef Stalin when he first came to power in 1924. For the CEEC, communist political systems and central planning were imposed after the Second World War as a consequence of occupation by the Soviet army.

In the same way other countries in Western Europe have experienced state control of resources, but through the rise to power of fascist governments to the right of the political spectrum rather than to the left. As well as the control of Germany and Italy by fascist parties in the 1930s, Spain and Portugal both remained under the control of fascist dictators until the 1970s, Franco in the case of Spain and Salazar in Portugal's case. Moreover, the late 1960s and early 1970s saw the operation of a military dictatorship in Greece.

■ 5.3 The failure of centrally planned economies

In 1991 the former Soviet spy George Blake, who escaped from Pentonville, an English prison, in 1965 after serving three years of a 42-year sentence for espionage, was quoted as saying 'Had the Soviet economy been able to produce consumer goods Soviet economists would now be in New York advising the Americans how to run their business, instead of the other way round'. This was clearly an exaggeration since there were fundamental problems in the centrally-planned economies of Central and Eastern Europe which successive governments failed to address. Nonetheless, insufficient consumer goods were a real symptom of the underlying problems.

All the command economies of the CEEC and the former Soviet Union had certain characteristics distinguishing them from market economies, most notably their emphasis on heavy industry (for armaments). Decisions were made by the bureaucracy, committees who lacked total knowledge yet who tried to undertake the functions of markets in terms of deciding how to allocate resources and what to produce. These decisions were normally made as part of a detailed planning process working to five-year national plans and setting production quotas for individual industries which were to be met regardless of actual consumer demand. After the collapse of communism investigation of production figures found that these targets were rarely fulfilled. Moreover, this did not affect those businesses not meeting their targets since the state was always willing to subsidise them. Consequently command economies were usually characterised by inefficiencies, operating inside their production possibility curves, misallocating resources and failing to match supply to demand. Worst of all, since resources were owned by the state there was little or no competition – hence there was no incentive to improve quality, upgrade design or improve productive efficiency. As a result, centrally-planned economies were characterised by long queues for basic amenities such as bread and meat, and waiting lists, often years, for consumer goods such as cars. The reader who is interested in observing a centrally-planned economy in action should look to North Korea, which is still largely clinging to the old model of the command economy.

Many reasons have been identified for the rapid fall of communism and with it centrally-planned economies in the late 1980s and early 1990s. One major factor is undoubtedly the slowdown in economic growth in the 1970s and 1980s reinforced by the reduction in easy credit which western banks had provided following significant defaulting by CEEC borrowers (known as sovereign debt). As a consequence of this, centrally-planned economies failed to supply consumers with the choice of goods and services available in Western Europe. Reception of Western European television programmes further reinforced in consumers' minds how far Central and Eastern Europe had fallen behind. Even though countries such as Hungary and, to a lesser extent, Czechoslovakia had made some progress in the 1980s towards a mixed economy, with private and public sectors, the continuing emphasis on the military, armaments and heavy industry such as coal and steel meant that resources were unnecessarily being diverted away from consumer goods. Other resources were diverted to unproductive bureaucracies rather than to the actual productive process while, very importantly, technological improvements and new investment were not implemented because of severe restrictions on foreign trade and capital flows causing production processes and goods produced to look very old fashioned and goods unattractively designed.

International trade, a major engine of economic development, was further stifled by the fact that Central and Eastern European currencies were not convertible. The net result was that industry was starved of modern investment, production techniques and design ideas while consumers were starved of consumer goods. As illustration the total redevelopment of the Skoda car manufacturer since being taken over by VW, and the redesign and re-engineering of its products, has resulted in a major growth in demand for cars previously derided for their poor quality and old-fashioned look.

A further factor preventing possible economic reform in most command economies was the perception that making profits was bad – so capitalism was a dirty word indicating the class-divided societies of Western Europe and the exploitation of the proletariat. This is best illustrated in the comparison of two men, Mikhail Kalashnikov and Eugene M. Stoner.

CASE STUDY   The AK47 and the M16

Mikhail Kalashnikov is the inventor of the AK47, the most famous assault rifle in the world. Over 55 million have been produced and it has been the stock weapon of the armies of the former Warsaw Pact (USSR and CEECs), China, Vietnam, the former Yugoslavia, and Finland. It has also been used widely in the Middle East and by terrorist and criminal organisations. It is compact, sturdy and reliable and its 30-shell magazine with its distinctive curve can be fired singly or in short automatic bursts. Because Kalashnikov never registered a patent, which was not supported in the former USSR anyway, he never received any royalties for his product. Had he lived in the West and registered his patent he would have been a multimillionaire. In fact when reported in 1994, the then 75-year-old was living in the provincial town of Izhevsk on a pension equivalent to £50 per month. In 1997 Boris Yeltsin awarded a medal to Kalashnikov for his life's work.

In contrast, Eugene M. Stoner was the designer of the M16 assault rifle, the American competitor to the AK47. The M16 was the standard issue for the US armed forces from 1963, and 85 000 were used during the Vietnam War, where the humidity of the jungle made them corrode. The M16 helped make Stoner a very wealthy man, with him owning several helicopters. His wealth was based on his holding more than a hundred patents. The M16 was also sold to a number of overseas armies, including those of South Korea, Israel and the Philippines. The two men often met at conferences with Stoner admitting to Kalashnikov 'Mikhail, your gun is more reliable than mine. It's simpler.' Stoner died in Palm Springs, Florida in May 1997.

■ 5.4 Making the transition to market economies

■ Different starting points

In the moves by Central and Eastern European countries to market economies, not all began at the same starting point. Hungary from 1968 with its liberalisation programme, and Poland from the late 1970s with its large-scale overseas borrowing, had sought to encourage a limited private sector, particularly in agriculture but also in retailing and manufacturing. A black-market economy also flourished unofficially. However, in spite of this Poland had seen only a tentative and limited introduction of economic reform by the early 1980s, partly in response to pressures from the Gdansk shipyard workers and their union Solidarity. Also these countries had sought to liberalise prices and develop trade with the West to reduce dependence on COMECON, the now defunct CEEC and Soviet Union trading agreement. As a consequence they have had a longer lead-in time to implement economic reform.

What is now the Czech Republic had through the 1980s actively opposed the development of a private sector, so consequently had more to do following the fall of the communist government. However, Czechoslovakia had been very careful in its borrowing from the West which helped it significantly. At the other end of the scale Albania, Bulgaria, Romania and Russia were still almost totally command economies in the early 1990s. Albania was largely an agriculturally-based subsistence economy due to being kept in total isolation for nearly 40 years as a consequence of the self-sufficiency policies of its dictator Enver Hoxha. It and Romania, who had adopted an austerity programme under Nikolai Ceausescu, interestingly both had no significant debts with the West. The Russian and Bulgarian economies, in contrast, relied very substantially on heavy industry while the Romanian economy was a mixture of heavy industry with a large agricultural base in the countryside surrounding the towns.

The problems which economies in transition have faced may also be extended to analyse progress in reform, which is undertaken in section 5.5. Estrin (1994) has argued that in comparing the relative positions of the former communist countries of Central and Eastern Europe the main differences between them are distinguished as the level of development, the degree of macroeconomic stability, the extent of microeconomic decentralisation and the exposure to international trade.

The level of development each country has achieved refers to the balance between the primary, secondary and tertiary sectors of the economy. It also applies to the country's progress towards market economies, which is discussed below. The degree of macroeconomic stability relates to the extent to which GDP has grown, or in the case of reforming countries in the early 1990s, the extent to which it fell. It also relates to such issues as the extent to which prices are stable, what is happening to government debt as a percentage of GDP, the trade balance and other macroeconomic variables discussed below. The extent of microeconomic decentralisation relates to the process of the state relinquishing its control of the means of production, particularly factories and farms. The process of privatisation is discussed elsewhere below. The exposure to international trade is a measure of its liberalisation process. COMECON nations always tended to look inwards and their ability to liberalise and turn to the West has been an important measure of their access to new sources of supply and to new markets. It has also been an important step in the process to convertible currencies and encouraging inward capital flows.

The difficulties faced by the governments of Central and Eastern Europe and the former USSR, in making the transition to market economies, have been formidable. They have had to undertake reform on a number of different fronts which are discussed below.

■ Macroeconomic stabilisation

This has involved stabilising and then turning around adverse trends in a number of key macroeconomic variables which are fundamental to achieving a stable and growth oriented market economy. These adverse variables have been rising levels of unemployment and inflation, negative economic growth, and deficit current account and fiscal balances. In virtually all cases, once initial transformation programmes had been launched, these key indicators accelerated sharply causing considerable economic, political and social difficulties.

During the Soviet era unemployment was officially zero for both the Soviet Union and the CEEC. In practice this was often due to disguised unemployment, that is, several people doing the work of one. Once reform commenced it became essential, especially in conjunction with privatisation programmes, to shed surplus labour as businesses sought to curtail costs and move to profitability. This was particularly so as subsidies were reduced and resources were switched from armaments and the military to consumer-goods production. Structural unemployment has, therefore, become a problem yet is not fully reflected in official statistics which do not always record an accurate picture. The current state of unemployment is discussed below in section 5.5.

The switch to producing consumer goods also required substantial investment programmes to update antiquated capital and production processes, investment which has not always been forthcoming. The lack of a modern financial infrastructure meant that, in the early 1990s, there were no stock markets, bank branch networks or financial instruments to channel funds from potential domestic savers to potential borrowers or investors. Where domestic savers had accumulated funds these were kept as cash (often US dollars) under mattresses, for example. However, rising inflation subsequently reduced very substantially the real value of these savings negating their potential benefits as sources to fund capital expenditure. Many savings have also been lost by bank failures, particularly in Russia.

Foreign direct investment into the CEEC and the former Soviet Union was deterred, in the early 1990s, by a number of factors, particularly uncertainty over political conditions. However, substantial investment, especially by Germany, and funding by the EU and international bodies such as the IMF and EBRD, have redressed this more in recent years. However, this inflow of capital has posed other problems in the late 1990s. Countries which have attracted large-scale inward capital flows – such as the Czech and Slovak Republics, Hungary and Poland – have experienced upward pressure on their currencies which has undermined the competitiveness of their exports and impacted on their current account balances.

Rising inflation, in the early years of transition, was caused by reducing the control over prices for food, fuel, accommodation and so on, and by the ending of soft loans to state enterprises such as oil and gas at negative real rates of interest. These rates had failed to reflect their opportunity cost and thus distorted business's true profitability. Enterprises which failed to repay loans were bailed out by the state rather then becoming bankrupt. When state aid was reduced businesses were forced to raise their prices to cover true production costs. Inflation was further aggravated by increasing money supply as governments borrowed from banks to finance their expenditure and, in the early stages of reform, by monetary overhang as people unwillingly acquired savings due to the lack of goods to spend their money on. When goods did become available excess money holdings enabled consumers to bid up prices to secure them. International lending agencies require governments to adopt tight monetary policies to combat inflation as part of the conditions of providing loans.

The heavy subsidisation of industry also manifested itself in high public sector debt which had to be reduced if government finances were to be stabilised and the budget balanced. Tight fiscal policy has also normally been a requirement of IMF and World Bank lending with the introduction of new taxes to take advantage of anticipated economic growth.

Externally, macroeconomic stabilisation requires reducing trade debt with the West and balance of payments deficits. The introduction of convertible currencies, with the consequent depreciation of their values against other currencies through market forces, was thought to be a way to correct balance of payments deficits over time but, as economies do stabilise and as capital inflows occur, as discussed above, exchange rates have risen, in some cases worsening current balances. Most importantly, economic stabilisation requires economic growth since without this people do not become better off and economic reform will therefore fail. The current position of the variables discussed here is analysed below in section 5.5.

■ Liberalisation

To enable markets to develop and function properly price controls and subsidies have had to be removed, although in practice this is not complete because of the adverse effects on unemployment and living costs. Of course, the aim is to allow markets to allocate resources effectively and for prices to equate supply and demand rather than attempts to do this by state planning officials. Positive real interest rates have been initiated to reflect the opportunity costs of borrowing and lending, and a financial infrastructure which did not previously exist has been introduced, both capital markets to act as a vehicle for both small savers and institutional investors to acquire company shares, and proper branch banking networks.

■ Institutional change

This has involved a need fundamentally to transform the whole pattern of ownership from state to private sector by dismantling bureaucracies which operated planning and control processes. New legal systems have had to be established to underpin these changes, including ownership of private property and meeting the claims of previous owners of property seized by communist governments, granting legal identity to corporations to enable them to own assets, hire and fire labour, sue and be sued and so on, and most importantly developing a recognition that the judicial system is politically independent of the government and government bureaucracies.

A programme of privatisation was begun on a scale not seen even in the West. This enabled production to be for profit rather than to meet former planning targets and has also made it harder for any political counter-reform movement to establish itself since it would no longer control economic assets.

■ Cultural change

Cultural change has been perhaps the hardest aspect to achieve. It has included changing the values and beliefs of the population to promote acceptance of the concepts of markets, profit, private ownership, competition and inequalities of income; that is, the characteristics of a business or capitalist culture. It involved acquiring the expertise and knowledge which was previously not allowed such as western accounting conventions, business administration skills, non-Marxist economics and the acquisition of English and German as foreign languages rather than Russian.

In the early years of reform, CEEC and Russia experienced real problems arising from increasing numbers of strikes as workers flexed newly acquired industrial muscle, the worry being that unrest would deter inward investment. In practice this has not been the problem that was initially feared. Indeed in many parts of Russia, even where people have not been paid for months, a mood of resignation has deterred major industrial action of the type seen in the early years of transition.

Corruption has been and continues to be a real problem which is harming reform, especially in Russia. Partly this has been through the opportunism of former communist apparatchiks reinventing themselves as modern capitalists by securing large shareholdings in privatised businesses at nominal prices, at times supported by Boris Yeltsin who has leaned on them for political support. The emergence of the Russian mafia with global links with criminal organisations in the US and elsewhere, links which enable the laundering of funds into legitimate enterprises, has also severely harmed transformation and deterred foreign direct investment. This is further exacerbated by large-scale tax evasion which hits the Russian government's fiscal balance and its management of the economy.

The other major area of concern is environmental pollution. The former Soviet government largely ignored the environmental harm caused by antiquated production methods and waste product disposal, while the Soviet army also had a totally irresponsible attitude to toxic waste disposal and has left a legacy which has caused harm not just to Russia but also to the Central and Eastern European countries it formerly occupied. This has been made worse by the lack of modern technology to dispose of such waste and the money to fund it. It is perhaps best typified by former nuclear-powered ships such as submarines and the nuclear ice-breaker *Lenin* which are rusting away with little attention being given to the safe disposal of their nuclear reactors and spent nuclear fuel.

A good example of such environmental damage is a report in the *New York Times* in the mid-1990s stating that since 1960 the USSR and Russia had dumped over half their nuclear waste, totalling billions of gallons, underground near to major rivers at Dimitrovgrad by the river Volga, Tomsk near the river Ob and Krasnoyarsk on the river Yenisei. This included Caesium-137 and Strontium-90 which by international standards should be stored in leak-proof containers in low-risk areas for thousands of years. At the time of the report Russian scientists said radioactive waste had leaked at one site and spread a wide distance.

■ External relations

This has involved re-entering the international economic community, joining international organisations such as the IMF, and gaining access to international capital from Western governments and institutions such as the European Bank for Reconstruction and Development (EBRD) and the World Bank (IBRD). It can most obviously be seen in the current proceeding applications of four Central and Eastern European countries and Estonia to join the EU, and Russia joining the former G7 group of nations. It has also required the establishment of new trade links with western nations rather than maintaining exclusive dependence on trade with former COMECON nations and, of necessity to achieve this, introducing convertible currencies.

■ Conclusions

As can be seen, the list of problems facing the new democratic governments of Central and Eastern Europe was virtually endless, requiring what seemed like a very long time to make any real progress. Yet ordinary citizens had high expectations after years of declining prosperity and were not prepared to wait the same length of time for reforms to be effected as it had taken for the former communist governments of these countries to get their economies into such a mess. This has posed significant problems for the reforming governments and the situation has been exacerbated by some countries turning back to reformed communist parties – often called social democrats – as a reaction against the failure of reformist governments to improve economic conditions sufficiently fast.

Having said that reformist governments have since been re-elected in these countries and, with the possible exception of Russia, political and economic reforms have progressed so far that it seems unlikely that regression is now possible. In the Ukraine and the Asian economies of the former USSR the position is, however, much less certain.

■ 5.5 Macroeconomic data: CEEC and Russia 1994–99

In this section key economic data are analysed for the period 1994–99, the period 1997–99 being estimates and projections by the OECD. Additionally, reference is made to the earlier part of the decade in the accompanying text although here much greater instability is in evidence. Also data in the early 1990s is much more unreliable.

The reader may wish to compare the economic performance of CEEC with that of EU countries discussed in Chapter 1, particularly comparing it with the requirements of the Maastricht convergence criteria as the benchmarks against which many of these countries will subsequently be evaluated.

■ Unemployment

Figure 5.1 shows the percentage of the labour force registered unemployed for the period 1994–99. In the early 1990s unemployment rose considerably as CEEC started the transition from command to market economies, peaking at around 15 per cent. This was partly through the removal of state subsidies and partly because of newly privatised firms seeking to cut costs by shedding surplus unproductive labour. It should also be noted that government statistics have been notoriously inaccurate, a real problem when seeking to manage economies. For example, in 1996 the International Labour Office (ILO) estimated 14m unemployed people in CEEC compared with official government estimates of eight million. Eurostat has also been very active in helping CEEC governments set up new accurate data-collection services.

The mid to late 1990s give a varied picture. Russia, slow or unstable in its reform programme, still experiences relatively high unemployment although this is, officially, lower than that in France, Germany or Spain. Hungary and Poland, where reform has been more effective, demonstrate progressive declines in their

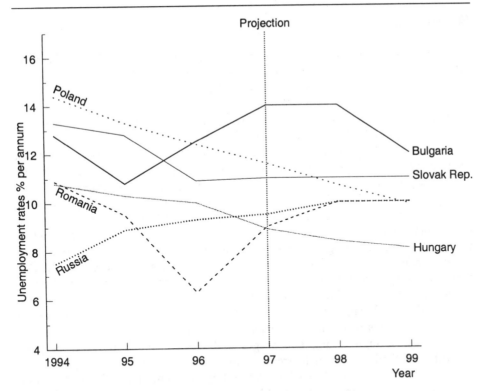

Data from OECD, *Economic Outlook*, December 1997, no. 62. Copyright OECD 1997.

Figure 5.1 **Percentage of labour force registered unemployed, 1994–99:**
▬▬▬▬▬ **selected CEEC**

unemployment rates, while the remaining three countries are less successful. The Slovak Republic has not implemented reform as effectively as other countries and has a large agricultural sector which is not ideal for fast economic growth. Nonetheless, the decline in unemployment from the 1994 peak shows it to be one of the faster growing CEEC. However, unemployment looks to stabilise at about 11 per cent for the remainder of the decade. Bulgaria and Romania also exhibit high unemployment for this period; the only exception is the Czech Republic with unemployment of only 3.5 per cent at the end of 1996.

Overall, the mid to late 1990s has exhibited a pattern where investment in CEEC is rising and industry has recovered from earlier low levels of capacity utilisation. This has caused labour productivity to increase and, consequently, firms have shed surplus labour. Unemployment has largely been concentrated on women and under-25-year-olds while large numbers of people are long-term unemployed, that is over one year. This latter group creates an economic underclass who effectively are no longer in the labour market and, of course, understates real unemployment.

■ Inflation

Figure 5.2 shows inflation rates since 1994. To accommodate the wide differences between different CEEC, a logarithmic scale is used on the vertical axis. In the early 1990s Russia's experience of inflation was horrendous, peaking at 1500 per cent in 1992, and even in 1995 running at 102 per cent compared with Bulgaria the next highest country with 60 per cent. All had rates much higher than EU countries (although Greece was not too far off some of these).

Broadly, the trend in CEEC during the mid to late 1990s has been one of continuous steady decline as with Poland and Hungary, for example, although some nasty blips can be seen in Romania and Bulgaria. The declines are due to countries seeking to operate tighter monetary policies partly through pressure from international bodies such as the IMF and the EBRD. For Russia there has been substantial progress since 1994, also due to the operation of a tight monetary policy, as well as a strong rouble and not paying many workers for months, thus reducing aggregate demand in the economy. This has also helped other CEEC in their battles against inflation since Russia is a major trading partner of theirs.

The main pressure mitigating against larger declines in inflation rates has been the growth of real wages at a faster rate than productivity. This has occurred for a number of reasons including workers seeking to make up for lost income in the early 1990s through falling real wages and the continued removal of price controls, particularly in such areas as housing rents, public transport fares, domestic heating costs, all of which figure large in domestic budgets. Additionally, transition economies have seen their service sectors grow most rapidly since the mid-1990s where labour productivity is lower, and they are less exposed to

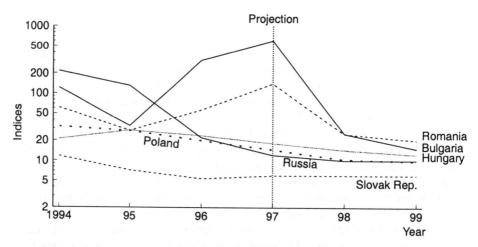

Data from OECD, *Economic Outlook*, December 1997, no. 62. Copyright OECD 1997.

Figure 5.2 Percentage change in average level of consumer prices over previous years, 1994–99: selected CEEC

foreign competition than manufactured goods. With price liberalisation also occurring here this has fed through to higher consumer prices. Further, because some countries have not progressed towards privatisation as fast as was hoped, investment has not grown as rapidly as it could have. Consequently labour costs are a bigger percentage of total production costs which further slows down the rate of decline of prices. Attempts by CEEC to operate tighter monetary and fiscal policy, at the behest of the IMF, have not always been totally successful in curbing inflation because of the lack of a fully developed financial infrastructure. Indeed in some countries, and particularly Russia, people positively distrust banks and are extremely reluctant to use them. In other countries, such as Bulgaria and Albania, monetary policy has been loosened prior to elections to win the support of voters – a strategy not unknown in EU countries.

◼ Changes in GDP

In the early 1990s all CEEC countries, embarking on the first steps to transforming their economies, experienced negative growth. Real GDP fell by 15 per cent in the Czech Republic, the Slovak Republic and Romania in 1991, while in Russia real GDP fell by over 20 per cent and hovered around −15 per cent for the two subsequent years. By 1993–94, however, the Czech Republic, Hungary, Poland, Romania and the Slovak Republic were all experiencing positive growth, some – such as Poland – sooner than others.

Figure 5.3 shows the position of these countries between 1994–99. Hungary, Poland, the Czech and Slovak Republics all exhibit positive if varying levels of annual growth in real GDP, some of which have been high – in the region of 6 per cent for Poland and 7 per cent for the Slovak Republic, for example, in the mid-1990s. Bulgaria and Romania show steady positive growth with the exception of 1996 in the case of Romania, and 1996–97 in the case of Bulgaria. Along with Albania, Bulgaria experienced severe problems which substantially hindered its economic reforms. In Albania's case they manifested themselves in the infamous collapse of the pyramid savings scheme which wiped out many peoples' savings and led to virtual civil war; while in Bulgaria the continuing power of the communist party, and its opposition to market reforms, again slowed progress. In both these countries the Communist Party had been more entrenched than virtually anywhere else and so, consequently, it was much harder to implement a reform programme. CEEC countries are likely to maintain steady growth, albeit a little lower, for the remainder of the decade, partly reflecting tough stabilisation programmes implemented by the Romanian and Bulgarian governments, and partly continuing uncertainty in Albania. These growth rates are likely to be mirrored in the Baltic Republics of Estonia, Latvia and Lithuania.

Only Russia, of the countries shown in Figure 5.3, demonstrates negative growth rates in each year of the time period, substantially through lurching from periods of reform to periods of stagnation. This has been aggravated by President Boris Yeltsin's ill-health and his use of this strategy to maintain his hold on

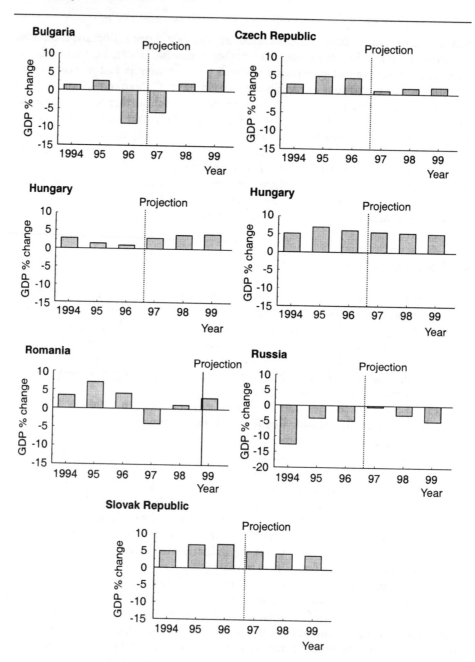

Source: © OECD, *Economic Outlook*, No. 62, 1997. Reproduced by permission of the OECD.

Figure 5.3   **Percentage change in GDP over previous year, 1994–99: selected CEEC**

power, by real and continuing opposition to reform by the relegalised Communist Party and by the extremist nationalists, and by substantial corruption which has reduced the effectiveness of government macroeconomic polices, for example, by hindering the collection of tax revenues.

■ Current account balances

In the 1980s the Soviet Union and most other CEEC showed strong current account surpluses through tight controls over imports, and subsidised exports mainly to secure hard currencies. Apart from the Czech Republic and Russia, for the early to mid-1990s, CEEC exhibited persistent deficits on their current account balances. Hungary, for example, was showing a deficit of US$4 billion for 1994 while Poland had run a deficit of nearly $3bn the year before that. Much of these deficits can be explained by the loosening of rigid controls over imports of goods and services as part of the process of transforming CEEC economies and the removal of exchange controls, allowing rapid increases in imports. Additionally as domestic output fell so did the goods available to export, while the removal of export subsidies meant that these goods lost much of their price competitiveness.

The period 1994–99, shown in Figure 5.4, shows continuing substantial deficit balances for many CEEC after large increases in deficits in 1996. These average around 5 per cent of GDP and are mainly through strong domestic demand for imports, not particularly by consumers but rather increasing imports of inputs as the economic transformation process continues; this also includes the Baltic states. The value of exports has declined through slower economic growth in the EU as these countries seek to meet the Maastricht convergence criteria, the need to build new productive capacity as existing slack capacity has been taken up, the failure to privatise as much as intended which deters foreign direct investment, rising labour costs as noted previously, and appreciating exchange rates, especially *vis-à-vis* the deutschemark, making exports less price-competitive. The redeeming feature for these countries' deficits is that they mostly have surpluses on their services, especially tourism which is growing fast, and on inward transfers of money from nationals living abroad.

Russia is clearly the exception to the above with a high and persistent current account surplus, while the Slovak Republic shows a brief surplus in 1994–95 and Bulgaria a small but continuing surplus through the late 1990s. With these two countries domestic adjustments caused a fall in imports. Russia has a much larger surplus on its visibles than on its current account as a whole, mainly because it has a large deficit on foreign travel.

So long as a country can finance its current account deficit then there are no problems. For CEEC at present this financing comes from a variety of sources including foreign direct investment, medium and long-term borrowing, portfolio investment (equity purchase) and short-term borrowing. It also looks to be sustainable in the medium-term future particularly as transition programmes

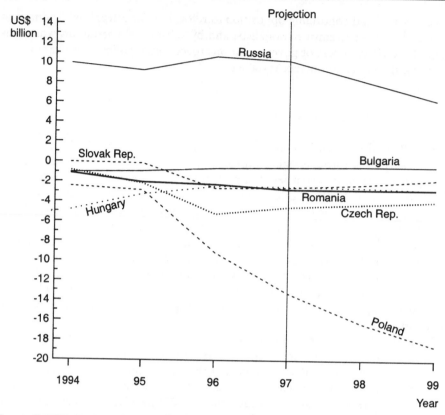

Source: © OECD, *Economic Outlook*, No. 62, 1997. Reproduced by permission of the OECD.

Figure 5.4   Current account balances, 1994–99: selected CEEC

are opening these economies still further to foreign direct investment, making them to be perceived as much less risky than previously – and indeed less risky than some Southeast Asian countries.

■ Fiscal balances

Figure 5.5 shows the fiscal balances of CEEC for the period 1994–99. Comparison with EU economies and the 3 per cent Maastricht convergence criterion show the Czech Republic and Poland to be likely to meet these by 1999, although the former's deficit is actually rising, while Hungary has a deficit of around 5 per cent. Romania, Bulgaria and the Slovak Republic are all within the 3 per cent limit and exhibit downward trends, while Russia, although also exhibiting a downward trend, still has a large deficit. One part of the problem is that as economic growth rates decline so do tax revenues, while social security payments

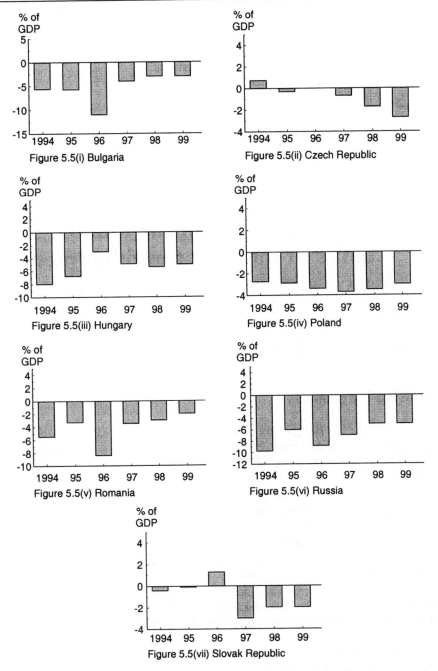

Figure 5.5(i) Bulgaria

Figure 5.5(ii) Czech Republic

Figure 5.5(iii) Hungary

Figure 5.5(iv) Poland

Figure 5.5(v) Romania

Figure 5.5(vi) Russia

Figure 5.5(vii) Slovak Republic

Source: © OECD, *Economic Outlook*, No. 62, 1997. Reproduced by permission of the OECD.

Figure 5.5   Fiscal balances, percentage of real GDP for 1994–99: selected CEEC

rise worsening fiscal balances. Additionally, CEEC tax collection is not as effective as it could be – both the range of taxes and the ability to collect them – while governments still incur heavy, albeit diminishing, expenditures as they seek to liberalise economies by removing subsidies.

■ Conclusions

Overall the reader should be seeing a picture of economies having gone through a difficult transition process in the early 1990s now coming under control; although some countries – particularly Albania, Bulgaria and Russia – are in a worse state than others and all still have major improvements to make.

■ 5.6 The introduction of the Market: case studies of different transition models

The debate which dominated the early 1990s in Central and Eastern Europe was how economic reform to market economies might best be effected. Essentially there were two schools of thought. These were whether reform should be very quick – known as the Big Bang approach – or whether it should be gradual. Furthermore, if the reform programme were gradual in what sequence should the reforms occur.

■ The Big Bang model

Proponents of the Big Bang or shock-therapy approach argued that the only way to achieve reform which would change the entire economy as quickly as possible was to change everything at once, or as nearly at once as possible. This programme of very rapid but total reform would effectively be a short, sharp shock which, in its initial stages, would be very painful. It would encompass a series of steps to address the problems identified at the beginning of section 5.4. Hence all price controls and subsidies would be rapidly removed, major privatisation would quickly be effected, foreign expertise and capital would be brought in through allowing foreign businesses to acquire part or all of some of the privatised businesses, and also by encouraging joint ventures between domestic and foreign firms. A financial and legal infrastructure would be established along with the introduction of tight monetary and fiscal policies and trade and currency liberalisation would be implemented – all as quickly as possible.

However, successful economic reform is also dependent on the policies of Western economies. Where these have run large budget deficits and, consequently, high interest rates, this has had the dual effect of increasing the debt burden of reforming economies and also reducing further borrowing due to the high cost. Once these reforms had been introduced the basis for the economic take-off would have been laid. However, the side-effects would be that output would initially fall, inflation rise and unemployment rise. This would mean for at least the first two to three years people would be significantly worse off, before things started to get better. Even with the promise that things will get better in future this is a very difficult stage to persuade a country to go through.

■ The gradual reform process

In contrast, the gradual reform (or gradualism) approach argued that severe shock therapy of the big-bang type was not acceptable and could not be sustained. Rather, reform needs to be undertaken slowly and one stage at a time, enabling it to be spread over a number of years to minimise hardship and economic dislocation and hence make it more acceptable to the population. One problem from this was what was termed sequencing, that is in what sequence would reforms be introduced. Should price and wage controls be lifted first, or would privatisation be a logical first step, or should the government get its own finances in order first by balancing its budget. Again does it make sense to lift trade barriers before or after privatisation? Or should financial systems such as banking networks be developed before or after privatisation?

In 1991 the World Bank produced a plan which was a summary of all the common factors agreed by economists, and which suggested a sequenced phasing-in over ten years. In reality the outcome has been that Central and Eastern European countries improvised dealing with problems as they arose, first tackling those things which seemed easiest to deal with.

■ The Polish reform model

The 1980s in Poland had been a time of political conflict between the trade union Solidarity, led by Lech Walesa with its power base in the Gdansk shipyard, and successive communist governments. Economic reforms introduced in the early 1980s to try and address the problems Poland faced were failing by the end of the decade, posing severe difficulties for the future. The problems facing the Polish economy were substantial. The major emphasis on heavy industry and the military had skewed production away from much needed consumer goods and created major shortages. The Polish government was forced to admit that inflation was causing severe problems, something COMECON governments had always argued only occurred in western capitalist economies. By 1989 this was running at approximately 640 per cent p.a. This was contributed to by the Polish government printing money to meet its internal (budget deficit) debts due to shortages of tax revenue. As inflation increased, the real value of tax revenues fell further. Additionally, while some prices were still fixed by the state, others were allowed to find their market level.

Poland faced a severe external (trade) debt problem with the rest of the world, aggravated by very heavy borrowing from western banks in the late 1970s, which it was subsequently unable to repay, although interest payments were maintained.

The exhaustion of Poland's hard foreign currencies and the non-convertibility of the zloty contributed still further to this problem. Because of the shortage of hard currencies, international trade also remained restricted and biased towards the USSR and COMECON, whereas what was needed was greater access to Western products and markets. The foreign debt rose from $20bn in 1982 to $40bn in 1989, $48.4bn in 1991 and $49.9bn in 1992.

As in other centrally-planned economies the bulk of the Polish economy was controlled by the state. Often it was difficult to determine precisely who owned what due to the complex organisational structure and ownership patterns of Polish industry and agriculture. Additionally, agriculture played too large a part in the economy compared with Western European countries, accounting for 13.2 per cent of the economy compared with 3.9 per cent for France, 4.1 per cent for Italy and 1.7 per cent for the UK. The low and falling effectiveness of the Polish administration also caused low living standards. In 1989, per capita GDP was $1954 p.a. for Poland compared with $13 057 p.a. for France, $10 466 for Italy and $9788 for the UK.

Tadeusz Mazowiecki's government, elected in 1989, sought to introduce a parliamentary democracy and a market economy. As noted above an essential co-requisite of the latter is a large-scale privatisation programme to shift the ownership of resources away from the public sector, and a liberalisation of prices and trade. However, before any significant reforms could be undertaken it was necessary to introduce a major programme of macroeconomic stabilisation to prevent the Polish economy from worsening.

Since the economic crisis was so severe a process of rapid and radical reform, which could not later be reversed, was chosen rather than one of gradual reform. A reform programme was introduced, subsequently known as the Stabilisation Plan and authored by Finance Minister Leszek Balcerowicz, which targeted inflation and the balance of payments as its two main objectives. Once this plan took effect subsequent economic reforms such as privatisation, the reform of local government and the creation of a stock market could be introduced, reinforced by political reforms. The stabilisation plan consisted of a number of items. Firstly there was the implementation of strict fiscal policy to bring down the budget deficit from 6 per cent of GDP in 1989 to 1 per cent. This included the imposition of taxes to reduce wage increases, a cause of cost inflation – in effect an incomes policy as was used in Western Europe in the 1960s and 1970s. A strict monetary policy was introduced to combat the growth in money supply and hence inflation through the use of positive real interest rates. This plus attempts to reduce inflation would also encourage Poles to save in zloty rather than purchase US dollars and deutschemarks on the black market. In turn this would make resources available for future investment.

Liberalisation of prices was introduced to allow them to be determined by market forces not the state bureaucracy – this was assisted by large reductions in state subsidies, which helped reduce the fiscal deficit. The Polish currency, the zloty, was devalued by 31.6 per cent to allow its official rate to reach the market rate in the unofficial free (or black) market and hence unify the two rates. Finally restrictions on international trade and payments were removed, although to reduce imports and help the balance of payments deficit a 20 per cent import duty was imposed.

In 1993, Mazowiecki's government was defeated in the Polish elections by a coalition of the Democratic Left Alliance (SLD) – in effect, former communists – and the Peasants Party (PSL). This was mainly due to disagreement between Leszek Balcerowicz on the one hand and Lech Walesa and other Solidarity leaders on the other over the pace of reform, causing Solidarity to splinter and its power base to dissipate, opening the way for the SLD victory. However, the harsh initial effects of the reform programme also turned many voters against the reformers. As has been demonstrated in other former CEEC, ex-communists are also pragmatists and so the SLD re-invented itself as a western-style conservative Social Democratic party, with policies widely supported by western businessmen. The coalition presided over four years of economic reform programmes which had been intitiated by the anti-communist Mazowiecki government. This achieved real economic growth and increasing real incomes, increasing foreign direct investment, rising productivity and revaluation of the zloty. In practice their economic policies were closer to those of Mazowiecki than were the policies of the anti-communist parties who, being strongly xenophobic, were opposed to further privatisation and the continuing market reforms needed to achieve EU membership. The political repositioning of the former communists was substantially helped by President Alexander Kwasniewski who defeated Lech Walesa in the 1995 presidential elections.

In spite of the economic progress made, in the general election of September 1997 the SLD were defeated by the Solidarity Alliance (AWS), a grouping of 36 parties including liberals, ultra-right nationalists and trade unionists which had not secured any seats in the 1993 election. As can be seen, political parties and alliances in Poland are still very fluid, as they also are in other former communist countries. To secure a sufficient majority to govern the country it formed a coalition with the Freedom Union, another anti-communist grouping, which is led by Leszek Balcerowicz the proponent of the original shock therapy or Big Bang programme of the early 1990s. This coalition is based mainly on mutual distrust of the former communists who are still intensely disliked in Poland.

As finance minister and deputy prime minister in the new government Balcerowicz, who believes that the reform programme has stalled in spite of the progress made by the SLD between 1993–97, launched a draft medium-term strategy in March 1998 to complete the reforms of the first Balcerowicz plan. This is to include structural reforms with key priority given to the completion of the privatisation programme including industry and banks, which has stagnated. Currently the state's share of output has fallen from 60 to 30 per cent in the 1990s, but the target is 15 per cent. Smaller and more profitable businesses have already been privatised quite painlessly. The problem will lie in privatising the remainder which include loss making large factories, mines and other businesses such as the telecomms monopoly TPSA, the national airline LOT, and the biggest bank Pekao. There is considerable opposition from many managers who would prefer to stay in the public sector. For heavy industry privatisation will result in the shedding of excess labour estimated to be 30 per cent. However, this is necessary to maintain sound public finances and address the large current account deficit. Membership of NATO and the EU is seen as another essential part of this programme to re-orient Poland to be like Western European countries.

Where problems could still arise is over Solidarity's position as a major supporter of Poland's nationalised industries such as shipbuilding, steel and coal mining. To maintain political support from these strong trade unionist workers it favours high wages and subsidies, polices which go against those of Balcerowicz. This could be detrimental to political and economic stability, factors crucial for the continuing inflow of foreign direct investment which has grown substantially under the SLD ($6.7bn in 1997) and which is crucial for continuing Polish economic progress. It is also important, this time, to ensure that the benefits of economic reform are spread more widely across the population, especially to the rural areas.

■ The Russian reform model

The Soviet Union was one of the later communist countries to reform and was handicapped by having had over 70 years of communist rule compared with 45 in the rest of Central and Eastern Europe; or as a particularly poignant poster, held by a protester in 1989 in the streets of Moscow read, '72 years down the road to nowhere'.

Yet Mikhail Gorbachev's period in office, 1985–91, was largely frittered away with promises of glasnost (political openness) and perestroika (economic re-structuring) but limited action. Partly this was because of the huge task facing him, as subsequent failures to effectively reform have demonstrated, and partly because Gorbachev was still essentially a communist with a desire to maintain the hegemony of the party. Talk by him of market socialism was merely an attempt to modify communism a little by attaching to it some features of market capitalism while still trying to preserve it largely unchanged. In reality what was needed was a fundamental restructuring of the Soviet economy. His failures to do this meant that the private sector virtually did not exist even in 1990. Gorbachev's main attempts to reform were introducing privatisation by permitting cooperatives to own assets, hire labour and make profits, with them required to be completely self-financing from profits or bank borrowing. However, they lacked flexibility and failed to make a significant impact on production. So Gorbachev's restruc-turing achieved little economic progress, rather causing falling output, rising prices, increased trade deficits and increased strikes. The attempted overthrow of him in August 1991, and his rescue by Boris Yeltsin, led inevitably to his fall from power.

With Yeltsin as Russian President the break up of the Soviet Union occurred at the end of December 1991 with the Belovezhskaya Pusha declaration which stated 'The USSR, as a subject of international law and geopolitical reality is ceasing its existence'. It was replaced by the CIS (Commonwealth of Independent States) and a much more vigorous programme of economic reform was planned based on the concept of a market economy and privatisation.

However, the Russian economy faced major problems including inflation of 1500 per cent p.a. inherited from the Gorbachev regime due to subsidised credits, negative real interest rates (at 10 per cent), and a monetary policy out of control. Plans to create a market economy had stalled while land reforms were minimal. Progress with privatisation and the creation of a stock exchange and commodity markets was slow. Additionally, high government debt imposed high interest payment burdens, and there were falling living standards and bureaucratic resistance to reform.

The Russian reform programme was launched in January 1992 by economist and first deputy prime minister Yegor Gaidar, and a group of other radical thinkers such as Boris Fyodorov. Its main aim was to follow the short, sharp shock programme of the Big Bang. As with the Polish programme it included restructuring the economy including the development of markets and land reform. It introduced strict monetarist-based macroeconomic policies, as recommended by the IMF. Fast privatisation was proposed to build on the new businesses which had come into existence in the last two years of Gorbachev's presidency, particularly the conversion of cooperatives into firms, and wholesale liberalisation of prices was to be implemented.

In practice prices and rents were liberalised but this contributed to severe inflation in 1992, and to resultant further falls in living standards and widening disparities between rich and poor. Implementation of the Big Bang programme had a major effect on the Russian economy causing GDP (or the Russian measure net material product) to fall substantially, in 1992 by over 15 per cent. The situation was worsened by farmers retaining produce for themselves and trying to sell it privately causing food shortages in cities. Additionally the rouble fell in value against the US dollar and other major currencies, while the US$ circulated freely in Russia as an alternative and frequently preferable currency to the rouble.

Conflict between President Yeltsin and the liberal reformers on the one hand, and hard-line members in the Congress of Deputies arose because of the opposition to this breakneck reform, aggravated by the hostilities over the breakup of the USSR and Russia's sudden decline as a superpower. By March 1993 arguments for a slower reform programme were becoming much stronger, including support for slower movement towards a market economy, looser monetary policy, slower privatisation, maintenance of state-controlled prices, and a continuation of state subsidies to inefficient state producers. The economic reform process was further complicated by a power struggle between President Boris Yeltsin and the Congress of Deputies led by Alexander Rutskoi and Rusian Khasbulatov. Although strictly the conflict was over who had exactly what power under the constitution it also impinged directly on the speed of economic reform and on its components; for example Yeltsin strongly argued for the privatisation of land while Rutskoi strongly opposed it.

In March 1993 Yeltsin declared that he would rule Russia by decree until 1 April when a referendum would be held. He won the national referendum obtaining a 58 per cent vote of confidence and 53 per cent support for his reforms. However, opposition continued from the Congress of Deputies and in October 1993 the showdown came with Yeltsin ordering troops to attack the White House, the building of the Congress of Deputies, and imprisoning the ringleaders. Nonetheless, by the beginning of 1994 Yegor Gaidar was obliged to resign his position as first deputy prime minister in the face of a communist and nationalist coalition in the State Duma, or lower house of parliament. Although he had brought Russia back from the brink of hyperinflation by following IMF-directed tight monetary policies, he had alienated the Russian electorate by the hardship these policies had brought. His replacement was Viktor Chernomyrdin, previously a bureaucrat in the gas industry who was much more pragmatic and moderate in his views, favouring a more gradual reform process.

From 1994 until early 1998 Viktor Chernomyrdin remained prime minister and Russia pursued a more gradual but at times erratic reform process, its variability being in part due to the political strategies and ill-health of Yeltsin. The war in Chechnya also proved a major distraction to reform so that by the mid-1990s there was little to show for several years of painful economic restructuring. Nonetheless in 1996, after a dramatic turnaround, Boris Yeltsin had been re-elected President of Russia for four more years, defeating ultra-nationalists and communists and permitting the reform programme to continue. This was largely due to his use of the infamous shares for loans privatisation scheme in Autumn 1995 when he transfered majority stakes in major Russian companies to potential allies and cronies at a fraction of their true value. In so doing he created large-scale financial–industrial groups, now major players in the economy, while the share owners became billionaires, for which Yeltsin won their aid and support.

It has therefore been argued that what Russia has not fully decided is whether it is seeking to develop a free-market liberal economy as in the EU, or whether it will continue to pursue a path of monopolist capitalism as typified by Latin America where big business and accompanying corruption run the economy. This is worsened by the failure of the state bureaucracy to assume a neutral stance but rather to become players in the power game, a consequence of Russia's history of absolute rulers, both Tsarist and communist.

Yeltsin has sought to reinforce his power by playing off his nominees for office against each other and this has contributed to reform being erratic. For example, in 1997 he brought reformers Anatoly Chubais and Boris Nemtsov into the government as deputy prime ministers to ginger up liberalisation. He re-emphasised the importance of liberalisation in his 'State of the Federation' address in March 1997, when he spoke of the entrenchment of democratic institutions and the strengthening of the judicial system to secure property rights and individual freedoms. Yet, a year later Chubais and Nemstov, along with Chernomyrdin, were dismissed from their posts allegedly for failing to implement sufficient reforms but in practice to isolate Chernomyrdin in his positioning of himself as a candidate in the presidential election of 2000. Chernomyrdin's replacement, the young and relatively inexperienced Sergei Kiriyenko, lasted barely six months before being replaced by Yevgeni Primakov, following the August 1998 collapse of the rouble in foreign exchange markets. Worryingly, at the time of writing, Primakov's main strategy to pay outstanding wages and bail out banks appears to be to print more money – which will contribute to already escalating inflation.

In terms of progress to economic reform, Russia continues to be plagued by the effects of crime, tax evasion contributing to the State's inability to pay workers' wages, falling living standards for most people while a minority become extremely wealthy, falling GDP, insufficient foreign direct investment entering the country, domestic businesses transferring funds abroad rather than investing them in Russia, and high and entrenched unemployment. Most important is the need for fiscal stability since tax evasion and arrears (facilitated by the wide-spread barter economy) mean unrealistic budgets are set and the government is unable to meet its committed expenditure. This is worsened by the complex and seemingly random taxation system. Additionally privatisation has created large private sector monopolies which either need to be regulated more effectively or broken up, while privatisation of some giant state monoplies such as Gazprom has proved very difficult to achieve.

What is needed is a restructuring of these big corporations with greater awareness of corporate governance and financial transparency. This needs to take place within an environment of economic and poltical stability. However, the resistance to reform by the bureaucracy, local government and industrialists who fear loss of power and privileges, has already been discussed as hindering such reform. It is these entrenched attitudes which in 1997 prompted Alfred Kokh, the Russian privatisation minister, to argue:

> for 70 years our people were taught one thing and a cult of the state was subconsciously programmed into the Russian people. But they must realise that the state can no longer manage everything. The state can no longer command people, it can only attempt to regulate.

Finally, there is also a need for effective legislation tested in the courts regarding property and contracts.

Having discussed the above problems there have been real reforms. In 1996 the EBRD estimated that 89 per cent of industrial output and 82 per cent of industrial employment were accounted for by non-state industrial enterprises, a major achievement in only six years of reform. The stock market and the government securities market have both developed rapidly as have branch banking networks. Price liberalisation has largely been effected although price controls remain at local levels. Additionally, import duties have been reduced, export quotas removed and the convertibility of the rouble introduced (and indeed the rouble was revalued in early 1998). Nonetheless the IMF and other western organisations still worry that Russia, pursuing its gradualist reform programme, is not operating tight enough policies and much structural reform needs to be under-taken if transition to a liberal market economy is to be achieved.

■ Comparing the two models

In comparing the two reform models of Poland and Russia, Poland has certainly made faster progress. Indeed, as far back as 1993 the European Commission concluded that, broadly speaking, the big-bang reform in Poland had been successful and the stabilisation programme had achieved its objectives. This was not the case with Russia where the shock-therapy model or Big Bang reform was soon abandoned and, with it, hopes of rapid progress.

At the end of the decade, however, one can see that Polish and Russian reform programmes both slowed down in the mid-1990s as more moderate pragmatists took the reins of power from market-oriented liberal theoreticians and, in both countries, opted for gradual reform models. This was partly through the adverse effects on the economy and the population of the transition effects of rapid movement from a command to a reform economy, and partly through the conservative beliefs of the reformed communists who acquired power. Nonetheless, the fact that Poland had already made some economic reforms by 1990 and its adoption of the Big Bang approach meant that by mid-1998 it had made more rapid progress than Russia. Whether Balcerowicz succeeds in implementing his second Big Bang programme for Poland, to complete his reforms, remains to be seen. Russia will continue to make slow but increasingly steadier progress subject, of course, to the political whims of Boris Yeltsin as he moves from reformer to conservative to reformer depending on political circumstances during the remainder of his presidency. Clearly such an approach is not helpful long-term.

This book does not have the space to explore all CEEC countries as they seek reform. However, the economic data provided above should give a reasonably clear picture of the progress made by these other countries. The reader is also referred to the references at the end of this chapter.

■ 5.7 Privatisation programmes

Privatisation is the process whereby a government, by various means, transfers ownership of resources from the public to the private sector of its economy. These resources include physical property such as factories, oil pipelines, electricity generating stations, rail tracks, land and so on. Privatisation also includes the organisations which own them – that is, the companies, farms and so on – although these have had to be modified to recognise their different ownership after privatisation.

■ Why privatise state-owned agriculture and industry?

Privatisation has been seen as a necessary step in the transition process towards the creation of market economies. The breaking up of state monopolies was perceived as crucial to the introduction of competition in countries, although in some countries such as Russia it has been replaced with financial–industrial complexes which, it is feared, might function as private sector monopolies. The creation of smaller enterprises also enables a property-owning middle class to be created who sustain the momentum of private ownership. Indeed it can be argued that ownership of shares is one way of developing the cultural change to liberalised economies and democratic societies. Privatisation also provides an incentive for managers in private sector firms to build up the business in terms of cost control, profitability, market capitalisation, quality of products, customer satisfaction, new investment programmes and so on. In other words a formal business strategy is implemented. With public sector businesses these incentives normally have not existed. So long as output quotas were achieved no one worried about the lack of other issues. Privatisation therefore provides motivation for managers, for example to exercise control over high wage claims, since failure to combat these could lead to the firm closing.

Privatisation also absolves the state from the need to provide funds to run businesses and to finance new investment, while preventing the state from crowding out the private sector in the newly emerging capital markets, that is forcing up interest rates through its borrowing power and thus preventing private business, which cannot afford the high rates, from borrowing to invest. Of major importance, also, is the fact that with privatisation foreign capital is able to bid for shares in companies, bringing in extra funding and also western expertise and technology.

■ The problems governments have faced in privatising

The biggest difficulty former communist countries have experienced is the sheer scale of privatisation needed. Although Western European countries have undertaken privatisation (or denationalisation as it used to be called) over intermittent periods since the Second World War none has undertaken it on the scale that Central and Eastern European countries have needed to.

Attempts to gain access to the savings of individuals has proved to be a problem because of the lack of an adequate banking infrastructure, accessible to all, and the lack of proper capital markets. Additionally, private savings have proved to be only a small percentage of the total value of the assets to be sold. Ownership of state-owned businesses also proved difficult to establish in the early days. Separate legal identities for businesses, as in the West, did not exist. Rather, some had been seized by managers and workers while for others there was a close interlinking with local government, other state bodies and their suppliers.

The lack of western financial and management accounting conventions and expertise made it very difficult to determine how businesses were actually performing economically, particularly as they lacked accurate valuation of assets and correct cash-flow estimates. Until this was completed it was difficult for governments to determine what businesses they owned. Also state businesses have been poorly managed and run inefficiently. This has meant that privatised industries have had to start from a low base making transformation of state-owned businesses that much more difficult.

■ How privatisation has been implemented

A number of different ways were considered by the governments of Central and Eastern Europe as means to privatise. However, before this could be undertaken commercialisation has been needed first, that is the state-owned asset has had to be transformed into a separate and legally recognisable identity.

Free distribution of shares to everyone was one model that has been used. This argument was based on the concept that private savings fell far short of the value of the assets being owned by the state, even assuming that these could be valued accurately by western accounting conventions. Since it would take decades for personal savings to match asset values then the remedy was to give shares freely to the entire population. What this method did not do was to raise much needed money to reduce government internal (budget) and external (trade) deficits. A variation on this is for the free shares to be in large investment trusts or funds which in turn hold shares in many different state-owned companies. The effect of this is to create organisations similar to Western European institutional investors. The trusts or funds can influence the direction of the companies whose shares they hold including prompting growth, mergers and takeovers and, where necessary, closure. This approach has been pursued by Poland.

An alternative concept was to give or sell shares of each state business to its employees and managers. There is logic in this argument since it re-establishes a link between work and corporate profits, which payment by wages has eliminated. This should provide an incentive for workers to make the businesses work. This method has been used in Russia.

A third model is to give or sell vouchers to each person. When used by Russia, each citizen was given vouchers up to 10 000 roubles, which could then be exchanged for shares in any company, or sold to someone else. Alternatively a person might sell his/her vouchers to someone else for immediate money. This happened a lot in Russia and since initially there was no stock market to set market prices many sold their vouchers for a pittance to buy bread. This enabled other people to accumulate substantial wealth very quickly. The Czech government adopted a voucher model whereby each person was offered vouchers for 1000 crowns. The holders of these vouchers then bid for shares in any of the companies being privatised. A second round was subsequently implemented after the sale of the first batch of vouchers. Approximately two-thirds of voucher holders entrusted their vouchers to privatisation investment funds. Also foreign investors were encouraged to purchase vouchers. This model has also been used in Poland and Romania.

Many people lost property and full or partial ownership of productive assets in the waves of nationalisation pursued by communist governments in the 1940s and 1950s. By restoring this property to its previous owners assets were transferred from the public to the private sector. This was particularly important in the former East Germany.

In the West European model of privatisation shares are sold by a government body, backed by advertising, with a fixed price quoted in advance. People may bid for whatever amount they want. This method has the advantage of maximising sales revenue and also allowing foreign investors to purchase shares. If the government is worried about losing control to foreign shareholders and institutional investors, it can impose a limit as to the amount that foreigners may hold. This method was used in the former East Germany and Hungary.

A final model has been the establishment of new firms. Although this may not sound like privatisation at first the idea here is for new firms to buy some of the assets of bankrupt state firms. These assets then enter the private sector and the state receives some revenue from the sale of the capital equipment.

■ Has privatisation been successful?

Space does not permit a detailed and exhaustive analysis of the privatisation progress of every CEEC; rather some countries will be examined in more detail and a broad picture will be presented of others.

In Poland, when in 1993 the SLD came to power in coalition with the PSL, their aim was to progress cautiously regarding privatisation with the aim of maximising revenue from the sale of state assets. As such they were less ideologically motivated than Solidarity, which had seen privatisation as a major weapon in the drive to a market economy. Indeed PSL believed that major sectors of the economy such as energy should remain under state control, even though external funding was urgently needed for modernisation and restructuring programmes. Having said that, the SDL did raise $600m a year from privatisations and in 1997 $830m. Overall, however, Polish privatisation has been too slow with significant industry including telecommunications, coal and oil still under state control. Also local investors still account for 80 per cent of all investment in stark contrast with Hungary, which is unlikely to provide suffcient funds for restructuring. Balcerowicz's commitment to 'privatise, privatise, privatise' is likely to change this in the course of the current administration.

Russia is another country where privatisation has been slower than is desirable, especially where plans have dragged on for years without coming to fruition. To illustrate, the last major oil company Rosneft was privatised in February 1998 but only 51 per cent was sold off (reduced from an original 70 per cent) while the government retained the balance as a golden share. However, foreigners have found it hard to invest in Russia although the country needs large inflows of funds, partly because of Russian opposition to foreign capital and partly because of the power of crony capitalism which was discussed in the analysis of Russia's reform programme.

Hungary, in contrast, is one of the most privatised countries in Europe with its privatisation programme almost complete. The government has sold large stakes in the state telecommunications company and other utilities through the Hungarian Privatisation and State Holding Company. This programme has included selling former state banks which had been very heavily subsidised to the tune of $3.5bn by 1995. As a result the range and quality of banking services offered has improved drastically, especially in corporate banking, while foreign competition has also stimulated innovation. In 1995 alone privatisation receipts totalled $4.5 billion. The focus of Hungarian privatisation has been attracting large-scale foreign investment in sharp contrast to the Czech voucher system discussed above. This has promoted substantial organisational restructuring, and investment in new technology which has helped lower unit labour costs and made Hungarian exports more competitive. The government also uses privatisation receipts to reduce its debt.

In the Czech Republic privatisation has occurred very rapidly under the guidance of Vaclav Klaus, the free market prime minister, using the voucher scheme discusssed previously. However, whereas Hungary has attracted substantial foreign investment, in the Czech Republic most shares are now held by the state-owned banks. Consequently few companies have been restructured, the stock market has been guilty of insider trading and suspect deals, and many banks have loaned large amounts which are now worth little.

Other countries have also encountered problems. Bulgarian privatisation ground to a halt as it was one of the countries most reluctant to privatise. Again loss-making organisations have not been restructured while croney capitalism has created barriers against foreign funds. In Romania, which has a reputation for corruption and an overstifling bureaucracy, the privatisation programme has been limited, although a reformist government elected in 1997 has started a programme of economic stabilisation based on the Polish programme which hopefully will lay the basis for future reform.

Clearly then, there is a patchy picture with some significant reforms while in other countries there is still much to do. This is not allowing for states like Belarus and some Asian countries of the former Soviet Union where reform has hardly begun. Also linked to this is the fact that most CEEC and the countries of the former Soviet Union still have much to do to create financial, legal, banking and other institutions to promote long-term savings which are needed to fund the rebuilding of the infrastructure run down under communism. Some of these countries have started tackling this by addressing pension and insurance reforms but much more is needed to mobilise domestic household savings and to develop properly funded insurance and pension schemes rather than existing pay as you go ones.

■ 5.8 Case study: The European Bank for Reconstruction and Development (EBRD)

The EBRD was established in 1991 to promote the transition of Central and Eastern European countries, including the former USSR, to market economies and to encourage private enterprise. It is owned by 57 countries, including 25 from the former Eastern bloc, the EU and the European Investment Bank. The intention of the EBRD was never to compete with investment banks or private sector financial institutions, but rather to encourage innovative deals. All activities must be commercially viable for the EBRD to fund them, which it does on a commercial basis.

Funding is obtained from initially subscribed capital of ECU 10 billion, an amount which was doubled in 1996, and by borrowing from the world's capital markets. In turn the money is loaned mainly to the private sector with the aim of also attracting commercial funds to creat a multiplier effect in these economies. Foreign direct investment is encouraged by the EBRD including as joint ventures. Additionally, domestic funds are sought, channelled through the new stock markets as equity capital and the new banking systems (as loans). Ultimately these must be the main source of funds for former command economies. There is normally a minimum lending requirement of ECU 5 million.

The EBRD seeks to assist these former Central and Eastern European economies to make the transition to market economies as promptly as possible, consistent with their own agenda. This also involves funding structural reforms therefore such as the reduction of state monopolies, privatisation of state enterprises and reducing the power of the state bureaucracy to permit markets to function properly. Finance is channelled to the public sector as well as the private sector, although, at the insistence of the US, the biggest individual shareholder, the EBRD has a commitment to allocate 60 per cent of its funds to private investment; currently this is running at 67 per cent. Funds are loaned to organisations which are capable of privatisation and also to finance infrastructure which will provide support for the new private sector. Additionally, the EBRD provides guarantees to other lenders such as commercial banks who might otherwise be unwilling to provide finance to this area.

One of the EBRD's functions has been to 'train' new borrowers to such western banking requirements as borrowing money and then fulfilling contracts by repaying it plus interest at the agreed times, corporate governance, international accounting standards, and so on. One-third of the EBRD's investments go into infrastructure projects, while the financial sector accounts for another third. Although privatisation is the preferred route, even if assets stay under state control the EBRD still seeks to ensure that they are run on commercial lines. As of 31 December 1997 the EBRD had approved investment projects in 26 countries totalling ECU 13.93bn. As the list is too long to include all of these, Table 5.1 gives a limited sample of Polish projects approved by the EBRD as of 31 December 1997.

■ The EBRD: the way forward

Although the EBRD has improved its performance significantly and made a substantial number of loans and other financial investments, its long-term activities have been questioned. Firstly it was established primarily to assist Central and Eastern Europe make the transition to market economies, that is, as a form of pump primer. As privatisation progresses this need is reduced.

Table 5.1   Limited sample of Polish projects partially funded by the EBRD to 31 December 1997

TYPE OF PROJECT	PROJECT NAME	SECTOR	TOTAL COST (ECU 000)	EBRD FINANCING (ECU 000)
Joint venture	Fiat/FSM	Vehicles	924 777	62 468
Polish corporate	Stalexport	Steel	171 196	28 986
Equity funds	Poland emerging growth fund	Equity fund	90 580	24 083
Mass privatisation/SRP	National investment fund	Investment funds	20 545	10 942
Banks/other financial institutions	American Bank in Poland	Bank	4529	4529
Transport	Railway modernisation	Railways	487 000	50 000
Telecomms	Netia	Communications	346 014	66 473
Energy	Bielsko-Biala power station	Energy transmission	90 132	30 310
Property	Poland housing	Housing	115 036	1 476
Total: All Polish projects approved (ECU 000)			5 868 631	1 186 325

Source: EBRD website http://www.ebrd.com/opera/country/polafact.htm

Furthermore, as private banking develops and people have mechanisms and indeed income to save this should enable capital to be generated domestically, both through the purchase of shares and through loans via banks. It is also the case that the EBRD is not a cheap source of loans. Normally it charges a margin over LIBOR – the London interbank offered rate (the rate at which London based banks lend to each other) – the exact margin depending on the extent of risk, duration of the loan and so on.

As commercial sources begin to offer cheaper rates the EBRD will become less attractive as a source of financing. International capital markets or institutional investors and multinationals may come to be more attractive. It has also been suggested that the EBRD should lend more to public sector organisations to enable it to increase its lending very significantly – in effect to lend as the World Bank does. This is because, in part, private sector organisations are high risk and therefore not all suitable for EBRD loans. Since the merging of its merchant banking and development functions, however, this has happened to some extent. It has even been questioned whether the EBRD is the best way to effect reform, since it is itself a bureaucracy which is trying to encourage the reform of state bureaucracies in Central and Eastern Europe.

■ Review questions

1. How and why did the command economies of Central and Eastern Europe fail before 1990?
2. Discuss why macroeconomic stabilisation is crucial to any economy in transition and how it might best be effected.
3. List the advantages and disadvantages of Big Bang and gradualist economic reform processes and discuss why both Poland and Russia have modified their initial policies during the 1990s. Use economic data to support your argument.
4. Critically review THREE different ways to privatise the state sector of an economy and discuss why privatisation has been perceived as a vital part of the transition process in Central and Eastern Europe.
5. Analyse the advantages and disadvantages of providing financial support to the private sector as opposed to the public sector in CEEC to promote economic reform.

■ Bibliography

Baylis, T. A., *The West and Eastern Europe: Economic Statecraft and Poltical Change* (Westport, Connecticut: Praeger, 1994).

Blanchard, O. J., Froot, K. A., Sachs, J. D. (eds), *The Transition in Eastern Europe*, Vol. 1: *Country Studies*. National Bureau of Economic Research (Chicago and London: The University of Chicago Press, 1994).

Blanchard, O. J., Froot, K. A., Sachs, J. D. (eds), *The Transition in Eastern Europe*, Vol. 2: *Restructuring*. National Bureau of Economic Research (Chicago and London: The University of Chicago Press, 1994).

Blejer, M. I. and Coricelli, F., *The Making of Economic Reform in Eastern Europe* (Aldershot: Edward Elgar, 1995).

Boycko, M., Shleifer, A. and Vishny, R., *Privatising Russia* (Cambridge, Massachusetts: The MIT Press, 1997).

Claudon, M. P. and Gutner, T. L., *Comrades Go Private: Strategies for Eastern European Privatisation* (New York: New York University Press, 1992).

Commission of the European Communities, *Partnership with the Commonwealth of Independent States and Georgia*. Background report, 18 November 1992, London.

Craner, J., 'Privatisation in Czechoslovakia and the EC Harmonisation of Financial Reporting: A Problem of Matching', *European Business and Economic Development*, October 1992.

Estrin, S. (ed.), *Privatisation in Central and Eastern Europe* (Harlow: Longman, 1994).

Fingleton, J., Fox, E., Neven, D., Seabright, P., *Competition Policy and the Transformation of Central Europe* (London: Centre for Economic Policy Research, 1996).

Major, I., *Privatisation in Eastern Europe: A Critical Approach* (Cheltenham: Ward, 1993).

Myant, M., Fleischer, F., Hornschild, K., Vintrovà, R., Zeman, K. and Soucek, Z., *Successful Transformations? The Creation of Market Economies in Eastern Europe and the Czech Republic: Studies of Communism in Transition* (Cheltenham: Edward Elgar, 1996).

Salvatore, D., *International Economics*, 5th edn (Hemel Hempstead: Prentice Hall International, 1995).

Smith, A. (ed.), *Challenges for Russian Economic Reform* (Washington DC: The Brookings Institution, 1995).

van Selm, B., *The Economics of the Soviet Break-up*, Routledge Studies of Societies in Transition (London: Routledge, 1997).

Also:

The Economist
The European
The Financial Times
The Times
EBRD website   http://www.ebrd.com

CHAPTER 6

European business organisations

■ 6.1 Introduction

Having taken a macro view of European business in the first five chapters, particularly the environment within which it operates, this chapter considers the micro perspective, focusing now on the business as an entity in its own right. In particular, consideration will be given to the main types of business organisation operating in Europe and the relative strengths and weaknesses of each. The structure of business organisations will be reviewed and the changes in them will be analysed. The chapter concludes with case studies to explore the issues more fully.

■ 6.2 The nature and objectives of European business organisations

European businesses exist for a variety of reasons. Each organisation has its own objectives, however, which should be common to all the employees in that business. These objectives determine their main activity which is to combine the resources available to them – land, labour, capital and enterprise, with capital including information technology while enterprise includes information – to produce one or more goods and/or services for profit.

Of course the task may not be to manufacture a product but rather to supply a component; car industry components firms would be examples of this. Similarly, the service output may be to design a product such as a new compact stereo system or to supply a service as part of the process of manufacture. For an airport or an hotel the concern will be throughput rather than output, for example the number of people passing through Copenhagen airport in any year, or the room occupancy rate at the Hotel Miramar in Amsterdam. In all cases, however, the essential process is the combining of inputs and their transformation into some form of output.

How any business is organised to achieve its objectives is what is understood by its nature. This involves an examination of the different types of European business which exist, their organisational structures and how and why these change. The process of managerial decision-making also needs to be considered within this framework. This includes the increasing emphasis on human resource management as labour is acknowledged as a valuable and costly input freed by automation from many of the repetitive production processes of the past. The impact of technological change, and their responses to it, also affect the nature and objectives of European businesses.

The rationale underlying the production process is assumed to be profit maximisation although, as is discussed elsewhere, other objectives may dominate. The nature of its activities, and indeed the magnitude of the profit a business can make, will vary with a number of factors both internal and external. Internal factors affecting a firm include the business's size, who owns it, its organisational structure and information systems, its culture including its ability both to initiate and to respond to change, the sources of finance it can secure, its staff and its human resource management policies. The introduction of automation, especially assembly-line robots, is an example of how businesses have had to demonstrate their dynamism in the transformation of their production processes in the last fifteen to twenty years. This has impacted significantly on corporate profitability. The investment and start-up costs have become much higher, but the reliability of production and the level and quality of output have also increased significantly.

European businesses are also substantially affected by external factors which impact on their profitability. The market structure within which a business operates, and hence the extent of competition, is of major importance influencing whether the firm has an ability to determine entry barriers, act as a price maker, collude with other firms and create brand and corporate loyalty through marketing. Other factors include the stage of the business cycle in which the country's economy is; national and EU legislation, for example relating to the environment; national cultural and social changes, such as the increasing Americanisation of European life; continuing reform in CEEC including widespread privatisation; the moves to the single currency within the EU; new technological developments, for example permitting teleworking; demographic changes; and increased provision of higher education and its impact on society. Figure 1.1 in Chapter 1 illustrates these influences.

This scenario, which has been described as an open systems model of business organisation, is clearly one where the business has to be adaptive to survive. Research has suggested that there are five functions which it must undertake:

- Firstly there is boundary spanning; this is to ensure that exchanges take place between an organisation and its environment concerning resources and information, and the exchange of goods and services.
- Secondly there is the technological function which relates to the production process and the need to incorporate the latest technological developments.
- A third function is that of control. An open systems organisation receives customer feedback about its performance and hence needs to respond appropriately.
- A fourth function is to be adaptive to external constraints and opportunities – as discussed above.
- Finally there is the institutional function – this relates to the establishment of performance norms for the organisation to ensure it maintains its organisational integrity in the long run.

This model has been criticised for not taking account of internal pressures such as conflict and different departments working to different goals. This has prompted the development of the political coalition model to explain organisational structure, and this is discussed later in this chapter.

Within Europe there is an imbalance between types of business in terms of their impact on the European economy. On the one hand there are a very large number of small and medium-sized enterprises (SMEs) which employ most of the labour force in the European Union. On the other hand there are a much smaller number of very large organisations which command considerable economic and political influence, which have grown organically or by mergers and acquisitions, and which increasingly are global players. Traditionally associated with heavy industry they include defence and aerospace, businesses with product assembly lines for goods such as automobiles and white goods, and the service sector such as financial services. The differences in these organisations are explored below.

■ 6.3 Types of European business organisation

There are a variety of different business organisations within Europe which have also been alluded to elsewhere in this book. This section briefly reviews the main ones in order to analyse the structure of European business more fully.

■ Sole trader

These comprise the bulk of European businesses and are distinguished by the fact that there is a sole owner or proprietor, even if s/he employees a number of assistants. Typical examples might be a builder working in Barcelona, Spain, or a person renting out holiday villas in the Algarve, Portugal, or a person running a computer repair business in Gothenburg, Sweden or a woman selling newspapers outside the Gare du Nord railway station in Paris. In recent years the growth of the computer software industry, particularly computer games, has seen many software designers start out as sole traders, although they have soon converted to a limited company when profits increase. EU job-creation initiatives have tended to stop at the SME level although national government initiatives may at times provide funds to help sole traders set up in business.

In terms of job-creation the sole trader is a relatively easy business organisation to establish, requiring minimum capital and an ability to move from sector to sector depending on economic circumstances and opportunity, and the sole trader's personal whim. Providers of domestic services such as the building trade, electricians and plumbers are frequently sole traders, although large regional and national industries can co-exist alongside them. Freedom to do as one wishes is commonly advanced as the reason why a person wishes to work for him/herself. Also all profits are kept by the person. However, downsides include that a sole trader has unlimited liability. Moreover the opportunity cost of being a sole trader is frequently high in that they can receive a low income.

CASE STUDY   the French Onion Seller

In the 1950s and 1960s a regular sight along the south coast of England in autumn was the French onion seller. Representing their families, who grew onions and other produce back in northern France, the onion seller would literally push his cycle round the streets of Portsmouth and other south coast cities carrying on it French onions secured together in long rows with twine. These were regarded as particularly good quality compared with English ones and households were pleased to buy a 'string of onions' when the onion seller called at their front door. Often several generations of male members of the French family had undertaken this sales activity.

In the 1960s and 1970s, with the spread of supermarkets at the expense of the corner shop, much greater choice of produce from around the world meant that this exclusive market for French onions contracted. This caused profits made by French onion sellers to decline to such an extent that the sellers virtually disappeared from English streets. The author was particularly surprised, therefore, when driving to work one grey wet November morning in 1997, to see a French onion seller complete with strings of onions pushing his bicycle along a main road, presumably having come to Portsmouth on that morning's ferry from France. It was good to see them still in business!

■ Partnership

Different types of partnership exist in Europe. At the one extreme are those associated with the professions, typically doctors, dentists, solicitors, architects, lawyers and so on. A partnership usually has unlimited liability with each partner being jointly and severally liable, that is if all other partners are unable to meet the partnership's debts due to lack of funds then the remaining partner has to, assuming s/he has sufficient money. Compared with the sole trader decisions are undertaken by all partners and this can cause delays to the decision-making process compared with a sole trader, for example. However, a partnership will typically have more capital and a wider spread of expertise compared with a sole trader.

In Germany the main types of partnership are the OHG (Offene Handelsgesellschaft), a general partnership, the KG (Kommanditgesellschaft) or limited partnership, and the GbR (Gesellschaft des burgerlichen Rechts) or civil law partnership. The OHG may be a partnership between people or business organisations and has unlimited liability. The KG differs from the OHG in that partners may limit their liability to the amount of the capital they contribute. The GbR might typically be a partnership between lawyers as discussed above. A similar arrangement exists in France with the SNC (Société en Nom Collectif) or general partnership and the Société en Commandite, or limited partnership. The former, as its name suggests requires its partners to have unlimited liability while the latter, although offering limited liability, is rarely used.

On a much larger scale a partnership may also exist as an agreement between two or more organisations to develop a new product or service, to move into new markets or simply to share scale economies from closer collaboration. Sometimes this is termed an alliance or joint venture and is discussed below. In such circumstances there may be cross share acquisition, that is each partner may own shares in the other, although this does not always have to be so. The same advantages apply as to pooling expertise and capital except that it is on a very much larger scale than the former example.

■ The limited company

Without the existence of the private sector company European business would never have developed in the way it has. Its importance in Western European production has also distinguished it clearly from production in Central and Eastern Europe since the Second World War. The private sector limited company is important for a number of reasons. Firstly, it is a legal entity in its own right with the ability to sue and be sued, own property and other assets, and employ and dismiss labour. Secondly, it has limited liability meaning that shareholders of the company who invest their money in it and receive shares in return are liable if the company has debts only up to the extent of their shareholding. So, if the company were to become bankrupt, they would lose the value of their initial investment (assuming they had not subsequently sold their shares), but not their personal assets – unlike the sole trader. Thirdly, the company enables investors to pool their resources and hence undertake activities no individual would be able to do. This is particularly important in the context of the wave of privatisations across Europe in the late 1990s.

In France the main type of limited company is the SA (société anonyme) which may or may not have its shares traded on the Bourse, the Paris stock exchange. It requires a minimum of seven shareholders and capital of FF 250 000, of which 25 per cent must be paid up. The main Spanish type of company is also denoted by SA (sociedad anonima) and again may be public or private and vary in size from the very large to the very small. It requires minimum capital of 3 000 000 pesetas.

For smaller French businesses there is the SARL (société à responsabilité limitée), a limited liability company requiring share capital of only FF 50 000 and between two and 50 shareholders. This is ideal for the family-based business of which there are many in France and indeed the EU since, as it grows and more capital is needed, more shareholders can be brought in relatively easily. The corresponding Spanish organisation is the SRL (sociedad de responsabilidad limitada); it is relatively easy to set up and has no minimum capital requirement making it very attractive for small businesses such as the building industry, retailing and tourism.

☐ 1 The public limited company

This type of organisation has its shares available for buying and selling on a stock exchange, for example in Frankfurt, Paris, London, Warsaw, Prague or a number of other European cities. Although private or individual shareholders are important as a source of capital, the bulk of shares in Western Europe are held by institutional investors such as banks, insurance companies, pension funds and other commercial organisations. Additionally, in both Central and Eastern Europe and Western Europe large numbers of companies have been owned by central governments or their agencies, although privatisation programmes are now seeing the divesting of such ownership. Chapter 7 provides a case study of French bank Crédit Lyonnais which has widespread shareholdings in a variety of French companies.

Additionally, markets exist for the issue of new shares when a company wishes to raise new capital, for example, to acquire a competitor or to finance new capital expenditure. Public and private limited companies may also be able to finance expansion by retained profits.

In Germany the only company whose shares may be traded on the stock market is the AG (aktiengesellschaft) or corporation, of which there are approximately 2000. Its minimum share capital is DM 100 000, of which at least 25 per cent must be paid up (as opposed to promised in future). Often an AG will have restrictions on shareholdings, for example no more than 5 per cent of total shares issued to prevent loss of control in a takeover bid. In the Netherlands the main business organisation, similar to the SA of France and Spain and the AG above, is the NV (naamloze vennootschap), a public limited company which may or may not be stock-market quoted. The minimum required paid up capital is 100 000 guilders.

CASE STUDY   Axel Springer Verlag

This German publishing company, an example of a private limited company, was founded by Axel Springer, who built it up into a major publishing house after the Second World War until his death in 1985. Pride of place in its portfolio goes to *Bild Zeitung*, a daily tabloid with a circulation of 4.5 million, while its main broadsheet is *Die Welt*, although sales are only 215 000. The company also publishes magazines across the spectrum including computer, car and womens' magazines. The company is family-controlled with Springer's widow (and fifth wife) Friede controlling just over 50 per cent of the shares. The rest are held by others in the family and another publisher Leo Kirsch.

Strategies for future development under its new chief executive Gus Fischer include controlling operating costs to boost profitability; entering new markets in France and especially Central and Eastern Europe; securing greater involvement in the development of digital broadcasting and Internet services; and, in Germany, challenging existing newspapers such as *Die Zeit* and *Frankfurter Allgemeine Zeitung* much more effectively. However, such expansion is expensive, even though Springer has substantial cash reserves, while its failure to develop significantly since Axel Springer's death makes such development much harder now against bigger competitors.

☐ 2 The private limited company

A private limited company is not quoted on stock markets. In Germany most businesses are either sole traders, partnerships or private limited companies. This is because there are very strict organisational requirements in Germany for public limited companies, who are the only ones able to issue ordinary shares in the capital markets.

There are a number of advantages with a private limited company, the main ones being that if it performs poorly in any year this will not reflect on its share prices and hence a falling capital value of the company, or in the inability to sell new shares. Additionally, the financial press, who can talk down the value of a company even if it is making a profit so long as it is not performing as well as they anticipate, will have no influence over the company's value. There is also no risk of a group of hostile shareholders gaining voting control of the company and changing strategic direction. This is the most important advantage of all. In the past some publicly quoted companies who have performed well and who are cash-rich therefore, have sought to buy back some or all of the shares they have previously issued in order to regain a strategic independence which they perceive themselves to have lost by going public. The British group Virgin which operates an airline, railway company, recording studies, record label, and financial services, among other things, has undertaken precisely this action.

In Germany the private company is the GmbH (gesellschaft mit beschrankter haftung). Easier to form than the AG it can have as little as one shareholder, although this is not typical. It is ideal for family-run businesses where the size of turnover requires limited liability. Although shares are not normally issued, if they are, they are not normally transferable. In the Netherlands the BV forms a similar function.

■ The role of the SME

Although European business is often perceived as consisting of multinational corporations, the majority of European businesses are sole tenders and small and medium-sized enterprises (SMEs), the latter often family operated and owned – indeed there are six million family run businesses in Europe, with Germany having 1.5 million and Italy over one million. SMEs have a workforce of less than 500 but in fact many are run by a sole trader, with family assisting, or as a cooperative, or a private limited company. This ownership structure is particularly common in Spain, Germany, Italy and Greece with the extended family an important economic unit in the Mediterranean countries, and where a stock market culture does not exist. This means that funding for such businesses is often from internal profits or, where outside funding is used, largely from the banking system.

In Europe the family business is currently in a state of decline. The generation due to take over from the founder of the business often has no wish to do so and, in many cases, the rising generation have chosen to live off the proceeds of the sale rather than take on the running of the family business themselves, or have opted to work for another organisation. Consequently, many family businesses have had to go public or accept management buyouts in order to survive. Even more likely to resist the pressures to take over the helm of the business is the third generation.

This has particularly been the case in Italy where the Italian employers' organisation Confindustria has warned that by 2000 some two-thirds of Italian businesses will face a generational crisis. Companies such as Fiat, the Marzotto textiles company, and Pirelli tyres and cables have been forced to surrender control to outsiders. Italian SMEs, built up on family-controlled businesses, state subsidies and other favourable interventions have also had to change. Although companies such as Benetton and Luxottica, the spectacles frame manufacturer, are successfully passing control to the next generation other Italian companies have experienced severe pressures due to generational change – such as long-departed small vehicles manufacturer Innocenti, fashion house Gucci, and investment bank Mediobanca which is a case study elsewhere in this chapter.

Going public or accepting a management buy-out (MBO) is never a desirable situation since when a company goes public, the family may well lose control of the business although this varies from country to country. In Germany, for example, over half of family businesses retained a majority of the shares in the floated family business compared with just over 10 per cent in the UK. The other problem with going public is that the newly floated company is forced into greater disclosure of its financial details.

The EU places considerable emphasis on the SME as a vehicle for wealth creation and especially as a source for generating employment – currently SMEs total 18 million across the EU and provide 66 per cent of EU jobs. This is particularly important since government attempts to reduce budget deficits mean less state funds can be spent on large-scale initiatives to create jobs, for example in the state sector, as has been done in the past. Measures in 1998 to promote SMEs, especially high-tech SMEs, have included the EU launching an initiative to promote an enterprise culture to encourage people to start up businesses, and to create a suitable environment within which these could flourish. This has involved better training courses for entrepreneurs and schemes to provide mentors to new companies to help them develop. Other suggestions, which national governments would need to implement, included tax incentives and better access to finance, especially venture capital.

The EU has also proposed the need to create a pan-European risk capital market which would significantly help the growth of new SMEs by providing easier and more effective finance to them. Simpler administrative procedures to start up new businesses would also help, the European Commission has asserted. This is most important in the light of a report in late 1997 which suggested that most new EU jobs are likely to come from small businesses with up to ten employees. One million new businesses start up each year in the EU and most of these are SMEs; although half have failed within five years the other half, which are less inclined to bankruptcy than bigger businesses, grow and provide jobs. Chapter 7 discusses this more fully.

CASE STUDY   Compagnie Générale des Eaux (CGE)

CGE is a classic example of a conglomerate, but one which is now seeking to reinvent itself. As well as being the largest water supplier in France it is also involved in both the public and private sectors with affiliated activities such as waste disposal, sewage treatment and street cleaning. Under its previous chairman, Guy Dejouany, it diversified into totally unrelated activities like car parking; motorway, hospital and property management; electronics and the media, including Canal Plus the French pay television company; and the railways with its acquisition of the privatised British company Connex South Central. In total it invested over £1bn in the UK between 1986–97, currently has a UK turnover of £1.7bn p.a. and employs 22 000 people. At one time CGE had 2700 subsidiaries; additional investments in other French companies totalling FF 13bn; over 204 000 staff; and group sales of almost FF 150bn. Subsequently, however, this empire suffered losses of FF 10 billion.

In 1996 its current chairman Jean-Marie Messier, who had begun rationalising CGE by selling off unprofitable subsidiaries and cutting costs, announced his intention to refocus CGE on three key activities – international electricity generation; the utility services of waste, water and energy; and telecommunications. In particular the revenue from the utilities division is to be used to finance the telecommunications growth.

In pursuing this latter area, CGE has agreed to a deal with AOL (America On Line) the Internet service provider to relaunch the latter's Internet service in France. In partnership with British Telecom CGE owns Cegetel, the main telecomms competitor to France Telecom. This will enable it to offer lower connection costs than France Telecom, which have inhibited French subscriptions to Internet providers so far. Cegetel is seeking a 20 per cent share of the French market by 2000. This was further developed in March 1998 with the next stage in its strategy to transform itself into a vertically-integrated international communications group focusing on the media and telecommunications, by its proposal to merge with the media group Havas, the world's fifth biggest media company, in which it already has a 30 per cent stake. Havas itself has a 34 per cent share of Canal Plus, Europe's biggest pay television company. This will enable CGE to provide French content to the Internet which is currently dominated by the English language. The merger will also provide synergistic gains.

In turn this merger has triggered interest by other companies. For example, Havas Advertising, the world's eighth biggest advertising agency and a subsidiary of Havas, is seeking to merge with a UK agency in a move which is likely to create excitement in the UK.

As noted above, there have been past problems with operating a conglomerate of this size. Since there was no clear focus of activity CGE became unwieldy, losing strategic direction in the 1980s and early 1990s, and dissipating its energy in too broad a spread of activities. In concentrating in future particularly on international communications, it is now seeking to redress that failure. Cost control and the operation of discrete profit centres without cross-subsidisation from profit-making to loss-making activities was also hard for CGE to effect, especially when operating in both public and private sectors. Profits for 1997, for the group as a whole, have been estimated at FF5bn.

CASE STUDY   Airbus Industrie – From Consortium to Company

From the 1960s world commercial aircraft manufacture was dominated by US companies, the most notable being Boeing, Lockheed and McDonnell Douglas (Boeing and McDonnell Douglas merged in 1997). Entry barriers to this industry are very high because of research and development costs and the production set-up costs of building new aircraft. This is aggravated by the long lead-in time before customers make payment.

To establish a major European presence in this market was beyond the resources of any one European country. In 1967 a collaborative project was therefore undertaken to design and produce a range of new aircraft through the consortium Airbus Industrie. The Airbus partners are France's Aérospatiale. (37.9 per cent share), Germany's DASA (Deutsche Aerospace) (37.9 per cent), the UK's British Aerospace (20 per cent) and Spain's Casa (4.2 per cent). Because Airbus is a consortium it does not release its financial figures, so there is no clear picture of how it is performing financially. It has been structured as a Groupement d'Intérêt Economique; as such it does not accrue profits or losses. Rather any surplus or deficit is shared among the four partners who are also responsible for any borrowings which Airbus needs to undertake. Work is allocated between the four partners by them bidding against each other. This has the effect of encouraging each partner to seek the highest profit margins it can on the components it supplies to each plane without being undercut by another partner. In practice, however, work is usually shared out in roughly equal proportions to each country's share in the consortium. This means that production costs are linked to those of the highest cost producers, Aérospatiale and Casa, which then reflects disadvantageously in the price at which Airbus planes compete against Boeing.

As a result Airbus has needed for some time to rationalise to enable it to be transformed into a public limited company. This would allow it to stand on its own feet, raise its own funds in financial markets, be much more responsive to market forces and make its own strategic decisions independently of the four members' governments. In this way it could drive down its costs of production and compete more effectively against Boeing which for a long time has cross-subsidised its other products with the profits it has long made from its market leader, the 747.

Negotiations began in 1996 but encountered problems over which assets and liabilities would be transferred from the existing partnership to the new company. Aérospatiale was particularly difficult in insisting for some time that it retain the research facilities dedicated to Airbus, although this issue has now been overcome. The French government has also agreed to surrender its majority stake in Aérospatiale, the state-owned aerospace group, due to pressure from the German and UK partners. Consequently, on 1 January 1999 it will be converted from a limited partnership to a more conventional corporation. Alenia of Italy, another aircraft manufacturer (which with BAe and Aérospatiale jointly owns Aero International Regional, another European regional planemaker) has now joined with Airbus while Saab of Sweden, who recently gave up aircraft manufacture, is also likely to join.

One major criticism of the US has been that Airbus is unfairly subsidised to enable it to compete with US planemakers. The EU's response has been that although this may have been true in the past it is not so now. Further, subsidisation was crucial to enable the consortium to establish itself against the might and market domination of Boeing and McDonnell Douglas. Also, the US subsidises its planemakers through military contracts it awards – McDonnell Douglas has manufactured both commercial and military aircraft, for example.

It is certainly true that Airbus has successfully acquired market-share against its US competitor with 35 per cent of the world market in 1997, and a commitment to increase this to 50 per cent. However, it has also faced problems. Most notably these have been the past political rivalry between the four partners and their governments, the early 1990s world recession which hit air travel, the complexities of Airbus's internal structure, R&D duplication, the extended cross border production line and the lack of an effective cost control and reduction programme, some of which have been discussed above.

At the end of 1997 Airbus had the largest share of new world aircraft orders in its history, totalling US$ 69.2 billion, compared with $25bn in 1993. This included 1997 orders of 292 aircraft (with $6bn accounted for by an order for up to 400 aircraft from US Airways) and a backlog of 1187 aircraft (compared with competitor Boeing's 1629 aircraft). This has been helped by the major growth in demand for passenger air transport in the mid to late 1990s and the need for airlines to replace ageing aircraft. Also, widening its product range, except in the jumbo class where the Boeing 747 still dominates, has helped Airbus gain market-share from Boeing – although Airbus does intend to launch a 500-seat new aircraft in 2003 at a cost of $8bn, with the aim of competing head on with Boeing's 450 seat 747-400. As a result, Airbus' output has increased from 93 in 1996, to 185 in 1997 to 234 in 1998. Of major importance in Airbus' success is its growing acceptance in the US market with nearly half of the biggest US airlines now buying from Airbus.

There were also plans for Airbus to design a new generation of long-haul aircraft capable of carrying 966 passengers, with a working title of A3XX-200. This was to be in conjunction with Boeing and was based on the assumption that by 2015 the number of passengers flying would increase threefold; however, subsequent market research found that there was only limited airline demand for such a project and so it has been halted.

Conclusions

The market conditions that promoted the development of the Airbus consortium are even more relevant today, particularly in the light of the Boeing–McDonnell Douglas merger. Also, Swedish company Saab has exited from independent plane manufacture. Further, the Dutch aerospace business Fokker, the world's biggest regional planemaker, has become bankrupt following majority owner Daimler Benz' withdrawal of its financial support in January 1996 and its inability to secure another buyer. These events clearly show that the day of the independent European planemaker is numbered. The global nature of the market and the very high R&D and production costs make mergers, collaboration and effective cost control essential. Moreover, as EU governments seek to limit expenditure increases in the light of the obligations of the EU's 1996 Growth and Stability Pact, financial support for aircraft manufacture, both regional and international, will be even harder to fund. Therefore it is absolutely vital that Airbus transforms itself into a limited company if it is to grow further. From the base it has established, it should then be able to compete even more successfully with Boeing–McDonnell Douglas.

■ The conglomerate

The term conglomerate is often used to describe a company, or more accurately a group of companies, operating in a wide range of different fields which may often be unrelated to each other. The parent or controlling company will own the subsidiary companies although each will have its own board of directors to make day-to-day operational decisions. Long-term or strategic decisions will probably be made by the parent company, however, taking a global view of operations.

■ The joint venture

This is similar to a partnership except that the companies involved do not own shares in each other. Rather, in this situation, two firms set up a separate company with each owning part of the capital of this new business. The benefits are essentially the same as those of the partnership with the added advantage of shared risk. Although it does not have to be multinational, increasingly this is likely to be the trend in the market which makes up the European Economic Area.

■ The consortium

This is very similar to a joint venture except that a number of firms are involved in this rather than merely two. All the same advantages accrue except on a bigger scale. The case study reviews European commercial aircraft manufacturer Airbus Industrie as an example. The reader should also see Chapter 8 where a discussion of the needed rationalisation of the European defence industry has some overlap with this case study.

The importance of both the joint venture and the consortium are strategic on a microeconomic and on a macroeconomic basis. Microeconomically they enable firms to enter markets or activities which they would not be able to do individually. This may be due to the high level of funding needed to undertake the activity or the level of risk which an individual firm might not feel able to sustain. As has been noted elsewhere in this chapter entry barriers are often so high as to be prohibitive to any one organisation. Without joint ventures and consortia, product development and the ability to compete would be inhibited.

Secondly, on a macroeconomic basis the need to compete, not just in the single European market but more importantly globally, means that a minimum critical size is needed. There is at times a dilemma between, on the one hand, the need for European champions big enough to compete on a large scale, and, on the other hand, the need to preserve competitive markets without monopolistic influences. This is discussed more fully elsewhere.

■ The cooperative

This is a business organisation which has been established and owned by a group of people who share common objectives, the collective risks incurred in running it and any profits it makes. Most typically, cooperatives have been found in retailing but, additionally, producer cooperatives exist. An example of the latter might be a group of French farmers who pool their resources to build barns and purchase wine presses and vats. All use the facilities and hence spread the high (to them) capital costs. Profits are shared according to initial investment.

As was seen in Chapter 5, cooperatives were perceived as one way to begin the move to a more market-based economy in Russia when Mikhail Gorbachev was president of the former USSR. However, their success was limited due to the lack of a market infrastructure to support them.

CASE STUDY Mondragon

Mondragon is a group of cooperatives founded in 1956 and based in the Basque region of Spain. Its 100 businesses were brought together in 1991. It produces and exports white goods (refrigerators and so on), car components and machine tools and is involved in the construction industry and agriculture, banking and medical care. Its output accounts for approximately 7 per cent of the Basque region's GDP. Each of its 26 000 workers is a member and owner of the cooperative and so has to make a financial contribution before s/he can work for Mondragon. A large amount of its output is exported. Additionally, it owns a chain of supermarkets in France and factories in Mexico and Thailand. In this sense it is untypical of most cooperatives by its sheer size of operations and is able to compete with limited companies in Europe. Turnover for 1994 was 497 billion pesetas, with profits exceeding 33.7bn pesetas. In May 1995, due to a liquidity shortage, Mondragon was forced to raise 12 billion pesetas ($96 million) by seeking a stock market flotation. For the first time this meant that part of the business was owned by non-employees including foreign investors.

   Although Mondragon is the most famous example of a cooperative, the Spanish government actively encourages the development of these, especially in agriculture, to make production more efficient through farming larger plots of land than if each farmer worked alone.

■ Europe's top companies

The term 'top companies' is a dubious phrase since it depends on which criteria are used to measure importance. In this case they are measured by their market capitalisation or share value. Other criteria which might have been used are profitability, profitability per employee, total sales, value of output produced or a number of other accounting measures. From Figure 6.1 it can be seen that seven of the companies are British, (British Petroleum Co.; HSBC Holdings; Glaxo Wellcome; Unilever; Lloyds TSB; SmithKline Beecham; and BT), five German (Deutsche Telekom; Allianz; Daimler-Benz; Siemens AG; and Bayer), three Swedish (ENI; Astra; and Ericsson), three Swiss (Novartis-Bearer; Roche-Holding Bearer; and Nestlé), one Dutch (ING Group) and one Anglo-Dutch (Royal Dutch Shell). Of these, pharmaceuticals account for six of the main European businesses (Novartis-Bearer; Roche-Holding Bearer; Glaxo Wellcome; SmithKline Beecham; Astra; and Bayer), while financial services account for four (HSBC Holdings; Allianz; Lloyds TSB; and ING Group). The oil sector is represented by Royal Dutch Shell, British Petroleum and ENI. The importance of communication and information technologies is shown by the presence of Ericsson, British Telecom and newly privatised Deutsche Telekom. Of the remainder Unilever and Nestlé are in the food processing industry while Siemens produces electrical equipment and Daimler-Benz manufactures automobiles.

■ 6.4 Traditional organisational structures: strengths and weaknesses

The reader may have concluded from section 6.3 above that it is difficult to talk of a typical organisational structure since there are a wide variety of different types of organisation. Nonetheless there is a standard traditional structure which is analysed here. For illustrative purposes a public limited company is assumed, with no subsidiary companies and owned by a mixture of private and institutional shareholders. It employs over 1000 staff.

■ Organisation by function

Figure 6.1 gives the company's organisation chart. As can be seen it is hierarchical in that there are clear levels of authority from the board of directors at the top of the chart to the workforce at the bottom. It is functional in that it has clearly defined departments such as production, marketing, finance and personnel, each with their specialist areas of responsibility to achieve the business's objectives. Although the benefits of specialisation and familiarity accrue from this structure there is a danger of overcompartmentalisation, particularly with a large organisation as in our example. This may cause a breakdown in horizontal communications, failure to work together effectively as a team and, at its worst, internal feuding with each department having its own agenda which might differ from that of the organisation as a whole.

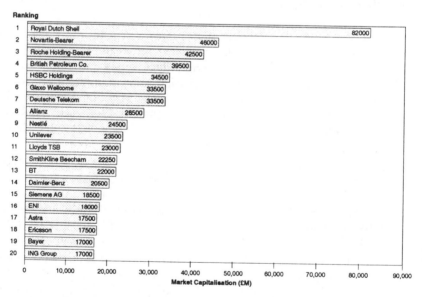

Figure 6.1   The leading 20 EU companies, 1998

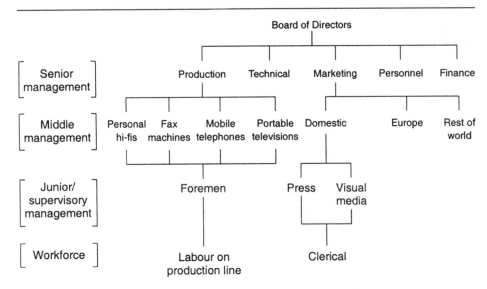

Figure 6.2 Hierarchical organisation of a public limited company

■ Organisation by product

In Figure 6.2 production is undertaken with four separate production lines for personal hi-fis, fax machines, mobile telephones and portable televisions. It may be the case that the company will be organised on the basis of products with a separate division for each product, although corporate functions such as human resources, marketing and so on will still be company-based. This can be an attractive structure in that resources and staff specialisms are allocated specifically to each product, and the ability to evaluate each on its own merits is easier. It may also promote more effective ownership by staff of the product with which they are exclusively involved. However, overall coordination may be a problem if staff relate exclusively to their product rather than the organisation as a whole. It may well also promote duplication of effort across different products.

■ Organisation by country

Where a company has a presence in a number of countries, in the EU for example, the organisational structure may reflect each separate market. In this case instead of distinguishing between production, technical, marketing and so on, the structure may read France, Italy, Austria as appropriate. In these circumstances local management will be responsible for all the organisation's functions in each country separately, an example of decentralisation. This structure offers a flexibility to adapt to local circumstances and change which the previous organisational structure may well not permit. However, overall coordination and control, including information flows, may again be difficult to achieve. The Volkswagen car company, with plants in Germany, the Czech Republic, the UK and Spain, is a good illustration of this.

■ Conglomerate organisation by company

The growth of cross-border mergers and takeovers creating conglomerate organisations and the increasing development of joint ventures and consortia, as discussed in Chapter 10, means that an all-embracing organisational structure based on departmental functions may not be appropriate in these circumstances. In the case of conglomerates it is quite probable that organisation will be on a company basis, each with its own separate structure. In this case the holding company may retain some functions which are undertaken on a group basis, for example marketing the corporate image or overall financial planning and control. However, day-to-day autonomy is delegated to the individual companies to exercise through their own organisational structures. Indeed decentralisation may extend to allowing each company to undertake all corporate functions. This model may even be extended to a greater or lesser extent to any of the above structures.

■ The matrix organisation

This type of organisational structure is a combination of two of the above structures – organisation by function and organisation by product. It might typically be found in businesses such as research and development organisations, marketing firms, universities, consultancy firms and hospitals. The main benefit of the functional structure was noted to be in bringing together specialist skills, but this was offset by the problems of coordinating different specialist teams to work in unison and ensuring that the goods are produced. With the product structure, on the other hand, it is easier to coordinate specialisms and produce goods on time and within budget, but duplication of costs and activities may be the downside.

The matrix organisation attempts to bring together the good aspects of the functional and product structures without their problems. Its key characteristic is that each employee has both a functional department manager and a product manager. Figure 6.3 shows such a structure for a European-wide marketing firm. The left-hand column lists the main functions which the firm undertakes, while the top row identifies the main products – or services provided in this case. Such an organisational structure promotes both communication and flexibility since each person is effectively in at least two teams, a functional and a product grouping. It also ensures resources are used most efficiently rather than being compartmentalised. So a new business studies graduate, recently employed by the firm, may be a member of the market research team yet also be working specifically on the marketing of new letterbox style digital televisions for a

Products (clients) / Functional Departments	New range of 4x4 off-road vehicles (car producer)	New range of digital TVs (Japanese Electronics Company)	Services of a newly merged Swiss investment bank	New strategic alliance of telecoms providers	UK supermarket chain which has lost market leader position
Creative					
Media					
Marketing Services					
Finance					
Human Resources					
Public Relations					

Figure 6.3   A matrix organisational structure: European wide marketing firm

Japanese business client. The danger of such a structure is that it may cause uncertainty or even confusion.

■ The board of directors

The function of a company's board is to determine the business strategy that the company will pursue in the long run; for example development of new products, diversifying into new markets, growth through mergers or acquisitions and so on, and the medium-run tactics for achieving it. They also delegate the day-to-day running of the company (operational management) to senior managers who may also sit on the board. They are elected by and answerable to the shareholders, and the annual general meeting (AGM) enables them to be challenged as to their (and hence the company's) performance during the last year.

In Figure 6.2 there is a unitary board of directors. This is the only possibility for the UK. It is also found in Germany for small private limited companies, and in France for a large majority of businesses. However, larger private and public limited German companies and some other French companies, mainly in the public sector, have a two-tier system with both a supervisory board and a management board.

□ 1 The supervisory board

This is required in Germany for companies with over 500 employees. The supervisory board consists of shareholders and employees' representatives, especially including representatives of banks, who make long-term loans to

German businesses and have close relationships with them, and representatives of the firm's customers and suppliers. Consisting of between three and 20 members its function is to supervise the management board, offer them general advice especially when major investment and strategic decisions are made, and appoint and dismiss senior management. In turn it is answerable to the AGM and may be appointed and dismissed by the shareholders attending it.

☐ 2 The management board

The management board consists of the company's top managers and they set the strategic direction of the company and ensure it is being run effectively and efficiently on a daily basis. They are also answerable to shareholders through the AGM. Although at times the two boards appear to work well together, at other times conflict between them appears inevitable, especially when there are disagreements over future strategy. Also, senior managers on the management board must inevitably look over their shoulders from time to time. Advocates of a two-tier system would argue that it gives extra input to strategic decision making and acts as an additional check on, and balance to, the management board.

A similar model operates in France for a limited number of companies, about 3 per cent, although for public companies listed on the CAC40 index the figure is 25 per cent. In these cases there is a supervisory board (the directoire) which performs similar functions to the German supervisory board. However, most French limited companies have a unitary board chaired by a chief executive (président directeur général, or PDG) with considerable delegated powers.

There are a number of reasons for this divergence of boards between different countries. Perhaps the most important is the much closer linkage between companies, and between companies and banks in Germany compared with France and especially the UK. Traditionally in Germany banks have worked closer with companies and made longer-term loans; hence they have a greater desire to be involved with their customers' decision-making processes. This linkage is explored more fully in the next chapter.

■ Production

The separation of the company in Figure 6.2 into a number of corporate functions such as production, engineering and marketing has already been alluded to. Two of these, production and marketing, have been traced through the organisational structure for illustrative purposes.

As noted above there are four different products manufactured, each having its own assembly line. Since there is continuous manufacture of each good, and the firm seeks to sell globally, then in our example it achieves economies of scale from volume production. Before the 1980s and the large-scale advent of capital intensive robotic production to European assembly lines, economies of scale depended on the two requirements of division of labour and specialisation. The former relates to the separation of a production task into a number of sub-tasks which can then be undertaken repetitively by labour; this was first defined by Adam Smith in *The Wealth of Nations*, published in 1776. Specialisation requires each worker to concentrate on one of these tasks to achieve manual dexterity and speed of working through constant repetition.

This bureaucratic concept of production, which has been described as a 'closed system or one best way model' on account of its belief that it is possible to determine scientifically various aspects of the organisation independent of external developments, owes its origins to the work of an American engineer Frederick Taylor. He sought to improve productive efficiency by breaking down tasks into their smallest components to permit labour, working with capital, to become as efficient as possible. This was supported by close and accurate measurement of each task to be undertaken and by a system of performance-related pay, where people were rewarded for their output; what was to become known as work study. The model also requires a strong hierarchical structure, with precise regulations and procedures governing operations. It was adopted by Henry Ford in the production of the Ford Model T, the first mass-produced car; this production process became known as Fordism and is typified by Henry Ford's famous comment about the model T Ford cars he produced – 'you can have any colour you want so long as it's black'. This exemplifies the problems associated with long production runs, namely their inflexibility. Taylorism, or scientific management as it was also called, dominated industrial production until the 1980s. In third-world countries, where capital is limited but labour plentiful and cheap, it is still highly influential.

Mass production of this sort offers obvious cost and efficiency advantages as discussed above. However, there are many disadvantages and these have told against it in recent years. Labour is treated as a machine denying each person's aspirations, ideas and contributions to the company's performance. Modern human resource management is, in part, a reaction to Taylorism (see section 6.7). Additionally, constant repetition of a production task creates boredom, loss of interest in the work and hence falling quality of output through mistakes. Industrial relations suffer and strikes can multiply to relieve the boredom of the job. In effect Taylorism reinforces divisions between management and labour by encouraging a tight and autocratic management structure. The different groups can, therefore, become antagonistic to each other rather than working as a team making the products; workers have no sense of ownership of the product since they do not produce a finished product, merely adding one component to a half-finished good. The decline of the British car-making industry in the 1960s and 1970s was partly due to this. Finally, establishing long-term production runs reduces operational flexibility for the company making it difficult to switch quickly from one good to another as consumer demand changes. Additionally, large markets with constant demand are needed to justify the high set-up costs of the assembly line.

The introduction of robotic production since the 1980s, especially in the European car industry, has meant that the very nature of the production process itself has changed, and with it the demands employers place on employees. These changes are discussed more fully in Chapter 9.4 when the concept of flexible specialisation is discussed.

Since the work of Taylor and the realisation of its limitations, much research has been undertaken into theories of motivation since the extent to which people are motivated in the workplace determines the level of their performance. This includes the now famous work by A. H. Maslow which identified the hierarchy of needs that people seek to fulfil, consisting in ascending order of physiological, security, social, esteem and self-actualisation needs. Work by David McGregor examined the X (people seek to minimise effort, lack ambition and are indifferent to the organisation employing them) and Y (people work hard, are self-motivated and actively seek responsibility rather than avoiding it) theories and concluded that the latter was more appropriate to workers' behaviour. In the same way, the work of Elton Mayo starting in the scientific management tradition emphasised the work of formal groups in the workplace and how boring and tedious work overcomes the efforts of managers seeking to motivate staff.

The importance of this research was to move thinking from the narrow almost robotic behaviour expected of workers with Taylorism to a realisation that workers are a valuable resource with their own aspirations who need to be developed and experience a sense of belonging, ownership and fulfilment if they are to work well.

■ Team assembly and job rotation at Volvo

One attempt to overcome the problems of mass production is the model which was adopted by Swedish car producers Volvo in the early 1980s. Instead of requiring each person to perform one task *ad nauseam*, workers were organised into teams with responsibility for producing the whole product themselves. Job rotation was practised so that each person would undertake a different task every few months. This gives product ownership and a sense of teamwork which assembly line production denies. It also enables staff to acquire an wider range of skills and achieve greater job satisfaction. However, it also imposes higher training costs on the company while new tasks are being learned.

■ Marketing

In Figure 6.2 marketing is assumed to be undertaken by this company on a geographical basis divided into domestic market, rest of Europe and rest of the world. With the advent of the single European market in 1992 firms have been very much less inclined to distinguish between domestic and rest-of-Europe markets. Indeed the advent of satellite and cable television has actively encouraged the development of intra-European brands and campaigns. The chocolate bar 'Marathon' which adopted the Europe-wide name 'Snickers' and the dried cat food 'Munchies' which became 'Brekkies' are examples of this.

A company may choose to structure its marketing organisation on the basis of products rather than geographic regions. So one campaign would cover mobile telephones, another fax machines and so on.

The advantage of grouping marketing on a regional basis is that cultural differences are already recognised and built into particular campaigns. Even grouping Europe into one area fails to recognise that there are significant cultural differences between different European countries, as was discussed in Chapter 1. Grouping marketing on a product basis focuses attention more precisely on products, each of which has its own special characteristics. In the end, whether the marketing is undertaken by product or region will be influenced in part by the type of organisational structure which the business has adopted.

This discussion is not intended to be exhaustive but rather to give examples of corporate organisational structure which may then be built on with further reading. The effectiveness of the structure is of course determined by how well it enables the business to achieve its objectives. Two characteristics of organisational structures which particularly are worth considering in this respect are hierarchical control and span of control.

■ Hierarchical structures and span of control

Figures 6.4 and 6.5 give two examples of companies with different hierarchical control structures and different spans of control. The hierarchical control structure relates to the number of layers that a company has – that is, its chain of command. The span of control relates to the number of people a manager has under his/her control or reporting to him/her. Figure 6.4 illustrates a European business with a tall hierarchical structure but narrow span of control. In contrast Figure 6.5 presents a business which has a short hierarchical structure but a wide span of control.

A hierarchy offers a coherent structure within which a business may be operated. Since it is clearly defined it gives the workforce knowledge and certainty of their place in that structure. It also enables the business to continue when the people who have established the structures no longer work for the organisation, a factor of increasing importance with the ending of jobs for life for most of the European workforce. However, it has been argued that although it is useful at limiting intra-organisational conflict it is not effective in determining solutions to these conflicts. Exactly how many layers of organisation a company has will depend on a number of factors including the complexity of the production process, the cultural attitudes in the country, and the preferences of the directors in terms of their perceptions of the minimum necessary to function effectively and global competition.

The business in Figure 6.4 may face vertical communication problems in that, because of the tall structure and long chain of command, it will prove more difficult for the board to get information to the workforce and to receive feedback, if that is what it wants. However, it does offer steady career prospects for the loyal worker to progress up the occupational ladder. From a managerial

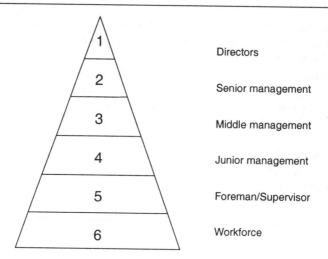

Figure 6.4   Organisational structure: tall hierarchy/narrow span

viewpoint the narrow span of control means that horizontal communication should certainly be effective – that is between people on the same level – and since managers only have a limited number of people to manage they should be able to do so more effectively.

The structure represented by Figure 6.5 faces the opposite problems. So although vertical communication may be better there may be a higher turnover of staff due to the lack of career prospects, although it can be argued that sideways development into new jobs at the same career and salary levels is a way of mitigating against this. Also managers may be stretched to the limit of their capabilities by the fact that their span of control is wide and therefore concentrate on operational aspects of their work rather than thinking strategically.

The pyramid shape is often used to represent a company structure since this is most typical of organisations. The reader will observe that the span of control narrows as one moves up the hierarchy reflecting the increasing complexity of work undertaken and needing to be supervised. However, the structure does not have to be a pyramid. Lane (1989), in her analysis of British, French and German companies, argued that German companies tend to have a short relatively flat structure (rather than pyramidical), with wide spans of control. They are also the least formalised and bureaucratised of the three countries and are best integrated horizontally. In contrast, the typical French business structure is much more hierarchical with rigid separation between levels of management and the work-force and, not surprisingly, serious vertical communication problems. Figure 6.3 probably best summarises the French structure. The UK business structure, certainly until recent delayering, was found to have a shape more like an inverted pyramid with increasing spans of control as one moved up the management

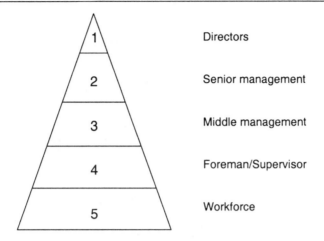

Figure 6.5   Organisational structure: short hierarchy/wide span

hierarchy, albeit these remained narrower than German companies'. Research by Bessant and Grunt (1985) shows that UK businesses have the worst horizontal integration and communication, with jobs being compartmentalised at each level. This in turn has adverse effects on vertical communications.

■ Delayering the organisational structure

Figure 6.6 represents the situation of the late 1980s and 1990s with the advent of delayering or downsizing (see also Chapter 4). The late 1970s and early 1980s in particular saw a substantial increase in the use of capital to replace labour (blue collar workers) in the assembly-line production process. Partly this was to take advantage of the latest technological developments first used widely by Japanese industry, and partly to effect operational cost savings. The consequence of this was a reduction in the demand for unskilled labour across Europe and rising unemployment as remaining demand was for semi-skilled and skilled labour.

With the impact of the recession of the early 1990s and the major increase in competition from low-cost cheap labour countries of the Pacific Rim, especially the Peoples' Republic (PR) of China, further cost-savings were needed. This time white collar workers or management were most affected by redundancies. Whole layers of management, junior, middle and senior, were removed from the organisational structure. This had the effect of creating businesses whose structure was shorter and squatter, giving much wider spans of control. It is argued that this gives more power to employees at the bottom of the organisational structure and creates a hierarchical structure as in Figure 6.6. However, it has also has the impact of increasing the workload of remaining staff significantly

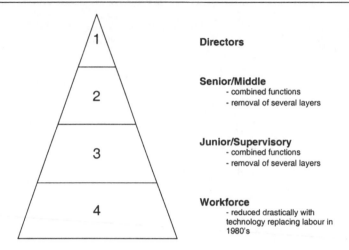

Figure 6.6   Effect of delayering on an organisation's structure

and causing increased stress. Moreover, delayering has the negative effect of undermining staff loyalty and making staff retention more difficult, particularly in times of economic boom.

The question to be asked about downsizing is whether companies can sustain production and quality as demand increases and/or the business cycle enters the upswing. Certainly the widespread use of computers, fax machines and other electronic devices has boosted productivity substantially, in the same way that the introduction of automation did for production line workers in the 1980s. This is reinforced by the increased use by businesses of contracting-out work, for example reprographics, Information Technology services to agencies, or employing workers either on short-term contracts for specific tasks or part-time so that when the need arises labour can easily be shed. This substantial saving of overhead costs helps significantly to contribute to corporate profitability. However, recent research has suggested that the profitability of firms which have substantially downsized has been adversely affected compared with firms who have not dismissed older staff or removed whole layers of the company.

■ 6.5 The changing business organisation

The models of organisational structure discussed above have relied heavily on departmentalisation, that is grouping together similar tasks to enable them to be coordinated effectively – organisation by function being the most common way of doing this, although organisation by country and by product was also examined.

Other options not discussed in this chapter include grouping by process, for example assembly of components as part of producing the final good; and grouping by customer, for example public sector and private sector. This chapter has also examined the concept of chains of command, although delayering has shortened these while communication and information technology such as Lotus

---

CASE STUDY   Boeing – Rethinking the Downsizing Strategy

Boeing, the world's largest producer of commercial airlines, suffered major production difficulties in late 1997 and 1998, in part due to an over-ambitious downsizing programme, although its merger with McDonnell Douglas at the same time as pursuing a strategy of doubling output also caused serious problems. As a result, although the cyclical demand for commercial airlines was on the upswing stage and near to its peak, Boeing was unable to meet demand for its products, resulting in a lengthening waiting list and loss of market share to Airbus. As such its third quarter 1996 profit of $466m slumped to a loss for the same period 1997.

In 1992 Boeing had announced a major organisational restructuring plan involving a considerable reduction in its labour force accompanied by a major capital expenditure programme. This, it argued, would result in an increase in production while costs would fall by 25 per cent between 1992–98. Not surprisingly this caused Airbus some considerable concern.

So how did Boeing get itself into its present position? Part of it relates to a visit by Boeing senior executives to the Toyota car plant in Japan in 1993 where its Just-in-Time philosophy was encountered (see also Chapter 9). Simply, the main principle of this minimalist philosophy is that a producer has close links with components suppliers who deliver materials just in time for the producer to use, even if a dozen deliveries a day are needed. This cuts the producer's stock holding costs substantially. Additionally the producer supplies just in time to meet identified customer demand rather than holding stocks of manufactured goods just in case there will be a demand.

Link to this increased production targets, and the downsizing principle which was very much in fashion in the late 1980s/early 1990s, and one can see major changes in how Boeing organised its production. Indeed between 1989 and 1997 Boeing dismissed one third of its workforce, totalling 60 000 employees. However, in taking this too far, Boeing was then unable to produce the planes for which there was an identified demand – hence the waiting list for 1629 aircraft. Add to that also the adjustment problems arising from the 1996 announcement of the merger with McDonnell Douglas and it is easy to see why Boeing encountered such production difficulties.

Consequently it was forced to hire thousands of new workers - who had to be trained, which cost time and money; rehire McDonnell Douglas staff sacked due to the recent merger; and poach staff from its main contractors, which worsened its ability to secure the components it needed and undermined the whole philosophy of just-in-time stocks. At the beginning of 1998 estimates were that it would take some eighteen months to get production back on stream, a situation aggravated by a month-long shutdown of its 737 and 747 assembly lines in October 1997 due to shortages of components and production mix-ups. However by July 1998 Boeing was admitting that the amount of work behind schedule at its 747 plant had doubled since November 1997. Also overtime was rising again increasing production costs and impacting on profit margins. The only saving grace was the inability of some Asian customers to pay for the aircraft they ordered because of the financial crisis (see Chapter 1) giving Boeing some extra breathing space.

Notes enables senior managers to bypass subordinate levels of authority and communicate directly with the workforce. Also the concept of span of control has been explored.

More recently organisational structures have been re-examined with the aim of making them work more efficiently. The aim of such a re-examination is to move from mechanistic structures – which are very centralised and formalised with rigid departments and limited interchange of information – to organic structures which are much less formal, exchange information effectively within the organisation, empower workers by enabling them to be a part of the decision-making process, and seek to transcend vertical hierarchies and narrow functional departments. As we saw, with the conventional organisation communication chains may be too long or spans of control too wide to enable the organisation to function totally effectively. Three alternative models which are briefly examined here are the team structure, the virtual organisation and the boundaryless organisation. These seek to address the problems of conventional structures.

- The **team structure** model is based on the concept of using teams as the means to centrally coordinate the organisation. Decision-making is therefore decentralised while teams cross departmental boundaries, enhancing communication and cross-fertilisation of ideas. This sort of organisational structure might be used by a marketing agency for example. The team approach is also good for developing new products or seeing through major projects such as designing a new car model. The team requires its members to be generalists rather than specialists so that each can contribute fully.
- The **virtual organisation** – or modular or network organisation – has already been encountered although not by this name. Simply, the idea is that the business retains its core functions, for example the design of new products, and outsources its other major business functions such as information technology, marketing, human resources and so on, to other businesses which can undertake them more cheaply. Hence there is little departmentalisation. European companies which assemble personal computers from components produced elsewhere are one example of a virtual organisation – for example monitors from Germany, chips from South Korea, keyboards from Taiwan and assembled in Sweden. The aim is to create an organisation which has maximum flexibility; however, the downside is inevitably some loss of control over key activities.
- The **boundaryless organisation**, which is a concept businesses work towards without expecting to achieve it, seeks to break down the business's internal and external barriers. The internal barriers, vertical and horizontal, have already been discussed; the external barriers separate the firm from its customers and suppliers. The reduction of hierarchical barriers makes the organisation look flatter as after delayering, while the replacement of departments by empowered cross-functional teams removes horizontal barriers. Eliminating external barriers is part of the process of a firm developing a global strategy – such as forming strategic alliances which have been discussed elsewhere in this book, or the use of foreign direct investment. The crucial requirement for the boundaryless business is, of course, the availability of computers for all enabling the use of an intranet for internal communications and the Internet for external – both with clients and for staff who telework from home.

In the end whether a business organisational structure is mechanistic or organic depends on a number of main factors – the strategy the business adopts; its size; its technology; and the environment in which it operates.

■ 6.6 Managing the European business

Deciding the strategy that a company will pursue to achieve its long-term goals or objectives is the responsibility of the board (of directors) of the company. They in turn delegate to the business's managers authority for achieving these objectives through their day-to-day or operational management. The setting of strategic objectives is discussed in detail in Chapter 8.

Many definitions of managers have been produced but perhaps the most famous is Mintzberg's which encompasses a range of tasks which, put together, provide an integrated whole. Broken down into their constituent parts they include interpersonal roles such as duties of a ceremonial nature, as leader in motivating the workforce and liaising with those outside his/her direct area of responsibility; as an information resource by monitoring information, sharing and distributing it to subordinates and to more senior managers; and undertaking decision-making as entrepreneur (that is, being proactive as an initiator of change), as a handler of disturbances and as an allocator of resources (Mintzberg, 1989).

This is best described by the 'political coalition model' of business organisations which was developed partly in response to the open-systems model discussed in section 6.2. The political coalition model argues that although an organisation may be divided into sub-groups, they may pursue their own agenda to further their own ends rather than those of the organisation as a whole. The manager's job therefore becomes, in part, one of seeking to ensure that departments and individuals all pull in the same direction, while the organisation needs to be designed in such a way as to ensure that this can happen. How an organisation has developed over time may well determine the nature of sub-groups within an organisation and hence conflicting agenda, as also might technological developments.

A manager needs therefore to be able to coordinate the use of the resources available to him/her in such a way as to utilise them most effectively, and to monitor whether performance is as intended. How s/he does this will depend on many factors including particularly the country's culture.

■ Employee-related versus job-centred styles of management

Lane (1989), whose work informs this section, distinguishes between leadership styles which are employee-related as opposed to job-centred. With the former style managers are much more concerned with the needs of their employees, considering their relationships with them, listening to their ideas and being good at rewarding good performance. With a job-centred management style much more stress is placed on the tasks being undertaken. Planning ahead is much more important with emphasis on deadlines. Employees are encouraged to achieve objectives and encouraged to get the work done. In reality some mixture of the two is also possible.

□ 1 The UK and Germany

Lane reports that research by Budde, Child, Francis and Kieser (1982), examining UK and German managers in the late 1970s, found that UK managers placed more emphasis on the well-being and personal development of their staff (employee-related), whereas German managers sought more to use procedures to minimise costs and wastage (job-centred). British managers tended to be concerned with maximising their own benefits (salary, promotion and so on) whereas German managers derived most satisfaction from solving problems arising in production. This was mainly because British managers tend to move from company to company for promotion whereas Germans are promoted within the same company.

Also German managerial authority rests on their technical expertise whereas for British managers it rests more on their authority as managers. This is because to a great extent engineering and technical apprenticeships have always been important in Germany, and indeed in France; in contrast, in the UK, accountants have tended to be senior managers and so the engineering culture does not have the same hold. Indeed most British children actively seek to avoid science-based subjects at school and engineering at university. The French and German emphasis on engineering is also because in both countries there are close links between industry and the banks, so managers are not so distracted by the need to obtain short-term finance. In the UK, in contrast, obtaining external funding is a major concern.

One thing that should be noted is that the survey of the UK and Germany which Lane quotes is very old. Certainly management styles have changed in the 1980s and 1990s and it is probable that British styles have now moved much more to a job-centred style. However, with the development of human resource management in the 1990s, the pendulum may now be swinging back towards employee-related management styles for all three countries.

□ 2 France

In France, Lane argues, the managerial style tends to make managers aloof and separate from the workforce. Its style also tends to be technology rather than production-oriented; that is, the French are excellent designers and innovators but weak on cost control. The large number of French industries which have been heavily dependent on state subsidies might be indicative of this.

■ Democratic versus autocratic styles of management

The other distinction made is between democratic and autocratic styles of management. The former encourages staff participation and a relationship of trust with employees. The latter is one where there is a lack of trust of employees, a paternalistic style and strong direction and control.

☐ 1 France

Lane argues that the French management style does tend to be autocratic and strongly centrally-controlled at all levels of the company; so workers are closely supervised and there is a wide social separation between management and workers, making the latter highly politicised. This also applies to other EU Mediterranean countries such as Greece, Italy, Portugal and Spain.

☐ 2 Germany

In the case of German managers up to the early 1980s, the belief that they are totally autocratic is not true since there were a number of management styles. However, it is more highly centralised than the UK, due to the fact that many German firms have grown organically rather than by takeover and merger. Increasingly, however, the trend in Germany is to participative management.

☐ 3 The UK

Here the management style sees subordinate involvement at all levels, including top management delegating strategy decisions such as investment to middle management. Also the workforce were widely consulted until the early 1980s whenever a change affected them. This is reinforced by Hofstede (1991) who argues that Northern European countries such as Germany, the Netherlands, Ireland, Scandinavia and the UK are less autocratic managerially, with power being more widely diffused across a flatter bureaucratic hierarchy than the Mediterranean nations.

This author would argue that with the trade union reforms of the 1980s under the Thatcher governments, however, this consultation disappeared to some extent from the mid-1980s and the present UK management style is more supervisory of the workforce.

■ 6.7 Human resource management: a European dimension

The most important of the resources or factors of production to which a European business has access is the human resource – the men and women who work for it. They are important not only in terms of their cost to the business but also because, by their actions, they will directly determine whether the business succeeds or fails. In spite of the trend to increasingly automated production, with capital replacing labour, those who still work for European businesses do have a direct impact. This in turn has been reflected in recent years by the development of personnel management into that of human resource management (HRM), particularly in the US and UK and, to a lesser extent, in continental Europe. The precise definition of HRM varies from author to author but may be said to include the role of labour as a special resource for a business, including its flow through the business from entry to exit; motivating, developing and retaining the human resource; and monitoring the performance of the human resource, the use of reward systems and so on.

The increased emphasis on HRM is due to a number of reasons. Firstly there have been changes in product markets in the 1980s which have impacted on management and business organisations, particularly emphasising the importance of the human resource – product design, and distinctive and imaginative product marketing are two examples. Secondly there has been a devolution of responsibility for the management of the human resource from a central function to senior line managers. This has meant that the latter have became much more involved with staff recruitment, development and training and promoting ownership among staff, that is the concept that by their labour staff are part-owners of the entire production process. This concept seeks to promote flexibility of working rather than a divisive worker versus management scenario, with close clock-watching. Effective communication within the organisation at each level (horizontal) and between levels (vertical) is crucial to this.

Closely linked to this is the idea of workforce empowerment, that is, that if within the overall constraints of the business workers are given some opportunity to influence their own working lives rather than having everything dictated centrally, they will be more self-fulfilled and productive and this should feed through to improved product quality. Additionally, there is a perceived need to enable HRM to play a key part in the formulation of business strategy (known as strategic HRM) since labour is such an important resource, rather than denying it any significant input as previously. As such it is a total contrast to Taylorism. As well as assisting in the formulation of strategic objectives, HRM plays an important role in terms of the organisational development of the business. This is important for our discussions in Chapter 8 of the impact of change on European business, since the human resource will be particularly affected. In particular the impact of delayering, that is the removal of levels of management which was examined above, is a direct consequence of the changing environment within which businesses operate, especially the competitive challenge from low labour-cost countries such as those of the Pacific Rim.

A number of tensions have developed in terms of this movement to HRM:

1. On the one hand European businesses are seeking to promote staff-ownership of the production process and more importantly the strategic objectives and the culture of the organisation. On the other hand, however, large-scale delayering and short-term temporary contracts are creating conditions where there is less likelihood of staff loyalty. However, this reinforces the importance of line managers having HRM competencies at a time when organisational structures (a movement towards leaner flatter organisational structures) and cultures have been changing. Unfortunately many see HRM in the context of assisting in this delayering rather than the positive benefits it can also bring to a business.

2. In some countries, such as Germany, HRM is perceived to be quite different from that in other countries such as the UK. In its old guise of personnel management it focuses

much more on the application of industrial relations and worker representation, with the emphasis on legal terms and procedures. Additionally, much of HRM theory, such as leadership, is based on American literature and, as discussed elsewhere, cultural differences within Europe mean that this may not be suitable to all countries at all times.

3. The role of the state and of trade unions means that European business often has a more paternalistic and corporatist approach to the organisation and hence HRM than the US. This means that European businesses thus have less freedom of operation than the US where much more emphasis is placed on the role of the individual business and on goal achievement. Additionally, in the US there is much greater opposition to unions. In contrast, at the board level of formulating strategy human resources play an important role in Sweden, France and Spain, but only to a limited extent in Germany and Italy. This latter may be because of the existing level of worker participation at boardroom level in Germany.

4. Developing a business culture where HRM is integrated into strategic formulation of objectives and taken on a par with economic and management inputs can take time to be accepted and then implemented. This is particularly a problem where the business is operating in several different EU countries each with their own approach and culture.

5. Line managers may well lack the HRM skills necessary to cope with these changing structures and cultures, and in particular to ensure that the right people are employed in the right jobs as and when needed. Yet increasingly in future, with the challenge of further change, it is precisely these skills which are needed.

6. With the increasing integration of the single market more people are now obliged to work on contract in a country other than their home. Research by the Economist Intelligence Unit in 1994 found that many businesses lack the background to put together staff remuneration packages, or to develop cross-border teamwork, or to cope with the jumbled situation which currently is EU pensions; there is no reason to expect this to have changed substantially at the end of the decade. Additionally, where joint ventures have been established the cultural differences between different races and the expectations each has of the other, as well as the human resource implications have contributed to higher than expected failure rates, with 67 per cent running into serious trouble within two years (Bleeke and Ernst, 1991, quoted in Lichtenberger and Naullau, 1994).

In conclusion human resource management has been recognised as an important development in the operations of European business. It may become increasingly important in future as the pace of change quickens affecting European business structures, their ability to respond to international challenges from the US and the Pacific Rim, and the changing nature of their own labour forces. As the EIU report argues, the vital question is whether human resource directors and managers are able and willing to respond. If they don't the consequences for European businesses could be serious.

■ 6.8 Case study: acquiring a new business – the battle for acquisition of Rolls-Royce Motor Cars

In late 1997 Rolls-Royce Motor Cars (hereafter RRMC), the luxury and last independent car producer of significance in the UK, was offered for sale by its owner Vickers, the engineering conglomerate. In May 1998 Vickers' Board of Directors agreed to sell RRMC to Germany's BMW (Bayerische Motoren Werke AG) for £340m subject to the approval of the AGM of shareholders in June 1998, in spite of rival bidder Volkswagen (VW) arguing that it was willing to offer £400m–£500m.

■ BMW

BMW is a stock market quoted company with a very distinctive corporate culture, over forty per cent of its shares being held by the Quandt family who are very secretive and conservative. As such, often BMW has not responded to pressures exerted by the market or market analysts preferring rather to pursue its own conservative strategy. Its most important car is the 3 Series which accounts for about sixty per cent of its total sales; however this had been losing market share which made the need to diversify from over-dependence on a narrow product range all the more important.

BMW had bought Rover cars from British Aerospace for £850m in 1994 and, in spite of heavy expenditure subsequently, continued losing money on its acquisition – in 1997 to the extent of £185m, while in mid 1998 it announced major redundancies, partly through the strength of Sterling hitting overseas sales. It also sought £100m of government aid to help finance investment at its Birmingham plant. Because of this it was questioned why BMW would want to acquire another British car company and indeed how effectively BMW might manage a range of products from the Mini Cooper at the bottom of the ladder, through the Rover range, to its existing 3, 5 and 7 series BMWs, to the top-of-the-range Bentley and Rolls-Royce. A number of reasons could be identified why BMW wanted RRMC, however.

Firstly, BMW's chairman, Bernd Pischetsrieder, owns a 66-year-old Phantom II and loves Rolls-Royce cars. Secondly, BMW perceived itself as the ideal owner for RRMC since the two companies had closely collaborated in production with the British company using a BMW V-12 engine in the £125 000 Silver Seraph, its first new model in 30 years. Also Pischetsrieder promised to treble Rolls-Royce production from 1900 to over 6000 cars p.a. and add two completely new model ranges, increasing the number of employees by 50 per cent. At least one of the new models was to be a Bentley (the other marque of RRMC) positioned at the lower end of the luxury car price range to enable BMW to compete more effectively against the Mercedes S class, Toyota's Lexus, VW's Audi 80 and Ford's revitalised Jaguar – although doubts were expressed as to how many super-luxury cars the top end of the market could take, with a top figure of 2660 p.a. being floated. BMW had been losing sales, especially in the US, to these competitors.

Were BMW successful in its bid, it was argued, it would gain a top of the range super-luxury car and, very importantly, a world renowned name. Having said that some analysts believed that BMW does best when it sticks closest to the markets it knows – mass production rather than luxury sales – and its traditional strength is the 3-series. However, the counter-argument was that BMW had learned much from its acquisition of Rover, lessons which it could apply to RRMC. The benefits outlined here might be termed the carrot of BMW's strategy. The stick was that if the takeover failed BMW said it would no longer supply RRMC with engines and instead would build its own super luxury car, probably based on the BMW 7-series; this would pose serious problems for RRMC.

■ Rolls-Royce

From RRMC's viewpoint production could clearly be increased yet it had been limited in its ability to expand by a lack of funds from its parent, Vickers. The Silver Seraph cost £200m to develop and had to be funded from RRMC's very limited annual output; in fact the company was not making money. If BMW bought RRMC then analysts forecast that it would need to spend at least an extra £1 billion to modernise the production facilities. This may have seemed a lot but Ford had paid £1.2bn for Jaguar and then spent another £3bn modernising production facilities. In general, the belief was that Ford had paid over the odds for Jaguar so the price for RRMC seemed reasonable even if another £1bn had to be spent subsequently.

Had BMW succeeded in its purchase RRMC would also have benefitted by the fact that it could have secured cheaper components due to BMW's ability to secure economies of bulk purchase. Additionally the German firm had substantial engineering expertise – this and its successful international network of dealers would also have helped the marketing of RRMC. Many of these arguments also applied were VW to be successful in its bid.

■ The competitors

In the German car-producing market there is considerable rivalry between the Big 3, Mercedes-Benz, Volkswagen and BMW. Nonetheless Mercedes-Benz declared that it was not interested in acquiring BMW and would concentrate on launching its own top of the range Maybach (a previously famous marque in Germany) to compete with RRMC. Additionally there was an announced merger of Daimler-Benz with American car producer Chrysler, the former generally perceived to be the dominant partner.

Volkswagen, in contrast, did table a bid of £430m for RRMC although it was initially prevented from doing so by a period of exclusivity in negotiations between BMW and Vickers. It also promised to invest a further £300m to expand output and develop new models. VW had talked of resurrecting another deceased marque – the Horsch – to challenge Mercedes-Benz and enter the top end of the super-luxury market. However, as with BMW, VW perceived that acquiring RRMC would give it immediate access to the super-luxury end of the market and the Rolls-Royce and Bentley names. The only worry from VW's viewpoint was that the name Rolls-Royce was not owned by Vickers but by Rolls-Royce plc, the aero-engine company. This had an aircraft engine joint venture with BMW in

Germany which after years of investment was starting to make profits; consequently it backed the BMW bid.

As well as its strategy of bypassing the Board of Directors and appealing directly to the AGM regarding its offer for RRMC, VW also needed a strategy to outflank BMW's threat no longer to supply its engines to RRMC if it failed to acquire the company. It therefore announced that it would bid for Cosworth engines (which had supplied engines for the Ford Cosworth 4x4 in the late 1980s, for example), which was also owned by Vickers. This would address the concerns of many British traditionalists about additional production shifting to Germany. In buying Cosworth and RRMC, VW would be bringing production back to the UK. As a further weapon in its strategy of appealing to Vickers shareholders it said it would increase production of RRMC cars fivefold to 10 000 p.a.

Other possible purchasers, American car producers Chrysler and General Motors, expressed no interest in RRMC because of their belief that Ford had been stung over the price it paid for Jaguar.

■ Conclusions

In the end (or almost so!) it was VW who acquired the ownership of RRMC with its £430m bid (worth £470m after a rise in Rolls-Royce's assets in 1998) as a result of a 97 per cent vote in favour at the AGM. Apart from the higher price compared with BMW's offer, its agreement with Vickers to buy specialist high-performance engine makers Cosworth for £117m to replace BMW's supply of engines to RRMC sealed the deal (VW then sold Cosworth Racing, the motor sport division of Cosworth to the Ford motor company, enabling Ford to continue its 30 year relationship with Cosworth which had seen engines developed for Formula 1 and US Indycar racing).

BMW refused to enter into a bidding war, perhaps confirming its reputation as secretive and conservative, while a third group, Crewe Motors, consisting of Rolls and Bentley owners, also failed in their bid in spite of offering £490m. The latter were handicapped by their inability to demonstrate the external funding guarantees necessary to undertake new investment and raise production levels. After the AGM BMW announced that it would cancel its contract to supply engines, seats, electronics and safety equipment for both the Rolls-Royce Seraph and Bentley Arnage models from July 1999 and would seek to develop its own rival to RRMC.

■ The final twist

In the end the triumph of VW over BMW was a pyrrhic victory. Rolls-Royce plc, the aero-engine company, which owned the Rolls-Royce name, sold it to BMW, their preferred owner of the entire company. This left VW with the Bentley marque and the ability to manufacture Rolls-Royce cars until 2003; after that BMW will be the sole manufacturer of Rolls-Royce cars. BMW will now still provide its V12 engines and components for the Rolls-Royce Silver Seraph and the

Bentley Arnage; subsequently it will build a new factory to manufacture Rolls-Royce cars in the UK.

Incidentally, having acquired Rolls-Royce, VW then purchased Italian luxury car producer Lamborghini for $111m. As the company only has a workforce of 310 and produced a mere 216 cars in 1997 it was purchased, as with Rolls-Royce (or so VW thought) mainly for its badge, to boost the corporate image of VW.

■ Review questions

1. Discuss why there is a need for such a variety of European business organisations in the EU, identifying the advantages and disadvantages of what you regard as the three most important.
2. Discuss the advantages and disadvantages of:

   (a) a formalised business organisational structure such as by function or product;
   (b) an organic business structure such as the team-structure model or the virtual organisation.

3. Write a report recommending that your company employ a human resources manager to implement a human resources policy.
4. Discuss the problems and benefits which Airbus might encounter when it becomes a company rather than a consortium.
5. Discuss the advantages and disadvantages to VW and RRMC of the acquisition of the latter by the former. What impact could VW's acquisition have on (1) the organisational structure (2) the management philosophy of RRMC?

■ Bibliography

Beaumont, P. B., *Human Resource Management – Key Concepts and Skills* (London: Sage, 1993).

Bessant, J. R. and Grant, M., *Management and Manufacturing Innovation in the United Kingdom and West Germany* (Aldershot: Gower, 1985).

Bowman, C., *Management in Practice*, revised edn (Oxford: Butterworth-Heinemann, 1987).

Brewster, C., 'European HRM: Reflection of or Challenge to the American Concept', in Kirkbridge, P. S. (ed.), *Human Resource Management: Perspectives for the 1990s* (London: Routledge, 1994).

Budde, A., Child, J., Francis, A. and Kieser, A., 'Corporate Goals, Managerial Objectives and Organisational Structures in British and West German Companies', *Organisational Studies*, vol. 3(1), pp. 1–32, 1982.

Butler, R., *Designing Organisations – A Decision-Making Perspective* (London: Routledge, 1991).

Cole, G. A., *Management Theory and Practice*, 3rd edn (London: DP Publications, 1990).

Farnham, D. and Pimlott, J., *Understanding Industrial Relations*, 5th edn (London: Cassell, 1995).

Gallagher, M., Austin, S. and Caffyn, S., *Continuous Improvement in Action – Strategies for Successful Implementation and Operation* (London: Kogan Page, 1997).

Hickson, D. J. (ed.), *Exploring Management Across the World* (Harmondsworth: Penguin Books, 1997).

Hofstede, G., *Cultures and Organisations* (Maidenhead: McGraw-Hill, 1991).

Kay, J., *Foundations of Corporate Success* (Oxford: Oxford University Press, 1993).

Lane, C., *Management and Labour in Europe* (Cheltenham: Edward Elgar, 1989).

Leavett, H. J., Dill, W. R. and Eyring, H. B., *The Organisational World: A Systematic View of Managers and Management* (London: Harcourt Brace Jovanovich, 1973).

Lester, T., *Managing People in Europe: Facing the Human Resource Challenge of Leaner Companies* (London: The Economist Intelligence Unit, 1994).

Lichtenberger, B. and Naulleau, G., 'Cultural Conflicts and Synergies in the Management of French–German Joint Ventures', in Kirkbridge, P. S. (ed.), *Human Resource Management: Perspectives for the 1990s* (London: Routledge, 1994).

Lock, D. (ed.), *Handbook of Management*, 3rd edn (Aldershot: Gower, 1993).

Lucey, T., *Business Administration* (Mendelsham: DP Publications, 1994).

Mintzberg, H., *Mintzberg on Management: Inside our Strange World of Organisations* (New York: The Free Press, 1989).

Peters, T., *Thriving on Chaos* (Basingstoke: Macmillan, 1988).

Preston, J. (ed.), *Cases in European Business* (London: Pitman, 1992).

Randlesome, C., Brierly, W., Bruton, K., Gordon, C. and King, P., *Business Cultures in Europe* (Oxford: Butterworth Heinemann, 1993).

Robbins, S. P., *Organisational Behavior*, 8th edn (New Jersey: Prentice Hall, 1998).

Also:

The Economic Review
The European
The Financial Times
The Independent
The Telegraph
The Times

CHAPTER 7

Financing European business

■ 7.1 Introduction

Having considered in the previous chapter the organisational structure of European businesses, this chapter considers the financial side of their operations. Profit maximising and other theories are reviewed. The cash flow and asset values of the European business are examined, as are the main sources of finance. The role of transfer pricing in multinational organisations is also analysed. The chapter concludes by looking in detail at attempts to complete the internal market in financial services, with case studies examining the pressures for change faced by financial services providers, the French bank Crédit Lyonnais and the problems the EU faces in developing new pensions schemes to cope with an aging population.

■ 7.2 Profit maximisation and other theories of the firm

So far the assumption has been made that businesses seek to maximise profits. In fact a wide range of different theories exist as to the motives of operating a business. These can be considered under a number of different headings:

■ Sales revenue maximisation

In 1959 the economist William J. Baumol developed a model which identified sales revenue maximisation rather than profit maximisation as an explanation of a firm's behaviour. His argument was that managers' success was judged on the level of their firm's sales; this in turn directly affected their salaries, bonuses and non-monetary rewards, for example car, size of office and so on. So long as the firm can achieve sufficient profits to keep shareholders happy, its managers will spend more on advertising to boost sales than if the business's main objective was profit maximising. In other words the managers are profit satisficers.

■ Management discretion

Economist Oliver Williamson developed a theory of management discretion in 1963. Like Baumol's theory this focused on the fact that, in most organisations, there is a separation of ownership (shareholders) and control (managers). Again, so long as managers can achieve satisfactory profits for shareholders they will pursue policies at their discretion to maximise their own utility. This will particularly involve increasing their salary and bonuses, job security and status and prestige; it has been seen in the UK in the 1980s and 1990s with the major increases in salaries that senior managers have awarded themselves. It has also occurred in the UK when building societies have opted to become banks. In recent years senior managers have increasingly been given share options as part of an overall financial package to provide them with incentives to maximise profit and to reduce this gap between owners and managers. Management buy-outs (MBOs) have had a similar effect.

■ Growth maximisation

Maximising growth may be another motive either by increasing existing market share or diversifying into new markets, either geographical or in terms of product, or by mergers or takeovers. Case studies developed elsewhere in this text will enable these philosophies to be explored more fully as part of the analysis of business strategy.

■ Public sector organisations

For public sector organisations such an assumption cannot be made. For organisations such as the partially privatised Gazprom, based in Russia, the aim may be partly to provide employment and hence reduce government expenditure on unemployment benefits. For European governments seeking to disentangle themselves from public ownership by pursuing a policy of privatisation, the main objective may be merely to minimise losses while enabling the organisation to survive until the business can be sold to the private sector. The use of 'creative' accounting to disguise real losses may also be employed. The French government's past rescue packages for computer manufacturer Bull and Air France are two such examples.

■ Profit maximisation

As a working hypothesis, however, the assumption will be that private-sector organisations (that is, not owned by the national or regional government of the state where the business is resident) do seek to maximise profits. It should be noted at this point that a business's undistributed profits are a major source of finance for its capital expenditure.

■ 7.3 Cash flow and asset values: the need for liquidity

■ Working capital

European businesses often have to buy components and raw materials, set up production runs and so on in anticipation that they will eventually receive payment. Yet suppliers will want their payment sooner rather than wait until a business eventually sells its goods. A business therefore needs a constant flow of money to be able to make payments. This is known as working capital and is the money needed to cover the business's short-term expenses. These are directly related to the volume of goods sold while waiting for the business's revenue to come in from selling these goods. It is of major importance in that it determines an organisation's liquidity, that is its ability to meet its daily payments in running the business – in effect a lubricant for the business.

The business's working capital or cash flow may be defined as its current assets (temporary assets such as goods for sale which management will convert into cash or consume, normally within a year) less its current liabilities (the company's debts or obligations falling due to its creditors within one year). It will be affected by a number of factors, including:

1. how large the business is;
2. how fast revenues follow expenses;
3. the extent to which revenues vary from month to month while expenses remain more steady;
4. the extent to which it makes cash payments to creditors or receives payments from its debtors;
5. the extent to which the business will be growing, staying steady or contracting;
6. the extent to which it makes cash purchases of working stocks, for example raw materials, or receives cash from sales of stocks, for example of work in progress or semi-manufactured goods;
7. changes in its long-term loans – banks and other institutions are normally willing to provide working capital in return for the expectation of a share of future profits;
8. whether it can issue new shares;
9. whether it is buying new fixed assets (or disinvesting by selling them);
10. the extent to which it has to make cash payments, for example to the tax authority, or, less likely, receives a refund from them.

If a European business is unable to meet its regular payments such as interest on loans or to trade creditors then this will affect it seriously. Banks may seek to call in loans, especially in the Anglo-Saxon economies; creditors will refuse to supply raw materials or other components and will seek payment for outstanding debts even more urgently. In the last resort if the business is unable to meet the demands of claimants it will be forced to stop trading. This can apply to large organisations as much as to small traders. One way to protect cash flow is for a business to monitor its stock levels carefully and regularly to avoid having too much cash tied up in unprofitable current assets. In Chapter 9 the just-in-time (JIT) stock control system is discussed as an alternative to the conventional model of holding, say, one month's or two month's supplies.

Similarly, the business needs to watch carefully its debtor position. The European Commission has been investigating the deliberate delaying of outstanding debts by firms to ease their own cash flows (one aspect of overtrading). This is understandable, particularly in recession where cash flow is less, but it merely passes the problems down the line. In the end the component and raw material suppliers and the firms who are smallest and weakest are those first driven to bankruptcy by non-paying firms. The large businesses may then survive at the expense of the smallest.

In the same way businesses need to carefully monitor their position regarding credit. Although they may be tempted to take all the credit they are offered, it still has to be paid back albeit at a later date, which can cause cash-flow problems subsequently. Credit will also incur interest payments and a firm can overstretch itself if not careful.

It is essential, therefore, that businesses regularly forecast their cash flows to ensure that incomings match outgoings in the short to medium term and that any short-term variances can be covered. Those forecasts must then be monitored and compared with practice to give real values. New businesses are particularly vulnerable to cash-flow problems, and the high European failure rate, particularly in time of recession, is evidence of this. However, even well-established and government-funded firms such as Air France, Bull Computers, Crédit Lyonnais, and most European state airlines are evidence of how large well-established firms can also suffer the same problems.

▪ Fixed capital

It should be noted that fixed capital is, in many ways, as important to a business as working capital since it constitutes the funds to purchase fixed assets such as machinery, new buildings, computers and so on which will yield a flow of services to the business over a number of years. Raising such money can be difficult and is discussed fully below. Businesses use investment appraisal techniques such as net present value (NPV) and internal rate of return (IRR) to assess the worth of new investment projects. Although it is not appropriate to consider these now, the reader should note that these techniques exist and are used to judge the financial merits of purchasing a fixed asset in terms of whether it should yield a profit over its life. Long-term capital repayments must be made independently of the volume of business activity.

▪ Depreciation

Fixed capital depreciates over time; that is, its physical usefulness and value diminish. As a result a percentage of the cost of assets will be charged as an expense every year – say 20 per cent over each of five years. This is to anticipate that in five years' time – in our example – the asset will need to be replaced.

With the rapid changes in technology this means that, in most cases, the asset will be replaced by another which will be more technologically advanced and, probably, more expensive – this applies especially to computers. As a result the business may well have to increase its depreciation provision during the life of the asset; for example this book was written using a (at the time of purchase) top specification 166 MHz computer which the author bought in October 1996 – by March 1998 firms had stopped making machines this slow.

CASE STUDY   Fokker – Dutch regional plane manufacturer

77-year-old Dutch company Fokker was wound up in 1997 when German industrial giant Daimler-Benz, who had acquired a 51 per cent share of the company in 1993, refused to provide further working capital because it could see no end to the company's losses, even though Fokker had shed 3900 staff between 1994–97. These losses were aggravated by Fokker's struggle for market-share with British Aerospace's Avro subsidiary. The Dutch government, a minority shareholder, also refused to contribute the 3bn guilder (£1.2bn) Daimler-Benz had demanded to help the regional plane manufacturer which had debts of $1.8bn, although it did offer short-term finance of 255m guilders.

Once Daimler-Benz refused to provide further credit then, understandably, component suppliers also refused to supply further parts. The first was Shorts of Belfast which stopped delivering wings. This in turn brought an end to rescue proposals by South Korean conglomerate Samsung Aerospace.

The main long-term reason why Fokker closed was its high cost base due to its failure to introduce capital intensive production methods to replace some of the 7900 high-cost Dutch workers it employed. It was also handicapped by the rising value of the deutsche-mark, and hence the guilder which is closely tied to it, against the dollar in which civil aircraft are priced, by continuing large financial risks, and continuous industrial over-capacity. However, the crucial final straw was the lack of working capital – a simple cash-flow problem.

■ 7.4 Sources of finance

This section looks in more detail at how European businesses raise finance. Funds may be provided either through internal or external sources. Internal funds are accumulated by undistributed profits, that is retained by the company rather than distributed to shareholders, and as noted above they are a major source for its investment expenditure. Obviously the amount retained varies depending on the success of the business during the previous year. In the recession of the early 1990s, for example, retained profits fell as businesses sought to cover costs, reduce debt and pay dividends to shareholders; by the mid-1990s, as the business cycle entered its upswing, they recovered.

External sources of finance are those where the business obtains funds from elsewhere, including European capital markets which are also explored here. The main types of finance are discussed below.

■ Short-term

☐ 1 Bank borrowing

This is in the form of loans and overdrafts. Overdraft facilities are short-term, in theory repayable on demand although, in reality, usually renewable. The bank will consider, *inter alia*, the credit rating of the business (as determined by rating agencies) or the strength of its balance sheet. The business has to offer security, for example in the form of a fixed charge on the business's assets, and, of course, the interest rate is variable. The introduction of the single currency is intended to converge interest rates downwards. A variable rate is attractive when interest rates are falling but when they are rising it can put a heavy cost burden on a business. The advantage of the overdraft to the business is that it evens out variations in working capital as discussed above.

☐ 2 Trade credit

This was discussed above and is the time period allowed by a supplier, say of raw materials, to the manufacturer before payment has to be made. Alternatively it may be that the manufacturer gives trade credit to his customer. Typically 30 days is the most common time-span although this may increase when the economy is in recession. This may be because the seller feels that a longer credit period is necessary to attract custom, or simply the customer delays payment longer than the agreed period to ease his/her cash-flow position. However, excess use of trade credit is not a desirable thing.

☐ 3 Factoring

A factoring company (or factor for short) buys a business's debts and makes an immediate payment to it, usually for 80 per cent of their outstanding value. These debts must be approved by the factor, that is it wants to be reasonably certain that it will be able to recover payment from the debtors in due course. Examination of the business's debt portfolio will therefore be the key to the factor giving support. Factors usually also offer a service of all aspects of sales accounting such as book keeping and credit control processes if the business wishes these as well. A factor may well also offer a guaranteed full payment on approved sales by the business which will be honoured even if the ultimate customer is subsequently unable to pay.

Usually factoring is only offered to businesses regularly selling to a wide range of customers; the total accrued sales will need to exceed £250 000. The factor usually charges between 1–3 per cent of sales value which makes this quite an expensive process, but it does free up cash for the business with liquidity problems. It may also enable the business to obtain support when secured bank lending (that is against direct security – provided by the business itself, or collateral security – provided by another party on behalf of the business) is as high as the lending bank wishes it to be.

Invoice discounting is a variation of factoring when one firm sells goods to another, submitting an invoice for payment. The factor will buy the invoice and make full payment, less its charges, to the vendor at once. It will subsequently collect from the debtor in due course.

CASE STUDY   The Problems of Late Payment

For the UK, a Dunn and Bradstreet survey of 86 000 businesses in late 1997 found that only 23 per cent of small businesses pay on time compared with the even worse position of 13.8 per cent for medium-sized companies and 9.7 per cent for large businesses. Another survey, by the Forum for Private Business, found that at any given time £20bn is owed to the business community. An earlier survey by National Opinion Polls for *Business Pages* had reinforced this finding that 70 per cent of small businesses identified late payment as a serious problem.

The UK government has set out plans to change the culture of late payments, which causes cashflow problems for companies, and to give small companies a statutory right to claim interest payments from those businesses that do not pay on time at base rate plus 8 per cent. The legislation was implemented in July 1998. However, small businesses expressed concern over this proposal arguing that businesses on whom they levied interest might simply take their custom elsewhere.

The EU is also addressing this issue. A directive put forward by the Commission in April 1998 proposed that companies would be able to claim compensation for late payment, including interest on the outstanding debt, and this would apply to transactions within the private sector and between companies and the public sector. Also, simplified debt-recovery procedures will be introduced for debts up to ECU 20 000, with a 60-day high-speed system to recover unchallenged debts. In Europe, 25 per cent of insolvencies are caused by late payments, especially SMEs.

◼ Medium-term

This period may cover as long as three to five years, or it may be as short as three months if trade credit is being considered. There are a number of different ways in which medium-term finance might be obtained:

☐ 1 Bank loans

These are normally used to finance the purchase of a fixed asset and the business will offer security either in the form of a charge on the asset being acquired or, more generally, on all the company's assets. Although fixed rates of interest may be employed, more typically the cost will be 3–5 per cent over base rate (or equivalent rate for other EU countries), the exact amount depending on the duration of the loan, the level of risk, the amount of the loan and the track record and reputation of the borrower. In Germany, fixed interest loans are more common than in the UK, partly helped by German exchange rate stability and the reduced risk of inflation.

Unsecured lending, that is with no security provided by the borrower, is more likely to be granted only to larger corporate businesses.

☐ 2 Leasing

This again frees up a business's resources by enabling it to obtain plant, heavy machinery, mainframe computers and so on without having to find the funds up front. Instead it contacts a leasing company, usually associated with a bank, and itemises precisely what it needs. The leasing company undertakes the purchase and then leases the equipment to the business in return for regular payments over a period of 3–5 years, with the option of extending the lease subsequently if the lessee (the business) wishes to. Leasing may also extend to long-term finance. Leasing can be a very effective way of financing equipment use which has a fast rate of depreciation because of rapid obsolescence, for example computer-related equipment.

☐ 3 Hire purchase

Another alternative is for a business to purchase capital equipment through hire purchase. As with leasing it avoids the need to find all the funds up front so that capital costs can be spread over a period of time. The main difference from leasing is that at the end of the period the business will own the asset, assuming that all payments have been kept up. The final choice between the two will be cost-related.

☐ 4 Using the European capital markets

In financial services terms capital consists of funds loaned for medium and long time periods, largely used by manufacturing and commercial businesses to finance expenditure on fixed investment such as factories, office premises and plant, diversification into new markets or products, or acquisition of competitor businesses. Providers of these funds have traditionally been banks, insurance companies and stock markets, with most emphasis on banks for Continental Europe and stock markets for the UK. A capital market deals with both new capital and also claims on existing capital, for example existing shares and debentures. Highly-developed capital markets are an inevitable consequence of mature market economies; indeed in recent years the focus has shifted from financial institutions such as banks to the money and capital markets as the prime sources of funds.

Banks, insurance companies and pension funds fulfil the functions of financial intermediaries. They accept deposits and savings and undertake risk transformation (bearing the risks of any loss through the investment), maturity transformation (accepting short-term deposits yet lending long-term) and aggregation (grouping large numbers of small deposits into fewer large amounts for lending) to provide the capital market with the surplus funds placed with them by both individuals and businesses. The capital market then channels these loanable funds or capital to where they are most needed, as determined by the return earned on that capital.

Liberalising and attempting to integrate the EU capital markets has afforded two specific benefits. Firstly, users can access a wider range of markets and investments enabling them to diversify their portfolios with the increased opportunities of risk-minimisation and profit-maximisation. The wider the range of investments over which funds are spread the less the risk if any one fails; similarly the greater are the opportunities for profit the more that investments perform above the market average. Secondly, in a free market there is only one price, if no transport costs are assumed. This is realistic for financial services and, although there will be transaction costs, these are not dependent on geographic distance. In the capital market this price is the real rate of interest. To the extent that one interest rate eventually emerges this will enable the capital market to allocate resources with greater efficiency, although the Cecchini Report suggested that these gains will not be large.

Other advantages of a largely unified capital market are greater freedom of movement for capital within the EU (one of the four freedoms of the single market), including greater choice for users; the ability to compete even more effectively with the US and Far East markets for global funds; wider adoption of existing financial services and products to enable financial institutions to compete more vigorously; the incentive for still further development of financial products and services to meet growing market sophistication; and lower costs for users as a consequence of greater competition. However, there is still not agreement between members regarding tax harmonisation, which will prevent total liberalisation of the capital market.

☐ 5 Venture capital

Venture capital has grown in importance in recent years and is particularly linked to the development of small and medium-sized enterprises (SMEs). Investment tends to be to help these develop and is often associated with high-risk industries such as information technology. The venture capital company raises funds from interested investors and offers the borrowing company business advice and so on. The investor will usually look for a significant return on his/her money within say 3–6 years, through the company subsequently being listed on the stock market or someone else buying out his/her stake. The reader is also referred to the Benetton case study in Chapter 8.

CASE STUDY	European and American Attitudes to Venture Capital

In the US, venture capital is a major source of finance for new businesses, particularly in growth areas such as biotechnology, computers and the media. As such, in 1996, US investors provided over $9bn of venture capital which increased, in 1997, to approximately $13bn. This type of capital led to over 7000 new companies being floated in the US between 1992–96, many of them in California's Silicon Valley which attracted over $1bn. Additionally a substantial amount of venture capital goes to existing US firms seeking to expand.

Chapter 1 looked at the importance of cultural differences; nowhere is this more obvious than in the attitudes of US and EU citizens towards venture capital. The cliché of American society as a melting pot of different nationalities who have had to travel from their home countries to the States to become Americans has much truth in it and may well explain why Americans are much more willing than Europeans to take risks by putting their money into venture capital. It has also been argued that Americans take failures as part of the learning experience whereas in Europe failure is something which bears extremely adverse connotations. In France, Germany and Italy owners of companies do not even consider selling them.

In general, therefore, European investors are much more cautious and unwilling to take risks. Although in 1996 in the EU $6.8bn of venture capital was provided, over 60 per cent of this was either investment in the UK or UK investment of funds overseas. As a result in the EU just over 700 new firms were established through venture capital between 1992–96. Yet the economic problems the EU faces in terms of its failure to create sufficient new jobs and to match other countries' high growth rates means that venture capital could play a major role in creating new European businesses. EU funds are being attracted to the stock markets in the wake of large-scale privatisations, mergers and acquisitions to achieve scale economies, and expectations of medium-term low inflation and low interest rates which are attractive to investors. However, these developments, and management buyouts, tend to lead to rationalisation and job losses rather than job creation which is clearly what the EU needs. Also venture capital needs to be long-term whereas Europeans tend to think medium-term at most, with bank lending typically of 3–5 years. It is only in the UK, Scandinavia and the Netherlands that institutional investors such as insurance companies and insurance funds have provided necessary long-term funds (as has the US).

US venture capital is also helped by the fact that there is a much better chance of new US firms making it to the stock market and hence yielding even greater returns for their investors. Venture capital also needs secondary markets to provide investors with exit routes for their capital – in the EU there is only London's Alternative Investment Market (AIM) and Frankfurt's Neumarket. Also the growth of the US high-tech stock market Nasdaq, compared with the European Easdaq, is a good illustration of this – this is discussed in more depth in the case study below. In general, EU stock markets are less developed than those of the US. There is also a much greater linkage between top technological universities and businesses in the US enabling new research and development to be translated into commercial activities.

Most recent EU attempts to promote venture capital have been by providing subsidies, while in Germany the government will at least match any approved private sector venture capital through the vehicle of the TBG (Technologie Beteilingings Gesellschaft). In April 1998 the Commission launched a new initiative to develop a pan-European risk (venture) capital market arguing that underdevelopment and fragmentation into a number of small markets are hindering risk capital. The six-point plan aims to (i) integrate the venture capital markets into one market; (ii) eliminate institutional and regulatory barriers; (iii) improve taxation regulations to further promote venture capital; (iv) promote the development of high-tech SMEs; (v) develop people to be better entrepreneurs; and (vi) reduce cultural barriers to enterprise.

Although this EU initiative addresses many of the issues discussed above there is still clearly much to be done, and even the non-cultural changes will take quite some time to implement.

■ Long-term

This might typically relate to a period between 5 and 10 years. The main choice facing a business in the long run is between debt and equity, that is whether to borrow money or to issue new shares in the company.

□ 1 Leasing

This has already been discussed above.

□ 2 Mortgages

When a business needs long-term finance it may be to acquire land, build new warehousing, a new factory and so on. The money may be advanced by one or more banks (a consortium) or some other institutional investor such as an insurance company or pension fund, against the security of the asset. The business borrowing the money may not dispose of the asset unless the loan has first been repaid. The business makes regular payments and at the end of the period owns the asset. If payments cannot be maintained then the mortgage is foreclosed and the asset sold to recover the purchase price, or as much as possible bearing in mind that physical equipment will depreciate.

□ 3 Debentures

A debenture is, simply, a fixed-interest fixed-term loan secured against all the assets of the company (known as a floating debenture) or against some particular asset (a fixed debenture). There is also a convertible debenture which offers the chance of being converted into ordinary shares at some fixed date and price. The interest on the debenture must be paid whether or not the business makes a profit, and if it cannot be paid the company's assets will have to be sold to raise the funds. The debenture holder has first claim in this case. A debenture deed, issued by the company, will contain such information as how and when capital will be repaid, payment of interest, what security the company will offer and so on.

A variation on debentures is unsecured loans, that is where no security is offered by the borrower against the loan. Since the risk is higher the investors will be seeking a higher return on their money to compensate them.

□ 4 Eurobonds

One form of capital which has grown significantly in importance in recent years is the use by firms, particularly multinational companies, of Eurobonds. These bonds are issued in European capital markets; for example Zurich, and typically do not mature for 10 to 15 years. They are often denominated in a currency differing from that of the country of origin and are sold globally. For example a French firm might float a sterling-denominated Eurobond issue, totalling £300 million, in the Frankfurt market to finance new capital expenditure. The issue might be taken up largely by US investors. The Eurobond market is one example of what is termed the globalisation of banking, which has rendered national banking boundaries less and less meaningful as businesses have demanded more international and less regulated financial markets.

CASE STUDY   Using Eurobonds to Raise Finance

A Swedish multinational public limited company, which manufactures furniture, wishes to use Eurobonds to raise a large (DM 500m) long-term (10 year) loan to finance major expansion of retail outlets in Germany, the Netherlands and the UK. The bonds are placed by an international consortium of Swedish, German, French, Italian and UK banks and other financial institutions. They will be managed by a lead bank. This means that the consortium will find banks and other financial institutions to underwrite the issue (that is guarantee to buy any unsold bonds), and others to take up the Eurobonds and place them with their clients. To facilitate this the take-up or selling banks will issue a prospectus itemising all the details of the deutschemark-denominated Eurobonds – for example terms and conditions; name of the multinational issuing the Eurobonds; purpose of the loan and so on. The Swedish company, to be able to make a Eurobond issue, must be credit-rated by an international agency whose job is to vet all publicly quoted companies.

□ 5 Preference shares

These shares are so named because their holders receive preference over ordinary shareholders when dividends are paid (although coming after debenture and other debt holders). However, unlike ordinary shareholders they usually have no voting rights at the annual general meeting (AGM) of the company. There are a variety of different types of preference shares such as cumulative preference and convertible preference. The interested reader may wish to pursue these further.

□ 6 Equity

A business's equity capital is its ordinary shares. The holder receives dividends after debenture holders and preference shareholders have been satisfied, assuming any money still remains. However, the ordinary shareholder usually has voting rights of one vote per share and, if dividends are not payable for some time, can in theory vote in a new board who will pay dividends.

In reality the board will try if at all possible to pay a dividend since if it does not do so the share price will fall and, if it falls so far that the share price does not truly reflect the value of the assets, the company may be vulnerable to a takeover. Additionally, since many public limited companies' shares are held by institutional investors, these are not likely to want to overthrow the board except in the most extreme circumstances. Boards are often therefore criticised as being self-perpetuating. Perhaps the German model of the two-level board is more appropriate in these circumstances.

■ The UK versus the continental European model of business finance

As discussed elsewhere, the Continental European model has traditionally been one where banks have loaned long-term to businesses due to the close relationship between each. In contrast, in the UK businesses have more traditionally raised funds on the capital markets via equity, for example, for long-term finance. This is because UK banks have always tended to lend to business only short-term.

This is only partly reinforced by a 1984 study by the Deutsche Bundesbank which considered the ratio of debt to equity for investment by UK and German firms (Henderson, 1993). For the UK it found the ratio to be 51:49 per cent (almost half of investment was financed by borrowings and half by share issues); for Germany the ratio was 81:19 per cent (that is, most investment is financed by borrowing). Although the German figure for debt financing is higher than the UK's, the UK's debt-financing figure is higher than expected – helped by the popularity of leasing in the UK in the 1970s. This indicates that UK firms have been relying more on long-term debt than previously supposed.

However, notes Henderson (1993), since the mid-1980s both the UK and Germany have switched more to equities as the source of finance and away from debt, partly encouraged by improved company earnings, generally rising stockmarkets since the early 1980s and especially the late 1990s, and by the improvements in public finances due to the Maastricht convergence criteria.

■ 7.5 Pricing strategies: transfer pricing and the transnational

Multinational corporations are considered elsewhere in this book in terms of their strategic objectives. Here we consider their activities in terms of transfer pricing, drawing particularly on the work of Maxwell (1991). There are several types of transfer pricing which may be distinguished.

CASE STUDY   The Transformation of EU Stockmarkets

Domestic stockmarkets

In Europe domestic stock markets, where equities are bought and sold, and futures and forwards exchanges, where it is possible to hedge against future changes in the value of exchange rates, interest rates, equities and commodities, are coming under attack from several directions simultaneously; these changes are forcing a major restructuring of exchanges across Europe. Firstly, the advent of the single currency will remove exchange rate barriers. Secondly, the development and application of new communication and information technologies have made the development of cross-border trading systems easier. Also consolidation in the global provision of financial services has concentrated custom, while the wave of privatisations across Europe has created an equity holding culture for the previously averse population.

It has been argued that the next logical step in this development is the creation of a pan-European stockmarket. However, until now national exchanges have been reluctant to surrender their sovereignty. Also they are owned by their members so it is difficult to secure one coherent strategy for expansion. In the 1990s, however, a number of stock exchanges have given up their mutual status in favour of being public limited companies, floated on their own exchanges or linked up with other exchanges. These include the Stockholm stock exchange in 1992, which demutualised and subsequently merged with the Swedish futures and derivatives market. The Milan and Amsterdam exchanges have also demutualised, while the Paris-based Société des Bourses Françaises has merged with the French derivatives market Matif and, at the time of writing, is considering floating as a public company.

There have also been cross-border strategic alliances. Germany's futures and options exchange, the Deutsche Terminbörse (DTB) – to be renamed Eurex – has, as noted elsewhere, linked with its Swiss counterpart – the Swiss Options and Financial Futures Exchange – and its French counterpart – Matif – to block the competitive challenge from the London International Financial Futures and Options Exchange (Liffe) and, in practice, has taken substantial custom from Liffe. These markets have also, in many cases, adopted new technology, moving from floor based (known as open outcry) to electronic or screen based trading allowing brokers remote access rather than having to be on the market floor, an example which Liffe is now being forced to follow; also the DTB is cheaper than Liffe.

Most significantly, albeit still a small step, in the moves to a pan-European stock market, however, has been the strategic alliance between the London Stock Exchange (LSE) and its rival Frankfurt's Deutsche Börse (the DTB is its derivatives exchange), with a combined market capitalisation of nearly £2000bn. From 1 January 1999, when the single currency is introduced, investors in each country will be given access to both countries' leading stocks. Subsequently the aim is to create a common electronic trading platform for 300 blue chip (leading companies) stocks. This alliance has been driven particularly by the twin forces of the advent of the euro and globalisation. However, additionally, Frankfurt has developed a higher volume of trading than London aided substantially by its cheaper and faster technology.

This alliance between LSE and Deutsche Börse has been partly encouraged by the strategic alliance between Deutsche Börse and Nasdaq (see below) which is likely to create an electronic market in continental Europe's biggest shares and could, therefore, have serious implications for the LSE, especially if it were to continue in isolation. Indeed Nasdaq has stated that it wants a strategic alliance with any pan-European electronic stock exchange which emerges, with the two systems linked together. A pan-European stock market covering say the top 300 European companies would improve liquidity and benefit share prices as well as introducing greater transparency. Although this arrangement has been attacked by the Paris Bourse, which feels excluded, it is seen as inevitable that other continental European exchanges will also join up creating a pan-European stockmarket with common trading systems (known as a common platform) by 2001–03. Although the LSE is twice as big as Frankfurt in terms of market capitalisation the perception is that Frankfurt will be the dominant partner due to Germany being in Euroland, while Frankfurt is also the home of the European Central Bank.

Nonetheless, barriers to a pan-European market still remain, including different regulatory requirements in each stock exchange, differences as to the amount traders must first deposit as security, differences in settlements (already a matter of dispute between the LSE and Deutsche Börse), and differences in how transparent information is. Also, compared with the US, European markets lack intellectual capital ie the depth of research and analysis which American investment banks have. So currently some sectors, for example, automobile industry or airlines are run on a pan-European basis which is achieving some, but not all, of what is needed. However, the London – Frankfurt alliance, if successful, lays the basis for a future pan-European stockmarket.

Alternative EU Stockmarkets – Easdaq and EuroNM

The pan-European integrated alternative stockmarket Easdaq, which opened in November 1996, is aimed specifically at small high-growth high-tech companies and was established as a rival to Nasdaq, the 25-year-old American high-tech stockmarket. So far it has performed considerably below expectations. It set itself a target of 500 listed European companies by 2002; in early 1998 this had reached just 26, of which 18 were also with Nasdaq.

Nasdaq has a clear competitive edge because it was established first. Its name is better known while it also has greater liquidity because of the reasons discussed in the previous case study about venture capital. As such its daily value of shares traded is around $17bn per day compared with Easdaq's $5m.

In contrast, EuroNM, which is currently more fragmented, links together the Neuer Markt (Germany), NMAX (the Netherlands), Le Nouveau Marché (France), and EuroNM (Belgium) in a grouping of linked screen-based (as opposed to trading on the floor) stockmarkets which similarly seeks to target high-tech growth stocks – in other words to beat Easdaq at its own game. It was also created in 1996 and at the end of 1997 its market capitalisation was over $6bn; issuers have raised over $1.2bn and its average daily turnover is approaching $47m. Although it does not currently have a single set of rules for listing companies and for settling contracts – known as a single platform – (whereas Easdaq does have this), its advantage over Easdaq is that it can be accessed more easily because of its range of partners. It is also working on the harmonisation of regulatory and operational standards among the four exchanges. Further, it reflects the growing trend among European stockmarkets to consolidation as the smaller markets find themselves unable to compete sufficiently. As such it has emerged as a real challenge to Easdaq.

Not in this grouping but also of importance is the UK's Alternative Investment Market (AIM). These alternative markets have come into existence due to a growing trend by small high-growth companies to access the capital markets for funds rather than borrowing from banks, the traditional continental European companies' method of securing finance.

Meanwhile in the background, like a prowling lion, Nasdaq is launching a major European advertising campaign through the media and its website and hoping to entice further European funds into its stock listing. It already has 100 European companies listed and is seeking to at least double this by 2001.

The reader is also referred to the previous case study on venture capital.

Table 7.1   European stockmarkets: share volume January 1997 (000s)

EXCHANGE	VOLUME
London	13 618 422
Milan	8 153 044
Frankfurt	2 221 185
Amsterdam	901 225
Stockholm	437 767
Paris	440 988
Warsaw	73 927
Athens	32 352
Vienna	21 880

Data reproduced by permission of Datastream/ICV.

■ Tax-driven transfer pricing

This is the process whereby a multinational corporation is able to minimise its tax liability and hence help increase its working capital through the prices its subsidiaries operating in different countries charge each other. It does not apply to trade with businesses outside the multinational. It does this by a subsidiary in one country (say Greece) artificially raising the prices of parts, semi-manufactures or services it charges a subsidiary in another country where taxes are high (say Sweden). Since the Swedish subsidiary faces high input costs, this minimises its tax liability. In the same way, when goods are shipped from the high-tax country, Sweden, to another country, say Germany, the price of the finished goods will be understated, reducing therefore the amount of tax which the Swedish subsidiary has to pay.

The reason for tax-based transfer pricing is that prices are set to benefit the multinational as a whole. The net effect is that profits are being moved from high-tax to low-tax countries. It is argued, however, that subsidiaries which have a specific country base and loyalty to that country may in fact wish to pay the full tax regardless of the cost, since this helps foster better relations with the government in future.

■ Manufacturing-driven transfer pricing

With this the transfer pricing is set to enable the manufacturer to obtain a standard profit margin on each good produced. This is based on the assumption that each good must make a positive contribution to profits if the company is to survive long-term. Yet it may lead to short-term decisions such as the manufacturing part of the business developing products which, although contributing to profit, are not what the marketing department wants.

■ Market-driven transfer pricing

With this strategy the importance of the market price in determining sales is recognised and the goods are sold by the subsidiary at the price it believes will be competitive in its country's market. It then deducts from this price the profit margin, administrative and selling costs, stock control costs and so on, and the residual is the transfer price paid to the manufacturing subsidiary of the multi-national.

However, with a market-driven sales strategy there may be the risk that the sales organisation, adopting an aggressive sales strategy, sells the wrong product or product mix resulting in lack of coordination between sales departments in the subsidiaries in the different countries.

The process of transfer pricing is illegal in most countries yet it is very hard to prove that it is occurring since it is difficult for tax authorities to know what the correct price should be. This is particularly so in the case of managerial or technical services transferred from the multinational headquarters to a subsidiary company. Strategically, the corporate treasurer of an European business may override market-driven transfer pricing with tax-driven transfer pricing if he or she feels that significant tax savings can be made in a high-tax country, such as Sweden. Although the multinational will benefit from reducing its tax bill the high-tax country loses important tax revenue. This is particularly significant if the high-tax country is a third-world country with limited income at the best of times, since the loss of potential revenue will harm its economic development.

Maxwell argues the need for a fourth type of transfer pricing namely

■ Strategy-driven transfer pricing

This has the aim of encouraging the organisation to consider its strategic objectives as a whole and to weigh the contributions of both the manufacturing part of the multinational and the sales part. It modifies the market-driven transfer pricing policy by firstly accepting that the market price does not necessarily have to be the lowest price at which the product is sold in the particular country's market. It could be sold, for example, at a premium if the product is felt to have a competitive edge in terms of marketing. This is a decision which needs to be taken strategically for the organisation as a whole since it will impact upon the transfer price charged.

Secondly, instead of applying a standard profit margin to each product sold in each market the profit margin will be allowed to vary from product to product depending on the level of demand. Those where demand is highest will be allowed to charge higher prices and hence transfer prices between manufacturing and sales will be higher. This in turn will allow resources to be allocated more efficiently to those products which face the highest demand. To make this work properly every subsidiary within the multinational will need full access to all information.

Finally, argues Maxwell, the currency at which transfer prices are agreed needs to be agreed. The problem of a variety of different EU currencies has been that exchange rate instability impacts upon the profitability of the business. The advantage of the single currency for European multinationals will be that it eliminates exchange rate fluctuations for the 11 countries participating.

■ 7.6 Completing the single market in financial services

Financial services underpin EU trade in many ways. Goods sold from Denmark to Sweden, for example, have to be paid for through the international banking network, perhaps with the Swedish firm being allowed three months' trade credit before payment. They must also be insured in case of loss or damage, probably through Lloyds of London. A German manufacturing company may wish to purchase a Spanish firm and finance it by issuing new equity capital on the Frankfurt and Madrid stock markets. The Cypriot government may wish to issue new securities to finance the purchase of anti-aircraft missiles from Russia. The purpose of the single market in financial services is, therefore, to provide unified European financial markets – banking, insurance and securities (stocks and shares) – which function freely and to which all might have free access, and to harmonise costs downwards.

Some of these issues have already been addressed in this chapter, particularly the need to integrate national capital markets, to promote more risk capital to help SMEs, through an integrated venture capital market, and to help the cash-flow difficulties of SMEs by addressing the problem of delays in payments. Other issues are explored below.

■ The European banking system

□ 1 The need for change

Before the single market programme of 1987 the EU lacked an open and competitive banking system. It was characterised by overbanking – that is, an excessive number of branches per thousand head of the population, especially in Belgium, France, the former West Germany, Italy and Spain. In Belgium, Eire, France, Greece and Italy there was market concentration of banking services by a few large banks stifling competition. Some countries, such as Greece, Italy and Spain, suffered overregulation of the banking system by their central banks. There was also a lack of internationalisation in the EU, that is foreign banks often had only a limited presence in the domestic economy. Belgium, Denmark, Eire, France and Italy were weak in this respect. Finally, in some EU countries there was a lack of development of banking and ancillary services. Spain, Greece and Portugal, perhaps not surprisingly, exhibited these characteristics the most. In contrast, in the UK financial deregulation enabled banks and building societies (savings and loan associations) to compete vigorously in each other's markets, albeit still overbanked.

The most open and deregulated banking systems in the EU were Denmark, Germany, the Netherlands and the UK. France and especially Luxembourg had very strong international presences in their banking systems, although France had defects in other areas as above. A variety of barriers to cross-border activity operated, both regulatory and non-regulatory. Regulatory barriers included the need to obtain permission from the host country's regulatory authority before establishing a presence in the host country, exchange controls and limitations on the range of financial services provided by the bank entering the market. Non-regulatory barriers included the sheer cost of establishing a significant presence in another country and the cultural conditioning of the host country's population, that is their unwillingness to trust foreign banks. These latter have been very hard to overcome but the use of communication and information technologies in banking, discussed below, is helping.

As well as the single market programme, significant global banking changes occurred during the 1970s and 1980s forcing EU banking to adapt. These changes included rapid growth in banking and associated financial services, the emergence of universal banks offering a very wide range of services, increased deregulation in different ways and different sectors of the European banking market, new competition from non-EU banks, the increase in funds bypassing banks (known as securitisation), and a greater awareness of and response to market pressures.

☐ 2 How the EU has effected change

The EU has addressed the issue of creating a single market in banking services by the introduction of seven basic banking directives and 12 amending directives. The two most important banking coordination directives – the First Banking Coordination Directive 1977 and the Second Banking Coordination Directive 1989 – are discussed below. These directives, and those applying to other areas of financial services, have now largely been implemented through EU members' national laws.

The First Banking Coordination Directive 1977 sought to coordinate the rules, regulations and laws governing credit institutions which accept deposits and make loans. To operate in any member states an institution had to have minimum adequate own capital (as opposed to its directors' capital) and at least two reputable directors. An institution operating in one EC country could no longer be refused permission to establish branches in another on the ground that there was insufficient economic need for it, so long as it met the requirements local banks had to fulfil. An advisory committee was also established to supervise EC banks.

The Second Banking Coordination Directive 1989, implemented from 1 January 1993, authorised banks approved by any one EC member state to operate in any other EC country with a single licence or 'passport'; that is, there was no need for a local licence by the host country (the principle of mutual recognition arising from the 1979 Cassis de Dijon ruling of the European Court). This included opening branches and providing banking services even if these were not provided by the host country's banks. Credit institutions operating outside their own country were to be controlled largely by the rules and regulations of their home country. However, non-EC countries' banks operating in the EC could not claim this home-country control, needing rather a local licence to bank in each separate EC country. Also new provisions were introduced regarding the minimum capital a credit institution was required to have (ECU 5m), what constituted suitable shareholders, including the monitoring of major ones, and limits on non-bank activities. This was to harmonise bank supervisory standards across all member states. The ten leading European banks as of June 1997 are shown in Figure 7.1. Their respective rankings are Deustche Bank (2nd), Crédit Agricole (3rd), HSBC Holdings (10th), Crédit Suisse (11th), Dresdner Bank (13th), BNP (14th), ABN-Amro Bank (15th), UBS (19th), Barclays Bank (20th), and Rabobank (44th).

Most recently the EU has proposed a need to replace these 19 banking directives with one simplifying 'banking code' directive. The aim is to make banking legislation more transparent and accessible for both customers and financial institutions. The banking code directive will include the rules on the need for only a single authorisation to operate in all EU countries and those relating to financial control, both from the second directive above.

■ The impact of the euro on financial services

It is estimated by the Union Bank of Switzerland that the introduction of the euro will cost world banking $7 billion per annum from lost opportunities for foreign exchange trading and from the bond and money markets. Costs will also rise short-term as the euro is phased in and banks have to deal with dual currencies. Elsewhere it has been suggested by the Centre for the Study of Financial Innovation that investment in new systems and technology could wipe out six years of cost-savings forecast from the single currency.

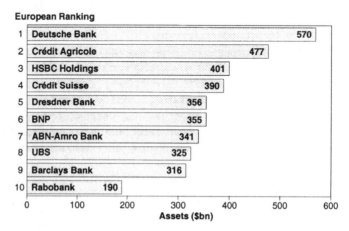

Figure 7.1   The ten leading European banks

■ Insurance

The above analysis has considered financial services and specifically capital and banking reforms in the context of the single market in financial services. Parallel developments have also occurred in the insurance sector of the financial services market covering the two wide areas of life assurance and non-life insurance. A series of directives have been issued covering both these areas with the aim of creating, as far as possible, a single market in insurance services. It applies the same principle as the banking directives, namely that an organisation approved in its home country is free to operate in any other EU country without the need for host country licences. Consumers also have the freedom to purchase any insurance service from a company anywhere in the EU. The most recent directive, with an amended draft in February 1998, seeks to offer greater flexibility in the supervision of insurance groups. The reader who is interested in pursuing this topic further is referred to the selected reading list at the end of this chapter.

■ Securities

The last area of the single market for financial services is the securities sector. This covers areas such as brokerage (buying shares or other financial assets on behalf of clients), managing portfolios of assets for clients (shares, government bonds, company debentures and so on), the underwriting of share issues by companies seeking to raise funds, financial futures (where a financial instrument is purchased for future delivery) and options (delivery may or may not be exercised in this case) including exchange rate and interest rate options. Under the 1990 Investment Services Directive, as with banking, credit institutions are now allowed to offer their services in any EU state on the basis of a home country licence. Exceptionally, Greece, Portugal and Spain were permitted to prohibit the direct access of banks to their markets until the year 2000. Again the aim of this directive has been standardisation of conditions for the whole securities market. This area of the internal market has been particularly important in recent years since many financial activities now bypass traditional banking services.

In January 1996 the Capital Adequacy Directive was implemented which identified minimum capital requirements for investment companies and banks dealing in investments. It stated that the provisions against risk which such businesses must make include foreign exchange risk, risks arising from trading and settlement, and large exposure risks. Again the aim was to protect the investors or clients whose funds these businesses manage.

If the British government decides to join the single currency British banks will have to place 1.5–2.5 per cent of their deposits with the European Central Bank, under new minimum reserve rules designed to bring stability to European money market rates and harmonise the treament of banks' solvency across the EU. This money may not be used by banks for lending but they will receive interest on it at near market rates. Currently UK banks are only required by the Bank of England to set aside 0.15 per cent of their deposits as a minimum reserve. Such a requirement will hit UK banks' ability to lend and hence their profitablility.

■ 7.7 Case study: European banks' responses to competitive pressures

This case study examines the change drivers impacting on the European financial services industry, the impact of these on four European countries and the responses of their banks.

The European retail banking industry has, in the late 1990s, been characterised by widespread mergers and acquisitions and this trend is likely to accelerate still further as banks seek to acquire critical mass to compete cost-effectively in Europe. The technological revolution currently sweeping banking, with the increased use of communication and information technologies, is typical of many industries. However, banking is more vulnerable than most because of its high labour content.

■ The UK

Telephone banking has had a major impact on the traditional retail branch network in the UK enabling branches to be closed and staff to be shed, although many EU countries including the UK are overbanked. Interactive banking through the Internet is now taking off with the ability of some banks' customers to transact business from their PCs at home linked via a modem and their telephone lines to a central bank computer. Attempts to shop and make payments using the Internet are accelerating rapidly as payment security has been solved. This is best shown with the use of Barclays Bank's virtual shopping mall, where purchases can be made from neighbouring virtual shops by credit card or, in future, smart cards or electronic purses, such as NatWest's Mondex – where a card can be credited with a certain amount of money from one's account. However, these developments lower entry barriers still further encouraging other firms to challenge traditional banks, particularly specialist technology companies. For example Digicash, an Amsterdam-based software provider, has developed 'e-cash', a form of digital money which can be used for Internet purchases. Increasingly, banks also have websites.

Also, in the UK, traditional banks are under pressure from a number of new financial services providers including supermarkets Sainsbury and Tesco, retailer Marks and Spencer, and Virgin Direct, as well as from building societies demutualising and becoming banks – such as the Halifax and the Woolwich all of which can undertake the banking functions of taking deposits and lending. These new providers have been able to bypass the traditional high entry barriers associated with setting up a retail branch banking network by their adoption of

24-hour telephone banking. Additionally, by offering higher interest rates for depositors, they have lured many customers from traditional banks. In all these areas the traditional banks are now being forced to compete on similar terms – or form strategic alliances with their competitors. For example, NatWest teamed up with Tesco for a while to provide staffed kiosks at selected branches which provided access to many more potential customers than a bank branch and were very much cheaper to provide. Natwest also handled Tesco's Clubcard Plus which is a payment card linked to a current account. The declining cost of processing financial services and less-restrictive government regulations as the internal market in financial services nears completion have also created increased pressures on traditional providers.

Mergers and acquisitions by financial institutions are likely to continue to address the issue of over-capacity in financial services provision and as a strategy to reduce operating costs and gain critical mass to compete in the internal market. The latter is crucial as providers pool resources to fund large-scale businesses and manage risks. This is happening across Europe, particularly in banking but also in insurance and, in the UK, with building societies. This in turn demonstrates the breaking down of barriers between formerly separate segments of the financial services market as banks provide insurance (the so-called bancassurers) and mortgages, building societies offer current accounts or are acquired by banks, and insurance companies offer telephone banking and mortgage services – for example the UK's First Direct provides all its services by ATM or telephone at much lower costs than traditional banks. Additionally, geographical borders are being crossed as illustrated by Dutch bank MBNA International's penetration of the UK financial services market with its telephone banking and credit card services.

■ Spain

Spanish banking is dominated by the big-5 – Banco Santander, Banco Bilbao-Vizcaya (BBV), Banco Central Hispano (BCH), Argentaria and Banco Popular – the latter being the most aggressive of the retail banks. Like other countries these banks came about by a process of consolidation, the last of which was Banco Santander's purchase of Banesto in 1994.

The domestic market is, therefore, highly competitive and dominated by the domestic banks with their huge branch networks and top-of-the-range technology – although the number of branches will reduce as new banking methods are introduced, lowering one major entry barrier. Currently foreign financial services providers have found it hard to gain a major foothold in the market. In the late 1980s and early 1990s, US banks Chase Manhattan and Citibank, Germany's Deutsche Bank, France's Crédit Lyonnais and BNP, and the UK's Barclays and NatWest all bought domestic branch networks to compete head-on with the Spanish domestics. All have now halted further growth, while NatWest has left the country. However, using their specialist skills they have now focused more on corporate banking, helped by the wave of privatisations in Spain.

Recently the Spanish banks' domestic lending strategy has shifted from corporate lending, their traditional market, which has been declining. Attention is now much more on retail banking, fuelled by growing consumer demand, and mortgages; this is aimed at consumers and currently accounts for 40 per cent of total lending. They have also been helped by a consumer switch from customer deposits to managed funds products such as pension funds and unit trusts enabling these domestic banks to gain customers from the Spanish savings banks. This sector of the market is very profitable and, as the barriers to the single market in financial services are minimised and the single currency comes into use, and consumers become more aware of a global financial sector, then foreign asset management companies able to offer high-return low-risk globally-diversified financial products are likely to seek an increasing share. Of the foreign banks Barclays (180 branches) and Citibank (83 branches) which entered the Spanish market with the intention of offering universal banking services (see section 7.7), are in the best position to gain a share of the private banking market – although both have suffered intense competition from domestic banks copying their products.

The Spanish banks – especially Banco Santander, BBV and BCH – have also been extremely active in their former colonies in Latin America accumulating extensive branch networks by acquisitions totalling over $6bn. Helped by new rules allowing foreign control and by common language and similar histories and culture they have felt most at home in expanding into this area – it has also proved to be a major battlefield between these main Spanish banks.

▪ Italy

Italy was one of the countries described at the beginning of this section as over-banked, over-regulated and over-protected from international influence in the late 1980s, at the beginning of the single market programme. Currently Italy has almost 1000 banks and 300 000 bank employees; analysts argue that at least 10 per cent of these staff will need to be shed if banks are to be competitive. Clearly Italian banks have to respond positively if they are to survive.

This has started to happen with three major mergers of Italian banks since mid-1997 as they abandon their previously inward-looking non-competitive mindset and seek to gain size to secure market influence and compete. After the merger of Credito Italiano and Unicredito, and then Banco Ambrosiano Intesa and savings bank Cariplo to create Banca Intesa, came the merger of San Paolo and IMI. San Paolo is a retail bank with a good branch network, while IMI is an investment bank with expertise in investment banking and asset management. As well as the wide spread of expertise in both retail and investment banking the new San Paolo–IMI will be Italy's largest bank with assets of 340 000bn lira ($200bn). San Paolo is also 5 per cent owned by the Agnelli family, who own Fiat, and political influence like this is still of importance in Italian banking.

More mergers are likely as this regrouping process continues.

■ Estonia

Since Estonia regained its independence from Russia in 1991 its banking system has grown substantially. Initial problems of bad lending, lack of experience and a lack of banking legislation led to many new banks failing. The remainder, learning from the mistakes which had been made, consolidated through mergers and acquisitions, while the central bank increased its supervision of the survivors and raised minimum capital requirements. Also, Estonian banks began harmonising their regulations with those of the EU. The remaining banks have pursued a programme of adopting leading-edge information technology based on telephone banking, the PC and the Internet. Hence paper cheques were bypassed with banks switching directly to ATMs and plastic bank cards. Estonian banks have also diversified into related activities such as stockbroking, insurance, leasing and asset management.

Following the Asian crisis of 1997, the performance of Estonian banks suffered as the central bank sought to slow down credit growth of 90 per cent in 1997. The stockmarket also fell 60 per cent, much of it consisting of bank shares which were held by each other. If the central bank raises capital adequacy ratios further, the smaller banks in a sector already overbanked may experience difficulties setting off another round of mergers and acquisitions – already two of the larger banks, Hansabank which is strong in the corporate sector, and Hoiubank, which has a strong retail base of 200 branches, are investigating merger possibilities. This will also prepare them better for when foreign banks enter the market, and enable them to expand into the other Baltic republics, Latvia and Lithuania. The other major Estonian bank Uhisbank, which was created by the merger of 10 banks which collapsed in 1992, has opened a branch in St Petersburg and is seeking to enter a partnership with a strategic foreign investor wishing to gain access to the Russian market.

■ 7.8 Universal banks versus financial disintermediation: a model for the future?

The traditional type of bank in a number of EU countries has engaged in relatively narrow activities, being primarily concerned with accepting customers' deposits which are then used to make short to medium-term loans to borrowers. These loans can be and are renewed periodically, but technically they may be called in by the bank at any time. In this sense banks perform financial intermediation, that is, time and risk transformation and aggregation. These types of banks conform to what is known as the market-based or Anglo-Saxon model of banking as typified by the UK and the US. In these economies businesses raise long-term funds by issuing securities such as shares and debentures through capital markets like the London Stock Exchange.

In other European countries, however, what is known as a bank-based model operates. Although still being financial intermediaries, here banks are much more linked to businesses and will make long-term loans to finance capital expenditure, for example. In such countries stockmarkets have therefore tended to be less fully developed. Germany, France and the Netherlands are countries with this type of banking system.

Within the bank-based system German banks stand out as particularly important because they are what are called 'Universal' banks. As the name suggests, these undertake a full range of activities within the one organisation without any geographical restrictions. Their activities include 'deposit-taking, lending, financial leasing, money transmission services and means of payment, trading in foreign exchange, money broking, credit reference services, safe custody services and investment activities' (Steinherr and Huveneers, 1992). In other words not only do they undertake the functions of the Anglo-Saxon banks, but also they are involved in underwriting and distributing securities. As such they are often held up as the model for European bank development in the future, including in the liberalising economies of Central and Eastern Europe.

In many cases universal banks will hold stock (shares) in other companies and exercise their right to be involved in the management of these companies. France's Crédit Lyonnais would be such an example, but as Crédit Lyonnais has found to its cost this can pose significant problems (see section 7.9). In such circumstances banks have voting power and influence over the strategic direction of the companies whose shares they hold. Whether this is economically desirable or whether there are conflicts of interest is an issue of concern. Furthermore, when companies run into severe financial difficulties this can put great pressure on the bank itself.

The universal bank is important because of the changes which have occurred in European banking in recent years and which will increasingly occur as a direct result of the single market in financial services. The two most important changes are what are termed Disintermediation and Securitisation.

Disintermediation simply means that when businesses want to borrow significant amounts of money they increasingly bypass banks and go directly to the capital markets. In London, the major EU financial centre, the main market is the Inter-bank market which charges interest at Libor (the London Inter-Bank Offered Rate). Since banks are bypassed this directly affects their profitability. Libor has also been the established international reference rate for transactions in US dollars and deutschemarks. Other comparable rates exist in the EU the most recent of which is Euribor which has been adopted by the Deutsche Terminbörse (DTB), Germany's derivatives exchange. This is the continental European reference rate and will be used for contracts denominated in euros. Its adoption is also part of the ongoing battle between the DTB and the London International Financial Futures and Options Exchange (Liffe) for supremacy in euro-denominated contracts after the introduction of the single currency.

Securitisation refers to the fact that securities firms (often called investment banks) have developed to directly challenge banks in this area. Whereas banks rely on depositors placing savings with them which they can then on-lend to borrowers, securities houses borrow directly from wholesale money markets such as the inter-bank markets. This gives them greater flexibility and the ability to achieve scale economies in borrowing through securing lower interest rates. In turn they on-lend these funds. They may also sell their debt to someone else whereas banks tend to hold their debt, such as bank loans, until they mature. Securities firms will also put cash-rich firms in touch with other businesses who wish to borrow funds long-term.

Added to the above is the fact that a large number of new financial products have developed in recent years to finance loans. The net effect of these developments is that European banks are under more pressure from competitors, and have themselves to offer a wider range of financial products and services than ever before. This is good for consumers but not for the banks!

Universal banks therefore offer, for banks, a hope to slow down the competition from the non-bank financial sector, such as securities firms, because they act both as deposit-takers (the Anglo-Saxon model) and also underwrite share issues, hold shares in other companies and so on (the universal bank model). They also offer significant economies of scope which Steinheer and Huveneers (1992) define as existing when, for a given scale of production for each good or service, the joint production total costs are less than the total costs of each product being produced separately. However, as discussed above, when such banks hold large amounts of shares in non-financial businesses, as is the case particularly in Germany, then there can be problems. At times there may be conflicts of interest between different sectors of the same universal bank. And, as with all banks, they will also face cultural problems of consumer acceptance as they seek to offer cross-border services within the single market.

This will not prevent, however, a continuing significant rationalisation of European banking which has been occurring in recent years. As seen above, a number of countries, particularly Italy and Spain which are heavily overbanked, have actively encouraged their largest banks to merge to permit rationalisation and greater competitiveness. The advent of the Euro is likely to increase still further the competitive pressures on EU banks. As noted elsewhere, mergers can impose high costs; however, particularly during the merging process which can often be quite long-term as a result of rationalisation, they may also fail to perform as anticipated.

Strategic alliances between banks are an alternative form of cooperation. Here each bank retains its own separate identity but cooperates in a number of other areas such as sharing the costs of developing into a third market, developing new shared services, and so on.

In either event, EU banks are going to face continuing heavy competitive pressures from credit cards, life assurance, money markets, software companies and a variety of other sources. Continuing widespread use of technology, including the development of virtual reality banks and the much wider use of less sophisticated telephone banking is likely to contribute to continuing large-scale labour reductions. Further, worldwide shopping through the Internet is also developing rapidly now that banks and retailers have developed secure payments processes. In this case national and cross-border mergers seem quite likely to meet the growing competitive environment.

■ 7.9 Case study one: Crédit Lyonnais – rediscovering retail banking

Crédit Lyonnais, one of the largest of European universal banks yet also renowned for its large losses, is an interesting example of government intervention in French industry. Its main shareholders are the government itself (which owns 57 per cent of Crédit's shares), the Thomson electronics group (27 per cent) and the French bank Caisse des Depots (6 per cent). It has a major branch network and subsidiary companies throughout the EU; additionally it has also been used as a conduit to finance French businesses, often taking shareholdings in these companies in return.

■ Non-banking activities in the 1980s and early 1990s

In the late 1980s and early 1990s, under the leadership of Jean-Yves Haberer, Crédit Lyonnais made very large losses. These were due to a combination of imprudent lending and investment against the background of the severe European recession, aggravated by high interest rates due to France's membership of the exchange rate mechanism. As a result, when property prices fell in the wake of the early 1990s recession, Crédit's assets also fell substantially in value. This was exacerbated by the poor supervision of the bank's activities internally and also by the French government.

Crédit's financial involvement included FF 550m to La Cinq, France's fifth television channel which went bankrupt in 1994; FF 1.5bn loaned to Bernard Tapie, the businessman, Socialist politician and former chairman of Olympique Marseille Football Club; FF 1.1bn in loans to the late Robert Maxwell, the discredited British businessman; and FF 2.6bn to Olympia and York, the Canadian firm responsible for the major redevelopment of the docks of East London, which project collapsed in 1992. In addition Crédit Lyonnais bought heavily into French industry, including a 20 per cent shareholding in the giant French steel producer Usinor Salicor, which is now privatised, and Airbus partner Aérospatiale, and ownership of MGM cinemas (by its Dutch subsidiary CLBN) and sports goods company Adidas (both of which have now been sold off).

In 1993 the government had to launch a rescue package totalling FF 135 billion to guarantee Crédit loans and save it from bankruptcy. This was followed in March 1994 by the French government effectively taking over FF 18.4bn of the bank's debt, and in July 1994 the granting of a further FF 4.9bn of credit facilities. In spite of this, in 1994, Crédit lost FF 12.1bn, the biggest French bank loss ever.

■ Turnaround strategy

Under new bank president Jean Peyrelevade a turnaround strategy was adopted in 1993 aimed at reducing Crédit Lyonnais's exposure in other companies and restoring the bank's liquidity. This sought to reduce the bank's asset holdings in other businesses by FF 20bn during 1994–95. The 1994 target of FF 10bn was achieved by reducing the Usinor Salicor shareholding to 10 per cent, selling its 19.9 per cent share in Adidas, the sporting wear manufacturer, and exchanging holdings in other state industries for more liquid investments (which can more easily be converted to cash). By 1998 much of its non-core activities had been split off and assigned to the Caisse des Dépôts et Consignations (CDC).

The report of a French parliamentary enquiry in late 1994 argued that the bank's problems had been exacerbated not only by the very large investments in other companies which had not always demonstrated good risk management, but also by property speculation. Blame was placed on the bank's directors, government ministers and the bank regulators.

■ The Commission and Crédit Lyonnais

There has been an ongoing struggle between the European Commission and Crédit Lyonnais over the large amounts of state aid which the latter has received from the French government. In August 1995 Karel van Miert, the EU competition Commissioner, agreed to the French government providing a further FF 45bn of state aid provided that 50 per cent of its total assets outside France were sold by 1998, especially its European retail banking holdings. This aid, the Commission argued, must subsequently be repaid by Crédit Lyonnais to the government.

On 23 March 1998, Crédit Lyonnais announced its annual results with a 400 per cent increase in net income to FF1.1bn ($172.6m). However, EU Competition Commissioner Karel van Miert immediately declared these results to be illegal, arguing that the real income statement should show a loss of FF2bn. His logic was that no agreement had been reached over the losses incurred by the bank's non-performing assets, removed in 1993. Van Miert also ordered Crédit Lyonnais chairman Jean Peyrelevade to submit a revised plan to restructure the bank and a timetable for privatisation or the EU would take action against it.

The 1995 EU-approved rescue package had required Crédit to sell half of its non-French European subsidiaries as one condition of the bail-out. However, in 1998 van Miert argued that as the French government had given Crédit further subsidies it should now be required to sell off all its European non-French businesses. This would be in return for a revised version of the rescue plan originally agreed in 1995 due to the growing financial costs of the rescue of Crédit Lyonnais which have risen to between FF 100 and 190bn. The existing 1995 plan only approved French government aid to FF45bn. In total, French taxpayers have provided over $32bn to the bank since 1993.

Crédit Lyonnais is soon likely to sell off some of its remaining profitable businesses such as Crédit Lyonnais Belgium and its subsidiaries in the UK, Germany, Spain and Switzerland. Additionally Crédit Lyonnais Securities Asia (CLSA) also offers potential for attracting serious customers.

■ Privatisation

Although it was originally planned to privatise Crédit in 1996, as part of the French government's ongoing programme of divesting state ownership of businesses, the government has now pledged privatisation by the year 2000. This, and the required asset sales, will impose much needed market discipline on the bank and force it to operate on profit-maximising commercial terms concentrating essentially on its core banking functions. By delaying privatisation and repaying French government loans, Jean Peyrelevade has, in practice, bought time for Crédit to recover prior to privatisation – and this recovery is happening. Also, in spite of its debt problems, Crédit is an attractive bank which will appeal to investors, particularly another bank, with the imminent arrival of the Euro and the increase in European banking mergers and acquisitions. It offers a regional retail banking network of over 2000 branches, and telephone and online banking services. Its main weakness is that very heavy expenditure will be needed to substantially develop its range of banking products which, currently, are limited.

Allianz, the German insurer, and Nippon Life are taking significant minority stakes in the bank. This fits in with the French government's preferred strategy for privatisation, namely to effect a partial privatisation of significant minority stakes to friendly investors. Prior to privatisation Crédit is likely to sell much of its remaining non-core business leaving only the banking business for sale to a buyer. What will most deter potential buyers, apart from the cost of developing new products will be the problems of needing to downsize labour. Crédit has 32 000 employees in France and another 19 000 worldwide, and any buyer will need to rationalise the number of branches – yet French labour laws make it very difficult to dismiss or pay-off staff.

■ 7.10 Case study two: European pensions

Europe, along with other countries such as Japan, is facing a crisis due to its aging population and, in particular, the problem of how to finance their retirement pensions. Traditionally EU countries, and those in Central and Eastern Europe, have used a system known as pay-as-you-go (PAYG). This means that those currently working contribute national insurance payments to provide the pensions of those who are retired; however, as more people retire and the working population shrinks the system is near to collapse. Also, as the extended family diminishes and divorces increase the state faces still greater pressures to help the aged.

Governments have attempted various measures to address this problem such as raising the retirement age, equalising retirement ages for males and females, and allowing a reduction in the real value of state pensions. However, many EU pension schemes are either in deficit – as in Germany – or rely on the state to fund the deficiency – as with Italy and France. Additionally, there are real problems in Central and Eastern European countries. In practice, governments in Europe and elsewhere are having to choose between three different models – maintaining the existing PAYG system alone, either as is or in some reformed state; adopting a mixed model of PAYG supplemented with a private scheme or schemes; or totally replacing PAYG with a private scheme.

Maintaining the PAYG scheme alone is clearly not viable long-term as currently it cannot be financed to provide sufficiently high levels of income for the growing numbers of pensioners. Nor can social security contributions be raised further since it is generally accepted that they are already at their highest sustainable levels – 11 per cent in the EU and 25 per cent in Poland. Traditionally, in Europe, most of pension and life assurance funds have been compulsorily invested in government bonds, often to finance the national debt. What is needed is pension schemes whose proceeds are invested in capital markets to generate new wealth – so-called funded pensions.

A mixed scheme is certainly viable. Hungary, Poland and Romania, for example, have all opted for a reformed PAYG scheme together with a compulsory private scheme and a carefully regulated private voluntary scheme. This means that everyone gets two sources of pension and those who wish to contribute to the private voluntary scheme get a third. The advantage of maintaining the PAYG scheme in parallel with private schemes, certainly for economies in transition, is that it offers greater security for pensioners since capital markets, which act as financial intermediaries channelling funds from contributors to investors, are by no means fully-developed in Central and Eastern Europe, nor stable.

The switch to a totally private-sector-funded scheme is the most radical model and is one currently being considered by the Ukraine and Russia, for example. However, such a scheme will not in itself solve the difficulties as the future problem facing countries is not a shortage of capital but a shortage of work. If people can't get work they can't contribute to such schemes and also need social security payments. Also the CEEC are having to battle with the legacy of low per capita incomes which, as incomes first grow, causes people to be more concerned with the acquisition of consumer goods than pensions, and also with large numbers of workers taking early retirement as privatised firms have downsized.

For both the second and third models the process is expensive and slow since the workforce will need to redirect some of their national insurance contributions to a private fund, unless they can be persuaded to save extra; in turn this will reduce contributions to PAYG and hence the value of the state pension. In some CEEC this has been addressed by using funds from the privatisation of state assets.

Where new fund-based pension schemes offer opportunities for European businesses is in the area of asset management, with pension fund assets in the EU totalling only one-third of those in the US. Within the EU there are considerable disparities – 90 per cent of EU pensions investments, currently totalling ECU 1200bn, is invested in the UK and the Netherlands. Asset management companies act as intermediaries between savers (who contribute funds for their pensions) and the capital markets. It is asset management companies in these countries, and Ireland and Switzerland, which are most likely to be able to use their expertise to provide services in the other EU countries with less-developed pension schemes. However, these other countries will need to relax their taxation and investment restrictions on pension funds – for example Denmark has restrictions on how much money may be invested in equities.

For CEEC, and to a lesser extent the EU, reform of the pensions sector is crucial since it will help stockmarkets develop faster and provide funds for new investments by businesses. Otherwise European businesses will have to rely too much on banks for their main source of investment funds.

■ Review questions

1. Discuss the main ways by which a European business might raise short-term and medium-term funds. Discuss critically the advantages and disadvantages to the business of each method.
2. Analyse why a fully functioning single market in financial services in essential to the full functioning of the single European market.
3. Discuss what is meant by transfer pricing and explain its importance to a multinational enterprise.
4. What advantages and disadvantages might an universal bank have compared with an Anglo-Saxon type of bank?
5. What might be the main advantages and disadvantages of a bank holding shares in another company to which it has loaned long-term funds?

■ Bibliography

Commission of the European Communities, Background Reports, London.

Dermine, J. (ed.), *European Banking in the 1990s*, 2nd edn (Oxford: Blackwell Business, 1993).

Dixon, R., *Banking in Europe: The Single Market* (London: Routledge, 1991).

Gardener, E. P. M., 'Banking Strategies and 1992', in Mullineux (1992) *op. cit.*

Gardener, E. P. M. and Molyneux, P., *Changes in Western European Banking: An International Banker's Guide* (London: Routledge, 1990).

Henderson, R., *European Finance* (Maidenhead: McGraw-Hill, 1993).

Landreth, O. L., *European Corporate Strategy: Heading for 2000* (London: Macmillan, 1992).

Lucey, T., *Business Administration* (Mendelsham: DP Publications, 1994).

Maxwell, A., 'International Transfer Pricing: Using Transfer Pricing to Gain Advantage in the European Market Place', *European Business Journal*, 1991.

Mullineux, A. (ed.), *European Banking* (Oxford: Blackwell, 1992).

Salvatore, D., *International Economics*, 5th edn (Hemel Hempstead: Prentice Hall, 1995).

Steinherr, A. and Huveneers, C., 'Institutional Competition and Innovation: Universal Banking in the Single European Market' in Mullineux (1992) *op. cit.*

Vickerman, R. W., *The Single European Market* (Hemel Hempstead: Harvester Wheatsheaf, 1992).

Winters, L. A., *International Economics*, 4th edn (London: Routledge, 1991).

Also:

The Chartered Banker
The Economist
The European
The Financial Times
The Times

CHAPTER 8

Formulating European business strategy

■ 8.1 Introduction

Having examined the organisational and financial aspects of European businesses, this chapter explores the strategic issues and problems facing them in their long-term operations. The strategic objectives of businesses are analysed and the role of change in influencing business strategy is examined. The role of the strategic audit is discussed as a tool for the business to evaluate its performance as a prerequisite to the formulation of competitive strategy. The strategic implications of diversification are considered. Finally, for the business encountering the threat of failure, the use of a turnaround strategy is analysed. Case studies are explored to discuss these issues in depth.

Obviously in a book on European business a detailed analysis of business strategy is not feasible. This chapter seeks rather to take the basic concepts of business strategy and to apply them to specific examples. The reader who wishes to pursue these issues in more depth than is possible here is referred to the references at the end of this chapter.

■ 8.2 Business strategy: types of strategic problem

■ What is business strategy?

Business strategy is the process of defining the medium- to long-term objectives of a business and how it seeks to achieve these. To succeed, any business must have clear answers to four main questions: what does it intend to achieve – that is, its objectives; why it intends to achieve them; how it intends to achieve them; and by when it intends to achieve them. Without these it is almost certainly doomed to failure.

Although it is difficult to define time-spans precisely, a business's strategy will relate typically to any period from one to five years. To plan beyond five years is immensely difficult because of an inability to predict the future, although businesses do try; indeed many would argue that even two years ahead is impossible to forecast accurately. Less than one year relates to tactical management, which is concerned with the short-term tactical decisions of the business, while operational management covers the business's day-to-day running.

Business strategy involves looking not just at the business itself and what it intends to achieve but also at the environment within which it operates. As was seen in Chapter 1, the term environment is all-encompassing and involves such issues as the nature and structure of the markets in which a business operates, the strength of the competition it faces, the extent and impact of change specific to the product (which may well include technological change) and also more generally in society and the economy. Chapters 3 and 4 have demonstrated the particular importance of the EU as an agent of change through the implementation of the single market programme, social policy, the single currency and so on.

■ The impact of the environment

Business environment issues of the type identified above will certainly affect a business and may well deflect it from its planned path. If so, then either new strategies will have to be adopted to ensure that the original objectives are still achieved, or the original objectives will have to be modified. Which of these is chosen is a strategic management decision. This means that senior management will need to monitor progress towards strategic objectives on an ongoing basis and take appropriate corrective action if there is significant divergence or variance.

To achieve its objectives a European business will need to consider how to best use its resources within this changing environment. The strategic decision of BMW to buy Rover in 1994 was partly to diversify into new products such as 4x4 vehicles without the R&D and capital costs of new assembly lines, and partly to gain a competitive advantage over rival German producers Mercedes and Volkswagen. Most importantly it was to acquire greater critical mass in an highly competitive market where growing concentration through mergers and takeovers is both inevitable and encouraged by the European Commission. The reader might like to review Chapter 6.8 and reflect on VW's strategy in acquiring RRMC. In the same way, particularly since privatisation, a number of European telecommunication companies have sought strategic alliances with each other and with American telecomms companies. This is for reasons which are discussed more fully elsewhere, but is particularly because of the opportunities afforded to EU telecomms companies since the creation of the 1996 single telecommunications market by the EU.

One way for a European business to assess the environment within which it operates is to undertake a PEST or PESTLE analysis, as was discussed in Chapter 1, to which the reader is referred. S/he will recall that, for PEST, this involves examining the political, economic, social and technological environments within which the European business operates and the likely impact of these factors on its strategy.

■ Types of strategic problem

Businesses face four main types of strategic constraint which are:

☐ 1 The nature of the industry

This will include the type of market structure within which the business operates; for example is it oligopolistic and, if so, is there any form of collusion? In turn the type of market structure will determine the ability of firms to determine price, the extent of entry barriers and the extent to which products are differentiated by advertising, branding and so on. The nature of the industry will also determine the extent to which production is capital or labour-intensive.

The European car industry has already been examined through the attempted acquisition of RRMC by BMW and Volkswagen. This industry is oligopolistic in that it is dominated by a small number of very large producers and there are high entry barriers through set-up and R&D costs and the Common External Tariff aimed against the products of foreign producers. Its highly competitive nature pushes it towards greater concentration through mergers and takeovers to permit survival of the remaining few; and the move in Europe towards greater privatisation has meant that privatised firms lose any fall-back on state aid.

☐ 2 The nature of the enterprise

This encompasses a wide range of issues which in turn will affect the strategy which the business adopts. They will include its size in terms of capitalisation, market share, number of employees and so on. Its structure will be relevant in terms of whether it is a single company or a conglomerate as will its ownership – for example, is it a limited company or a state-owned enterprise? If the former, who owns the shares? And so on. The balance of its markets between domestic and international will also significantly affect the strategy it pursues.

☐ 3 The current circumstances of the firm

These will be affected by the stage of the business cycle at which the company find itself operating. During the downturn sales will fall as household incomes reduce and the firm will need to consider how it will address diminishing sales. It will also need to carefully time new product launches to ensure they occur, if possible, on the upturn of the cycle. Of equal importance is the stage of the life-cycle at which its products are. If all are reaching the end of their life-cycle, with no new ones coming on stream, then the business has serious strategic problems. The business's gearing ratio, that is its ratio of fixed debt such as debentures to equity, is also vital. If this is too high it means the company has large ongoing interest payments on its debentures, which must be met. Unless these borrowings have been used to finance new investment which is generating revenue flows this will reduce the funds available to spend on new investment.

☐ 4 The type of economy

Europe has a wide mixture of economies which are in fact a mixture of public and private sectors, the exact balance varying from country to country. The level of prosperity also varies significantly from country to country with Albania setting the one extreme and Switzerland the other. Whatever the type of economy it will generate problems of a strategic nature for the businesses which operate within it.

■ 8.3 Strategy and the organisation: objectives

Although every European business has objectives, these will vary depending on a host of factors including its nature, size, product mix, ownership and the dynamism of its managers. Most importantly, objectives identify the goals of the business and so are what it intends to have achieved by the end of a specific time period. A goal may be defined as a general statement of the purpose of the business (Johnson and Scholes, 1993). If the goal of a German company is to diversify into CEEC then its objective will be, for example, to achieve a specified market share in Romania, Slovakia and Slovenia by 2002.

Objectives therefore provide the focus and direction which a European business will take, and its strategy is how it seeks to achieve these. In our example the strategy for achieving market presence in CEEC will be to establish a network of company-specific agents and to undertake a marketing campaign. In setting objectives any European business will inevitably face a series of conflicting interests from different parties within or connected with the organisation.

In summary the important point to note about the objectives of any European business is that they will cover a diversity of activities within an organisation and external to it. They may relate to the business's human resources, production, marketing and so on. Additionally, they will apply to the position of the business in its environment, and in relation to its competitors who form part of that environment.

■ The mission statement

To complete the picture many companies also have mission statements. A mission statement encapsulates briefly in general terms the overall rationale for the business. In terms of priorities the mission statement will be at the apex of a pyramid. Below that lie the goals of the organisation, then the strategic objectives and finally the means to implement them. Perhaps the most famous example of a mission statement is that of Star Trek's *USS Enterprise* with its five-year mission 'To boldly go where no one has gone before'.

CASE STUDY   Juventus FC – Developing New Income Sources

As an illustration of the above constraints Juventus Football Club, a private limited company which admittedly is untypical of most European businesses, plays in the Italian Serie A, a market regulated by the Italian football association, with extremely high entry barriers determined by any club's ability to gain promotion to this league. It is now seeking to take commercial advantage of its name, which is, in effect, a world-renowned trademark. Italian football clubs have been notoriously slow to benefit from marketing compared with German and UK clubs, relying on people passing through the turnstiles and television rights as their main sources of revenue. For example, according to a study by accountants Deloitte and Latouche, wages account for almost 50 per cent of Juventus' turnover, while for Inter Milan the figure is 69 per cent. In contrast, for the UK's Manchester United the figure is 25 per cent, while it earned £20m from merchandising. Indeed, in early 1998 Manchester United encountered criticism for introducing its thirteenth change of team strip in five years, with a shirt costing on average £45.

Juventus' strategy encompasses a number of steps which are perhaps best summed up in its slogan *Vendere e Vincere* (sell and win). This has been prompted by a realisation, generally, that Italian football clubs have to compete within a wider entertainment industry which also includes TV, cinema, other sports and so on, rather than just within a narrow soccer market. This includes diversifying income sources.

Firstly, Juventus has established a joint partnership with a network of schools, called Punto Juve, under which the schools guarantee their children regular physical education which the state does not provide. In return, Punto Juve encourage supermarkets and hypermarkets, filling stations, banks and so on to sell Juventus merchandise and hence generate revenue for the club. This addresses the fundamental problem of any Italian club – a poor distribution network. Also, of course, any outstanding youngsters can be appraised by Juventus before other clubs see them. Secondly, as a consequence of the Bosman ruling by which any player can transfer to another club once his contract has expired without any transfer fee (and hence secure higher wages than pre-Bosman), Juventus are now selling their top players before their contracts expire in order to be able to charge a transfer fee – as with players such as Fabrizio Ravanelli, Roberto Baggio and Gianluca Vialli. Thirdly, Juventus has established a summer training camp in the Valle d'Aosta where 2000 fans take their holidays to watch their team undertake pre-season training. In return the regional government, mindful of the tourism benefits from this, has paid Juventus 1500m lira to train there.

Juventus is also planning to build its own stadium since, like most Serie A clubs, it currently rents its ground. However, due to the cost of this Juventus will need to go public which is not likely to happen until about 2002. Where Juventus has a problem is that fashion conscious Italians do not regard it as cool to walk around in replicas of their first team's strip, a problem from which UK soccer fans do not suffer! To generate steady income streams Juventus has secured 'institutional sponsors' whose names are permanently exhibited on stadium hoardings – organisations such as the mobile phone company TIM, whose outlets can be used to sell Juventus merchandise.

■ How strategy is formulated

How business strategy is formulated really depends upon the structure and nature of the organisation. For a one-person or small family business the actual process may be minimal and not specified in writing or, if it is, is for the benefit of a bank when seeking a loan. In the hierarchically structured businesses considered earlier, much depends on the attitude of senior man board of directors, led by the chairman or equivalent, will formulat strategy of the organisation including its strategic objectives. Some may seek the views of various levels of management and mem workforce as a means to secure as diverse a range of views as pos create corporate-wide ownership. However, other businesses may ch do so.

Many firms in the UK and the US now make widespread use of management consultants. In the UK these are often linked to large accountancy firms. One or more consultants will visit the firm for either a specific period of time such as two weeks or on an ongoing basis – perhaps one day a month. On the basis of information gathered they will formulate a strategic plan for the business usually addressing a problem for which they have been called in. However, the advice may relate to the total future strategic direction of the company. The advantage of bringing in outside consultants is that they may have new ideas which existing staff, being very close to the business, may not have the perspective or the time to consider.

This use of management consultants is not usually found outside the Anglo-Saxon economies. In continental Europe and in Japan the concept of bringing in outsiders to gain a snapshot picture of the organisation and then give detailed advice is not part of the business culture. It is seen as making little sense and is not normally used – particularly as consultants charge very high fees. Rather such businesses prefer to use their own staff who have expertise and deep knowledge of every aspect of the business for which they work. Also involving existing staff creates ownership. In the end whichever system works is the one that a business should opt for. However, management theory is often criticised for its tendency to embrace the latest fashion and some argue that management consultants are an example of this.

■ 8.4 Business strategy and operational management

If strategic relates to the long-term activities of a business, then operational relates to the short term. It is concerned with the day-to-day running of the business and, depending on its precise nature, will encompass a number of different activities. These might include ensuring that daily production targets are met – for European car manufacturers this will be in terms of the number and quality of completed cars coming off the assembly line. When production is disrupted for any reason this has to be remedied as soon as possible. In the case of Eurotunnel, for example, this would involve ensuring that trains leave on time and, if a breakdown occurs or a fire starts (both experiences which have occurred, the latter closing the tunnel for some months), this is remedied as soon as possible.

CASE STUDY   Benetton – European Business Objectives

Introduction

Since its founding in 1965, by Luciano Benetton, the Italian clothing manufacturer Benetton has grown to be the fourth biggest business in Italy as well as a $1.1bn global corporation (7000 shops in 120 countries by the early 1990s) with one of the twenty best-known names in the world. Its initial strength was in product design; limited resources forced it into a series of partnerships with small workshops manufacturing its products throughout northern Italy, while the goods were sold to licensed retailers who then on-sold them.

It continued to expand until the early 1990s when it was hit by economic recession and by competitors with production facilities in low-cost developing nations. Rather than relocate to match its competitors' costs and lose the links with its 250 000 sub-contract workers on whom its success had been built, the 72 per cent family-owned Benetton decided to invest $60 million in new plant – one to cut the clothes and another to finish the processing and handle the dispatching (fully automated production is not feasible for clothing assembly). By centralising production in this way and with management nearby, Benetton has been able to respond quickly to changing market circumstances. It is also linked to its overseas locations by a global computer network to enable it to track the location of each style of good ordered by a customer and where exactly it is.

In recent years Benetton has diversified into other activities building upon its initial experience. Since the early 1990s the holding company, *Edizione Holding*, has diversified into venture capital, provided finance through its subsidiary *21 Investamenti*, for small and medium-sized firms in Italy which have sales of $30–50m. Now it has also moved into the UK with a British subsidiary *21 Invest* to provide finance to riskier British medium-sized firms for periods of 3–5 years.

Benetton has also diversified into sports equipment and leisure lines for the male, acquiring in 1997 Benetton Sportsystem at a cost of $200m to use up some of the $513m of cash it has accumulated from its highly profitable clothing production. Sportsystem is a collection of sports goods manufacturing companies including Nordica ski boots and Prince tennis rackets. The acquisition also recognises the increasing overlap between leisure and sports wear which other companies such as Adidas and Nike have taken advantage of in recent years; Benetton intends to boost the clothing production from 10 to 50 per cent of Sportsystem sales. Benetton also sponsors a Formula 1 racing team and has acquired over 2 million acres of land in Patagonia, South America where they breed 270 000 sheep for the wool which is exported to Italy.

Business objectives

Recent Benetton objectives have been:

- to diversify into sportswear and sports equipment, and venture capital activities, to continue global expansion as opportunities for opening retail outlets in third-world countries become exhausted (having run out of countries);
- to encourage greater competition among existing franchisees in developed markets to enhance corporate profitability;
- to continue to adapt production and distribution methods to meet the competition from other chains of retailers who copy the Benetton style and can produce their goods cheaply in low-labour-cost third-world countries;
- to ease the transition as Luciano Benetton passes over more control to his children in anticipation of his eventual retirement – a real problem for family-owned businesses as noted elsewhere;

- to maintain the reputation for quality and middle-price-range style which it has developed for Benetton goods, and to establish this for Sportsystem goods;
- to avoid the adverse publicity of the early to mid-1990s which arose from its controversial advertising campaigns; although in early 1998 Benetton has produced a series of pictures set in Israel showing an Israeli girl kissing her Bedouin boyfriend.

This case study is also explored more fully later in this chapter. The reader might also like to refer back to the Juventus case study above and list what that club's objectives are likely to be.

Movements of stocks and completed goods as part of the production process need to be undertaken as planned and required – in the case of Benetton, for instance, its ability to supply goods to any franchisee anywhere in the world within eight days is a direct consequence of its massive and highly automated stock control system. Required maintenance also needs to be undertaken as prescribed while marketing to promote the business's goods and/or services is crucial. Finally, although not an exhaustive list, personnel relations need at least to be satisfactory.

It has been noted that in the past a separate level of management known as tactical management has existed, involving the functions of middle management. However, improvements in information technology such as LANs (local access networks) where, for example, any authorised person in a business can access corporate databases etc means that senior mangers can obtain information directly from operations rather than having it filtered through middle management. The discussion in a previous chapter on delayering within businesses emphasises this point. Operational management is therefore taken to be that aspect of the management of the business undertaken by middle and junior management on a daily basis to achieve the strategic objectives discussed above. To illustrate, the strategic objective is to reach North Cape, Norway. The operational management is equivalent to the driving from Paris to get there, as numbers of French do each summer.

■ 8.5 The strategic implications of change in the business environment

As discussed elsewhere, the biggest issue facing businesses in the EU, and globally, is change which is occurring at a faster and faster pace. This shows itself in the speed of technological innovation and its implementation in business, particularly the replacement of labour by capital in the production of both goods and services, and in both the public and private sectors of economies. It appears in the development of new goods and services; political, economic and social change within the EU including its widening and deepening; the new global political order with the end of communism and state planning; the continued, if temporarily interrupted, rise of the Pacific Rim countries . . . the list is endless and much of it is technology-driven.

A century ago most Europeans never moved further than ten miles from their homes in their entire life. Distance was measured by kilometres or miles. Now it is measured by time – eight hours from Paris to New York; 23 hours from Rome to Australia. Furthermore, change affects peoples' very lives, their possessions and their expectations for the future. It may not be possible to predict realistically what life will be like in the year 2050, but it will be more different than life was in the year 1950 compared with now. Consumer goods and services which many of us now take for granted, such as microwave ovens, personal computers, cellular telephones, satellite and cable television, the Internet, relatively cheap world travel, did not exist 30 years ago. For those in work, holidays to Disneyworld, Florida or to Africa are increasingly the norm whereas two generations ago many people could not afford a holiday, or if they could it was a week in a local resort. Indeed, in recent years a market which has grown substantially is to marry in an exotic location such as Kenya, the Dominican Republic or the West Indies, combining it with the honeymoon rather than marrying in one's local church or register office.

This poses big challenges to any European business and simplistically might be summed up as the choice between being reactive and proactive. Reactive businesses respond to change taking place around them – that is externally. The speed with which they respond determines whether they survive or not but still they are accepting agenda set by other organisations. The alternative strategy to change is to be proactive and to initiate change within the existing business – then other firms must respond to your agenda. In reality managing strategic change is likely to be a mixture of both reactive and proactive.

■ 8.6 The role of the strategic audit

Since change has been identified as the greatest challenge to European business in the late twentieth and twenty-first centuries, one immediate response of firms is to assess how capable they are of meeting such change. This involves employees undertaking a strategic audit of the business which will involve considering its past developments and its present position and undertaking a forecast of its future. To appraise its present position it needs to consider both the environment within which it is located and its resources as a European business.

Analysing the external environment will include reviewing external factors which have influenced the business in the past and are likely to continue doing so in future (for example EU legislation; exchange rate movements; the single currency; the changing nature of work and of labour markets; the business cycle), analysing the stability of the environment (for example the impact of continuing privatisation on CEEC markets, whether competition from the Pacific Rim will intensify), and identifying the key forces at work in the environment (new technology). On the basis of this the key opportunities and threats facing the business can then be identified and analysed (Johnson and Scholes, 1993). Opportunities will include building on existing products and markets or developing new ones, for example. Threats will need to consider environmental factors which can adversely affect the business such as new competition, decline of existing markets, skilled labour shortages for example in the software industry, environmental legislation imposing new production costs, EU social policy and so on.

To analyse its internal resources as a business, staff will need to consider a number of issues These will include its portfolio of existing goods and/or services, for example VW's acquisition of Bentley and Rolls-Royce to gain a presence at the super-luxury end of the car market. The type and quality of existing goods and services is another, as with Fiat's 1993 realisation of its need for more distinctive marques with a better quality reputation and their position in their product life-cycles, if it was to survive as an independent company; this involved it undertaking a major new investment programme. The markets in which products are sold are also important; for example the Swedish car producer Volvo has sought to diversify realising its overdependence on the UK, Swedish and US markets. And a company's financial position needs to be considered. Eurotunnel, which has £8.7bn of debt and is unable to meet its own traffic and profit forecasts, is an extreme example since it has had constant battles with the financing banks to reschedule its debts. Its latest promise is that the first dividends will be paid to shareholders by 2006. Also production processes have to be looked at very carefully; for example, when the Japanese acquired a share in Rover Cars before its acquisition by BMW, this Japanese involvement led to the introduction of such practices as total quality management (TQM), and Just-in-Time (JIT) stock-control methods (see Chapter 9).

Considering its previous development is important, since a business can learn from its past experience how it has reached its current level of success, or lack of success. However, an audit is more than just extrapolating from the past to the present. From analysing its past and present a European business can then identify and evaluate its internal strengths and its internal weaknesses, determining which can be built on and which need to be rectified.

Forecasting is notoriously difficult, yet, for an audit to be effective, estimates of changes in the future business environment are necessary. This requires identifying potential opportunities and threats which face the business. The most widely used tool to assist in conducting a strategic audit is the SWOT analysis. To be effective it should provoke discussion as part of the process to reaching decisions about future strategy.

S = Strengths
W = Weaknesses
O = Opportunities
T = Threats

Once this appraisal has been undertaken the business should be able to obtain a clearer picture of why it is doing well or not so well.

■ 8.7 Case study: Disneyland, Paris – choosing the best location?

This exercise will be taken in the context of a case study of Disneyland, Paris. Before we attempt this it will be useful to provide some background information.

EuroDisney (as Disneyland was then known) was opened as part of an ongoing strategy of diversification from the original core functions of cinema cartoons and subsequently films. The first Disneyland was opened in Anaheim, California in 1965, shortly before Walt Disney's death, thanks to the judicious buying up of orange groves years before. Its success prompted the subsequent building of Disneyworld in Orlando, Florida and then the geographic diversification to Disneyland, Tokyo in 1983. The substantial success of this last development was offset by the error of signing away most merchandising and sponsorship rights, an important part of total income, to a local company. It therefore seemed logical when considering further geographic diversification, to look to Europe where American cultural influence is very strong.

A number of sites were considered, among them Barcelona, Spain, which offered the advantages of an excellent climate and a well-established holiday base around the Costa Brava. However, in the mid/late 1980s Spanish tourism was not growing as vigorously as previously due to its image of being cheap, with little ethnic character and a growing reputation for troublemakers. Additionally, it is an airplane flight from European cities with big centres of population (Europeans do not use internal flights to the same extent as Americans do) and its trade is seasonal between May and the beginning of October.

In contrast the site finally chosen, to the east of Paris, was very much more accessible to core EU cities and not dependent on the seasonal holiday trade. France had a history of theme parks such as the famous Asterix the Gaul park. Also, the French government, being anxious to secure a prestigious project, offered Walt Disney Inc., the US parent company, a very attractive package which eventually tempted them to France. This included the government funding autoroute (motorway) and high-speed rail links to EuroDisney, generous loan provisions and the promise of tax breaks.

Management consultants Arthur Andersen, who undertook the initial feasibility study for Walt Disney Inc., argued that demand would be enormous and estimated that nearly 18m people would visit in the first year generating receipts of US$ 1.1 billion. In fact less than half that number materialised.

What Disney did not take account of was the cold climate in autumn and winter, the fact that Disney is quintessentially American whereas the French government has sought to limit American films and the use of English in the media, and that, given the prices initially charged by EuroDisney, Europeans could go to the real America at Disneyworld, Florida more cheaply than to Paris. Also, demand had been falling at Disneyworld as people looked for more sophisticated holidays. Ironically Disney had recognised this in the US with plans to build an historical theme park in Virginia (until blocked after protests by local residents). Further, Disney incurred costs far greater than anticipated building hotels which overran budget by 30 per cent.

Walt Disney Inc. owned 49 per cent of EuroDisney. Of the remaining 51 per cent some was held by private investors and the rest by the consortium of banks which provided most of the very significant financing necessary to build the park; however, this imposed high fixed costs on EuroDisney in the form of interest payments. Seeking to avoid the mistakes incurred at Disneyland (Tokyo), heavy licensing fees and royalty payments had to be met by EuroDisney and this put further financial burdens on it as soon as the theme park opened.

■ Question:

Assume that you were hired by Walt Disney Inc. to undertake a SWOT analysis of EuroDisney, Paris before the decision to go ahead with its construction. What might your conclusions be? (Cover up the rest of this page if you wish to work this out for yourself.)

(NB: As only limited information has been provided, a full SWOT analysis is not possible – however, a flavour of the process can certainly be obtained.)

- **Strengths**
    1. Past experience of running theme parks.
    2. Globally-known brand names of Disney and characters such as Mickey Mouse, Donald Duck, etc.
    3. Popularity of American culture with most consumers.

- **Weaknesses**
    1. High prices charged could deter customers.
    2. High royalty payments to be made to Walt Disney Inc. for use of names.
    3. High gearing ratio, that is large amounts borrowed from a consortium of banks means high interest payments.
    4. Wrong location.

- **Opportunities**
    1. Generous financing by French government.
    2. Nearness to main centres of population.
    3. Advent of the single market with the absence of frontier controls, making travel to France easier.

- **Threats**
    1. Competition from other European theme parks.
    2. French government antipathy to American culture.
    3. Poor climate.

4.   Competition from Disneyworld, Florida.
5.   Problems involved if exchange rates were to become unstable again.

Of course just presenting a list of points is not totally helpful. It is how each point is weighted in terms of the importance attached to it which finally enables a business to decide what it will do next. In the case of Walt Disney Inc. the determination to expand into Europe, the generous financing by the French government, and the nearness to major population centres outweighed other detrimental factors such as climate and the very high debt burden. Additionally, Disney was trying to offset the mistake in Tokyo regarding royalty payments by making unrealistically high demands on EuroDisney, yet failing to realise the problems this would create for the new enterprise.

■ 8.8 Responding to change: adopting a competitive strategy

Having undertaken a SWOT analysis as part of the strategic audit the directors of any European business will be in a very much stronger position to make decisions regarding future strategy. Although it is not the intention of this chapter to discuss in depth the processes of formulating and implementing strategy, a very brief oversight is necessary.

The business's senior decision-makers will need to constantly keep in mind the objectives which have been set for the business and how these might best be achieved in the light of both the organisation's internal structure and the external environment within which it operates. Since there will be a number of ways of achieving each goal, some less efficient than others, then a coherent process of decision-making is needed. An outline is identified below:

1.   Remind decision-makers of defined objectives of the organisation.
2.   Identify the main strategic alternatives to achieve these goals.
3.   Evaluate each in terms of marketing research undertaken, investment needs, new staff, training needs, financial and time costs, new product development, after sales service, legal issues, potential growth and so on.
4.   Make choices in the light of information presented.
5.   Implement adopted strategy/strategies.
6.   Monitor to evaluate actual against predicted performance.
7.   Keeping the initial objectives in mind, and take remedial action if necessary to restore actual performance nearer to predicted.

A body of literature exists on the actual criteria to be employed by any business in evaluating and choosing one of the alternative strategies facing it. Since space does not permit a discussion of these the reader is referred to the texts at the end of this chapter.

There are of course a wide number of strategies which might be adopted, depending on the individual business and its specific objectives. These include:

1. the No Change strategy – that is, let things continue as before;
2. organic growth in existing markets – that is financed internally from the company's own resources or through external borrowing and/or issuing new shares;
3. diversification into other markets, for example abroad, while selling the same products;
4. diversification into other products – which may or may not be related.

The last two strategies might also be financed internally and/or by acquiring other businesses by acquisition (through a cash and/or shares exchange) or by merger. Continuing the list:

5. cost leadership – that is, being the cheapest producer in the market – yet, as noted, this can be risky if profit margins are pared too low;
6. product differentiation – by marketing to create consumer perception of differences between similar products;
7. specialisation by creating a market niche – that is concentrating on a small segment of the market which others have neglected.

Here just three options are briefly explored and applied to a case study. Figure 8.1 illustrates the various options which can be pursued.

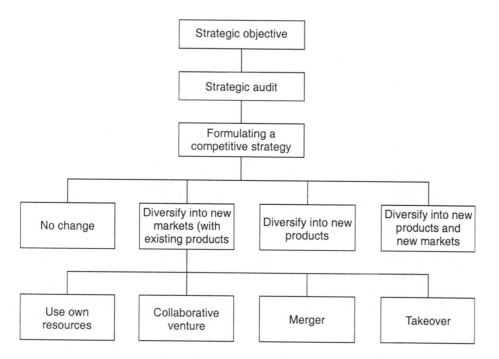

Figure 8.1   Adopting a competitive strategy

■ The No Change strategy

The decision following an audit may be to do nothing. A business may be actively alert to such issues as changes in market structure, innovations by competitors, the extent of competition from abroad, changing consumer preferences and demands and new technology.

It may already be initiating change in its own right forcing other firms to respond to its actions. In these cases what a business can still do is to ensure it maintains this competitive advantage. To be successful the No Change strategy really implies no change from ongoing awareness and self-challenge. If these are the reasons for a business not changing its existing strategy then that is acceptable. The problem arises when a No Change strategy is adopted out of inertia, because the firm that stands still in these circumstances will soon get overtaken . . . and then left far behind.

■ Diversify into other markets

This might mean getting into other markets before one's competitors do. The opening up of the markets of Central and Eastern Europe in the 1990s has shown the scrambling for position from Western European and US firms. Tobacco companies have sought to gain market share through local cheap production since cigarette consumption is much higher there and public health warnings are less common. One key factor affecting potential success is the ability of Western managers to cope with different cultures and the inevitable extra workload expansion brings.

■ Diversify into new products

The success of this strategy will be determined by such internal factors as the financial strength of the business itself, how good its market research has been in forecasting market demand, the strength of its R&D and other technology to develop new products, and the ability of its staff to cope with the production and sale of the new goods or services. Additionally, external factors will include the strength of the competition who are already established in the markets for this new product, and the whereabouts of the product in its life-cycle.

The product life-cycle is obviously an important concept in that it gives an indication of how long the product may be expected to yield a profit. Figure 8.2 below shows a typical product's life-cycle although not all products conform to this pattern. The confectionery Mars bars, the Irish stout Guinness and the Danish Carlsberg lager all appear to be permanently in the maturity stage, without any obvious sign of decline. However, such products are revitalised and sustained by marketing strategies. In contrast, other products such as the Sinclair C5 never get beyond the innovation stage – which makes it all the harder to give many examples!

Assuming that the European business adopts a new competitive strategy by diversifying into new products, then this is obviously higher in risk than the

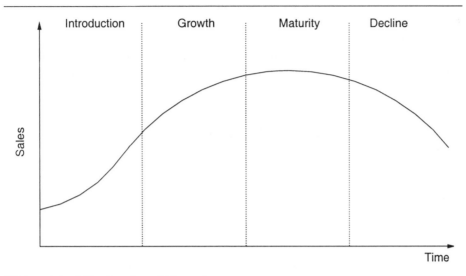

Figure 8.2   The Product Life-cycle

previous two strategies. This is because the business will have no experience of producing and marketing the new products. However, if the launch is confined to the same geographical areas as the other products already manufactured then at least some of the problems will already be known.

With both diversification into new markets and new products, one crucial distinction any firm must consider is the extent to which this is related to previous activities. Diversification into unrelated activities poses much greater operational problems for management and, certainly in the early years, may not contribute as much to profits as hoped.

■ Managing strategic change

Managing strategic change is by a process of delegation through the organisational structure, from the board of directors through senior and middle to junior managers, and hence to the workforce. It is therefore of fundamental importance that all should have involvement in earlier detailed discussions before the strategic plan is formulated to create a sense of ownership. The responsibility for daily operations rests with senior managers of departments or centres who will be budget holders. They will have to ensure the meeting of the weekly, monthly and annual targets as laid down in the strategic plan or explain significant variances if these occur.

One model of managing strategic change suggests a process whereby managers continuously monitor the business environment within which they operate and make small or marginal adjustments to the business as needs dictate. The important issue is to ensure that the business continues to function properly and effectively and that all its stakeholders are happy with what is being done (Johnson and Scholes, 1993).

Synergistic gains are often an important reason for diversification by means of takeovers and mergers, as well as integrating existing organisations under the same corporate umbrella. Quoted in nearly all texts as $2 + 2 = 5$, it relates to the fact that after combining activities the whole is greater than the sum of the parts. The case study below, which examines the potential for mergers among European defence contractors, highlights the synergy which would arise from such mergers.

CASE STUDY   Mediobanca

The Italian bank Mediobanca is a revealing example of a business which is seeking to change itself from a domestic organisation into a European investment bank, particularly with the advent of the euro. Currently it has substantial shareholdings in almost every Italian industrial company – such as Fiat (3 per cent), Pirelli (9 per cent) and Generali (12 per cent) – but little presence outside its domestic market. Within Italy it is also losing custom to foreign and other Italian banks, as with its failure to secure the contract for the 1996 privatisation of the state oil company ENI. This, and the restructuring of the Italian economy as privatisation continues and the single market is completed, is forcing it to review its strategy if it is to survive. To raise money for its restructuring it intends both to issue new shares and to sell existing shareholdings in other companies – this money will be used to develop the investment banking side of its activities and its asset management functions. But it has been argued that to succeed as a bank it needs to divest itself rapidly of its interests in these other companies and to act more like a bank.

As importantly as the physical restructuring is the need for a change in its corporate culture. In the past it has always relied on its contacts and position of influence, doing deals behind closed doors – but now times are changing. Instead of bidding for contracts it is said that Mediobanca still expects to be invited to organise deals as the lead bank – hence its failure to secure the ENI privatisation by its refusal to bid for the contract. Its research publication record is also extremely poor. Most seriously its senior management appears resistant to modern management ideas. Analysts argue that unless Mediobanca changes, its influence in Italy will continue to suffer. Indeed it might be argued that, in practice, Mediobanca is almost adopting a no-change strategy.

■ 8.9 Case study: the European defence industry – the need for a united EU strategy

■ The background

One of the legacies of the fall of Communism and the ending of the political, economic and military divisions in Europe was the so-called peace dividend – the fact that defence budgets could be cut by governments and the resources devoted to other activities. This has led to a contraction in the number of armed forces in the countries of NATO and the former Warsaw Pact (the Soviet and CEEC equivalent of NATO) and in the military equipment needed to service them. However, the links between governments and defence industries are strong and valuable in terms of the defence contracts the former award the latter. Also defence industries have a real strategic value, are symbols of national identity, employ thousands of people and are valuable sources of exports (currently 30 per cent of European total sales). As a result the promised peace dividend has been harder to realise in the EU while EU defence contractors have been slow to adopt appropriate strategies to respond to these changing circumstances. In practice some have operated on the assumption that nothing has changed although this is clearly not so.

The same situation was experienced in the US in the early 1990s. As a result, in 1993, the then US Defence Secretary Les Aspin invited the heads of the top American defence and aerospace companies to dinner at the White House – a meeting now dubbed 'the last supper'. He informed them that the US Government expected them to rationalise through mergers in order to maintain their global competitiveness and to reduce US government defence procurement costs. Quite simply there were too many to survive. The US government would not use its antitrust legislation to block such mergers. Consequently, by 1997, the top fifteen defence corporations had contracted to three conglomerates – Boeing–McDonnell Douglas, Lockheed Martin and Northrop Grumman. However, attempts to complete a £11.6bn merger by the latter two were, in March 1998, disrupted by a challenge from the US anti-trust regulators, the Department of Justice, which announced that it was fundamentally opposed to the deal. The concerns were essentially over the fact that rationalisation has reached its limits consistent with maintaining competition and that any future merger activity is likely to hinder competition and innovation.

■ The problems of the EU defence and aerospace industries

The EU defence and aerospace industries are currently where the US industry was in 1993. There is substantial over-capacity, with too many small firms, preventing the achievement of scale economies in the production of new high-tech weapons, aircraft and warships. For example one major European weapons procurement programme is for 6000 multi-role armoured vehicles (the so-called battlefield taxi) for the French, German and British armies – yet there are 23 different European manufacturers in this sector of the industry, compared with two in the US. The sheer size of potential contracts from EU governments – currently estimated to be nearly $60bn – means that there are only limited incentives for these firms to rationalise.

Nonetheless in the global marketplace, where EU firms compete against US firms for valuable contracts in such places as the Middle East, Latin America, the

---

CASE STUDY   The Promotion of Digital Broadcasting

The promotion of digital television broadcasting highlights a number of the issues above. The broadcasting companies claim that digital broadcasting is a quantum leap forward which will offer households hundreds more tv and audio channels, with CD-quality sound and access to the Internet, home banking, home shopping, radio broadcasts and so on, as well as pay-on-demand channels with just-released films, real-time sports events and so forth.

For the terrestrial and satellite television companies it illustrates diversification into a new, albeit related, product. Also analogue broadcasting – the existing system – is clearly reaching the downturn in its life-cycle and it is proposed to end analogue broadcasting by 2010 to force consumers to switch to digital broadcasting to enable companies to recoup the very high investment costs.

Surveys of UK consumers show little enthusiasm for digital television or for the massive increase in the number of channels available. Indeed very large choice tends to promote poorer quality programmes to fill the time available and 'channel surfing' by viewers as those who holiday in the US soon discover. So the companies launching this new service have substantial consumer resistance to overcome, with much work to be done to differentiate the digital from the analogue service, and a lengthy lead-in time before profits are made.

The strategy to market digital television in the UK was to have been the creation of a new consortium – British Digital Broadcasting (BDB) – consisting of the terrestrial commercial television companies Granada and Carlton Television, and the satellite company (BSkyB). The proposed strategy was that they would ensure the production of a plug-in box to sit on the top of a television and enable household reception of both terrestrial and satellite digital broadcasts. However, the Independent Television Commission (ITC), the UK's television regulator, has forced Rupert Murdoch's BSkyB to leave this consortium for fear that it would give him too much control over digital tv.

This intervention poses a real marketing problem in that the terrestrial and satellite companies have each been forced, therefore, to develop their own non-compatible set-top boxes for digital reception, at a time when compatibility was needed to make the launch a success. So now the UK has three different digital television services coming on stream. One is from the BBC, another is from BSkyB and the third is from ONdigital (the new name for Carlton and Granada). BSkyB will offer the greatest number of new channels – 200, while Ondigital will only offer 30 extra. Unfortunately each digital provider will require a different set-top box to receive the broadcasts, none of which is compatible with the others. A viewer wishing access to all three services would have to pay £600 for the 3 different set-top boxes as well as extra fees to watch the channels (BSkyB estimate a cost of £10 per month). A widescreen television to take full advantage of the new digital broadcasts will cost, initially, an extra £1000. (France, in contrast, has been broadcasting many digital channels since 1996).

Consumers with long memories recall the choice they faced between Betamax and VHS video recorder systems. Although Betamax was regarded as technically superior, VHS won out because it had access to major libraries of films which it brought out in the VHS format. Similarly consumers are reluctant at present to give up CDs and adopt mini-CDs or the digital compact cassette since converting from one system to another is expensive and, if the wrong system is chosen, extremely frustrating. The same logic applies to the set-top boxes for digital broadcasting. So not only has the original collaborative strategy failed through ITC intervention, but marketing the diversification into new products will be very difficult because of the incompatible systems being developed.

Indian sub-continent and Central Europe, economic efficiency, as well as technological innovation, is crucial. Hungary, Poland and the Czech Republic, for example, all have major expenditure increases on defence for a number of years as they seek to replace dated Soviet equipment with NATO-compatible new technology equipment. Additionally the EU faces competition from the US defence contractors within its home markets. For example the contract for the Future Large Aircraft has the potential European manufacturers facing competition from the Russian-Ukrainian Antonov-77 and Boeing's C-17 Globemaster planes; additionally there is talk in Germany of possible EU – Russian–Ukrainian long-term cooperation in this area.

Table 8.1 shows the EU's leading defence contractors. For comparison the leading three companies in the world (all American) in 1995 were firstly Lockheed Northrop ($25.09bn), secondly Boeing–McDonnell Douglas, although in 1995 they were separate companies ($17.90bn) and thirdly Raytheon/Hughes/Texas Instruments ($11.67bn). The biggest EU defence firm was BAe, lying fourth.

There is also disagreement between EU countries over the role of the projects identified in Table 8.2. For example, the proposed construction of the two large aircraft carriers has provoked a debate over the aircraft they will carry. One suggestion is for a naval version of the Eurofighter, which might in practice be too heavy, while an alternative proposal is the next generation of US strike fighter being developed as a successor to the British Harrier jump jet which the US Navy currently uses. Again with the construction of new frigates (codenamed Project Horizon) there is disagreement over the role they will fulfill, with France and Italy wanting them as escort ships defending specific targets while the UK wants them capable of defending a convoy over a wide area. There is also disagreement over the anti-air missile system these ships will operate.

Where there has been multinational cooperation between EU defence contractors it is in the form of ad hoc consortia which have a dubious record, as is shown by the £40 billion Eurofighter, a top-of-the-range bomber and combat jet, which is to be produced by a consortium of British Aerospace, Dasa (Germany – owned by Daimler-Benz), Alenia (Italy) and Casa (Spain), probably from 2001. This project has dragged on since the late 1980s to the extent that it is now questioned whether it actually has a function to fulfill other than as a horrendously expensive job creation scheme. It has been plagued by soaring costs, duplication of effort and national hostilities between the partner countries as to how many planes each country should buy and which components should be produced by each country. Further, it faces competition from rival planes the Swedish Grippen, the French Rafale and the American F22. However, the estimated cost of £50m per aircraft puts it £20m below the F22, while it is allegedly more manoeuvrable than the Rafale and 'a better plane' than the Grippen. The future producers of this plane see it as a potential export success, although a number of doubts have been raised about this, including the extent to which there will be a future demand for jet fighters, and whether the name Eurofighter will be attractive in the US (the major market for arms sales) and Asia, a problem subsequently overcome by renaming the plane 'the Typhoon'.

Table 8.1   The EU's leading weapons companies

COMPANY	PRODUCTS	SALES ($bn)	COUNTRY
Aérospatiale	Aerospace/missiles/satellites	8.7	France
Thomson CSF	Electronics/missiles/communications	6.25	France
Lagardère	Missiles	3.30	France
DCN	Warships	2.6	France
Dassault	Military airplanes	2.25	France
Snecma	Aircraft engines	1.55	France
Giat	Armoured vehicles	1.0	France
DASA	Aerospace/missiles	3.25	Germany
Finmeccanica	Aerospace	2.80	Italy
British Aerospace	Aerospace	6.60	UK
GEC	Electronics	4.30	UK

Source: The European; the Times

Table 8.2   Key weapons procurement programmes, 1998

PROJECT	COUNTRIES INVOLVED	NO. OF UNITS	VALUE OF CONTRACT (US$b)
Future Large Aircraft	UK; France Germany; Italy	300	30.0
Frigates	UK; France; Italy	22	10.0
Aircraft Carriers	UK, France	2	13.0
Battlefield Taxis (multi-role armoured vehicles)	UK; France: Germany	6000	5.0

■ Adopting an EU competitive strategy

What EU defence and aerospace industries need to do is to undertake major restructuring with estimates suggesting that a 20 per cent capacity reduction is needed. Because of this the British, French and German governments called on their main defence contractors to develop a formal plan to promote mergers and strategic alliances within Europe by 31 March 1998; they also argued that the commercial aircraft consortium Airbus needs to be urgently restructured as a single company, which is meant to occur in 1999, although there were worries that this proposal would be hindered by the French government's ownership of Aérospatiale, which has a 37.5 per cent share of Airbus. The UK Defence Secretary, George Robertson, reinforced this need for mergers by his argument that British aerospace and defence industries must 'rationalise or die'. However, it is possible that EU companies may also seek strategic alliances with US companies.

Some consolidation has already occurred. For example, British Aerospace (BAe) and Lagardère's Matra are cooperating in missile production through Matra BAe Dynamics. The French government strategy, although also seeking to rationalise, has been francocentric putting Thomson-CSF, the defence electronics group it 58 per cent owns, at the centre of a new French defence grouping and blocking non-French companies such as the UK's GEC from merging with it. Indeed the large scale French state ownership of its defence and aerospace industries, with their overmanning and high operating costs, was seen as a real barrier to future European integration.

However, in July 1998 the French government surprised analysts by announcing that it was creating a new aircraft and defence group through the merging, on 1 January 1999, of Aérospatiale with the Matra Hautes Technologies defence arm of Lagardère, the privately owned French conglomerate (rather than merging its aerospace section with Dassault and its missiles group with the newly privatised Thomson-CSF as expected). Part of this merger is the partial privatisation of Aérospatiale, with Matra holding 33 per cent of Aérospatiale's shares, 20 per cent floated on the stock market, 5 per cent given to employees and the remainder held by the government. The government will also retain a golden share giving it a final say in decisions made by the merged company. The French government also argued that it believed BAe and Dasa would join the new aircraft and defence group, while the co-director of Lagardère stated that he expected Thomson-CSF and Alenia of Italy to merge their missile businesses with Matra BAe Dynamics.

Additionally, in April 1998, the UK's GEC and Finmeccanica of Italy announced a defence joint venture. This means that the two companies stay separate which makes cost savings and other scale economies hard to realise – not the boldest of steps in the light of what the European defence industry needs.

British Aerospace's Managing Director John Weston, appearing before a French parliamentary commission in 1997, had argued that the first step in consolidation was to make a single defence company from BAe, Dasa of Germany and Aérospatiale and Dassault; at the time of speaking the former of which was one hundred per cent owned by the French government and the latter fifty per cent. He asserted that full privatisation would have to occur in France before this were possible, something which the French government is clearly not envisaging yet. From this, he argued, it would be possible to seek integration with such companies as Alenia (Italy), Saab (Sweden) and Casa (Spain). However, any integration should adopt a fast step-by-step approach rather than a multiple merger of a number of companies simultaneously. His suggestion was for the establishment of a shell company in which all the partners would have a stake and into which they could subsequently transfer their assets as integration developed. Market analysts believe that Europe is still some way away from a single European defence company however.

Another model for integration of the defence and aerospace industries is to link them to the restructuring of Airbus when it is converted into a public limited company, creating one European aerospace company. Germany and France have already indicated that they wish to do this. A third approach which has been suggested is to create a European aerospace company from those currently working on the Eurofighter project, using the same restructuring strategy as is proposed for Airbus. This could then integrate with Dassault and then merge with Airbus, giving joint civilian–military aircraft production in the same way as Boeing–McDonnell Douglas. Yet another model might see transatlantic partnerships and ultimately mergers if the European defence and aerospace industries fail to respond to these global competitive pressures. What is clearly a non-starter is the no change strategy.

There are a number of stumbling blocks to any such integration programme to create a united European aerospace company big enough to compete with Boeing–McDonnell Douglas. Firstly, national pride is at stake and may prove a problem, particularly with the French. Within the Airbus consortium, Aérospatiale, which has a 37.5 per cent share, will still be considerably influenced by the French government, even after the 1999 partial privatisation. The government have indicated that they would want to maintain this 37.5 per cent ownership in any new Airbus public limited company which is formed. Yet this would deter the other partners who, rightly, want full privatisation of Aérospatiale, fearing otherwise French government interference in the company's activities in order best to represent French interests. This, of course, is characteristic of French state corporatism. In the same way another stumbling block is that rationalisation leads to job losses to cut costs, an issue that would be hard to accept in high-cost France and Germany which both have high levels of unemployment. Also, assuming rationalisation does occur, national governments will need to target contracts to these new European companies to ensure they can, at least initially, survive against US competition. This may go against the arguments for free markets and competition but it has happened even more extremely with, for example, EU subsidies for Airbus and it does happen in the US with indirect subsidies to defence contractors via the defence contracts awarded by the Federal government.

■ Conclusions

The rapid US integration of the early 1990s has had the effect of making European efforts at integration look weak, although progress is starting to be made, as evidenced by BAe's acquisition of a 35 per cent stake in Saab, the Swedish aerospace and defence group, in May 1998. Additionally, the March 1998 declaration by the Airbus partners that they had agreed on a possible merger – creating a single European aerospace company called Eurco – further offers hope, although continuing French government partial ownership of Aérospatiale is particularly problematic in this respect.

The US defence conglomerates can offer a full range of competitively priced military equipment to domestic and overseas (including European) markets thanks to the rationalisation and integration which has occurred reducing manning costs and overheads. Until the EU required blueprint for the future of the defence industries is finally agreed and implemented – two major steps forward in the light of previous European responses to global pressures for change – European defence contractors will continue to struggle in the face of the onslaught from the US.

∎ 8.10 Strategy and the multinational company

The benefits of a barrier-free single European market are undoubtedly real and important as has been demonstrated elsewhere. European businesses have been able to grow in size and profitability through the opportunities afforded by easier access to other European countries, and by the ease of establishing a production presence there. In turn, the opportunities afforded by expansion into the EU have attracted non-European investors, most notably US and Japanese multinational enterprises. The full effects of competition from the Pacific Rim countries have yet to be seen, and in 25 years the global market will be very different from what it is now, and much tougher.

Multinational enterprises (MNEs) must make strategic decisions covering a wide range of countries and goods and services. It has been argued that in the foreseeable future, whereas Pacific Rim countries will increasingly compete globally and win on price grounds due to low labour costs, particularly in the growth markets of the Pacific Rim, EU businesses will need to compete on the grounds of quality and style. This is because, even with cost-control programmes and the replacement of labour by capital in production processes, EU-located companies will still not be able to match Pacific Rim labour costs. It is true that more European businesses are now locating production facilities in NICs (newly industrialised countries) both in the Pacific Rim and CEEC. This is certainly a way to compete with Pacific Rim and other countries on cost terms. Equally importantly, however, is the development by the EU of new products and a greater move to services, leaving more established products to these cheaper producers.

The actual process of formulating strategy is hard to generalise for the multinational enterprise. For some, overall strategy will be decided by the parent company, say in Paris or London, then implemented separately by subsidiaries in each individual country. In other cases strategy is formulated at the level of the subsidiary then fed upwards to produce a global strategy.

The case study considered next, Benetton, is not a multinational in the sense of a parent company with a number of subsidiary companies operating in different countries, since everything is controlled tightly from Treveso, Italy by the Benetton family. However, it operates in over 100 countries in the world, is enormously successful in terms of growth and consumer awareness, and is a major European business. The reader might like to look again at section 8.3 before considering this.

■ 8.11 Turnaround strategies: how to fight back!

Section 8.6, the role of the strategic audit, considered the use of a SWOT analysis of EuroDisney during the period of time before the theme park was opened. This section returns to EuroDisney to examine the turnaround strategy adopted to try and stave off liquidation at the hands of its creditors, most notably EU and US banks.

The reasons why a turnaround strategy is needed will vary from business to business. They may include problems associated with diversification into new products or markets; overborrowing then failing to generate the revenues to repay the debt from the new activity; higher than anticipated operating costs; and lack of sufficient financial control (which may be linked to higher than anticipated production costs). All of these may be applied to EuroDisney.

It has been argued that the essential problem facing any business seeking to implement a turnaround strategy is the lack of time available to get things right. Certainly this applied to EuroDisney. A turnaround strategy therefore involves two aspects. Firstly, there is the operational side – trying to stabilise cash outflows, boost revenue and improve the daily running of the business. Secondly, there is the strategic side – seeking new strategies to move the business from its current difficulties to a situation where it can return to profit. Part of this strategic approach may involve the sale of some of the business's assets and reducing the labour employed. Ultimately, if all this fails the business will need to withdraw from this sector of activities or, if this is its only activity, cease trading.

■ Case study: EuroDisney revisited – background

EuroDisney officially opened on 12 April 1992, employing 10 000 people and covering an area one-fifth the size of Paris. It soon became apparent that the projected attendance figures of 17.7m were wildly optimistic and with them anticipated profits, so much so that when first-year trading figures were released in November 1993 they showed that EuroDisney had made a loss of FF 5.3bn (£610m).

CASE STUDY   Benetton: Global Expansion through Family Control

As noted previously, in just over 30 years the Benetton organisation has grown from a small family-run business to a global enterprise. To analyse its strategy is to look at a number of factors all of which have contributed to its success:

1. **Product characteristics**: The distinctive bright colours, fashionable yet safe designs and above-medium prices have given Benetton woollen products an image of affordable style and quality.
2. **Retail outlets**: Its distinctive retail outlets, meeting a standard format with the 'United Colours of Benetton' name, good customer service, and accessibility of products for handling have all created a 'customer friendly' environment.
3. **Franchising agreements**: The use of these – strictly termed independent retailers since franchise agreements were not signed – between Benetton in Italy and its retailer outlets throughout the world has meant that, during its rapid global expansion, Benetton has not had to bear the cost of this itself. All stock supplied is bought by the franchisee with no option of return if not sold. Additionally, the franchisee must rent premises for his/her shop and bear all the setting-up costs. Not having to undertake this financing itself has enormously helped Benetton cash flow. The number of Benetton owned outlets is very limited.
4. **Agents**: The decision to use a series of agents to act as the link between the parent company and the retail outlets has proved to be vital in ensuring Benetton maintains the required standards and quality. The agent also feeds back to Treveso monthly sales figures, places orders and so on.
5. **Retail competition**: To promote competition and hence profits Benetton encourages new retailers to open in close proximity to existing ones. Although this is not liked by the latter the Benetton argument is that existing firms can become lax after some time. New competition will spur them to new efforts – or finish them.
6. **Global expansion**: To become a global player Benetton has expanded into third-world countries such as Somalia, Cuba and Armenia where there would not seem to be much demand. The strategy here is that when economic take-off does occur, Benetton will be in the right place at the right time. Meanwhile there are always foreign customers resident in the country, as tourists or in the diplomatic services and trade missions.
7. **Marketing**: This has been boosted further by an advertising series which, over the years, has sought to shock by portraying scenes which would not normally be regarded as desirable for public exhibition. Benetton has argued this is to promote social awareness; others have argued that the company is following the old maxim 'any publicity is good publicity'. The campaign was dropped in late 1994.
8. **Control**: Although Benetton is now a public limited company the majority shareholding (72 per cent) is still controlled by the Benetton family, which enables it to exercise the particular strategic direction which it wishes.
9. **Inventory control**: A highly efficient stock or inventory control system is operated by Benetton which enables retail outlets to be provided with new goods very quickly. This gives a substantial start over other fashion chains, since normally there is a long lead time between new fashions on the catwalk and their appearance in shops.
10. **Quality control**: The final design and wool dying processes, which make Benetton products so distinctive, are still closely controlled by the family. This quality control process is very important in ensuring that standards are maintained.

The projected attendance for 1994 was 11 million people, including almost five million from France, which seems a very high percentage of the population. However, even 11 million visitors seemed unlikely considering that between October 1993 and March 1994 only 3.13 million people visited the theme park, even allowing for this being the autumn and winter. The biggest worry was the fact that attendances were continuing to decline, as was the amount of money each person was spending (merchandising being a very important part of total revenue). The 3.13m above had fallen from 3.32m for the same period the previous year.

This rapid downward spiral was, understandably, also reflected in the price of EuroDisney ordinary shares on the London stockmarket. When the shares were offered to the public in late 1989 at a price of 707p, they were oversubscribed ten times; on the first day of trading they shot up to 887p and by April 1992 were trading at 1700p. By early 1993 they had slipped to 1173p and by late 1993, following investigations of insider dealing on shares traded on the Paris Bourse, trading in EuroDisney shares was temporarily suspended. When it resumed they stood at 338p and, by October 1994, they were trading at 90p per share. (At the end of July 1998 they were 109p.)

In the same way the FF 3 billion of debt relating to the hotels which had been built around the park was being traded at around 25 per cent of face value. Debt attaching to the theme park itself – about FF 6.6bn – was selling for 55–60 per cent of face value.

■ Causes of the problem

Some of these have been discussed previously. Others include the economic recession in Europe, the very high prices charged for both entry to the theme park and staying at EuroDisney hotels, the lack of effective cost-control programmes, the strong French franc deterring visitors from outside France, and high interest rates deterring French consumption and hence visitors to theme parks.

■ Devising a turnaround strategy

Faced with the very large loss in 1992, EuroDisney realised that this could not be sustained and that a turnaround strategy needed to be devised promptly. It also acknowledged that it would face liquidity problems unless something was done soon. The main focus had to be the financial side of the turnaround strategy, and therefore its initial steps were to:

1. ask parent company Walt Disney Inc. for financial support until it could negotiate a deal with the financing banks;
2. introduce new management, including new chairman Philippe Bourguignon;
3. develop a new marketing plan with the aim of reducing entry and hotel prices;
4. improve cost control to minimise unnecessary expenditure – such as closing down parts of the hotels not needed in winter through lack of demand; and

5. delay constructing Phase 2 of EuroDisney, the building of film studios and a cinema theme park at Marne la Vallée.

During these negotiations Walt Disney Inc. promised finance until the end of March 1994. However, as a minority shareholder (49 per cent) it argued that it was primarily the responsibility of the financing banks to help EuroDisney. If by 31 March 1994 this help was not forthcoming, Disney would withdraw its support and EuroDisney would close. It was also extremely reluctant to renegotiate its royalty and franchising payments which would have eased the financial burden on EuroDisney.

In contrast, the financing banks, over 60 and mainly French, had contributed most of the funding and were now owed approximately FF 20.3bn (US$ 3.43bn). They were antagonised by Disney's demand that half the loans be written off to enable EuroDisney to survive. They were also looking for a greater commitment from Disney which had so far only invested US$160m yet was threatening to abandon EuroDisney; they argued that Disney should be much more involved in the rescue programme. Its offer to reduce its fees and royalties was one step in the right direction but not sufficient by itself.

It should be remembered that there was a considerable element of brinkmanship in these negotiations. The more either party could push the other to accept the bulk of the responsibility for the financial restructuring of EuroDisney, the easier it would be for them to escape with minimum loss. Nonetheless, it appears to be true that had financial help not been forthcoming Disney would have seen the closure of EuroDisney after March 1994.

■ The proposed financial strategy

A rescue package to save EuroDisney was finally agreed in March 1994, just before the expiry of Disney's deadline, but only after negotiations.

□ 1 Disney's proposals

1. Banks should accept proposals to halve EuroDisney's debt through a FF 5bn rights issue of shares and a debt for equity swop (that is, exchanging shares for fixed interest debt to reduce the interest burden EuroDisney had to pay).
2. The consortium of banks to put up at least half the money needed in total to rescue the company.
3. Caisse de Depots, the French government financial institution and one of the lead banks in the consortium, which held EuroDisney's FF 4.8bn fixed interest rate debt should reduce the rate payable from the then 7.8 per cent.

□ 2 Banks' proposals

Understandably the banks' main concern was to avoid exposure to even more risk of debt; they also wanted Disney to take more responsibility as a member of the rescue package. Their proposals were that:

1. Disney should be fully involved in the proposed rights issue, that is buying some of the shares to be issued.
2. It should use its influence to attract new equity investors for the proposed issue.
3. It should buy assets from EuroDisney, particularly its hotels.
4. It should reduce its royalty fees on EuroDisney's revenue (worth FF 262m the previous year).
5. The management structure and strategy at EuroDisney should be reviewed to assess how effective both were.

An agreement to financially restructure EuroDisney was finally reached in late May 1994 with creditor banks approving the financial restructuring of the theme park and agreeing to underwrite 51 per cent of a $1bn investment package.

■ The Saudis to the rescue!

Just as the cinema has a tradition of the hero turning up in the last reel to rescue the woman in distress, so EuroDisney was rescued by an unlikely hero in the form of a Saudi Arabian prince. In early June 1994 Prince Al-Waleed Bin Talal announced that he would buy between 13–24.5 per cent of the group's shares for approximately $1bn, if they were not taken up in the rights issue. He decided to invest in the ailing company because he believed the turnaround strategy EuroDisney had adopted, including the operational part discussed below, would enable it to turn the corner.

- Under the terms of the prince's involvement, the United Saudi Commercial Bank (of which he is chairman) would be involved in the issue of the new shares. Technically it would act as a sub-underwriter to the three leading underwriting banks in the EuroDisney rights issue (BNP; Indosuez; Caisse des Depots et Cosignations).
- 51 per cent of the rights issue was to be offered publicly, with Disney subscribing to the outstanding 49 per cent. The proceeds would be used to pay part of EuroDisney's FF 20bn debt.
- If Talal acquired less than $1.9bn of Euro Disney shares in the rights issue, Walt Disney would sell him the balance up to $1bn at the issue price (if the full $1bn were sold it would cut the Disney share holding to 36 per cent).
- Talal and the United Saudi Commercial Bank agreed to limit their total stake to FF2.4bn under any circumstance.

The prince also declared his intention to invest $100m in a convention centre in the EuroDisney complex to help fill the theme park's hotels in the low season.

■ The final package

□ 1 Financial

Following Talal's intervention a final deal, agreed by all, was assembled. Simply it consisted of the following:

- FF 13bn of debts were restructured, that is payment deadlines were deferred.
- FF 6bn (£700m) of new shares were made available as a rights issue, with shareholders offered 7 new shares for every 2 held. In August 1994 Euro Disney was able to pay FF 5.8bn proceeds from its recent rights issue to its banking syndicate.

☐ 2 Operational

An audit of EuroDisney's operations, which had been required by the bank consortium, found that generally the strategies of the new chairman, Philippe Bourguignon, were effective. Nonetheless, major action had to be taken to increase operational efficiency and change the theme park's image from one of high costs and financial failure. The following measures were adopted:

1. A further name change from EuroDisney to Disneyland, Paris (having used the name EuroDisneyland during 1994).
2. 20 per cent reduced entrance fees from April 1995 (a long overdue remedy to strong complaints).
3. Reduced accommodation fees.
4. Reduced cost of food.
5. The provision of new attractions such as 'Space Mountain', a highly popular 'white knuckle' ride found in other Disney theme parks.
6. The building of a 12-screen cinema complex.
7. The introduction of seasonal pricing.
8. The opening of plans for a 600-unit property development with a golf course to generate revenue independently of the theme park.

■ How successful has the strategy been?

Four years after the 1994 reform package the picture at Disneyland, Paris is still patchy. It is mainly one of improving operational profits but increasing financing costs arising from the delayed debt repayments coming on-stream. Strategically, the company also sees property and shopping village developments south of the theme park as major additional revenue sources.

For the three months March–June 1995, Disneyland Paris made a first-time net profit of FF 170m (£22.36m) against a loss of FF 546m for the same period, 1994. The upturn was assisted by a number of factors, including growing revenue and profit margins on operations – helped by increasing attendance through reduced hotel prices (boosting hotel room occupancy rates) and reduced entry prices; a new marketing strategy; the opening of Space Mountain, (at a cost of £100m); the financial restructuring addressed above – including the temporary suspension of debt interest payments (worth £600m per annum until 1997) and reduced payments to Disney; and increased usage by big French companies and government ministries for Christmas parties, conferences and so on.

However, net profits have not been maintained, and indeed losses have been more common. For example, for the period October 1996 to end March 1997, losses at Disneyland, Paris rose as a result of an increase in the interest payments of FF 68m to FF 356m on its FF 15bn debts. This contributed to a loss of FF 120m compared with losses of FF 169m for the same period the previous year. The interest payments, which began again in 1995 after the interest payment holiday in 1994, require a year-on-year rise in revenue of 5 per cent to meet the extra finance and leasing costs. As the year progressed, however, and peak summer attendance occurred this changed the picture so that, in 1996 as a whole, Disneyland made a profit before exceptionals of FF 156m, only its second profit since opening.

In late 1997 the proposed new cinema and conference centre was opened. Rising visitor numbers coupled with increased spending, increased hotel occupancy, themed events to boost winter revenues and efficiency gains meant that for 1997 as a whole the theme park losses totalled FF 205m ($34.2m). Management had felt that demand was sufficiently well-established to raise entrance prices without impacting visitor numbers. Indeed park turnover rose by 9 per cent while for the park, hotels and Disney village as a whole the increase in turnover was 15 per cent. Disney village, located just outside the park, has proved to be a major and important revenue source for the company with its restaurants, shops and entertainment complex. What is interesting to note is that operational profits ahead of financial charges rose from FF 107m to FF 227m for the year. Where the company is still being hit, however, is by the continuing increases in net financial charges to FF 436m, due to the restructuring begun in 1994, compared with FF 356m in the first half of 1996. However, Disneyland has argued that its strategy of providing a new attraction and developing its shopping centre and other property activities south of the theme park will allow it to cope with these rising financial charges.

■ 8.12 Measuring successful strategies

If a business strategy is implemented, then subsequently it needs also to be measured to determine the extent of its success. A successful strategy might be measured by looking at a number of characteristics, both financial and non-financial (Cole, 1994):

- **Financial**:
    1. Rate of return on capital.
    2. High growth rates in profit, turnover etc.
    3. Rising share value.
    4. Ability to maintain satisfactory cash flow.
    5. Ability to repay bank and other debt.

- **Non-financial**:
    1. Personnel: number of industrial disputes; good effective training programmes (measured by staff performance subsequently).
    2. Sales: by goods/services produced; by market.
    3. Technical innovation: extent to which employed.
    4. Investment expenditure: linked with 3 above and measured by amount spent and contribution to operations.
    5. Expenditure on Research and Development.

6. Marketing expenditure: as a percentage of total production costs and as compared with competitors.
7. Extent to which the business has become environmentally friendly.
8. Market share.
9. Scale of plant and operations.

The reader may think of other measures which would help to assess how successful a strategy has been. Often, of course, the problem is how to measure them accurately.

An alternative measure of successful strategy is added value (Kay, 1993). This is defined as the margin by which the value of a company's output (goods and services) exceeds the value of its inputs (labour, capital and so on). On this basis Benetton in our example above has been very successful in its strategy as judged by the value its production processes (including all stages from raw materials to the franchisee) have added, although a significant amount of the difference is of course due to that part of the input costs borne by the franchisees. However, since it has exhausted much of the potential arising from its distinct and individual character (the most vital part of a company's success in adding value), then its growth in clothing sales is destined to be much slower in future.

In contrast, argues Kay, the Dutch multinational Phillips has added negative value, that is it has reduced its wealth at the end of the production process compared with at the beginning. This may be attributed to a range of reasons including missed opportunities with some products – for example, the compact disc which Phillips invented (not the Japanese as many think), and lack of demand for other goods such as the laser disc and the DCC (digital compact cassette).

Value added, a concept also used in education to assess the contribution each college and university makes to a student's intellectual development, is a useful summary statistic. However, it is a blanket statistic and in that sense variables such as those above give a more discriminatory assessment of separate parts of an organisation. In the end, of course, the most vital statistic of all is the profit a firm makes – and its ability to increase it over time.

■ Review questions

1. Discuss why a European business needs to have a strategy rather than merely responding to events as and when they occur. Illustrate your answer with reference to case studies in this book.
2. Critically discuss Benetton's strategy of global expansion rather than concentrating just on the EU.
3. Discuss the advantages and disadvantages to a firm of diversifying into (a) new products, (b) new markets.
4. Write a one-page position paper to the European Commissioner for competition Karel van Miert, itemising the advantages and disadvantages of European defence firms merging.

5.   Discuss the main problems EuroDisney encountered in formulating a turn-around strategy. Can you think of anything else that might have been done to make the turnaround strategy more effective?

■ Bibliography

Anon, *Benetton S.p.A.* (Boston: HBS Case Services, Harvard Business School, 1988).

Ansoff, H. I., *Corporate Planning* (Harmondsworth: Penguin, 1975).

Calori, R. and Lawrence, P. (eds), *The Business of Europe: Managing Change* (London: Sage, 1992).

Cole, G. A., *Strategic Management* (Mendlesham: DP Publications Ltd, 1994).

de Rouffignac, P. Danton, *Europe's New Business Culture* (London: Pitman, 1991).

Drew, J., *Doing Business in the European Community*, 3rd edn (London: Whurr, 1992).

Houlden, B., *Understanding Company Strategy: An Introduction to Thinking and Acting Strategically* (Oxford: Blackwell, 1993).

Johnson, G. and Scholes, K., *Exploring Corporate Strategy*, 4th edn (Hemel Hempstead: Prentice Hall, 1997).

Kay, J., *Foundations of Corporate Success* (Oxford: Oxford University Press, 1993).

Mayes, D. G. (ed.), *The European Challenge: Industry's Response to the 1992 Programme* (Hemel Hempstead: Harvester Wheatsheaf, 1991).

Preston, J. (ed.), *Cases in European Business* (London: Pitman, 1991).

Scholes, K. and Klemm, M., *An Introduction to Business Planning* (Basingstoke: Macmillan, 1987).

Smith, J. G., *Business Strategy – an Introduction*, 2nd edn (Oxford: Blackwell, 1990).

Thurley, K. and Wirdenius, H., *Towards European Management* (London: Pitman, 1989).

Wilson, R. M. S., Gilligan, C. and Pearson, D. J., *Strategic Marketing Management* (Oxford: Butterworth-Heinemann, 1992).

Also:

The Economist
The European
The Financial Times
The Independent
The Times

CHAPTER 9

Alternative models of the European business organisation

■ 9.1 Introduction

Since the beginning of the second industrial revolution in the 1970s, with the advent of automation and communication and information technologies, European and US businesses have been forced to re-evaluate their entire production philosophies and processes. This self-appraisal was emphasised particularly by their relative lack of competitiveness against Japanese and other Pacific Rim businesses. It has been an ongoing process affecting all involved in production. Many side-effects of this revolution have already been seen, such as the growth of long-term structural unemployment across the EU as staple industries have declined.

This chapter looks at Japanese production methods and philosophies, how they differ from conventional production methods and the impact of this on organisational structures and philosophies as embodied by European businesses in the past. New philosophies such as Business Process Re-engineering and benchmarking are examined. Teleworking, hot-desking and other contemporary business working practices, which apply particularly to the provision of services, are also examined.

■ 9.2 European business organisations: the need for change

Earlier in this book the strengths and weaknesses of larger European business organisations were considered. Two aspects of this were particularly identified. Firstly there were problems arising from the large-scale production methods associated with Frederick Taylor. These had been implemented by Henry Ford's assembly-line production, the aims of which were to achieve économies of scale, that is, the cost-savings incurred when all inputs are increased in the same proportion. This became known as the Fordist production method. Unfortunately, the side-effect of lowering unit production costs was often found to be declining product quality.

Secondly, on an organisational or management basis such production methods have tended to accentuate divisions between management and the workforce leading at times to industrial conflict. This is particularly so where a top-down style of management has been employed. The implication of this is that suggestions for improving the operations of the business have tended to come from senior management and then to be implemented by middle management. A comparison with alternative production and management models as typified by Japanese firms is therefore essential.

■ The rise of Japanese production methods

In the 1950s, when Japan was rebuilding its industry to recover from the effects of the Second World War, its goods were considered to be of poor quality and only bought by those who could not afford dearer but superior-quality European goods. By the 1970s, however, the situation had to some extent reversed itself. Japanese goods had acquired a reputation for quality, reliability and attractive design while European goods were neither reliable nor of high quality – the Italian car producer Lancia and the UK car producer British Leyland were prime examples of this. Japanese success was a result of its manufacturers taking US and European products and production methods and modifying them to suit the peculiar needs of their culture. Most people associate the quality-control philosophy and processes with Japan – yet the origins of this are to be found in the US with the work of W. Edwards Deming and Joseph Juran. Similarly, many think of the compact disc as a Japanese invention – yet it was developed by Dutch firm Phillips.

Today Japanese specialisation in automobiles and electronics and electrical consumer goods has enabled them to dominate the world's markets. Additionally, they have been able to produce these goods at a cost much lower than that of the EU and indeed the US. Consequently, both of the latter have a large trade deficit with Japan, as was seen in Chapter 1, although this is not the only reason.

European businesses were therefore obliged to review their production and management methods and consider in turn how they might adopt and adapt Japanese methods to improve their competitiveness in world markets. This was particularly important in the light of increasing competition from other Pacific Rim countries, such as Taiwan, Malaysia, South Korea and Indonesia. Because European and Japanese cultures are so different, then even where Japanese plants have located within the EU the production processes have had to be translated to fit the culture of the country within which they are operating. For example, the traditional start-of-day exercises for all staff which are regarded as typical of businesses in Japan are not normally required in the EU.

■ 9.3 The failure of the traditional corporate model

■ The traditional European business model

Although the bulk of EU organisations are small and medium-sized enterprises (less than 500 employees) and many are family owned, it is the large-scale plant which this section focuses on particularly.

European industry has, in the past, been typified by a number of characteristics including:

1. An assembly line using mass production to manufacture only one type or design of good in a period of time.
2. Employment of a batch production process (often using EOQ or economic order quantity) whereby a product passes through a series of stages, each of these processing the good. However, there are risks of bottlenecks at various points.
3. By producing very large quantities of each good it is possible to achieve economies of scale, that is falling unit costs of production.
4. To mass produce entails holding large stocks of components and works in progress.
5. Quality has not been of fundamental importance to the organisation since defects can be repaired or, at worst, faulty goods destroyed.
6. Since large-scale manufacturing was in anticipation of demand, large-scale marketing campaigns had to create the demand for the product. Where this was not achieved large losses were incurred.
7. Since supply and demand often did not match, firms carried large stocks of finished goods – what has been called a just-in-case method of production, that is in case demand for the product suddenly increases.
8. When the assembly line has to be changed to a new product set-up, or change over times are lengthy, there are attendant disruptions to production and high costs. Additionally, there are extended lead-in times before customers can be supplied with the new product.

■ Problems associated with this model

It is fairly obvious that there are problems with this approach. Above all it is slow and cumbersome to adapt to sudden changes in consumer demand. The lead-in time for retooling the assembly line production to enable another good to be produced is sufficiently long to prevent the plant suddenly meeting demand fluctuations, for example a small demand for a specialised modification to the existing product. Setting up the assembly line for a new production run is costly, and while it is being undertaken the line and employees are not working.

Holding stocks of components and raw materials in anticipation of production, and finished goods in anticipation of sales, is both expensive in terms of factory space occupied and in terms of money tied up. The opportunity cost of this is likely to be high, particularly where a firm might have cash-flow problems.

Since quality is not of fundamental importance in pervading the whole culture of the business, errors and mistakes carry less weight since the perception is that they can be rectified – and anyway they are someone else's responsibility. Deficiencies in manufacture obviously create extra costs since these must be repaired; these may well offset the benefits of falling unit costs from economies of scale. More importantly, deficiencies in quality will lose custom and diminish future sales.

Since production is in anticipation of demand, and since volume production is necessary to achieve scale economies, any failure to secure high sales may cause substantial losses to the business. This lack of flexibility is of serious concern to any business since it imposes a constraint on its ability to modify its competitive strategy as external factors change. For example, its ability to respond rapidly to new products or new suppliers entering the market will be impaired.

■ 9.4 The Japanese production model

In contrast to the traditional production model outlined above, Figure 9.1 illustrates the fundamental differences of the Japanese model compared with the traditional European model. This diagram focuses on four main aspects of Japanese production:

1. The adoption of a Flexible Management system.
2. The use of a just-in-time production system.
3. The adoption of Total Quality Management as an operating philosophy.
4. Quality circles.

Each of these is explored below.

Of major importance to Japanese production is the concept of teamwork. Each member of the workforce, from managing director to floor sweeper, is a member

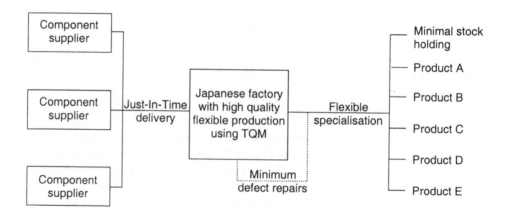

Figure 9.1   Japanese Production Systems

of the team and as such has an equal contribution to play in the quality of the production process. Japanese teams are much less overtly hierarchical than European companies, with all employees wearing the same company overalls, dining in the same area, starting and leaving work at the same time, and so on.

In contrast European businesses are, as we have seen, much more obviously hierarchical, with clear dress distinctions between management and employees, separate car parking spaces, separate dining rooms, provision of company cars for managers, and so forth. Most importantly it has been noted that any suggestions for improvement tend to be top-down rather than from any level of the company. However, Europeans who have worked for Japanese companies argue that in fact they are also hierarchical in their attitudes, but this is more concealed. For example the name tag, the size of the desk, the type of car provided all determine status in the Japanese business, albeit more subtly.

■ Flexible management systems (FMS)

The traditional European model of business production has been seen to involve large-scale production of one good at a time with long lead-in periods before the assembly line could be retooled for another product. In contrast, FMS, or Flexible Specialisation as it is also known, seeks to operate a multi-product model with a number of different goods being produced at the same time, and each assembly line being capable of switching to another product with relative speed and ease. This means that the batch size of each good (that is the amount produced) is smaller compared with the traditional European model. In addition, computer control of the machinery to enable components to be handled, assembled, tested and passed on to the next stage, with minimum delay, reduces the amount of down-time when production is not occurring. This is achieved by the use of Computer Numerically Controlled (CNC) machinery and the use of robotics.

To illustrate the ongoing improvement and effectiveness of Japanese production methods Jewitt (1994) argued that change-over times for the Hitachi Zoren 3000 tonne double-action press have been reduced from 130 minutes in 1988 to 10 minutes in 1994. Shingo (1986) asserted that Japanese techniques mean their production set-up times take one-fiftieth of the time taken in Europe and the US.

There are several requirements for flexible specialisation to work effectively. The workforce must be sufficiently skilled to be able to cope with producing a range of different products, and this requires an ongoing training programme. The marketing/forecasting department must be capable of clearly identifying changing market conditions to permit production to meet anticipated demand changes. Most importantly the capital equipment must be multi-purpose to be capable of producing different outputs.

The benefit derived from flexible specialisation is not that of economies of scale but rather economies of scope. These occur as a result of reduced average total costs due to producing more and different products. In this way overheads such as information technology, marketing, premises and so on can be spread over a number of products. This makes it cheaper for one firm to produce this range rather than a number of different small firms each producing one or two products.

There are a number of other advantages derived from flexible specialisation:

1. The business can easily switch from one product to another to meet sudden or short-term changes in demand between the different products it manufactures, and to pre-empt competitors.
2. Additionally, different goods may be produced at the same time on different production runs.
3. Because of the adaptability they offer to a business, short production runs can become as profitable as long runs.
4. Since production is to meet existing demand rather than in anticipation of potential demand, large stocks of unsold goods are not accumulated.
5. If a customised product is required, for example a summer sales campaign to sell a limited edition of a car, this can easily be produced.
6. Because production is in more limited runs quality problems arising from employee boredom are minimised.

■ Just-in-time (JIT) management

Although developed in the US, originally, this was also adopted most effectively by the Japanese in the 1950s. Its main aim is to exercise very tight control over all stages of the production process, to ensure that just sufficient components are brought in or produced just as they are needed, that is just-in-time (as opposed to the European just-in-case model). This begins from the initial stock or inventory levels by operating with the minimum possible levels consistent with producing to the required levels of output. Typically a large-scale producer such as a Nissan or Honda car plant might use this method. Component suppliers are located in a hinterland near to the plant with the responsibility for servicing its stock needs by making up to 16 deliveries a day. They take full responsibility for the quality of the components they deliver, absolving the producer from the need to carry large volumes of stock, or spending time to check their quality on delivery. As seen above this minimises inventory costs.

Schniederjans (1993) argues that JIT consists of eight main principles, which are:

1. Only when the customer has placed an order does the manufacturer begin production of the good or service.
2. To permit maximum flexibility in production each unit of each good produced should be viewed as a separate order to avoid being locked into long production runs. Quality is therefore paramount for each unit as well.
3. Work is towards the concept of zero waste to minimise production costs.
4. The workforce should continuously seek to improve the flow of products through the factory to avoid bottlenecks so typical of EU factories in the past.
5. Everyone should strive to produce goods with zero defects.
6. People working on the assembly lines should be afforded maximum respect since they are the most important (human) resource.

7. Since stocks held in case are a wasted resource, then managers should seek to eliminate unforeseen eventualities – this of course links back to the idea of producing on demand instead of in anticipation of it.
8. Allocating resources to JIT is part of a long-term process of continuous improvement.

So JIT extends to every stage in the production process from the receipt of orders until the goods finally leave the plant. At each stage of production just sufficient output is supplied to the next stage just as it is needed. Each employee therefore has responsibility to ensure that this does happen and that what is supplied has been produced to the highest quality possible. It also avoids the problems of bottlenecks. Linked to other quality assurance systems such as TQM (discussed below), this ownership of the production process ensures that what does not happen is that defective goods are only detected when the production process has been completed – as with the past European business model. Hence waste is minimised. JIT also requires minimum set-up times since the quicker each stage of a new production run can be undertaken, the lower the costs and the less revenue lost.

The classic example of JIT was developed by Toyota with its card-based or *kanban* system (literally meaning a visible record). Each time a stage of the production line needs components to undertake its part of the work it releases a card or *kanban* authorising the previous stage of production to produce the components it needs, and a similar card to deliver them. Since the whole system is driven from the ordered number of goods needed at the final output stage, overproduction and hence wastage is eliminated. The system has often been described as one where output is 'pulled through' the production process by final demand rather than being 'pushed through' the system by production forces as with traditional or batch production methods, that is from the inputting of resources. Figure 9.2 illustrates this.

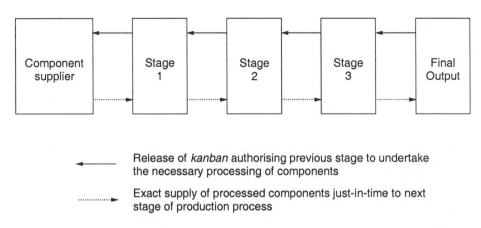

Release of *kanban* authorising previous stage to undertake the necessary processing of components

Exact supply of processed components just-in-time to next stage of production process

Figure 9.2   Just-in-Time Production

CASE STUDY   JIT and the Supplier Park System

Jaguar, which is the luxury car division of Ford, will begin the manufacture of its first high-volume car – the X400 – in 2001–2002. Helped by £43m of government aid the new model will create 500 extra jobs and will be based at its Halewood plant in Merseyside, NW England, where, currently, Ford Escorts are being produced. Already senior executives have decided that they want to be able to draw on suppliers located next to the production site – effectively using a supplier park, which is like a conventional industrial park but geared to one major producer. This is for a number of reasons the most important of which is that the proximity of suppliers will permit just-in-time delivery to the Jaguar assembly lines offering significantly lower inventory costs. Another linked reason is that growing traffic congestion on UK roads costs manufacturers an estimated £8bn a year through delays, extra fuel, vehicle wear and tear, extra time taken by employees, and so on. With nearness of component suppliers the manufacturer gains certainty regarding delivery. The components suppliers are happy because the new car will generate extra income of nearly £400m a year.

Outsourcing is clearly an important part of just-in-time or lean production and lean process stocks, and it is argued that as much as possible of a car's components should be outsourced to specialists who are experts in their field – who can therefore provide components which are of the highest quality and lowest cost and produced with the best technology – although sometimes this technology is in-house requiring components also to be produced in-house. In the case of Nissan at Sunderland, UK over 70 per cent of the car's value is outsourced.

What is also happening is that car manufacture is increasingly becoming modular in its assembly processes which speeds assembly time and reduces costs. So components suppliers are providing not just parts but whole component systems or sub-assembly modules such as seating, plug-in dashboard modules, suspension and even, for Chrysler's light truck plant in Brazil, a complete chassis with wheels that is rolled to the assembly line. These component systems total 60 per cent of the value of most cars – and the suppliers are being renamed systems integrators. Therefore the major global car producers, such as General Motors and Ford, increasingly see themselves as assemblers of these high-value component systems and are happy to delegate to the systems integrators the responsibility for researching, developing and manufacturing these component systems in return for providing them with long-term high-value supply contracts.

Other car producers such as Skoda, in the Czech Republic, are taking the supplier park system even further with component suppliers actually located within the car plant itself manufacturing component systems and transferring them directly to the assembly line. A similar situation occurs at Ellesmere Port, in the North West of England, where the Vauxhall Astra is being built. Here components suppliers located in the supplier park provide component modules by small trains directly to the exact point on the assembly line where they are needed and at the right time. They can do this because Vauxhall provide the suppliers several times daily with assembly schedules. This system is known as 'supply in-line sequence' or SILS. At Nissan, Sunderland, the facia for the Nissan Micra is put together on a conveyor assembly line close to the main assembly line and then transferred by rack to the appropriate point on the line.

However, there is a limit to how far this just-in-time development is permitted. Suppliers have been pushing to take it even further, for example to develop modules for the entire interior of the car and also to fit the sub-assembly modules. Manufacturers currently are reluctant to hand over so much responsibility for assembly and quality and hence so much control. Outsourcing does pose more control problems for manufacturers, particularly regarding the quality of assembly and the investigation of any problems arising. It has further been argued that outsourcing may be detrimental to just-in-time or lean production since the use of sub-assembly incurs more handling and associated costs and generates in-process stocks, since components are produced before needed at the point of assembly.

☐ The problems of JIT

The main problems any company faces when it introduces JIT management are:

1. the cost involved in introducing such a system;
2. the time involved, since the adoption of such a process is lengthy;
3. the problem of changing the whole philosophy and culture of the business – with the risk of staff resistance; and
4. how this fits within existing production processes – since JIT cannot just be grafted on to existing systems, there has to be a fundamental rethink of the whole philosophy of production and of the existence of the business.

■ Total Quality Management (TQM)

Although flexible specialisation and just-in-time might be regarded substantially as production and stock control processes, total quality management can be regarded much more as a management philosophy. Nonetheless, it is quite likely that a firm employing the first two production methods will also want to employ TQM as the underpinning philosophy. TQM aims to run the business in such a way that recognition of the need for optimum quality pervades every aspect of the organisation's activities and at every level from chairman to workforce. The failure to achieve this quality generates costs which detract from profitability and hence competitiveness. In particular, rather than solving problems once they have occurred TQM seeks to prevent them occurring in the first place; prevention rather than cure minimises costs. Prices of finished products can then be reduced to make them more competitive, market share can be increased and profitability enhanced.

Each member of the business is responsible for the quality of the work they undertake and hence for the quality of the final goods or services delivered. This means that the business must strive for zero defects in all work undertaken, since any errors or defects must be rectified and this generates extra and unnecessary costs. As noted previously it is not therefore acceptable for any faults to be detected only when the product is finished. Where faults do occur, they should be picked up along the line during the production process.

☐ 1 Internal and external customers

TQM in turn links to the concept of internal and external customers. The external customers are those who buy the finished product – the car or the video recorder; the internal customer is the next person in the assembly line production process to whom the semi-manufactured goods are being passed.

In Figure 9.2 the people working at stage 2 are the internal customers of those at stage 1 from whom they receive the goods to undertake their stage of production. In turn when they pass the goods to stage 3 these workers are the internal customers of stage 2. The same logic also applies to all services in the business – human resources, finance, computing, marketing, transport and so on. All other employees are their internal customers.

In summary, TQM might, therefore, be defined as having the following characteristics:

- It is a philosophy which underlies every aspect of the business's planning and organisational activities.
- It seeks to achieve zero defects in all aspects of production as a means to minimise production costs by anticipating and hence preventing problems before they occur. Although in reality this is unobtainable, nonetheless continuous improvement which underpins it (known as *kaizen*) is feasible through monitoring all aspects of production and exercising control over them.
- Production must be customer centred – both internal and external.
- All employees have a crucial role to play in their team to ensure that TQM is fully implemented.
- There is effective communication between all members of each team and hence the business as a whole. Quality is not driven solely by senior managers.
- An effective stock control system to minimise holdings and hence costs (such as JIT) is essential.

The similarities between JIT as a stock-control system and TQM as a management philosophy can be clearly seen in this analysis.

One aspect of TQM which can be distinguished is that quality is regarded both as a personal or individual issue and as a team activity.

☐ 2 Individual

As noted before, each individual is responsible for the quality of his/her work. Additionally plants may seek to encourage initiative still further by the use of a number of management tools, two of which are reviewed here:

1. **The Suggestion Box**: Here staff are rewarded for any suggestions which they put forward to save money for the business. These may relate to production processes or management, or any other quality aspect. Rewards include a cash payment or trips abroad or extra holiday. What they do is create a sense of involvement and ownership by staff.
2. **Performance-related pay (PRP)**: there are a number of variations but essentially staff receive part of their pay in proportion to their contribution to the business, as determined by certain pre-defined criteria. Normally this is paid as a once-a-year lump sum. In its extreme form for the sales force all pay might be performance related in the form of sales commission. In reality PRP may discourage those who either do not receive it or who feel that it is beyond them and hence are deterred from improving the quality of their work.

Recent research suggests that it has little effect upon the overall performance of a business.

Nonetheless, in Japan in the late 1990s there has been a move away from the traditional employment model of a job for life for staff, due to increased competitive pressures from the reduction of import barriers as a result of the work of GATT and the WTO, deregulation in the Japanese economy and recession. Voluntary redundancies and reduced recruitment are reducing employee numbers in Japanese businesses while, for the remaining workforce, an element of PRP is being introduced. Toyota has employed this since the late 1980s, calling it merit-based pay – although salaries are not revealed to other staff, which mitigates against PRP as a motivational tool. Nissan also employs PRP where it can create differences of up to 20 per cent in salaries for people doing the same job, although they do employ transparency with everyone knowing each other's pay.

☐ 3 Teamwork

An important and distinctive characteristic of Japanese culture as opposed to European culture is the role of teamwork. In the European and US models each individual is responsible for his/her own work. If a colleague fails to perform as he/she should, then that is a problem to be dealt with by management.

In contrast, Japanese businesses put much more emphasis on teamwork. If one member of the team is not performing as well as he/she should, then the rest of the team have an obligation to help until the person can catch up or otherwise rectify the problems. It is this inherent difference which enables the emphasis on quality to assume such a major role in Japanese businesses. One particular example of teamwork is quality circles.

☐ 4 Quality circles

One aspect of TQM which has worked well in Japan, but which has not translated so successfully to the EU, is the concept of the quality circle. The quality circle is a means to an end in that it helps to develop the total quality philosophy in the business. Workers meet regularly – say one hour per week – to discuss all aspects of work and how they might improve the quality of what they do. Suggestions are then fed to management. In this way ownership of all aspects of operations is created and staff are encouraged to be proactive rather than reactive – what is known as staff empowerment. To be effective, quality circles need to be voluntary. In reality managers have at times forced employees into membership of a quality circle which is counter-productive. Little is then achieved and employees remain resentful.

■ Lean production

A variation of the above quality production and management models is that of lean production. It is very similar to TQM and seeks to create a competitive advantage for the business using it by striving to achieve perfection, reduced costs, zero defects, zero inventory, endless variety for customers, a motivated multi-skilled workforce using highly flexible increasingly automated machines, a batch size of one and high volume production together with the elimination of wasted effort, time and materials. (Stewart, 1994)

The reason for its distinction is that lean production is particularly associated with global car producer Toyota. It was developed by them as Japan sought to recover after the devastation of the Second World War, and was necessary because of shortages of raw materials meaning that all waste had to be avoided. The case study below examines Toyota's quality development and its growth based on this quality control and assurance.

Table 9.1 compares Toyota's production system with traditional European batch production methods.

■ 9.5 The 1980s revolution in European industry

The 1980s and 1990s have seen what has become known as the era of post-Fordist production. This is because the relatively poorer performance of European businesses has forced many to look at their own and at Japanese production and management methods to determine what might be changed and the extent to which Japanese methods might be adapted to Europe. The essential problem of Fordist production processes has been its inflexibility towards changes in demand and market conditions.

Table 9.1   Comparison of Toyota and traditional European batch production methods

TOYOTA PRODUCTION SYSTEM	WESTERN BATCH PRODUCTION SYSTEM
1. Market demand pulls products through the production process.	1. Production forces push goods through the production system, starting from raw material inputs.
2. Toyota accurately estimates demand from customer feedback.	2. Market research seeks to estimate demand, which may not be totally accurate.
3. Work in progress is minimised.	
4. Quality assurance remedies problems as they arise.	3. Work in progress may exceed the capacity of a production stage causing bottlenecks.
5. Final supply accurately matches final demand.	4. Quality problems are only identified once goods are produced.
	5. Excess output may cause large stock holdings.

Case Study   Toyota and Lean Production

The origins of Toyota lay in the late nineteenth/early twentieth centuries, in work by Sakichi Toyoda to develop a business to produce automatic power looms. However, it was not until 1926 that the Toyoda Automatic Loom Works was created. An automobile subsidiary was established in 1934.

In the post-Second World War period, due to low Japanese per capita incomes after wartime devastation and shortages of raw materials, Toyota had to adapt its production to meet these new circumstances. Inspired by Taiichi Ohno, Toyota adopted a strategy aimed at reducing costs through minimising defects and introducing automation hence enabling workers to undertake a range of other tasks. The use of machinery was particularly important where tasks were hazardous and long repetition created boredom and hence mistakes and waste. This was reinforced by a 1949 financial crisis causing producers to hold far less stocks and hence ending economies of scale.

In 1950 Toyota undertook a five-year plan to double capacity with no extra employees. This was financed by a 50/50 mix of external sources (banks) and internal funds. In 1961 it introduced a five year quality control programme and between 1960 and 1970 this resulted in rapid improvements in output volume and its quality. At times, capacity utilisation was running at over 100 per cent due to the use of unscheduled overtime, the introduction of extra shifts and increasing production speeds. By the late 1960s, new technologically advanced plant was being built with computerised automated production, including the use of multi-purpose robots, to replace staff as they retired.

Domestic growth and expansion into the US and to a lesser extent the EU, both by exports and foreign direct investment, continued during the 1970s to 1990s again using lean production methods as the basis for the cost-effective manufacture of quality output. By 1992 Toyota had higher output at lower unit cost than any other company in the US where it has increasingly built up sales during this period. Since then Toyota has continued a programme of substantial capital expenditure. The Japanese domestic market is near to maturity and the situation has been worsened by economic recession in the late 1990s. As part of its strategy of global diversification Toyota, along with Nissan, Honda, Mazda and Mitsubishi Motors, sees the EU as a major market for future expansion. This is to maintain capacity utilisation of its domestic plant by absorbing excess output. This is particularly important as Japanese penetration of the US market has now reached 24 per cent which is causing serious concerns in the US.

In early 1998 Toyota also continued its plans to expand its presence in the EU by proposing to invest another £150m in the UK and to expand engine production; this followed an earlier decision to invest FF4bn in a second EU car plant in northern France to produce an extra 150 000 cars p.a. The French plant will use lean production methods, as does the UK plant. The purpose of this investment is to increase its EU market share to 5 per cent from current levels which are regarded as unsatisfactory, and to gain from cheaper EU labour costs – Toyota is estimated to make Y450 000 on each car it produces in the EU compared with Y350 000 in Japan. Sales will be further helped when, from 1999, a voluntary export restraint (VER) monitoring Japanese car exports to the EU expires. Also Japanese car producers in general are able to bring new products to the market much faster than EU car manufacturers which will help EU expansion plans still further.

The reader should note that the Just-in-Time (JIT) production model developed from the Toyota system.

Lean production techniques have been used, not just by Japanese transplant businesses but also by more and more indigenous European businesses as was confirmed by a 1998 survey by the European Foundation of 5800 European managers from manufacturing and services in the private and public sectors. Most of the businesses for whom the managers worked were closer to the Toyota or lean production method of production than to the Scandinavian model of well-trained and qualified employees working in groups with organisational high levels of trust. (See Chapter 6.4: Team Assembly and Job Rotation at Volvo.)

The survey also concluded that worker participation, an important part of Japanese production methods, has only been introduced in the last five years for 60 per cent of the firms surveyed. When a business does change its work organisation this is difficult and time-consuming and pay-backs may not be obvious or direct, especially with brownfield sites, ie city sites with existing premises that need to be converted or cleared.

One approach which developed in the US in the 1960s and, to a lesser extent has been adopted in Europe, is computer-based stock control systems such as Materials Requirement Planning and Manufacturing Resource Planning.

■ Materials Requirement Planning (MRP)

Developed in the early 1960s this computerised system seeks to minimise the stock holding of components and raw materials in a batch production process unless current production requires that they be held. The system is used to plan and calculate when items are needed, usually on a weekly basis, and the minimum quantities required; it then authorises the purchase of these.

■ Manufacturing Resource Planning (MRP II)

This is an extended version of Materials Requirement Planning. It is a computerised and fully integrated planning and monitoring system which encompasses the entire operations of a business, including its financial performance, purchasing and marketing. Essentially it simulates the demand for resources, including stocks, at each stage of the production process for each of a number of different levels of output. In this way business managers can plan precisely what are their resource requirements, since information is shared among a number of different personnel instead of just the production manager as with MRP. Its drawback is that it lacks the flexibility to respond to changes in demand.

Although MRP may seem at first glance to be very similar to JIT, it is essentially different. JIT is driven backwards through the system from the point of sale, that is, in Figure 9.2 every item of stock held is determined from the final orders placed for the goods. However, with MRP stock holdings are determined by known demand plus forecasts of potential demand; so in Figure 9.2 the requirements at each stage from the components supplier to final output would be estimated at the same time. As a result, MRP is described as a 'push' system since stocks are pushed through the production system to meet forecast demand, whereas JIT, the reader may recall, was a 'pull' system. Since its stock holdings are less, JIT needs less storage space and so saves overhead costs for the firm.

CASE STUDY   Lean Production at Dek Printing Machines

Dek Printing Machines is a SME (small and medium-sized enterprise) based in Weymouth, Southern England. In 1984 the company was sold to the American Dover Corporation; at this time it realised it was experiencing a major decline in demand for its products, which were automated systems for printing electronic inks to make circuits on electronic plates. The management of DEK decided that, if they were to survive, they needed to change not just the range of products they manufactured but also the production philosophy they employed to produce them.

The product range was changed so that now the company manufactures mobile telephones, and machines that apply conductive solder paste to printed computer circuit boards and other electronic goods. The company also implemented lean production techniques using a just-in-time system for the supply of components. This employs the *kanban* system as discussed previously in this chapter. Since JIT can put pressure on suppliers, the company supplies to them annual and revised weekly forecasts; it also has two-year agreements with single-component suppliers for them to supply on a seven-day-a-week basis which enables the suppliers to plan more effectively.

As part of the increased emphasis on quality, all staff are strongly encouraged to solve problems themselves rather than doing nothing since supervision has been reduced substantially. This is reinforced by an assembly area has been designed for maximum flexibility and by a productivity-boosting incentive scheme for zero defects in assembly work, which encourages staff to check each other's work. Also the American parent gives Dek total autonomy in what it is doing.

The effect of these reforms has been an increase in turnover from $20m to $100m between 1990–97 and a 225 per cent staff increase to 650 employees. Much of its sales are in overseas markets where the major competitors are Japanese firms.

The move to Japanese models

The move to Japanese production and management methods has been helped by the number of Japanese businesses which have established themselves in the EU and especially the UK – the so-called transplant businesses. Where European businesses have turned to such methods as JIT or TQM it has at times been done without total commitment or in an adapted form which has not worked so well. Having said that there have been successful adoptions of Japanese methods and more firms do now profess a commitment to some form of TQM. Such firms as Massey-Fergusson (tractor manufacturers), GKN, IBM (computers), 3M (Minnesota Mining and Manufacturing) and Lucas have all successfully employed TQM.

A major constraint to the adoption of Japanese methods has been the significant differences in culture between Japanese and EU businesses. The role of Japanese teamwork as opposed to European individualism has already been discussed. Another problem is that until recently Japanese businesses had a commitment to lifelong employment for their staff; this was a natural concomitant to the requirement that each employee take full responsibility for quality. In contrast Europe, with a greater tendency to hire and fire, has found the requirement of staff loyalty and total commitment to quality not surprisingly much harder to achieve.

Nonetheless, flexible specialisation has been adopted as an essential requirement for many European businesses and this in turn has been helped by the increasing use of robotics which can more quickly be modified to produce different products. The main drawbacks of FMS are the costs of setting up such a system and the time it takes to get the system up and running. In the same way quality is now a key word for nearly all firms.

■ The adoption of quality in the EU

This section has focused particularly on large-scale production as that most suitable to the adoption of Japanese production methods. The spread of Japanese production methods has been most influential in the Anglo-Saxon economies of the UK and the US; in the rest of the EU its influence has been less but is growing. After its initial arrival in the early 1980s, TQM has endured as a philosophy in the EU, something to note in an area (management theory) where new ideas and new fads are commonplace.

In reality the bulk of European businesses are small and medium-sized enterprises (SMEs). Where these are components suppliers for large plants the emphasis on a quality culture is a fundamental requirement of the ability of the main producer to operate a TQM or other system. For others, while the emphasis may increasingly be on quality the feasibility of adopting a full quality system may be less realistic.

It has been noted that many examples of flexible management systems (FMS) and total quality management (TQM) exist in Italy and Germany. For Italy there is a culture of small and medium-sized businesses, often family-run. Even where these have grown large, as in the case of Benetton, Fiat and Fininvest, family links have remained strong. Certainly Benetton's ability to supply retail outlets anywhere in the world in only eight days with the specific types of products they demand demonstrates the flexibility of production which has been considered above. The problem in terms of time and money of EU businesses having to acquire European wide certification such as ISO 9000 to satisfy their customers has certainly deterred some businesses from pursuing the quality issue fully.

Fiat, which in the 1980s had a reputation for poor quality products with its Lancia range, and a sameness of design in its Lancia, Fiat and Alfa Romeo ranges, undertook a major reinvestment programme in 1992. This sought to distinguish much more clearly the design characteristics of the three ranges as well as the introduction of a new generation of assembly robots to bring a flexibility of production and hence offer small batch sizes – a key characteristic of FMS.

■ 9.6 Management theories of the 1990s

■ Business process re-engineering (BPR)

This was first made popular by American consultants Michael Hammer and James Champy. In essence it seeks to focus the business's activities on the goods or services which it produces. This is undertaken by reassessing the production activities of the business and then removing the barriers between the different departments involved in their production, that is the bureaucracy which involves time and resources but does not contribute to efficient production. A computer system is needed which provides all the data connected to the production and which all key personnel can access. This reduces the need for resources to be devoted to transferring information between separated departments. Non-core activities not specifically involved in production are contracted out to specialist firms (outsourced). This might include the marketing function and the IT provision.

If BPR is to work properly then the removal of barriers between departments must also affect staff, who will need to become more flexible in their work patterns and able to offer a number of different skills. Teams of cross-functional staff covering the spectrum of skills necessary to produce the goods or services then cut across previous departmental barriers. By delegating more authority to such teams – that is almost creating mini-businesses – the emphasis is clearly placed on empowerment of staff which was discussed above, that is giving staff more responsibility and involvement in how the business is run, for example in recruiting new team members. In parallel, staff will also be more accountable of course. BPR also seeks to encourage staff to continually improve themselves; from this comes the idea of 'value-added'. This means that value can be added to the business not just at each stage of the production process but also at each level of the business; this is in contrast to the traditional company philosophy which says that value is added essentially at the top, by management.

The reader may notice parallels here with quality circles. Indeed some have argued that there is little difference between TQM and BPR, except for the greater speed of implementing the latter. S/he will also note that BPR is the antithesis of Taylorism and Fordism which were examined previously, with their emphasis on breaking the production process down into narrow and discrete tasks which can be clearly supervised. Layers of management, who are no longer needed, may be removed as part of this process (delayering), as may part of the workforce due to increased use of automation as a result of the reassessment of the production processes. Those managers who do remain need to be flexible leaders not autocrats.

The benefits of BPR to the business are increased productivity, cost reduction, making the business more efficient and effective, and improving the quality of the output and of the employees producing it. The main disadvantage appears to be that because of the speed of introduction there is a high failure rate with the use of

BPR, partly due to the failure to clarify from the beginning the objectives to be achieved.

■ Benchmarking

This is the process whereby a business continuously measures all aspects of its activities against those of its most successful competitors. This will include its production processes, the quality of its products, after-sales service, marketing and so on. Although benchmarking has been advanced as a management philosophy since 1980, it is only recently that it has become important, along with TQM and BPR, as a means to improve the competitive position of EU

CASE STUDY   Leyland Trucks

Based in northeast England, Leyland Trucks came into its latest form after a management buy-out (MBO) from the receivers of Leyland Daf. Previously, in the 1960s, it had been part of the huge state-subsidised corporation British Leyland which, in turn, was broken up into three companies in the 1970s. One of these was Leyland Trucks. This was subsequently taken over by Dutch car (until acquired by Volvo) and truck manufacturer Daf. The history of Leyland, certainly until the early 1980s was characterised by low investment, poor quality of product, lack of new models, management surrender to the unions (in the 1960s) and over bureaucratic organisation.

Since 1989, Leyland Trucks has adopted a form of lean production encompassing TQM and JIT, in an attempt to recover EU market share which had fallen to only 7.5 per cent of the 5–15 tonne market sector. Major investment in the early 1980s has made Leyland one of the most advanced plants in the EU and has provided the basis on which to build the new production and management processes; however, it alone did not turn Leyland around. MRP II was then tried in the mid-1980s, again without great success; so lean production was the next obvious step. Currently output is less than half the potential available which poses problems for unnecessary accumulation of stocks and works in progress, the very opposite of what a JIT system should be. Options to remedy this include finding new work (outsourcing for another producer), or at worst closing part of the factory until demand revives.

Estimates by Leyland Trucks' managing director are that since the introduction of lean manufacturing, as the reforms are called, £10 million p.a. has been saved through improved quality of product (leading to less mistakes), less stocks and some redundancies. Compared to the initial introduction costs of £100 000 (to cover staff training including the idea of targets, set up costs and so on), this represents a massive return on money invested. This is shown by the ability of Leyland to reduce their break-even point from 11 500 trucks p.a. to 5000 p.a. The development of flexible staffing has reduced the number of job descriptions, substantially enabling people to be used wherever they are needed, and is supported by the union. In the 1960s the nightmare of British Leyland was the numerous inter-union disputes over job descriptions and who did what job.

Most importantly, in line with Japanese quality methods, trucks are now built after orders are received rather than in anticipation of demand as previously. The high stockholdings are greater than the company would like but, as the business is producing at less than half of potential output, it is not realistic to expect suppliers to make the sixteen deliveries per day of the Toyota model discussed above.

industry. First employed by US photocopier company Xerox, which was facing severe challenges from the Pacific Rim countries, recent emphasis has been placed more on why the leading companies are superior, rather than trying mainly to establish measures or benchmarks of superiority.

A 1993 survey of the top 1000 UK companies by the Confederation of British Industry (the UK employers' organisation) and management consultants Coopers & Lybrand found that over 65 per cent of businesses who replied used some form of benchmarking.

■ 9.7 Flexible working

As has been noted elsewhere, the European labour market is changing faster than at any time in its history through the impact of global competition, driven significantly by information technology. As discussed in Chapter 4 this has shown itself in a number of ways including a greater access to work by women, more part-time work, job-sharing and more temporary contracts. Staple industries have declined significantly while service industries, often using information technology, have grown, albeit not enough, in Europe to offset the former. Additionally, as the population of the EU ages, less young people will enter the market, creating a need to employ more people aged over 55 who, in the 1980s and 1990s, might have expected to retire early. Indeed this is already happening in the US.

■ Flexitime

For many years office-based businesses have employed flexitime working. This enables staff, within reason, to work hours which suit them so long as they do complete the requisite number per week. There is normally a core time when everyone must be at work – say from 9.00 a.m. to 3.00 p.m. (allowing for a lunch break). Outside of this a person may, for example, come in at 6.30 a.m. on Tuesday and go home at 3.30 p.m., while on Friday s/he comes in at 9.00 a.m. and works until 7.00 p.m.

It is argued that this flexibility helps avoid the problem of people bringing their emotional baggage to work with them and therefore combats absenteeism, boosts productivity, creates a more content workforce who can better manage their working and personal lives, and eases travelling to and from work by the ability to miss peak traffic times.

■ Job sharing

This allows two people to share one job between them, each receiving half the pay for half the work. The flexibility this offers is particularly suitable for, say, two women with young children who only want to work part-time, but do not want to leave the labour market, lose income and face the problems of rejoining it later. Coordination between the two employees is obviously important and normally a handover period of at least an hour is necessary when both are at work together to make sure that the second person knows what the first one has been doing. As long as this happens properly the business can benefit from having two half-time employees with more energy and ideas than one full-time person.

■ Breaking down work barriers

In recent years some office-based businesses have sought to promote a more creative working environment by removing conventional workplace barriers such as individual offices, separating screens creating personal working space in large offices, and, in the extreme case, even individual desks. When several staff share one desk this is known as hot-desking. The argument for this is that by enabling staff more effectively to communicate with each other, new ideas can be more effectively generated, departmental barriers both physical and psychological are removed and new more effective working practices adopted.

■ Working from home

There has long been a trend in some industries for women to be employed and work from home. In the UK this has been most typical in the fashion industry where women might be employed to knit sweaters or stitch together garments supplied from the factory in parts. Other women are employed to make small cuddly toys, while, in recent years, particularly in the US and UK there has been a growth in sales through womens' evening parties meeting in one woman's home to sell 'Tupperware' plastic containers such as lunch boxes, womens' makeup, womens' underwear and most recently sexual aids. Recently some wine retailers have moved into this area, offering wine-tastings in one's own home before purchase. Pay is normally related to performance in terms of the number of garments produced, or sales revenue in terms of the total value of items sold. Typically, pay is also relatively low compared with the national average. Nonetheless, for some of these businesses there has been major economic growth, for example the formerly successful but now defunct jewellery supplier Cabouchon which retailed its products to homes and offices where its women customers were most accessible.

   As can be seen, these are very much targeted at women who see the jobs as offering some income, perhaps to supplement the husband's. Increasingly, however, as the rate of divorce continues to rise this may be the main source of income for a single parent. What it does offer a woman is flexibility to enable her to look after young children at home during the day and still earn some money. Most importantly, the decline in EU jobs in recent years has been in manufacturing, the male bastion of employment, while the main growth area has been services, where women are more attractive to employ than men. The concept of the male as breadwinner therefore, is already dated and will be even more so in future.

   What the employer gains from such arrangements is essentially cheap labour, reduced need for factory space, reduced operating costs associated with this such as heating and lighting, local property taxes, maintenance and repairs and so on. What society gains from people who work at home is less demand for transport services, less congestion on roads at peak times because people do not use cars, reduced air pollution arising from this, and a general freeing up of resources to be used elsewhere.

CASE STUDY   Radical Office Mobility Programme

The UK's Pearl Assurance Insurance Company, based in Peterborough, has been experimenting in one 12-person department with a new office layout called ROMP – short for Radical Office Mobility Programme. This was devised by an advertising agency HHCL and its aim is to create a more fluid and interactive system by mixing up people to generate new ideas through enhanced communications. Offices, they argue have been based on the old factory production-line system which is now outmoded. What is needed is to escape from this philosophy.

The ROMPing area is an open workspace where staff do not have fixed personal desks, phones or computers; nor are there desk dividers. As a result the staff feel obliged to sit at a different desk each day and so have contact with different colleagues to those they normally encounter. For more formal meetings three rooms have been set aside and decorated so as not to look like an office environment. The customer room looks like a kitchen with a big pine table and chairs and big colour pictures of customers on the walls – to promote awareness that the customer is the centre of their work. The pit lane is a room for short, quick meetings and has a yellow decor and pictures of a racing car pit team on the walls. It has a large clock on the wall which can be set to time meetings. The third special room is dark green with a large goldfish tank. The decor of all three rooms therefore distinguishes them from a conventional office.

Although the lack of individual space and personal effects on desks at first caused some discomfort, it has subsequently worked well as staff have been forced to be more open compared with the previous system. Also one person now deals with a customer through all stages of a query, compared with previously when the customer would be passed from person to person at Pearl Assurance. Although there was initial suspicion, staff who have been involved in this experiment feel that the quality of their work has improved and that they have been empowered. However, there has been jealously from staff not involved in ROMPing.

In other environments such an approach has been perceived as less successful. A university in northern England introduced an open-plan office for its business school staff. Although each member of staff had his/her own desk, an academic environment needs quiet places where the academics can think and concentrate without disruption, especially when undertaking research. Hence the open-plan office was perceived by many who worked there as a disaster. As a result it has now been sub-divided into smaller rooms.

■ Teleworking

The telecommunications revolution of the last decade, which has seen the sale of cheap personal computers (PCs), modems enabling computers to communicate with each other via telecommunications links, and fax machines, has taken this a stage further. Whereas the examples above relate at times to low-skilled low-paid work, modern technology enables this to be extended to many high-skilled high-paid jobs, both temporary and permanent. Typically, this might include secretarial services, translation work, copywriting for advertising agencies, provision of correspondence courses and so on, and has been dubbed 'teleworking'. There is no reason why a firm should pay high rates for temporary secretarial staff in Brussels, or Helsinki or Rome when staff living in the provinces can be employed at a cheaper rate. From the typist's viewpoint, as long as the work is done on time whether s/he works during normal office hours or evenings does not matter to the employer.

Currently, in most cases, it applies to a person working perhaps three days at work and two days at home. A report written at home, for example, can be downloaded from the computer and sent via the telephone line to be printed out in the office 100 kilometres away in a matter of minutes.

Furthermore, the rapid arrival of visual telephones means that even working at home a person will not feel so separated from colleagues. This is an important point to note because there are downsides to working at home. The main one is that work is partly a social activity and so the social isolation of home working can pose problems. Also there is the fact that the less a person is 'in work' the greater the danger that s/he will feel independent of the organisation and the less s/he will subscribe to the corporate ethos. However, the increasing trend towards part-time work and temporary contracts makes even this argument less applicable.

Interestingly, recent research has found people work harder and longer hours from home compared with actually being in work. Commuting two to three hours per day to and from the centre of Stockholm or Milan or Athens is tiring and work colleagues are often distracting. Also, as part of the delayering process which many European businesses have gone through those still in work now work much harder than say ten years ago.

In the Western Isles of Scotland people have long suffered from seasonal unemployment and low income prospects. Additionally, many young people leave for jobs on the UK mainland never to return. The local council and enterprise board has employed an information technology expert to coordinate bids for teleworking contracts. The first to be secured was to undertake an abstracting service of press cuttings which are then summarised and indexed. The final work can then be downloaded to the customer on the mainland. The islands are also linking to the Internet to establish the world's first computer university – the University of the Highlands and Islands – able to access sources from anywhere in the world. Many universities, particularly in the US, offer their courses to students via the Internet anywhere in the world – so long as they pay.

If the peripheral regions of the EU can be brought closer to the core as is happening here, then this has very important implications for all those parts of the EU which are remote from the centres of business and power and the main markets. The Greek islands, Northern Finland and Sweden, Southern Italy, Eire . . . the possibilities for economic growth, and hence for redressing income inequalities, are enormous.

> **CASE STUDY** Birmingham City Council – teleworking and hot-desking
>
> In 1996 the UK local authority Birmingham City Council asked hundreds of its employees to work from home or share desks in an effort to save £50m per annum. It would do this by cutting its 750 000 sq ft of office space by 20 per cent in 1996 and by 10 per cent in 1997. If successful, the council argued, it would be able to sell off 225 000 sq ft of prime office space.
>
> A few volunteer employees were provided with a £3000 home office including a computer, an extra phone line and answering machine, and a fax and modem to link them to the main offices – although eventually this would grow to several hundred. Additionally those council workers who spend a lot of time out of the office were asked to hot-desk, that is share their desk with others. If they needed it they could book a time to use it, hence avoiding equipment standing idle for long periods of time.
>
> The council anticipated that by early 1998 about 7000 of its 39 000 staff would no longer be using normal office space – although most would not be issued with full home offices but rather with such equipment as electronic notepads with modems. Also as part of this programme it was proposed to store documents by image processing to free up space currently used for records.
>
> Teleworking, it has been argued by Alan Deighton, the executive director of the Teleworker Centre Association, increases staff productivity, decreases turnover of staff and solves the costs and time incurred in commuting.

■ Teleconferencing

An extension to the above is the concept of tele-conferencing or video-conferencing. Under this system a number of people situated in different parts of the world can converse with each other simultaneously, and through a small camera attached to the PC can see each other through their computers or on a large screen. So real-time interactive discussion is possible. Latest software allows each member of the video-conference to contribute to a common document presented on all screens no matter where in the world each person is, and permits the sending of computer files from any person to anyone else in the conference.

Teleconferencing is much cheaper than people undertaking real journeys to hold a conference in Majorca for example. It saves time and enables busy executives to maintain their important ongoing office work without interruption. As the EU continues to expand and as multinational corporations come to play an increasingly important role in European business development, tele-conferencing will offer these organisations enormous advantages. This is particularly so if, through teleworking, some executives live and work largely in periphery areas many kilometres from head office.

The next stage in this development, although perhaps not in the next ten years, is likely to be the development of the virtual reality conference. People wearing the virtual reality headset will be able to sit in a virtual conference room, see and interact with their virtual colleagues, while the real ones are situated in other parts of the world.

■ 9.8 The impact of new technology

■ Computer Aided Design (CAD) and Computer Aided Manufacture (CAM)

The role of computerised systems in the production process, known as computer aided manufacture (CAM), has already been discussed in the context of inventory control systems such as MRP and MRP II. Where automation has become of major importance is in terms of multi-purpose robots which underpin the use of flexible management systems and computer aided design (CAD) of products ranging from cars to aircraft. Additionally the development of virtual reality techniques mean that major construction works such as office blocks as well as large manufactured goods such as aircraft can now be simulated, explored and tested before any work is undertaken in reality.

These are likely to play an increasing role in manufacture in the next ten years. The concern of new technology is that increasingly it is replacing human labour, both in the manufacture of goods and in the provision of services, with the implications for long term employment.

■ Services

Banking and financial services are areas which continue to offer substantial scope for new technology. The use of ATMs (automated telling machines) or cash dispensers has already demonstrated this. The provision of telephone banking services reduces the need for local branches and hence staff to service them. With moves towards the cashless society by the increasing use of smart debit cards which can keep an update of each owner's bank balance, computers will undertake activities previously provided by staff. Chapter 7 has discussed this.

■ Retailing

In supermarkets and hypermarkets experiments with new technology permit customers to check out and pay for goods without the need for checkout staff. Through satellite and cable television many people already have access to home shopping channels. By far the biggest growth area, however, in the next five years will be Internet shopping.

■ Implications for the labour force

The increasing use of new technology has serious implications for the European labour market in a number of areas. Firstly, unless new jobs are created the EU will face the danger of an increasing pool of unemployed labour as machines take over work previously undertaken by humans. For 25 years inflation was the major cause of macroeconomic concern but this has been superseded by unemployment.

The danger of a high rate of natural unemployment is that it creates social tensions as well as creating an increasing internal or government debt problem through the need for the payment of unemployment benefits.

Secondly, those people who do work will increasingly need specialist skills to meet the new demands of the rapidly changing labour markets – since fragmentation into a greater number of increasingly specialised areas is more and more likely. This suggests that the provision of education services is likely to be of even greater importance in future. Not only will people face a greater need to acquire knowledge through greater access to education; they will also need to acquire employment-useful personal and transferable skills such as information technology, communication and personal skills (the ability to work by oneself and in groups). These transferable skills will enable them to move from job to job as circumstances dictate. They will also be important as people are encouraged to create jobs for themselves.

The EU also faces severe competition from the cheaper labour producers of the developing countries. The increased use of new technology will enable the EU to compete to some extent on cost grounds, but mainly, however, it needs to compete on the grounds of quality. If EU goods are to be perceived as desirable in the global marketplace they must have distinctive characteristics which confer a uniqueness on them. The adoption of Japanese production and management methods, where quality underpins all activities, is therefore of crucial importance.

If new technology allied to quality is to enable European businesses to compete effectively then a greater emphasis on corporate investment is needed. Throughout the EU the role of the state as a provider of resources is diminishing as responsibility is handed back to the private sector. As has been discussed elsewhere new mechanisms to promote investment are needed which in turn requires a cultural change to encourage people to save more to provide the funds for this investment.

In summary, new technology may well destroy more jobs than it creates – this has yet to be seen. However, without heavier investment in new technology than is currently being undertaken the EU will not be able to compete globally in the next century. This needs to be underpinned by an increasing emphasis on quality in all aspects of production and a greater examination of the feasibility of further adopting Japanese production and management methods to support this new technology.

■ Review questions

1. To what extent have the traditional organisations of European businesses contributed to their competitive decline *vis-à-vis* Japanese businesses?
2. Why is the 'quality revolution' so important to European business?
3. Discuss the benefits and disbenefits of Just-in-Time compared with traditional stock holding.

4. Why might home working not always be a good thing:

    (a) to the business?
    (b) to the employee?

5. Your company is thinking of adopting tele-conferencing to cut down on transport costs for its executives. Discuss the pros and cons of this.

■ Bibliography

Calori, R. and Lawrence, P., *The Business of Europe Managing Change* (London: Sage Publications, 1991).

Garrison, T. and Rees, D. (eds), *Managing People Across Europe* (Oxford: Butterworth-Heinemann, 1994).

Harrison, M., *Advanced Manufacturing Technology Management* (London: Pitman, 1990).

Jewitt, R., *Just in Time: an Executive Guide to JIT* (London: Department of Trade and Industry, 1994).

Pinder, M., *Personnel Management for the Single European Market* (London: Pitman, 1990).

Schniederjans, M. J., *Topics in Just in Time Management* (Boston, USA: Allyn & Bacon, 1993).

Shingo, S., *Zero Quality Control: Source Inspection and Poka-Yoke System* (USA: Productivity Press, 1986).

Stewart, H., 'Lean Production', unpublished MBA dissertation (Henley Business School, 1994).

Stoner, J. A. F. and Freeman, R. E. F., *Management*, 5th edn (Hemel Hempstead: Prentice Hall, 1992).

Wood, S., *The Transformation of Work* (London: Unwin Hyman Ltd, 1989).

Also:

The European
The Financial Times
The Guardian
The Observer
The Telegraph
The Times

CHAPTER 10

Accessing European markets

■ 10.1 Introduction

This chapter considers how and why European businesses need to access new markets, and in this context the importance of market intelligence is analysed. The role of international marketing is considered as a means to achieve strategic objectives of accessing new markets. Linked to this the problems of barriers to entry, first developed in Chapter 4, are explored in more depth. Exporting, foreign direct investment and joint ventures are examined as means of market entry and then applied to CEEC markets, developing issues introduced in Chapter 5.

■ 10.2 Why seek new markets?

EU firms have experienced many opportunities opening to them in the last decade in terms of new markets. The Single European Act has largely completed the process of removing the barriers to the internal market, a market which was further extended with the creation of the European Economic Area in 1994 and the accession of Austria, Finland and Sweden to the EU on 1 January 1995. The transition of the countries of Central and Eastern Europe to free market economies has also opened these to trade and investment in the 1990s. Finally, until the Asian crisis of 1997 the growth of the economies of the Pacific Rim offered European businesses considerable opportunities both for trade and investment, and are likely to do so again in the future.

The single market was, of course, an external change imposed upon businesses to which they have had to respond – as evidenced by the waves of mergers in banking, pharmaceuticals and the car industry. Government privatisation programmes have also been, in part, a response to the internal market. Strategically, however, a business may decide to initiate action itself by diversifying into a new market. This may be undertaken because the domestic market will not sustain further growth or begins to contract. There may be competition in the home market, from either domestic or foreign producers, reducing profit margins and encouraging businesses to look for new markets – or in the case of foreign firms to retaliate against them. Expansion into new markets may also be to achieve economies of scale from larger markets or to take advantage of foreign market demand which foreign producers are unable to meet. Finally, diversification spreads the risks of concentration in one market.

The new market strategy may involve exporting to the new country or it may mean establishing a physical presence there through some form of foreign direct investment, either individually or jointly with a domestic business. In either case it is important that any such diversification complements existing activities to enable them to fit the same corporate concept. In other words the activities need to be linked to enable the workforce to be familiar with the new activities or market.

In essence, therefore, the strategic decisions which a business has to make concerning new markets are:

1. Whether or not to diversify – that is, do forecast profits justify the new strategy?
2. Into which markets to diversify.
3. Whether to export from the home country or establish a presence in the new market by investment.
4. Whether to go it alone or to seek a collaborative venture with another organisation in the new market.
5. Whether to supply goods and/or services to the full market or to concentrate on a niche market.

If a firm fails to initiate a positive strategy of diversification it may lose out to competitors who do.

■ 10.3 Barriers to market entry

The success of any business in diversifying into new markets will depend upon a number of factors, including the structure of the market it is seeking to enter. This in turn will determine the extent and height of the barriers to entry facing that firm and also the exit barriers deterring that firm from leaving the market subsequently.

Entry barriers are factors which seek to deter new firms from entering an industry and hence to preserve market share and supernormal profits for existing firms. Examples include:

- the capital costs to a new entrant of competing against existing businesses;
- the need for a high R&D (research and development) budget;
- the existence of economies of scale (falling total costs the larger the scale of production);
- the existence of economies of scope (falling total costs as more, and different, goods are produced);
- the number of competitors – the more concentrated the industry the harder it will be for new firms to gain access;
- pricing policies, for example setting prices at a low level to deter entrants;
- product differentiation through marketing and branding to create customer loyalty to existing brands;
- the cost of access to distribution channels to get the goods into retail outlets;

- access to strategic raw materials, for example oil or uranium;
- technology which deters new firms without the same level of expertise;
- legal means, typically state ownership of businesses.

CASE STUDY   Car Makers Move Eastwards

Car manufacturers have invested heavily in Central and Eastern European countries (CEEC) in the 1990s attracted by the cheap labour, compared with that in Germany for example, and by investment grants and tax incentives. Other factors attracting foreign direct investment include the near permanent over-capacity in car production in the EU and the slow growth in demand for new cars as the market reaches saturation. Most important, however, is the current and potential growth in car sales in the CEEC as household real incomes rise and hence demand for cars rises – and most importantly in the still untapped markets of the former USSR. The investing companies also argue that they are investing in the future since current investment buys goodwill.

The main investors in the region have been Volkswagen (DM7.95bn), Opel (DM2.23bn), Fiat (DM3.2bn), Ford (DM96m), Suzuki (DM 250m) and Daewoo (DM 2.39bn), while General Motors is also now investing heavily in Poland both in its own right (DM 530m) and through its Japanese affiliate Isuzu (DM 300m). The main recipients have been Eastern Germany (DM 4.2bn), the Czech Republic (DM3.7bn), Hungary (DM2bn) and Poland (DM6.3bn). Indeed Poland is now the sixth largest car producer in Europe after Germany, France, Italy, the UK and Spain. Volkswagen is 20 per cent owned by the West German state government of Lower Saxony and its choice of Eastern Germany for new engine and car plants rather than other CEEC is partly through political pressures. Its construction of new factories on greenfield sites in CEEC also enables it to test new and more flexible production practices which would be resisted by the unionised workforce in Germany, as well as to enable management to put pressures on its workforce through the threat of production relocation to the East.

Fiat's expenditure is partly on new plant and the development of new models; its Cinquecento city model is produced for worldwide sales solely at its Tychy plant in Poland, for example. The remainder is on the acquisition of 78 per cent of FSM, the former Polish government-owned car manufacturer, while Daewoo is acquiring FSO. The practices learned in Central and Eastern Europe will subsequently be transferred back to the West, enabling these companies to compete more effectively against cheap imports from Asian countries. Fiat has also signed a DM1.5bn deal with Gaz, Russia's second biggest car maker, to produce 150 000 Fiat cars per annum in Russia.

Other car companies, although believing that demand for new cars in CEEC will pick up in time prefer, for the present, to export them from their domestic plants rather then build new factories. This is partly because of the cost of building new plant and also through a belief that the benefits of cheaper labour will diminish as real wages rise in line with economic growth in Central and Eastern Europe. Also labour only accounts for 10 per cent of total production costs – although those investing in new plant argue that it will still take years for wages to catch up with those of the periphery countries of the EU such as Portugal and Greece. Additionally, fringe benefits are much less.

Karakaya and Stahl (1991) classify entry barriers into two main types. Firstly, there are those which are activated by would-be competitors or are controllable. These are usually generated by firms already in the industry, for example cost advantages through economies of scale; pricing; R&D. They argue that these do not always stop new firms entering the market but they do influence their marketing strategies. Secondly, there are entry barriers which are uncontrollable and would-be entrants can do little about these – for example, government licensing; the number of competitors; possession of strategic raw materials.

■ Entry barriers to international markets

Of particular concern in this section are the specific problems faced by any European business seeking to diversify into another country's market. Not only does this apply to within the EU, but also to EU firms seeking access to other markets such as the CEEC, the US, the Third World and Japan. These include:

- **Language** – although translators are readily available in all countries, and English is the international business language for communicating with agents and others in the new market, language still presents a significant real barrier. With electrical consumer goods, for example, operating instructions and guarantees must be in the consumer's language, totally clear and without translation errors which render them nonsensical. Since language also embodies the cultural values of its country this needs to be recognised in sales and promotions campaigns to win new customers.
- **Culture** – this was discussed in Chapter 1. To illustrate its importance as a barrier Mediterranean countries, for example, give a high priority to the family and its values, whereas this is not so obvious in other countries. A sales and promotion campaign for consumer goods might want to reflect this.
- **Import controls** to EU markets were removed with the advent of the Single European Market in January 1993. However, in other countries, especially Japan, EU firms face significant barriers through complex and delaying administrative procedures and differential pricing against EU goods. The Uruguay Round of GATT talks and the subsequent work of the WTO have sought to reduce these.
- **Exchange rate movements** – these can also act as a significant barrier inhibiting access to new markets. The single currency will remove this problem for the EU11 who are participating, although this still will not remove euro fluctuations against the US dollar and the yen, for example.
- **Joint ventures** – some countries require EU firms entering their markets to work through a joint venture to give the home country more control. This involves, typically, a third company being established and owned jointly by the EU company and the indigenous company. This is discussed more fully below.
- **Technical differences** – these can also cause entry barriers. Until 1995 the mains voltage differed in EU countries affecting electrical goods produced. Although this is now standardised different plugs are still used. Most clearly the UK and Ireland driving on the left-hand side of the road and all other EU countries on the right is a barrier for car producers. Until 1965 Sweden also drove on the left but changed to the right, literally overnight, to address precisely these problems.
- **Risk** is the biggest barrier to entering a new market. If there is a risk that businesses are unable to repatriate profits, or there is an inadequate financial and legal infrastructure, then they will be deterred from entering that market. It is possible to take out insurance to protect against non-payment for exports or state appropriation of investments, but this is costly and never covers the full amount which might be lost.

As with all entry barriers market research is needed before the new market is accessed. However, this is particularly important with foreign markets.

CASE STUDY   Why Not to Invest in Russia

During the 1990s Russia has been perceived by foreigners as the riskiest place in Central and Eastern Europe in which to invest. Therefore, although foreign direct investment (FDI) has been urgently needed to modernise the economic infrastructure and to generate growth in GDP, in practice this has not been forthcoming. For example, between 1989–96 Russia received $5.3bn of inward funds compared with Hungary's receipt of $11.5bn.

The main reasons why investors are deterred from investing as much in Russia as elsewhere are:

1. **The complex taxation system.** Investing foreign businesses find it hard to understand the complex and constantly changing tax structures. Also these are enforced randomly, while tax evasion means that only 40 per cent of tax revenues are collected by the state. Foreign firms are therefore often hit hardest because they have transparent accounts. There is an urgent need for a fair and transparent tax code.
2. **Bias against foreign firms.** Local politicians and businessmen who are friends of Boris Yeltsin and his allies are treated preferentially compared with foreign investors. This has been seen most clearly with the privatisation programme enabling Yeltsin's most influential supporters to become multimillionaires by acquiring large blocks of shares at low cost.
3. **Bureaucratic regulations.** Many current bureaucrats formerly worked for the communist regime and still find it hard not to get involved in political decisions. Also the same attitudes have carried over from the former regime – that bureaucracy is a necessary and deliberate obstruction rather than a means to facilitate progress. This means that would-be investors are deterred by bureaucratic barriers rather than being encouraged to invest in Russia.
4. **Property and contract safeguards.** These are often weak and ineffective, not giving the same degree of protection to the parties to a contract as one would expect within the EU or US. Also, property and contract law has not been properly tested in the courts creating still further uncertainly.

■ Entry barriers and the product life cycle

Karakaya and Stahl (1991) suggest that the extent to which entry barriers influence businesses to enter markets will depend on the stage of the product life-cycle their good is at. In turn the length of each stage of the product life-cycle will determine the height of the barrier; the longer the stage the lower the barrier towards the middle and end.

They argue that if a firm enters a market at the introduction stage there are significant potential gains, for example increased market share and lower costs due to economies of scale. However, entry barriers can be high, particularly the capital costs and risk of loss if the product does not take off. Barriers remain high during the growth stage but some of the uncertainties disappear as the product establishes itself and profits increase. By the maturity stage sales peak and profits decline as firms are forced to advertise more due to intense competition; barriers remain high. It is only in the decline stage that barriers become lower.

■ 10.4 Assessing the market: the need for market intelligence

■ What is market intelligence?

Market intelligence or research is the gathering of relevant information by a business to inform its decision-making. A database of relevant information is necessary to enable executives to make appropriate decisions. However, its gathering needs to be cost-effective and some businesses will buy-in data from outside. Such an agency may be situated in the domestic country or in the exporting market, or it can be an international marketing agency.

The data will include a variety of different areas which might best be illustrated by reference to the previous case study of the penetration of CEEC markets by US, EU and other car producers.

☐ 1 National characteristics

These will include such factors as:

- The political stability of individual CEEC, especially Russia.
- Population size – especially of adults, and with driving licences.
- Demography of the population, for example age and sex distribution (men are more likely than women to own the first car); average family size (affecting the number of cars per family).
- The level of income and its distribution, for example urban–rural divisions (incomes are normally higher in cities).
- Market size, that is the percentage of the population which has a car, new or secondhand; and the percentage likely to buy one in the next year, two years and so on.
- Percentage of per capita disposable income currently spent on automobiles; the extent of provision and use of credit facilities to finance new car purchases.
- National attitudes towards cars; for example does the government wish to limit their use on environmental grounds as in the UK, or is car ownership perceived as a symbol of Western European wealth which needs to be supported?
- Quality of the state education scheme; that is, the level of education and literacy.

☐ 2 Industry characteristics

This will cover such issues as:

- To what extent do forecasts indicate likely market growth?
- The extent and height of entry barriers, for example import duties; or alternatively tax benefits, provision of grants and so on by the host-country government.
- The number of domestic firms in the market, if any, and the extent to which they have modernised – for example Skoda through its acquisition by VW.
- The number of foreign firms which have entered the market.
- Market share each company has, that is, the competition facing the new entrant.

- Division of market by models – for example family hatchback; four-wheel drive; luxury.
- Pricing strategy each company operates.
- Extent of advertising budgets employed, for example promotional campaigns in the press, motoring magazines, cinema and so on.
- Cost of setting up dealerships or other sales outlets.
- What are labour relations like – for example the power of unions; incidence of strikes; ease of dismissing staff?
- The technology of existing producers – can lean production processes be established; outsourcing of components and so forth.
- Production costs – for example wage and bonus rates for labour; employers' social welfare contribution costs.

☐ 3 Business characteristics

These will include:

- In which products is the producer proposing to enter CEEC markets likely to have the greatest strengths?
- What are the estimated sales and profitability of the new premises?
- If it builds a factory as opposed to exporting cars from Western Europe how many can it produce per annum?
- What capital expenditure will be necessary and how will it be financed?
- Will the western business be allowed total ownership of the production facility or will it be forced to accept a joint venture (not a problem in CEEC)?
- Will it create a new company or take over a privatised one, for example Fiat'a acquisition of FSM?
- What existing rival models most closely approximate the proposed new ones?
- What share of the market does it seek to obtain within one, three and five years?
- What are the costs of exiting the market in the unlikely event of this being necessary?

There are many other questions which any business will need to answer, but these give some illustration of the range of market intelligence which is needed.

■ What is the purpose of market intelligence?

As can be seen from the above, the aim of market intelligence gathering is to enable a business to make more informed strategic judgements. This doesn't guarantee that such judgements will automatically be better, but it does increase the probability that they will be, due to the decision-makers of the business having more information from which to work. When a business therefore seeks to forecast such outcomes as potential market share, the strength and direction of the competitive response to its market entry and its potential profits, it will have a wide range of data gathered from a variety of sources. These will include:

1. **Primary research** – interviewing potential customers to determine existing brand loyalty, what it would take to encourage them to switch to a new brand, and so on.
2. **Secondary research** – gathering information from libraries, trade journals and so on to build up the picture of the characteristics of the industry and its market.

CASE STUDY   The PC Product Life-Cycle

In the personal computer (PC) market, rapid technological change makes each stage of a product's life relatively short and hence barriers stay higher. The introduction by Intel of the Pentium processor in 1995 made previous 486 machines obsolete through their relative slowness, even though prices were soon cut drastically to shift remaining stocks. Moreover, the Pentium was much more effective in running Microsoft's Windows 95, the upgrade of Windows 3.11. As rival chip producers began producing competitors to the Pentium – such as IBM's Cyrix-designed 6x86 processor – Intel then raised the stakes by introducing, at the beginning of 1997, the Pentium chip with MMX technology. This, consumers were assured, enabled graphics and animation packages and games to be run much faster and more smoothly. Add to that hard disks with greater memory (3 gigabytes), CD-ROMs with greater speeds (12x) and higher speed modems and the product life of PCs began to shorten still further.

In mid-1998 PCs have the Pentium II processor which, it is argued, is a major improvement on the Pentium with MMX technology, which stores are now selling at approximately 50 per cent of the price they were 18 months ago. Hard disks now have 11.5 gigabytes capacity or more, while 32-speed CD-ROMs are the norm. Additionally Windows 98 has been released, replacing Windows 95.

Manufacturers talk of the 'future-proof PC' which can be upgraded to keep up with the latest technology, even though most users only employ a small part of their machine's capabilities. In reality today's most advanced machines will be creaking with age by the time the reader first sees these words. Because the product life-cycle of a machine is now so short entry barriers remain high since each stage within the cycle is even shorter. Hence, although PC assembly firms may still set up and compete, processor manufacturers face very high time and cost barriers in seeking to compete with Intel. By the decline phase the processor is obsolete so there is no point in entering the market. Intel also advertises very heavily to generate entry barriers such that consumers feel a non-Intel processor is inferior.

Microsoft has achieved the same consumer perception towards its products. It also has very high entry barriers protecting its markets but this is due to its globally-established brand name and the provision of its Windows software, linked to an Internet browser, with most new machines. Indeed, for the home user it is hard to imagine employing any other operating system than Microsoft Windows.

The reader might like to draw a product life-cycle for a new model of PC and discuss what factors are likely to influence each stage of this cycle.

The business may have a market intelligence department which will undertake this work itself or it may use an agency which has a more specialist knowledge of a country.

■ How to use market intelligence strategically

In section 10.3 above, the problem of market barriers to entry was discussed. If sufficiently good market intelligence is available to identify the magnitude and extent of entry barriers then a firm can adopt a competitive strategy which will enable it to overcome these. It is important to do so because barriers will create difficulties for the business and hence impose costs. Although it is not desirable to confront the established market leader in direct conflict, in reality this is what will happen. Karakaya and Stahl (1991) suggest that ways to overcome entry barriers include:

☐ 1 Advertising and marketing

This can be used to distinguish the business's product from other existing ones in the consumer's mind. In the case of entry to the CEEC car industry the quality, style and reliability of western-produced cars and the importing of the technology to achieve this has been the most potent form of advertising against the low-standard indigenously produced cars. Within the Central and Eastern European economies the new entrant producers have segmented the market to achieve maximum sales, with appropriate advertising and marketing as in Western Europe. In practice, Western Europe and Central and Eastern Europe are becoming one extended (single) market, if not in law.

In the same way Dutch conglomerate Phillips' promotion of its digital compact cassette (DCC) as an alternative to the compact disc (CD), which it invented yet which has been most successfully marketed by the Japanese, is another example of market segmentation. The DCC is claimed to produce the same quality as a CD yet with the flexibility of a cassette. Phillips also tried in the past to achieve the same effect with the laser disc but failed to generate consumer demand, losing out to the VHS video cassette. Most recently Mini Disc technology has been marketed as a potential replacement for the conventional CD.

Perhaps the best example of market segmentation as a barrier is Japanese sales of cassette recorders, invented in the US, back to the Americans and to the EU. These are sold as Walkmans, as part of ghetto blasters, as stacking systems, mini systems, radio/cassette players, in cars – the list is almost endless. By creating perceived differences between the same product in terms of how it is used, the Japanese have expanded the market enormously while creating barriers.

☐ 2 Reducing customer switching costs

By designing their products to be compatible with existing systems which have high shares of the market, Microsoft with its Windows 95 and Windows 98, and Windows NT for businesses, has enabled consumers to switch from PC to PC and still use the same software. Even the Apple company with its Apple Macintosh computer has now been obliged to use Microsoft software, even though it pioneered the use of a Windows-type software.

☐ 3 Entering the market through takeovers of, or mergers with, existing firms

For the single European market one of the major benefits of tariff and non-tariff barriers being removed is the lowering of some entry barriers, although of course others still remain. Certainly the continuing spate of cross-border mergers and takeovers is a symptom of the ability to transcend entry barriers. In many cases it is also a preparation for the increased global competition the EU faces.

CASE STUDY　Using Market Intelligence – the Low Cost Airlines

In recent years European skies have seen the emergence of new low-cost budget airlines such as *Ryanair* and *easy-Jet* which have sought to skim the cream from major routes where the large well-established airlines charge high fares. They offer cheap fares to major European destinations with no-frills services to save costs; for example, *Ryanair* charges £99 for its midweek return flight from Stansted (near London) to Stockholm, compared with British Airway's £500. This is done partly by cutting out travel agent middlemen and selling tickets directly to customers.

The number of passengers using budget airlines has increased by 100 per cent between 1996-98 carrying eight million passengers and achieving sales of some $1000m. Market research suggests that this sector of the market is likely to increase in size by 400 per cent between 1998–2003, accounting for nearly 14 per cent of total passenger traffic and approximately 5 per cent of sales. This intelligence is important since it determines the investment strategies of the operators. *Ryanair*, for example, intends to spend $2bn over 1998–2003 on 25 new Boeing 737-800s (and up to 20 options), doubling the size of its passenger fleet. The other independent, *easy-Jet*, is considering diversifying into other geographic markets by opening a base in Amsterdam. Other new low-cost entrants include Debonair and Virgin Express, although these offer a full-service flight.

The major airlines have adopted competitive strategies to address this challenge to their profitability, based in part on the market intelligence forecasts of high potential passenger demand for this type of service. British Airways has just entered the market with its low-cost subsidiary Go to combat *Ryanair* and *easy-Jet*. Italy's Alitalia has established Team Alitalia to combat Italian budget airline Air One; however, the latter has now entered into a strategic alliance with Swissair to resist Alitalia's pressure. Spain's Iberia is also setting up a low-cost subsidiary as is Lufthansa. However, most continental European airlines will not be over-affected by these developments

Other parts of the strategy of the major airlines are buying up the opposition (BA offered to buy *easy-Jet* in 1997 but later withdrew its offer) and, *easy-Jet* has alleged, trying to drive the budget airline out of business by cross-subsidisation of Go – as it has been alleged British Airways sought to do with Laker Airlines on the trans-Atlantic route in the 1970s (this was settled out of court with BA paying a large undisclosed sum in £ millions).

■ 10.5 International marketing

For a firm to successfully access foreign markets it needs to use international marketing to achieve its strategic objectives. Precisely how it might access these markets is discussed more fully below. Here the concern is with how marketing can develop demand for the business's products in foreign markets; these products can then be matched to the specific needs of the foreign customers. For a new exporter there are major constraints which deter some businesses from taking the first step. These include:

1. perceived greater risks through lack of specific market knowledge, for example strength of competitors and the counter strategies they will adopt;
2. different legal systems;
3. different languages, cultures and so on;
4. costs of market diversification, for example marketing and establishing distribution channels;
5. exchange risks;
6. the need to offer credit facilities to new customers; and
7. greater risks of non-payment through greater distance.

Some of these have been discussed more fully above as examples of entry barriers so are not pursued further here.

A business needs to calculate its anticipated share of any new market since, if it falls short of a certain percentage of the market, it will not be cost- or price-competitive. For small businesses, however, where market share is not feasible in the short to medium run, an appropriate strategy is to concentrate on a niche market. As an example of niche marketing, Crewe Motors, the company set up by Rolls-Royce and Bentley owners to buy Rolls-Royce Motor Cars (RRMC), will continue in existence, even though it was defeated by Volkswagen over the acquisition of RRMC (see Chapter 6.8). It will now seek a niche financing Formula 1 racing as a result of the contacts it has built around the world with wealthy Rolls-Royce and Bentley owners.

■ Formulating an appropriate strategy

Previously, in Chapter 8, there was consideration of the strategic problems any European business faces. One of these is clearly whether or not to diversify into other EU markets. The tools developed in that chapter may be applied to the situation of entering foreign markets, as shown below:

Stage 1: Identify from alternatives that one strategic option is to diversify into new (EU) markets.
Stage 2: Undertake a strategic audit or SWOT (Strengths; Weaknesses; Opportunities; Threats) analysis of the business and its potential market to determine its capabilities and deficiencies regarding the proposed strategy. This will relate to both the present and forecast positions of the business.
Stage 3: Undertake a business environment PEST(LE) (Political; Economic; Social; Technological; Legal; Environmental/Ethical) analysis of the proposed markets to identify which are most suitable. This will relate to both present and forecast environments.
Stage 4: Select the market which is most appropriate in the light of the above analysis and in the context of the business's strengths and weaknesses, that is, in Michael Porter's words, where competitive advantage is greatest.
Stage 5: Identify the marketing strategy to adopt for the new market and implement it, that is marketing planning. This involves identifying the marketing mix to be employed.

Stage 6: Monitor performance to determine whether it is profitable staying in the market or withdrawing.

☐ 1 The products to be sold

These may be products already produced or new products specifically for the overseas market. Alternatively the home market products may need to be modified to meet the tastes and preferences of the overseas market; for example French cars sold in the UK, where the steering wheel is on the right side of the car.

☐ 2 The pricing strategy to be pursued

This will be determined by four main factors. These are: the pricing objectives (that is, does the firm seek to maximise profit or sales); the cost of production; the strength and extent of the competition in the target market; and the demand for the product.

A number of different strategies consequently exist of which alternatives are:

- **Competitive pricing**: that is, charging basically the same prices as the existing producers – this is usually a cost-plus based system (that is, cost + a mark up of X per cent of cost for profit). The cross-channel transport prices of ferries, hovercraft, air, and the Channel Tunnel are examples of this.
- **Penetration pricing**: that is, seeking to undercut existing suppliers to build market share – yet this could provoke retaliation. Global media magnate Rupert Murdoch's News Corporation cut the price of *The Times* substantially in 1994, primarily to target sales of a rival newspaper, *The Independent*. In so doing it also stole custom from other newspapers, forcing them to drop their prices, although not to the same extent. The reduced price is still continued on Mondays with the main target being the *Daily Telegraph*.
- **'skimming the cream'**: if it is a niche market which the business is entering it may be able to charge high prices because of limited supply and hence scarcity value. The proposed letterbox-screen televisions will command a high price until high demand and hence sales drive down costs and prices. Forecasts are that the initial UK price will be £1000. However, after two years this will drop to £500.
- **Dumping pricing**: this was a tactic used by the old COMECON countries to obtain hard currencies and involves selling at below cost price to get rid of stocks which could not be sold in the home market.

The pricing strategy also depends on the stage of the product life-cycle; for example in the introduction and growth stages firms may 'skim the cream'. When the product reaches the maturity and then the decline stages, a more appropriate strategy might be to lower price to maximise sales and deter late entrants, that is penetration pricing.

For sales in the EU factors such as transport costs, different VAT rates and exchange rate movements all affect the ability of a firm to charge standard prices in different countries.

☐ 3 How the products will be marketed, that is their promotion

This will involve devising a strategy to create and reinforce public awareness by covering such issues as:

(a) advertising – through TV and radio; the press; cinema; billboards etc
(b) sales promotions eg, trade fairs; special offers in supermarkets and hypermarkets eg introductory two for the price on one; free gifts or competitions; special packaging to attract the eye of potential purchasers; attractive product design
(c) public relations (PR) – ie a campaign to make the product known eg to potential retailers through promotions and interviews in trade journals, the business press etc
(d) personal selling ie salesmen in the market's retail outlets and to other potential customers

---

CASE STUDY   The US Invasion of EU Retailing

On 31 December 1997, American retailer Wal-Mart announced its intention of expanding into Europe by its acquisition of Wertkauf, the chain of 21 German hypermarkets, with a turnover of DM 3bn per annum. Using a penetration pricing strategy the enormous Wal-Mart stores sell quality branded goods at large discounts, backed by excellent customer service; as such they can be found in many American shopping malls. They also have stores in Canada, Argentina and Puerto Rico, and franchised stores in Mexico, Brazil, Indonesia and China, totalling 3300 in all. This number also includes their supercentres (which also sell groceries) and Sam's Club stores which are warehouse stores requiring membership cards.

In seeking to expand, Wal-Mart faces a number of difficulties. Planning permission for their huge stores will generally be hard to secure, although the UK is probably the easiest country from which to get permission. It may also be difficult for Wal-Mart to persuade manufacturers to allow their goods to be sold at lower prices. This will apply to electrical goods and white goods (for example, deep freezers) and especially to branded goods like Levi and Nike which have operated a 'skimming the cream' policy whereby they are sold at very high prices. Analysts have also suggested that the European market has consumers who are more sophisticated than American consumers, and that the market is mature and so low-growth – hence offering limited opportunities for the Wal-Mart philosophy of 'pile them high, sell them cheap', which characterised the EU when supermarkets first came into existence 40 years ago. Also Wal-Mart may find it difficult to compete from an initial base of just 21 stores compared with the much more established position of its competitors such as German-based Markant (DM 44bn annual turnover) or Aldi (DM 33bn turnover).

Having said that, there are also factors in their favour. European retailing is high-cost with not particularly good consumer service – both in terms of distribution costs for continental Europe and profit margins for the UK. For example, Wal-Mart operates on net profit margins of 2–3 per cent which is comparable with the privately owned continental European stores; in the UK, in contrast, major stores such as Tesco and Sainsbury operate with net margins of 5–6 per cent, making them more vulnerable to Wal-Mart competition. It has also been suggested that Central and Eastern Europe might offer conditions more favourable to Wal-Mart-style growth than Western Europe, typifying a fast-growing market and eager consumers – conditions more similar to the US than the EU is.

The precise combination to be used will need to be appraised in terms of its cost-effectiveness and for many businesses will involve the use of an agency. A cost-benefit analysis (CBA) may be undertaken to quantify these more precisely.

☐ 4 Where the products will be sold, that is the market

This will depend on market research as to which markets are most suitable for the product(s) to be sold. Factors likely to influence this decision will include:

- the strength of existing demand and hence potential sales volume;
- the ease with which distribution channels may be established and operated and their cost;
- nearness to large centres of population, that is large markets to ease transport costs; ability to meet sudden increases in demand;
- how easily markets may be segmented if sales are for a niche market.

This marketing mix which has been discussed above is also known as 'the 4 Ps', that is:

- Product
- Price
- Promotion
- Place

CASE STUDY   Direct Selling in the Home – Cabouchon

Cabouchon embodied what in the 1960s was known as pyramid selling and, in the 1990s, is known as multi-level marketing. This works by a company recruiting agents. Each agent sells the company's products (on which commission is received) and in turn recruits more agents, receiving some of the commission on their sales. In turn those agents recruit more agents. . . and so on. The visual image of the pyramid with the first agent at the apex is clear.

Cabouchon sold costume jewellery, similar to expensive products but with non-experts unable to tell the difference, it was claimed, at a fraction of the cost. This similarity of the product, bought from suppliers in the Far East, was one of the main marketing messages of the company. The other was the ease of purchase in one's own home. Promotion was frequently by word of mouth.

Founded in 1990 by German Petra Doring it grew into a multimillion pound business. In 1994 sales totalled £84m ($126m), and Cabouchon made its founder a multi-millionairess, while top sales executives each earned several hundred thousand pounds p.a. Sales frequently occurred in peoples' homes through organising jewellery parties, or through presentations at offices, womens' organisations and so on. Having started in the UK, Cabouchon soon located in many European countries including Germany, France, the Netherlands, Belgium and Norway.

Sadly, however, in 1998 the receiver was called in and the company was forced to seek liquidation with debts of more than £7m, having struggled financially for two years. As encountered in Chapter 6, this was essentially due to a cash-flow crisis with the company unable to pay its creditors.

The actual strategy a business adopts will be determined by a combination of the maturity of the industry the firm is proposing to enter and its own competitive position. Industry maturity is discussed in detail in section 10.4 under the heading 'Industry Characteristics'. The competitive position of the firm may vary from dominant through strong, favourable, tenable to weak, and then non-viable. For multinational enterprises, dominant (can determine the strategies of competitors), strong (ability to take an independent attitude without harming its long-run position) or favourable (can exploit its strengths if conditions are favourable) are likely to the positions in which it finds itself.

For small and medium-sized enterprises (SMEs), the bulk of EU businesses, the competitive position may only be tenable (potential strengths to justify continuing in the business) or even weak (unsatisfactory but may be able to create improvements). In this latter case, as noted above, an appropriate strategy may be to gain a small or niche market share through competitive pricing (to avoid retaliation from established businesses), and seek to build on its existing strengths to grow as the market grows or even to gain a larger market share over time.

For the larger business with an initially strong position an appropriate strategy may be head-to-head competition from the beginning seeking to grow rapidly and gain a significant market share. This might involve large marketing campaigns and penetration pricing to gain market share.

■ 10.6 Business strategies to enter EU markets

With the opportunities afforded by the single market, EU firms have reviewed their strategies to access new markets beyond their own countries. As the previous sections have shown, market intelligence is of major importance in this context if firms are to gather sufficient information to determine whether a market is worth entering. Additionally, it reveals the extent to which barriers are likely to obstruct entry.

If a business does decide to enter a foreign market, rather than merely accepting any orders that happen to come from abroad, it needs to use market intelligence to formulate alternative strategies. These strategies are discussed below.

■ Exporting

☐ 1 Direct exporting

This is the process whereby a firm produces and sells its goods directly from the home market to the overseas market. Many businesses do this, especially those which are small and/or new to international trade. It offers advantages of direct control over what is happening, cuts out the need for middlemen (agents), reduces the resulting overheads, and permits a business to grow gradually without the need for sudden rapid expansion and the attendant costs and risks. Most importantly it is a low-risk strategy.

The major disadvantage of trading this way is that, even if executives of the business visit the new market regularly, as they should, they are still relatively remote from it. This may create a competitive disadvantage *vis-à-vis* other businesses who either have agents in the market or a physical presence themselves, such as a sales office or even production facilities. A variation on this is for the potential exporter to enter into a collaborative arrangement, either with another business in the exporter's own country or with a business in the country to which the goods are being exported. This shares the costs of the activity and spreads the risks, while with the latter arrangement local expertise is being acquired at low cost. Although such arrangements can work well they can also pose problems when the businesses' strategies begin to diverge.

☐ 2 Indirect exporting

This involves the use of an agency to sell the exporting business's goods on its behalf. The agent may work exclusively for the exporting firm or, if the volume of work does not justify full-time employment, for a number of firms producing different products. The risk here is that it is difficult to ensure that an agent will spend the full amount of time on the exporter's product rather than other businesses' goods. Payment may be made on a salary and commission basis or just by commission.

The advantages of indirect exporting are that the exporter has a presence in the overseas market. Personal contact is always more desirable to generate new custom and to reinforce previous sales. The agent can also feed back to the exporter up to date information about current market conditions. Most importantly it is a cheap option for establishing a market presence. However, it does suffer from the problem of difficulty of coordination and influence over the marketing strategy employed in the export market. It should also be noted that agents may not hold stocks of goods for the exporter.

If sales increase and can be sustained the exporting business may wish to establish its own premises in the overseas market employing more staff. This will permit a better integration of domestic production and foreign sales and enable the producer to exercise more control over operations.

Variations on the above are the use of:

1. **Distributors** – who buy goods and hold them on their own account. These are the most widely used arrangement by exporters.
2. **Export houses** – who will act both as an agent and also as principal; that is, buy goods from the exporter as if a domestic sale and then find a buyer in a foreign market on their own behalf (since they now own the goods).
3. **Confirming houses** – who represent foreign buyers. They will handle all the documentation of the transaction and buy on behalf of the foreign purchaser, that is acting as his agent. The exporter receives payment in the same way as a domestic sale.

Insuring against non-payment   The advantages to an exporter of an organisation buying directly from him or her is that it minimises the risks of non-payment. The ideal situation for an exporter is payment in advance but this is not always forthcoming. The exporter is therefore often obliged to offer credit facilities to potential buyers.

To minimise the risk of non-payment an exporter can take out credit insurance with either a specialist organisation or with a bank. For payment of a premium the exporter gains some security in that, if payment is not forthcoming, the insurer will pay some percentage of the value of the exports – typically 90 per cent. This can relate both to consumer goods and to capital goods, construction work in a foreign market which may be spread over a year or more, or to services. If the exporter's profits are not to be affected the cost of this will need to be incorporated in the quoted price.

■ Foreign Direct Investment (FDI): what is FDI?

One of the four freedoms established by the implementation of the single European market was that of the movement of capital across EU national boundaries. Capital movements may be of two types (Salvatore, 1995).

□ 1 Foreign Direct Investment (FDI)

This involves establishing a subsidiary business in another country by the construction of factories, offices or other commercial or industrial premises; or the acquisition of existing ones, for example as a result of privatisation. This type of investment gives the investor direct control over the asset. Its purpose is to produce and market a product in the foreign or recipient country.

□ 2 Foreign Portfolio Investment

As distinct from FDI, foreign portfolio investment is the acquisition of shares, bonds or other financial assets of a company, usually through the intermediation of a bank or investment fund. In this case control is indirect since the company's strategy will be determined by the board and implemented operationally by senior managers. Foreign portfolio investment may also involve the acquisition of foreign government bonds.

Until the First World War the bulk of foreign investment was portfolio, the three major investors being the UK (50 per cent of total investment), France and Germany, with these countries investing mainly in Europe, North America, Australia and Latin America. In the 1980s and 1990s direct investment has been the major component. The largest foreign investors have been Japan, the US and the UK, with the main recipients being the EU (especially the UK), the US and less-developed countries (LDCs) – especially PR China. The bulk of FDI is undertaken by multinational enterprises (MNEs) such as Dutch firm Phillips, or German car manufacturer Volkswagen, organisations which have production facilities in more

than one country. In 1980 the total stock of FDI was $470bn; by 1993 it had risen
to $1800bn. In 1997 the annual flow of FDI totalled $350bn. The members of the
OECD are the source of 85 per cent of all FDI and recipients of 60 per cent, and
the leading European recipients are shown in Table 10.1. However, the major
growth has been towards developing countries and in the service sectors.

■ Why undertake FDI?

The end-result of any business activity should be that it increases profitability.
However, this does not mean that increased profitability is a direct consequence
of the action; it may occur subsequently as a result of another action which is the
initial rationale for FDI. For example, FDI might occur for the following reasons:

1. To diversify horizontally, that is by acquiring another business involved in the same
   activities.
2. To diversify vertically, either backwards to acquire raw materials, for example EU oil
   companies acquiring Middle East oil fields in the past; or forwards to acquire retail
   outlets, for example oil companies running filling stations. This is to reduce risk.
3. Conglomerate diversification; that is, the opportunity in a new market to introduce
   products unrelated to existing outputs in the domestic market.
4. The opportunity to seize strategic advantage by gaining early entry to an emerging
   market.
5. The opportunity to make monopoly profits in a market due to patent rights or technological, managerial or marketing advantage.

Table 10.1 Leading European recipients of FDI, January–June 1997

COUNTRY	EXPANSION OF CURRENT INVESTMENTS	NEW INVESTMENTS	TOTAL INVESTMENTS	PERCENTAGE OF TOTAL INVESTMENTS
UK	152	274	426	34.5
Ireland	35	60	95	7.7
Germany	13	77	90	7.3
France	28	54	82	6.7
Poland	21	60	81	6.6
Russia	10	54	64	5.2
Belgium	16	33	49	4.0
Hungary	16	32	48	3.9
Spain	18	26	44	3.6
Netherlands	10	32	42	3.4
Czech Rep.	9	24	33	2.7
Switzerland	4	18	22	1.8
Others	39	118	157	12.7
Total	371	862	1233	100

Source: Ernst & Young.

6. To counter a rival gaining a dominant share in the foreign market and hence threatening the domestic market in due course.
7. To utilise surplus funds by firms which are cash-rich due to asset sales, for example.
8. To spread risks due to over dependence on certain markets.
9. To address problems encountered with direct or indirect exporting.
10. For outsourcing purposes.

In summary foreign direct investment may occur due to attractive forces from the overseas or recipient market drawing funds to that country, such as the ability to produce more cheaply overseas or a country liberalising its trading policies, as with CEEC. This is particularly important for global car producers. Or it may be due to repelling factors forcing funds from the investing or donor country such as declining industrial sectors or products. Whatever the reason, intra-firm trade then becomes a major factor in international trade between the donor and recipient countries.

■ Theoretical models to explain FDI

Foreign direct investment is a consequence of the fact that markets are imperfect. If they were perfect then there would be perfect knowledge, similar input costs, and so on. Hence profitability would be the same in each country and in each industry and there would be no incentive to undertake foreign direct investment. A number of models have therefore been developed as theoretical underpinnings to explain the process of FDI. Although there is not the opportunity here to examine all of these in depth, it might be useful to briefly review some of them and to examine one in a little more detail. The reader is also referred to the texts in the bibliography for further reading and especially Sodersten and Reed's book on which the next section draws.

☐ 1 Internalisation Theories

These theories (Coase, 1937; Kindleberger, 1969; Hymer, 1976; Caves, 1982) try to explain FDI in terms of market imperfections. Some firms may enjoy specific advantages which enable them to gain economic advantages; these may include technological and/or managerial expertise in manufacturing, for example lean production; patents and copyright on production processes, products such as pharmaceuticals, and intellectual property; managerial expertise; famous brand names, and so on. If these confer greater benefits from exploiting them through foreign direct investment than the costs of the FDI it is worth undertaking. In other words, the bigger the market where the products can be sold which arise from the specific advantages the greater the returns to the company. There is also the argument that by undertaking FDI, one can gain control over one's competitors by setting up a subsidiary in a new market before they can do so.

In contrast, licensing may give away expertise to the licensee which may then be used against the licensor subsequently in his home market; also the company supplying the expertise loses control over the production process. One reason why McDonalds will not set up burger restaurants in India is doubts as to Indian licensees' ability to achieve its hygiene standards (the other is that the cow is sacred to many Indians!). The investing company may also have doubts as to the ability of licensees to build up maximum market-share and prefer to invest directly. In these circumstances FDI is preferable to licensing or franchising.

☐ 2 The product life-cycle theory

This follows the logic of the product life-cycle in arguing that, at each stage of a product's life, a particular form of foreign trading is appropriate (Vernon, 1966, 1971, 1977). In the early stages of introduction and growth the business will concentrate on exporting to overseas markets since this is the most cost-effective way. As the product reaches the maturity and then decline stages in its life, and competitors' products are available, the business will look for new cost-effective means to retain its competitive edge. One option is to invest overseas (FDI) in other developed countries as demand in these markets develops sufficiently to produce locally. Finally, to cut production costs by gaining access to cheaper labour and accessing new markets, FDI will take place in developing countries such as Central and Eastern Europe.

It may also be possible for firms to gain scale-economies by locating component and assembly plants at different sites in different economies – microprocessors produced in one country, PC monitors in another, keyboards in a third, and assembly in a fourth for example. As noted elsewhere, this will generate intra-firm trade between countries. One main criticism of this theory is its failure to explain why the firm does not just continue to export, or use licensing rather than FDI, once the local market reaches a certain size.

☐ 3 Knickerbocker's follow-the-leader model

This theory (Knickerbocker, 1973) is particularly relevant to the oligopolistic nature of modern global industries with their interdependence. It argues that as one firm undertakes FDI in a country, its rivals will be forced to copy so as not to lose competitive advantages. Japanese car investment in the EU is one clear example of this, while a similar situation can be seen with the global automobile industry investing in Central and Eastern Europe in the late 1990s. What this theory fails to do is to explain how the first firm decides to invest, unlike the market imperfections theory.

☐ 4 Dunning's eclectic or OLI model

Dunning's eclectic model (Dunning, 1977) is also known as the OLI model and examines whether a business or industry or country will be a FDI donor, a FDI recipient or neither. In this context OLI stands for:

O = Ownership advantages
L = Locational aspects
I = Internalisation benefits

Ownership consists of advantages accruing particularly to the firm, industry or country. Concentrating just on the business these include:

- organisational and management advantages;
- accessibility to supplies of raw materials and other inputs necessary for production;
- technological advantages;
- size of the business, permitting economies of scale;
- ease of access to finance – larger firms have access advantages over smaller;
- ability to diversify;
- ability of the business to move production between counties.

Location consists of such aspects as:

- entry barriers;
- transport costs of goods to markets, for example;
- political stability in the FDI-receiving country;
- taxation regimes in both donor and recipient countries, for example are there advantages of ownership in the recipient country;
- cultural differences or similarities between donor and recipient countries.

These essentially reflect comparative advantage (Winters, 1991).

Internalisation consists of benefits making it worthwhile to undertake transactions within the firm rather than in external markets, for example by franchising, licensing and so on. It offers:

- avoiding uncertainty;
- benefits of unexploited economies of scale;
- reduction of tax liability through transfer pricing (see Chapter 6).

For FDI to result, all three of OLI must occur.

▮ Methods of FDI

☐ 1 Establishing a subsidiary

This is a step beyond the use of the agent, since now the exporting firm establishes a presence in the foreign market. This gives it an immediacy which was lacking when it exported from the home country. The manager of the branch in the foreign country can now exercise closer control, determine more immediately the effectiveness of marketing campaigns, and more actively secure custom. Although it will generate greater costs it should also contribute more than this to profitability in the medium term. If it does not then its existence cannot be justified.

☐ 2 Acquisition of a business

There are various ways in which a firm may acquire total control of a business in another country. The two most obvious ways are:

1. Incorporate a new company (direct investment).
2. Acquire an existing company (portfolio investment).

In either case this is a high-cost strategy since it involves large expenditure. In the former case this will be capital expenditure incurred in acquiring premises, machinery, hiring staff and so on. Suppliers of materials will have to be established, a customer base acquired through marketing campaigns and so on. However, it does enable the foreign investor to start afresh and establish production facilities exactly to requirements.

In the latter case it will involve buying a majority of the shares of the 'victim' company. In this case the predator company acquires sources of materials, existing staff, customer base, distribution channels and so on. This means that new products can be introduced more quickly since the business is already up and running. However, there are costs of training, possible new capital expenditure, the risk of resentment of a foreign takeover causing existing staff to leave and so forth. Buying a newly privatised company is another way of acquiring an existing business.

☐ 3 Joint ventures

Joint ventures exist where a company wishing to enter a foreign market acquires a stake in another business based in that market, for example by purchasing a certain percentage of its shares. Usually it also exercises control over some management functions of the foreign company. The benefits of a joint venture to the acquiring company are the expertise of a local firm, the cost saving of not purchasing 100 per cent of a company, usually better returns and the ability to exercise fairly close control over the foreign company's activities.

The foreign or recipient company acquires an extension to its product range, foreign expertise and perhaps some new investment financed from overseas. CEEC governments such as Russia favour joint ventures in that control resides with the domestic firm not the foreign firm seeking access to the Russian market. Problems inevitably arise from time to time over future strategy, shared investment costs, and the foreign entrant's desire to make operational changes such as reducing the labour force and so on. Also, the receiving/domestic firm may, after a while, require a larger share of the profits as it gains greater confidence. Additionally, cultural differences between the two companies, both organisationally and nationally, may prove too great to handle.

CASE STUDY   LDV–Daewoo Joint Venture

A joint venture was agreed in 1998 between LDV, the UK truck manufacturer, (see Chapter 9.6) and Daewoo of South Korea. This is to produce two new vans, with production occurring at LDV's factory in Birmingham, UK, where up to 2000 new jobs will be created and 1500 safeguarded, and Daewoo's plant in Lubin, Poland. A total of £160m is being invested by the two companies in the joint venture while the UK's Department of Trade and Industry are providing £25m under the regional-aid banner. A third of this will be spent on product development and the rest on transforming the Birmingham factory.

At Birmingham the investment will boost production from 17 000 to 80 000 vehicles a year. 40 000 of these will bear the Daewoo name and are earmarked for Eastern Europe; the other half will have the LDV marque of which half will be sold in the UK and the other half in continental Europe. Daewoo will invest £25m in LDV and take a significant but not controlling stake.

☐ 4 Licensing

In this situation the licensor (the company granting the licence or patent) authorises the licensee (the foreign firm receiving permission to undertake the activity) to undertake one or more activities in its own right. These include:

- Manufacturing and marketing the good with the same brand name, for example Coca-Cola manufactured under licence in India.
- Manufacturing and marketing the good with a different brand name.
- Assembling and marketing the product from supplied components or components, some which are manufactured locally: for example, the Polski Fiat which was manufactured in Poland under licence from Fiat in the 1980s.
- Manufacturing other goods with the same brand name, for example clothes manufactured with the Guinness logo on them.

This arrangement offers the licensor a number of advantages, including licence fees/royalties; reduced costs and risks (since these are born by the licensee); easier access to foreign markets than exporting; local knowledge and established distribution channels; and avoidance of the need for capital expenditure.

However, there are also disadvantages, the main one of which is that having acquired the technology and expertise the licensee may dispense with the licence and continue by itself – the sale of Rover to BMW by British Aerospace demonstrates this, as Honda found to their cost. Other problems are that the licensor needs to monitor the licensee to ensure that agreed output levels and product quality standards are maintained.

☐ 5 Franchising

This is similar to licensing except that it tends to be longer term. Also the franchisee acquires not only the trademark of the company but also the obligation to meet certain requirements. This may involve such issues as the layout and design of the store, for example, how staff dress, the menu and how food is cooked, staffing policies and so on. In return the franchisee pays a fee and often royalties linked to sales. Examples of this would be Burger King, Domino Pizzas, Pizza Hut and so on. Among European businesses the Swedish furnishings firm IKEA, which has stores in 28 countries including West and East Europe, has expanded by the use of franchises. In contrast, UK department store Marks and Spencer have relied on a mixture of franchises, joint ventures and wholly-owned businesses, while Benetton has relied on franchises and agents.

☐ 6 Conclusions

The main advantages of FDI may be identified as placing the firm nearer to the market and permitting better market access, overcoming tariff and non-tariff barriers, reduced transport costs, a greater spread of risks through diversifying into new markets, and at times government incentives, financial or otherwise.

The main disadvantages of FDI are the high cost of capital involved in establishing an overseas presence, the risk that host government policies may be hostile, the risk of being accused of exploiting the host country, possible problems of repatriating profits (the last three applying to countries outside the EU), and cultural or legal problems.

■ 10.7 Trade and investment in CEEC markets

The opening of CEEC markets in the 1990s has offered considerable opportunities for Western European businesses, both in terms of export/import and in terms of direct foreign investment. With the former USSR having a population of approximately 280 million and CEEC having 113m, a market larger than the EU has opened up.

■ Differences posed by the CEEC

Although some of the problems of trading or investing are similar to those encountered elsewhere, the distinctive processes which the former USSR and CEEC are still going through means that there are also significant differences:

1. A variety of new languages, cultures and customs – although there are many cultural similarities with the EU and 45 years of communist rule failed to eradicate these.
2. Lack of market intelligence; that is knowledge about consumer preferences, income distribution, competition and so on. However, this has now improved significantly as advertising agencies and consultancy firms have moved into the CEEC.

3. Although potential demand for Western products is very high, actual demand is still much lower because of a lack of consumer purchasing power.
4. Low domestic output is still aggravated by outdated technology, production methods and distribution networks in many industries, in spite of loans from the EBRD, the EU and so on.
5. As seen in Chapter 5, the pace of liberalisation differs significantly from country to country with some nations of the former USSR having made limited progress, while others such as the Czech Republic, Hungary and Poland have made such substantial progress towards economic reform that they hope to join the EU by 2002, although failure to complete privatisation programmes remains a problem. Particularly this involves the business infrastructure of modern industrial economies.

The reader will observe that there are considerable similarities with the previous section. Gaining access to CEEC markets may be viewed therefore from the two different approaches of trading with existing CEEC businesses and investing in CEEC.

■ Trading with CEEC

The basic approach for trading with CEEC is now much closer to that of trading between EU nations than it was in the 1980s and before. In particular, there has been major decentralisation so that exports and imports no longer have to go through state trading organisations. When these existed in the past they acted as a mechanism for screening imports to ensure that only those which were needed for economic development were purchased. This prevented scarce hard currencies being spent on 'unnecessary' Western consumer goods. Now EU firms can trade directly with CEEC firms, although, in some of the relatively unreformed countries of the former USSR, particularly the Asian republics, the old constraints still exist to a considerable extent.

However, there are still differences in trading with EU countries compared with CEEC and the less a country has moved along the path of economic reform the greater these differences will be.

The strategy for diversifying into foreign markets which was formulated above may therefore be applied here, and the steps outlined above for entering foreign markets are also applicable. What is important is that potential exporters and investors must be proactive and seek out opportunities in the markets of CEEC, rather than waiting for CEEC firms to come to them. This implies that before making strategic decisions any exporters or investors should visit the proposed country since field research can offer considerable advantages over desk research. They should also consider employing any of the growing number of agencies specialising in CEEC to research the market in detail. Until recently these have been largely based in Western European countries but now offices of Western European and US agencies exist in CEEC cities.

Obviously the level of sophistication of market analysis is limited by the lack of consumer and specialist market data compared with a Western European country.

Apart from the conventional ways of securing custom through marketing campaigns there are a number of other specific ways to access potential customers. These include:

- **Trade fairs**: These have been widely used in CEEC in the past and are still a useful vehicle for bringing together potential buyers and sellers in specific areas. The most famous one is held in Leipzig in Eastern Germany.
- **Trade missions**: Organised by chambers of commerce these can offer assistance on making contacts with potential customers and will group together a number of firms to spread the promotional and administrative costs.
- **National weeks in department stores**: The aim of these is to promote a country's consumer goods in the store. The store is provided with detailed promotional material, demonstrations are laid on, competitions set up, product tasting sessions organised – for example wines, cheeses and so on. These are used in EU and US stores and prove very successful.

■ Countertrade

When trade occurs it is normal for the exporting firm to give the purchaser a period of credit before payment has to be made. This will vary, typically, from 30 to 90 days. Payment is usually made through the banking system and involves a number of different options including bills of exchange and documentary credits. The interested reader should contact his or her local bank who will be able to advise on the alternatives available.

One problem faced in trading with some countries of the former USSR is that shortages of hard currencies still exist, although most CEEC currencies are now largely convertible. Additionally some CEEC may find it difficult to obtain credit from EU suppliers, for example, particularly if there are doubts about repayment. Although trade between companies has significantly replaced trade by state trading organisations, some countries of the former USSR are, therefore, still forced to some extent to use measures from the pre-reform days to enable foreign trade to take place. These may be considered under the heading of countertrade.

Essentially, countertrade occurs when trade in one good is dependent on trade in another good in the opposite direction to finance it. For example, oil from Russia traded for grain from the US was a common form of countertrade in the 1980s. It is still widely used in its various forms by developing nations. The advantages of countertrade are that it promotes international trade which would not otherwise occur. It also enables newly-industrialised countries (NICs) to engage actively in international trade

Its disadvantages are that it can prove to be very complex, particularly if more than two parties are involved. It can also prove to be very bureaucratic and hence time-consuming. It is expensive because of the number of parties involved and the charges levied by each, for example banks, insurance companies, lawyers and so on. Also its suitability for small and medium-sized enterprises (SMEs) is debatable because of the cost aspect. Hence it has been undertaken mainly by government trading agencies or by large organisations.

A number of different types of countertrade exist and some of these are briefly reviewed here.

☐ 1 Barter

This type of trading arrangement is not commonly used. Simply it involves good X being exchanged for good Y in a single transaction without any money payments occurring. In reality it is not quite so simple. If US grain is shipped to Russia and in return oil is supplied by Russia to the US, the US firm will sell it to obtain payment for its wheat. The money will be held by a US bank in our example, in what is called a trust or escrow account. Any surplus funds after sufficient has been set aside to pay the US supplier will be remitted to the Russian exporter.

☐ 2 Counterpurchase

In this case two separate and parallel contracts are established which effectively cancel each other out. For example, the Republic of Armenia supplies silk and cotton to France in exchange for womens' fashion clothing. The silk and cotton are paid for by the French importer in francs. A separate French firm supplies the womens' clothing to a separate Armenian firm in Armenia. They may be for the same value as the silk and cotton or more. There is no reason for the transactions or the businesses to be related. The main advantage of this type of trade is to ensure that by matching imports and exports Armenia does not experience a large balance of payments deficit.

☐ 3 Compensation

Sometimes known as a buy-back deal this usually applies to heavy machinery and mining equipment. With this form of countertrade the exporter of the equipment agrees to be paid in the future from the proceeds of the goods manufactured with the exported equipment. For example, if specialised coal extraction equipment is exported payment would be from the sale proceeds of the coal mined using this equipment. Russia in particular favoured this approach in the 1980s.

There are also a number of other types of countertrade including offset and switch trading which the interested reader may wish to pursue.

■ Investing in CEEC

Eastern Europe offers many attractions to the Western investor. Apart from the enormous pent-up demand Eastern European labour is cheap, well-educated and relatively compliant because of anxieties about employment prospects, although strikes in the early 1990s caused some concerns over this. Further, because of the past culture of working to production targets rather than for profit, and the lack of capital investment, labour productivity is low. The continued existence of the nomenklatura, the old communist party bureaucrats, working to different agenda but still in place and largely doing the same work, has certainly inhibited development, in some countries more than others. Also privatisation still needs to be completed.

There are also tensions and conflicts, particularly in the form of resurgent nationalism which at times has cast doubts on the long-term profitability of investment. In its worst form it is exhibited in the conflict in former Yugoslavia; in its peaceful form in the break up of Czechoslovakia. It has also manifested itself in tensions between Albania and Serbia and Albania and Hungary. Furthermore, particularly in Russia, organised crime is a major problem with severe implications for deterring investors in the same way that it has in Southern Italy.

Worst of all, CEEC industry is dated with technology still lagging behind that of Western Europe, although foreign direct investment has improved the capital base significantly, of some countries more than others. Since the mid-1990s tourism has proved to be a major source of income for the countries of Central and Eastern Europe, particularly the cultural cities of Prague and Budapest, rural Poland and parts of Romania (the Carpathian mountains). However, this has not been applicable to a number of other industries.

A number of strategies exist for investing in CEEC economies, each offering advantages and disadvantages. These are largely the same as those for investing in EU countries, and this section will focus on the particular differences involved in establishing these in CEEC compared with the EU.

☐ 1 Direct investment

One important decision any investor must make is whether to invest in a greenfield site; that is, build from scratch as an independent company constructing premises on former agricultural land, for example, or buy into a privatised business.

1. **Manufacturing locally as an independent company**   There are inevitably both advantages and disadvantages in a greenfield site strategy. The disadvantages are:

- There will be substantial set-up costs in spite of the fact that capital and land costs are generally much lower than in the EU.
- There will inevitably be delays before production can begin.
- The costs of training local staff, establishing distribution links and so on, which have been discussed elsewhere, must be taken into account.

The advantages are:

- The production facility can be located at an optimal site, for example near road links.
- The factory can be designed as wanted.
- New equipment is immediately available for use.

2. **Buying into a privatised organisation** This is certainly a feasible option as more and more businesses are privatised in CEEC. The advantages of this strategy are:

- premises already exist;
- a cheap trained workforce exists;
- production is already occurring;
- existing customer base;
- existing distribution network exists;
- local knowledge.

Significant disadvantages are:

- How to value the assets being purchased – different accounting conventions from those of the EU can make for serious problems, although this is now less of a problem in many countries as Western accounting methods are employed.
- Premises may not be particularly suitable, or in a state of disrepair.
- Labour skills may not be suitable for new production processes.
- Capital equipment is likely to be dated.
- Heavy overmanning exists.
- Resistance from existing management (the nomenklatura).
- Possible costs of previous environmental pollution which need clearing up.

A very careful estimation of the costs of each strategy is needed here. Although an existing CEEC business may seem attractive at first, the costs of bringing it up to EU standards may be significant as the federal government found in Eastern Germany.

3. **Joint ventures** When a joint venture is established between an EU and a CEEC company this might be achieved by buying shares in the local company. However, in some countries total ownership of certain assets is not allowed; for example Russia will not allow total ownership by foreigners of its energy resources. Additionally, if the domestic partner is subsequently privatised the investor may suddenly find it is dealing with another company, possibly from the EU or US. Other alternatives are establishing collaborative links while still maintaining legal independence, or setting up a third company jointly owned by the Western and Eastern European companies.

Each party to the relationship seeks specific gains. For the Western firm these include local knowledge of the local markets and culture; an easily acquired labour force and management; (often) land and premises ready to be used; existing distribution networks; favourable taxation; cancelling past debts of the partner and other concessions from national governments anxious to attract new investment; and synergistic gains from linking into similar activities in the CEEC. The CEEC partner acquires financial and managerial expertise; funding from the new partner; access to new technology; licenses to produce new products from the West; and much easier access to Western markets.

| CASE STUDY Greenfield Sites in Hungary and the Czech Republic |

Greenfield sites are generally perceived as preferable to brownfield sites; the latter are existing industrial sites which need to be cleared of previous premises, or at minimum converted to new usage. Either option can prove very expensive, especially when the costs of clearing up pollution effects from previous production are allowed for – a common problem in CEEC.

In Hungary the main plank of the government's privatisation programme has involved selling state-owned assets for cash to strategic investors – especially public utilities, banks and industrial enterprises. This has accounted for some 30 per cent of the foreign direct investment into the country in the 1990s, and has facilitated the upgrading of technology and management skills as well as creating access to foreign capital – none of which the Hungarian state or local authorities could provide.

However, new investment has also occurred in greenfield sites as well as existing brownfield ones. This has including the construction of new facilities and plant for the recently privatised industries and for new industries, and for new retail outlets such as the UK's Marks & Spencer and Tesco in city centres, entertainment complexes and suburban shopping malls. The head of the government's task force on European integration, Andreas Inotai, has argued that these greenfield site investments have provided the greatest benefit to the Hungarian economy since they are often export-oriented – over 70 per cent of exports now coming from foreign-owned plants. Greenfield investment has created new industries such as automobile assembly and components industries, as well as resurrecting existing ones such as pharmaceuticals and electronics. Businesses such as IBM and Phillips have located in Hungary and started production since late 1997, adding further to GDP and exports.

In the Czech Republic the ability to attract overseas businesses to greenfield sites has proved less successful. Matsushita, a leading Japanese consumer electronics group, was one of the first to invest in a greenfield site at Plzen in Western Bohemia, constructing a television assembly plant at a cost of $66m. The management is delighted with the fact that it took only one year from acquisition of the land to achieving the first line of volume production – 1000 sets per day; also the quality standards are very high. However, critics argue that in a fiercely competitive market for FDI, the limited range of investment incentives provided by the government is failing to attract new investors in competition with other countries offering greenfield sites plus better financial incentives. The chief executive of the Czech investment promotion agency, CzechInvest, has argued that FDI is the only reliable source of capital and know-how as the Czech stockmarket is not working very well, the currency the crown is floating, and there are debt problems at the banks. Foreign firms account for 40–50 per cent of Czech exports. CzechInvest also argues that the businesses performing best today are those that were sold to foreign businesses or started on a greenfield site.

☐ 2 Portfolio investment

When buying into a privatised company an EU company may do so merely by purchasing shares or bonds without the intention of being involved in its running, that is as a sleeping partner, although this is very unlikely. In any event there are difficulties in being engaged in portfolio investment since stockmarkets are not yet very developed, and those that do exist trade only in a few shares compared to EU centres. Even though the volume of shares is being increased with the scale of privatisations that are occurring, the fact that true market prices are not emerging reinforces the difficulties of a properly functioning stockmarket.

■ Review questions

1. Discuss the reasons why a European business might diversify into CEEC and the problems it might face.
2. How does international marketing differ from domestic marketing?
3. What sort of pricing policy might be applied for:

   (a) a new 4-wheel drive model of car marketed in Germany;
   (b) a new cat food with flavours which drive the cats wild!
   (c) a range of 486-computers bought as a job lot from a bankrupt manufacturer.

4. What advantages and disadvantages does FDI have over exporting for the sale of white goods to the Czech Republic?
5. Discuss the advantages and disadvantages of compensation trading with a firm in the Ukraine.

■ Bibliography

Branch, A. E., *Elements of Export Marketing and Management* (London: Chapman & Hall, 1990).

Caves, R. E., *Multinational Enterprise and Economic Analysis* (Cambridge: Cambridge University Press, 1982).

Coase, R. H., (1937) 'The Nature of the Firm', *Economica*, vol. 4, pp. 386–405.

de Rouffignac, P. Danton, *Doing Business In Eastern Europe: A Guide for the 1990s* (London: Pitman, 1991).

Drew, J., *Doing Business in the European Community*, 3rd edn (London: Whurr Publishers, 1992).

Dudley, J. W., *Exporting* (London: Pitman, 1989).

Dunning, J. H., 'Trade Location of Economic Activity and the MNE: A Search for an Eclectic Approach', in Ohlin, B., Hesselborn, P. O. and Wijkman, P. K. (eds), *The International Allocation of Economic Activity* (London: Macmillan, 1977).

Dunning, J. H., (1979) 'Explaining Changing Patterns of International Investment: In Defence of the Eclectic Theory', *Oxford Bulletin of Economics and Statistics*, vol. 41, pp. 269–96.

Gilligan, C. and Hird, M., *International Marketing: Strategy and Management* (London: Routledge, 1986).

Hallenstein, D., *Doing Business in Italy* (London: BBC Books, 1991).

Hymer, S. H., *The International Operations of National Firms: A Study of Direct Foreign Investment* (Cambridge, MA.: MIT Press, 1976).

Houlden, B., *Understanding Company Strategy: An Introduction to Thinking and Acting Strategically* (Oxford: Blackwell, 1993).

Jain, S. C., *Marketing Planning and Strategy*, 4th edn (USA: South-Western Publishing Co., 1993).

Karakaya, F. and Stahl, M. J., *Entry Barriers and Market Entry Decisions: A Guide for Marketing Executives* (USA: Quorum Books, 1991).

Ketelhohn, W., *International Business Strategy* (Oxford: Butterworth-Heinemann, 1993).

Kindleberger, C. P., *American Business Abroad: Six Lectures on Direct Investment* (New Haven: Yale University Press, 1969).

Knickerbocker, F. T., *Oligopolistic Reaction and Multinational Enterprise* (Boston: Harvard University Graduate Business School of Business Administration, 1973).

Liebreich, K., *Doing Business in Eastern Europe* (London: BBC Books, 1991).

Paliwoda, S. J., *Investing in Eastern Europe: Capitalising on Emerging Markets* (Wokingham: Addison-Wesley, 1995).

Randlesome, C., Brierly, W., Bruton, K., Gordon, C. and King, P., *Business Cultures in Europe*, 2nd edn (Oxford: Butterworth-Heinemann, 1993).

Salvatore, D., *International Economics*, 5th edn (Hemel Hempstead: Prentice Hall, 1995).

Sodersten, B. and Reed, G., *International Economics*, 3rd edn (Basingstoke: Macmillan Press, 1994).

Swann, D. (ed.), *The Single European Market and Beyond* (London: Routledge, 1992).

Terpstra, V. and Sarathy, R., *International Marketing* (Orlando: The Dryden Press, 1991).

Vernon, R., (1966) 'International Investment and International Trade in the Product Cycle', *Quarterly Journal of Economics*, vol. 80, pp. 190–207.

Vernon, R., *Sovereignty at Bay: The Multinational Spread of US Enterprises* (London: Basic Books, 1971).

Vernon, R., *Storm Over Multinationals: The Real Issues* (Cambridge, MA: Harvard University Press, 1977).

Winters, L. A., *International Economics*, 4th edn (London: Routledge, 1991).

Also:

The Economist
The European
The Financial Times
The Times

The Green European business

■ 11.1 Introduction

This chapter considers two major issues of increasing importance to European business in the near future. They are considered both from the macro approach of the policies of the EU and from the micro basis of individual businesses and how they respond within the European business environment.

One area of increasing concern to European businesses and consumers is that of the environment. In the next decade businesses will have to respond much more positively to environmental issues as a result of pressures from the EU itself, consumers and lobby groups such as Greenpeace. This will inevitably force businesses to look carefully at their production processes and the costs imposed by the need to effect change. Allied to this is the increasing awareness that businesses have an obligation to behave ethically rather than just seek to maximise profits. This may again have environmental aspects or it may relate to the treatment of employees, including those in third-world countries, by European multinationals. There may also be clashes with the EU over competition and social policies. Both these issues are considered here.

■ 11.2 European business and the environment

■ The impact of environmental problems

> Our survival is only a question of 25, 50 or 100 years. It is absurd and dangerous for those who live in prosperity to think that the world economy is a cycle and its riches will circulate for ever. Unrenewable resources are being squandered. Waste is building up. Valuable goods are vanishing while rubbish thrives.
>
> (*The Man, the Octopus and the Orchid*, the autobiography of Jacques Cousteau)

European businesses and their purpose in supplying goods and/or services have already been examined, as have new production and management processes which emphasise cost-reduction through placing quality at centre-stage. However, production also generates outputs other than goods, which might be described as bads; these include pollution and waste and are either side-effects or a direct consequence of production. They impose external costs on society in terms of their effects and in terms of the need to redress these, but are not reflected in a business's accounts nor, except partially with petrol, in the price paid by the consumer in the marketplace. However, these costs are borne indirectly both by the consumer and by society at large. Figure 11.1 shows how a European business uses resources to produce not just goods and services but also other outputs termed bads.

Estimates of the effect on the German economy of environmental damage in the early 1990s totalled approximately DM200 billion, or between 6–10 per cent of GDP (Hopfenbeck, 1993). The harmful effects of economic growth are manifested in the following ways:

1. **Pollution**: This is clearly evidenced by the growth of respiratory illnesses such as asthma, and the number of cities which have air quality poorer than EU and World Health Organisation limits, often by significant amounts. The major contributor to this, and hence to the harming of the ozone layer, is transport and specifically automobiles although other sources such as power stations and aeroplanes also contribute. This has implications in terms of rising hospital costs, lost working days and the increasing incidence of cancer. In the medium to long term the EU, in conjunction with national governments, will have to shift the balance of transport provision from automobiles to public transport, whether funded privately or by the public sector, if this is to be stabilised let alone reduced.

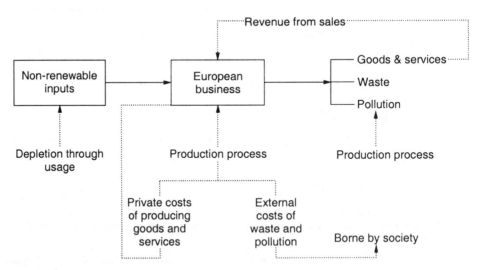

Figure 11.1 Production Processes Reflecting External Costs

2. **Damage to the ozone layer**: Although environmental scientists are at present reluctant to state categorically that sustained global warming is occurring, probable evidence of its existence has been well-documented in recent years. Emissions of pollutants such as carbon dioxide, nitrous dioxide, sulphur dioxide and CFCs (chlorofluorocarbons) are harming the ozone layer which shields the planet from the sun's harmful ultraviolet rays. This is currently demonstrated by the increasing incidence of skin cancer with its attendant hospital costs both in the EU and elsewhere. In the long term this destruction may have profound effects on regions of the EU such as the Mediterranean, which are dependent on sun and sea-based tourism for economic prosperity.

   The reader should note that, although ozone is needed as a layer above the earth to shield humans from the harmful effects of the sun, when inhaled at ground level it is injurious to us.

3. **Climatic change**: Global warming which contributes to climatic change will cause the polar ice caps to melt, a process which already has started to occur. This has implications for EU coastal regions at sea level requiring major expenditure on sea defence systems in the short to medium term. In the long term the risk is that areas may have to be abandoned if sea levels rise very high. In extremis, if both ice caps were fully to melt estimates suggest that the sea level would rise 50 metres (160 feet). The increasing risk of unstable weather patterns, such as severe hurricanes or rivers flooding, will impose costs on households and businesses both in terms of clearing up and repairing the damage and through rising insurance premiums, assuming insurance companies will still take this business. In other parts of Europe, such as Southern Spain, severe and prolonged drought is already a problem. This will have major implications for EU agriculture and hence employment in terms of the changing pattern of crops which will and will not be able to be grown. It will also result in the extinction of even more species of flora and fauna – currently three species of flora and fauna are lost every hour in the world due to environmental destruction.

4. **Waste generation and disposal**: The EU is a major generator of waste, both household and industrial. This ranges from waste products to non-biodegradable packaging, scrap to domestic refuse. In the past this has been disposed of by the use of landfill sites, incineration, sewage treatment, or at worst discharge untreated into the North and Irish Seas, the Mediterranean and Aegean and into rivers such as the Rhine. Not only has this led to seas unfit to bathe in, but also to the death of marine life including fish, one of the EU's major food sources. As landfill sites are used up the EU will have to find new ways to dispose of its growing mountains and lakes of waste.

CASE STUDY   Air Pollution in the UK

In 1997, pressure group Friends of the Earth published a report showing that air pollution reaches levels harmful to health every five days in the UK. Ozone levels and particulates, which contribute to lung and heart disease and worsen asthma for the UK's 3.5 million sufferers, frequently exceed standards in the government's national air quality strategy. Particulates are minuscule flecks of soot coated with petroleum-based chemicals such as benzene. These enter deep into the lungs and, it is estimated, cause the UK 10 000 premature deaths each year.

   The worst place in the UK for ozone levels in 1996 was in Lullington Heath in East Sussex with a total of 55 days when standards were exceeded, while the worst for particulates was Port Talbot, South Wales and Leeds city centre, each with more than 40 days.

Table 11.1 shows the per capita emissions of pollutants for EU countries in 1993–95.

The most important aspect of all this is that pollution and waste from present production and consumption is passed on to future generations through polluted seas and air, a thinner ozone layer and depleted resources.

■ 11.3 EU environmental policies

■ The 1970s and 1980s

Following the 1972 Paris summit, the first EC environmental action programme (EAP) was implemented in 1973 and followed by a second programme in 1977. In both programmes the emphasis was largely reactive to problems which already

Table 11.1 Per capita emissions by EU countries, 1993–95

COUNTRY	CARBON DIOXIDE EMISSIONS	SULPHUR DIOXIDE EMISSIONS	NITROUS EMISSIONS	MUNICIPAL WASTE (IN TONNES)
Austria	7.1	8	22*	556
Belgium	11.0	25*	35*	343**
Denmark	11.5	30*	53*	521*
Finland	11.1	22	54	414*
France	6.0	18*	26*	360**
Germany	10.4	37*	27*	333**
Greece	7.5	. . .	15**	296**
Ireland	8.9	50**	. . .	312**
Italy	7.1	34**	35**	471
Luxembourg	21.4	26**	. . .	536
Netherlands	11.1	10	35	598*
Portugal	4.1	26*	26*	257**
Spain	6.1	53**	31**	381
Sweden	6.1	11	45*	364*
UK	9.1	40	39*	348**

Notes:
(i)   * 1994
      ** 1993
      Other figures, 1995. Where data is missing it is not available.
(ii)   Carbon dioxide emissions from fossil fuel – measured in tonnes.
(iii) Sulphur dioxide emissions from all sources – measured in kilograms.
(iv)   Nitrous dioxide emissions from all sources – measured in kilograms.
(v)   Municipal waste – kilograms per inhabitant.

Sources: Eurostat, *Yearbook, 1997; Environment Statistics Yearbook, 1996,* European Commission.

existed. The third EAP of 1983 saw a change of approach with emphasis on the need to prevent problems before they occur. It also stressed the constraints imposed on future economic and social growth by finite resources and the need for future EC policies to have an environmental dimension.

CASE STUDY   The Threat to the Coto de Doñana National Park, SW Spain

In April 1998, Europe's most important wetland breeding ground for birds and its biggest natural park was threatened when, following a dam breach, five million cubic metres of toxic mining waste water escaped from a reservoir at a mine on the River Guadiamar. The mine produces zinc, lead, copper and silver.

Doñana was declared a UN World Heritage site in 1994. It covers 579 sq miles of natural beauty and has 125 different bird species including some of the few remaining Spanish imperial eagles, and other birds very rare in the rest of Europe. It is also a stop-over point for more than one million birds migrating from northern Europe every winter. The river Guadiamar feeds huge areas of the marshlands of the Coto de Doñana national park before it joins the river Guadalquivir near its estuary. Its sediments support large numbers of small fish and other creatures which are food for the birds; however, these sediments are extremely vulnerable to toxic wastes which could result in long-term damage to the environment and hence food supplies and the very existence of many of these birds.

The Spanish authorities diverted much of the waste water into canals around the park and then into the river Guadalquivir in the hope that the waters of the river would dilute the waste and flush it into the ocean, although, at the time of writing, this did not prove very successful. Subsequent assessment found that very severe damage had been done. The park is also under constant threat from modern agriculture, tourism and industry.

Where it was weak was in terms of treating each sector – for example air, water, land – separately rather than pursuing an integrated policy. There was also a failure to recognise fully that pollution will harm countries not generating it – hence any environmental policy needed to be EC-wide.

However, the Single European Act 1987, in introducing amendments to the Treaty of Rome, extended the proposals of the third EAP. In particular there was concern that if the economic growth forecast by the Cecchini Report was to materialise, then the environmental effects of this would be substantial. Consequently a.100A and a.130R, S and T were incorporated into the Treaty of Rome to protect the quality of the EC environment, health and resources, to stress the principle that 'the polluter pays' and to ensure that EC-wide measures were adopted since, if barriers to intra-EU trade were to be removed, EU-wide environmental policies should logically be introduced. This would also prevent the emergence of environmental standards imposed by some countries which might act as new non-tariff barriers (NTBs) to countries with lower environmental standards, and hence limit the benefits to be derived from the internal market.

The Single European Act also embodied, through its reforms of the Treaty of Rome, the principle that in future every piece of EU legislation would need, where feasible, to have an environmental aspect. In particular this means considering the effects on the environment of this legislation and whether it might incorporate aspects to promote EU environmental policy.

■ EU environmental policies in the 1990s

The reforms introduced in the Single European Act were strengthened through the Treaty of Maastricht which emphasised the aim of integrating a green dimension into all areas of EU policy. This has been reinforced by the Commission's emphasis in its fifth EAP (1993–2000) on the need for an integrated pollution prevention and control (IPPC) approach to air, water and land, rather than treating them separately as in the 1970s and 1980s. Most recently the Commission put forward a proposal in June 1998 to integrate environmental factors into all EU policies.

Since the 1987 Brundland Report of the World Commission on the Environment and Development, and especially since the 1992 Earth Summit in Rio de Janeiro, however, EU policy has changed in terms of its nature, direction and approach. The adoption of the fifth EAP has seen a proactive focus, seeking to prevent problems occurring at the potential source of pollution as much as to redress problems already existing. Specifically emphasis has been placed on:

1. Managing future EU economic and social growth so that it is sustainable (known as sustainable development), that is without depleting scarce non-renewable resources further. This encompasses producing to market demand rather than in anticipation of possible demand (compare this with the ideas of TQM), introducing more efficient and less wasteful and waste-creating production processes (hence minimising production costs), and where possible recycling previously used materials and excess production. These new production processes are known as Best Available Techniques (BAT). It also includes educating consumers away from the idea of the 'throwaway society' where consumer goods are replaced rather than repaired when they break down, and persuading producers to make more durable goods.
2. Establishing minimum environmental standards for business and society. In particular emphasis has been placed on:

   - **businesses** – with the development of green economics. This encompasses the use of state-of-the-art technology to permit cleaner production, and the integration of environmental costs and risks into all production estimates.
   - **energy creation and use** – particularly renewable and non-polluting sources such as hydro-electric power, wind power and solar power.
   - **transport** – the need to shift from private to public ownership of transport services to reduce congestion and carbon dioxide emissions. Yet roads are essential to link the separate regions of the EU and as a generator of wealth through industrial location and the multiplier effects of the road building investment – so a balance has to be struck.
   - **agriculture** – with the harmful effects of chemical fertilisers and pesticides on the environment and EU citizens, and the waste of overproduction of crops.

- **tourism** – with a need to address the dichotomy between the harmful environmental effects of mass tourism yet its economic benefits to the receiving regions. This explains growing research into sustainable tourism.
- **the urban environment** – since cities and towns are the greatest consumers of resources and the greatest polluters
- **waste management** – both in terms of recycling waste and in terms of minimising waste generation. Where waste has to be disposed of then more environmentally-friendly methods need to be found. This is nowhere more important than in the decommissioning of old nuclear power stations.

3. Creating a partnership between the EU, national governments (particularly in the light of subsidiarity), European business and consumers to develop these policies.

The Amsterdam European Council meeting, June 1997, ratified as the Treaty of Amsterdam in December 1998, although not producing anything radically new reinforced the above. It urged that the Rio process initiated at the 1992 summit be speeded up to reach a point whereby worldwide economic development is sustainable, and argued for the coordination and integration of economic, social and environmental policies to eliminate poverty and change consumption and production patterns. It also supported a strong response to the risks of climatic change and strengthened treaty provisions on the environment.

Also in June 1997, Commission President Jacques Santer launched the 32-nation pan-European Consultative Forum on the Environment and Sustainable Development. He argued that Europe must take a political lead to promote sustainable development at a global level and said that the Commission would give a new stimulus to integrating economic, social and environmental objectives in Europe. This has been reinforced by an ECU 1.8bn fund, established by the European Commission and the European Investment Fund, to enable small and medium-sized enterprises (SMEs) with less than 100 employers and especially less than 50 to obtain loans for environmental purposes of up to 50 per cent of the cost. Projects for funding can include ways to save energy, pollution reduction or prevention, and ways to make goods and services more environmentally friendly. As discussed elsewhere SMEs are major employers and perceived by the Commission as an important source of future economic growth and job creation. However, as they are seen as higher risk by banks it is more difficult for them to obtain loans.

In parallel with the above, June 1997 also saw the second Earth Summit in New York, a follow-up to the Rio summit of 1992, which sought to assess progress in sustainable development during the last five years. The general assessment has been that the world's main industrialised nations have failed substantially to honour the commitments of the Rio summit – the so-called Agenda 21 – specifically with failure to:

- Increase aid to help developing countries fight poverty (with the environmental side-effects of increasing population and poor use of natural resources) – the developed nations agreed to provide aid to 0.7 per cent of their GDP, but in practice it has fallen.
- Combat deforestation (which has increased) and desertification.

- Reduce carbon dioxide levels to those of 1990 by the year 2000. There has also been a subsequent failure by leading nations to agree on new targets for carbon dioxide reductions, with the US and Japan refusing to accept EU proposals to cut carbon dioxide by 15 per cent compared with their 1990 level, by 2010.
- Reduce the use of subsidies and tax regimes to promote the wasteful use of resources (over two-thirds of which are provided by developed nations). The main success of Rio has been the greater involvement of non-governmental organisations (NGOs), for example in promoting sustainable forestry.

The outcome of the New York summit was essentially a reaffirmation of the environmental goals set by Rio, while at Kyoto the US also promised a strong commitment to binding limits on greenhouse gas emissions.

The First Conference of the parties to the climate change convention – also known as the Kyoto Conference – was held in Japan in December 1997 to introduce legally binding targets for emissions of greenhouse gases. One main outcome was an agreement by the US and the EU to reach a compromise on stabilising greenhouse gas emissions through agreeing a 7 per cent cut from 1990 levels by 2010, as against the original EU proposal of 15 per cent. The conference also proposed that industrialised nations, and developing nations which undertake voluntary restraints, be allowed to buy and sell fixed amounts of greenhouse gas pollution – the exact details to be determined subsequently. More efficient countries which can cut pollution quickly will be able to sell the part of their pollution permits they don't use to less efficient ones – who, effectively, will be able to buy time to control their greenhouse gas emissions by employing the unused part of the quotas of the more efficient countries – for a price. Countries who exceed their limits – allocated and purchased – will be fined. There were also proposals to increase the amount of trees that remove from the air carbon dioxide pollution caused by transport and industry.

■ Other recent EU initiatives

These have included:

- The provision of ECU 13.4m to protect EU forests against pollution and fires, the EU having monitored forest health since 1987. This is important due to the declining health of European forests as measured by leaf or needle loss. Less than 50 per cent of broad leaf trees sampled were undamaged, a 1997 survey found, while 42 per cent of forest soils sampled were very acidic or had low levels of base saturation. This means that further acidification could cause serious damage to tree roots.
- The Life II programme to protect the environment, co-financed by the Commission and totalling ECU 90.2m (£57m) for 1997. This covers such issues as waste and water for industry; planning and water for local authorities; the conservation of natural habitats for wild flowers and fauna, and establishing a European network of protected areas.
- A draft directive imposing tighter limits on four types of air pollutants – sulphur dioxide, nitrogen dioxide, lead and particulates – based on 1996 World Health Organisation (WHO) guidelines. This is to include monitoring and public information. In the case of carbon dioxide this has been extended to a policy to halve projected growth. Based on agreement at Kyoto, this is by means of action to improve the fuel economy of automobiles; progress on fair and efficient transport pricing; completion of the internal

market in rail transport; and methods to better integrate freight and passenger transport into intermodal systems. Without coordinated action carbon dioxide emissions are expected to increase from 26 to 40 per cent of all emissions by 2010.

- Legal action by the Commission against 13 member states in October 1997 for failing to produce waste management plans, and against 10 EU countries for failing to produce lists of natural habitat sites.
- A directive for the mandatory labelling of genetically modified products.

CASE STUDY   The Destruction of European Forests

A survey published in late 1997 by the World-Wide Fund for Nature (WWF) found that 62 per cent of Europe's original forest has been lost while, for the UK the figure is 97 per cent. 98 per cent of Europe's remaining forests are unprotected and at risk from overgrazing, pollution – especially acid rain, and from clearance to make room for housing, industrial development and roads. Also, there is insufficient new planting of broadleaf trees such as the oak, and too much planting of fast-growing conifers, not indigenous to areas, for timber. The WWF has called on European governments to follow the example of the Finnish government which has used £530m to buy and protect valuable old growth forests.

■ How to achieve environmentally friendly policies

A number of proposals have been advanced by the EU to tackle the problems posed by environmental degradation. These involve the use of both incentives and disincentives to promote environmentally friendly actions.

□ 1 Incentives

These seek to reward businesses and consumers for the adoption of environmentally friendly practices and can include:

- Tax concessions for green production processes and goods. In late 1997 the Commission proposed that some countries which export to the EU and receive trade concessions under the generalised system of preferences (GSP) could receive further tariff reductions on their exports if they implemented internationally agreed standards on labour and environmental protection
- Financial support to promote research and development into environmentally-friendly goods and production such as renewable energy sources (RES).

  A white paper, published by the Commission in December 1997, proposed a strategy to promote the use of renewable energy sources (RES). It argues that for the period 1997–2010 the strategy could save ECU 21bn in fuel costs, create a significant number of jobs, and reduce fuel imports by 17.4 per cent, based on net investment of ECU 95bn. This would cut carbon dioxide emissions by 402m tonnes a year by 2010 and provide economic opportunities through the growth of the renewable technologies industry – including solar cells, decentralised village electricity systems, biomass power stations and windfarms.
- Campaigns to promote public awareness of global warming; for example encouraging the reduction of domestic heating levels in winter.

- Financial grants to promote the increased use of effective house insulation materials, solar energy panels and so on.
- Funds channelled to the peripheral regions of the EU, particularly Eire, Greece, Portugal and Spain, via the European Social Fund, the European Agricultural Guidance and Guarantee Fund (EAGGF), the European Regional Development Fund (ERDF) and the Cohesion Fund. This is because the poorest regions are usually those which have the worst environmental record. Although not yet EU members, the evidence from CEEC demonstrates this most clearly. Since 1984 the European Investment Bank (EIB) has also lent funds for environmental investment purposes.
- Training programmes to change the culture of energy consumers by creating an EU-wide awareness of the need for using renewable energy sources as an alternative to non-renewable sources such as oil, coal and gas.
- The launch in July 1993 of the 'eco-label' by the Commission to enable manufacturers to apply for accreditation. The award of the label to their products (except food, drink and pharmaceuticals) identifies the products as environmentally friendly in their usage. Its initial application was to washing machines and dishwashers, but as standards are determined for each product group other manufacturers may apply to use this. Currently over 160 products have the eco-label including, as well as washing machines, paint, toilet paper, laundry detergent and bed linen. Refrigerators are expected to be the next products to be covered by the scheme.

☐ 2 Disincentives

The EU has accepted the principle that 'the polluter pays' – in other words whoever causes pollution or other adverse environmental effects should bear the costs of it. This applies both to businesses which generate pollution in producing goods and services and consumers for example in using cars. This has been reinforced recently by the introduction of civil liability for those responsible for creating waste. Disincentives include:

- The use of EU directives to prevent polluting activities or improve the environment. The most famous is probably that concerning the cleanliness of coastal bathing waters, with the ability to fly a blue flag awarded to those beaches which meet specified standards. These directives have to be passed by national governments then implemented; however, the European Court of Justice can take action against governments who fail to meet these standards.

  However directives are increasingly perceived not to be the most effective way to achieve pollution control in future and much more emphasis is now being placed upon the idea of civil liability for damage to the environment.

CASE STUDY   Keeping EU Coastal Waters Clean

The most recent report on EU coastal bathing waters, published in May 1998, found that they hardly improved between 1996–97. 93 per cent met minimum standards, but only 83 per cent met the more stringent guide values of the bathing water directive. The UK fell below these levels on both counts with values of 88.3 per cent and 43.4 per cent respectively. For EU freshwater, 60 per cent met the basic standards and 60 per cent the guide values.

- Eco-taxes: such as the EU proposal, at the 2nd Earth Summit, Rio de Janeiro, June 1997, for a tax on aviation fuel to recognise the pollution caused by civil aircraft. This is an example of making the polluter pay. Another example floated by the EU in the mid-1990s was for a carbon or energy tax on oil equivalent to $10 per barrel by 2000 to reduce carbon dioxide emissions by energy users and to encourage greater energy efficiency. If implemented it was believed that it would deter car and other road users and encourage a move to rail transport or other power modes, for example electrically powered cars. However, consumer surveys have found that motorists value their car usage very highly and are willing to pay very high fuel prices to be able to continue using them. UK government policies of raising fuel prices by 5 per cent above the rate of inflation each year have had little effect on the use of automobiles in the UK.

    Those supporting eco-taxes argue that businesses will also find it financially beneficial to adopt cleaner production methods. A tax is necessary because the price of crude oil is low in real terms so there no incentive by users to switch to other energy sources. Renewable and non-polluting energy sources would be exempted. The eco-tax is an example of the green accounting policies being developed by the EU as part of the process of getting users to pay the real cost of environmental damage. Road tolls either in the form of toll barriers or electronic metering of cars is another option.

    The main problem with the principle of making the polluter pay is in terms of measuring the cost of environmental damage – pricing environmental values can be very difficult. For resource consumption, for example, the problem is to determine which part of social costs are private costs and which part are external; this in turn will impact upon cost–benefit calculations for new environmentally-friendly investments. More useful is internalisation of the effects of the pollution, not just by raising the business's costs but also by requiring the polluter to reduce the amount of the pollution, and subsequently to prevent it, for example by legislation.

- National legislation to ban cars from city centres when air quality falls below a certain level. Rationing has been used in Athens with cars with odd numbered plates allowed in on one day and even numbered plates the next.

- The use of the Environmental Impact Assessment Directive (1988) requiring environmentally sensitive projects such as proposed oil refineries to be subject to an impact assessment to determine their effect on the environment, and how harmful effects might be minimised.

- The use of a voluntary eco-audit or environmental audits of existing businesses to reassure all interested parties as to the greenness of the organisation; for example the workforce, shareholders, customers, and so on. This is discussed in more detail below.

- Tradeable permits such as are used in California. Companies buy a permit to create a maximum amount of actual or potential pollution each year as part of their production processes (the allowable limits are lowered over time). A firm which does not reach the limit of its allowable pollution may sell the remainder to another firm which has exceeded its limit. In this way the polluter clearly pays while the revenue can be used to promote clean technology. (See also the previous case study relating to this.)

■ 11.4 How European businesses might become greener

In both EU and OECD countries there is clearly considerable pressure for businesses to adopt strategies which incorporate and implement an environmental dimension. For this to succeed it cannot merely be added in as an extra, to be considered after other issues; rather it must encompass all aspects of the business's operations and indeed underpin and drive them. Hence it needs to be a fundamental part of the business's strategy.

In this section it is not possible to discuss such strategies in any detail. A brief overview of the main areas which a business's green strategy needs to focus on will therefore be given. Then greater consideration will be given to three aspects of these, the environmental impact analysis (EIA), the relationship of management methods such as total quality management (TQM) and just-in-time (JIT) systems to the environmental strategy, and the use of the environmental audit. The reader is directed to the suggested reading at the end of the chapter if s/he wishes to pursue this subject further.

■ Why adopt a green strategy?

It has been seen above that the EU can pursue both a carrot and a stick approach to implementing green policies directed towards European business. For the businesses themselves there is a considerable advantage in pursuing a voluntary or self-regulatory strategy for a number of reasons:

1. if a business fails to do anything to make its operations more environmentally friendly then its national government or the EU will increasingly put pressure on it to do so.
2. Consumers are very much more environmentally concerned than say five years ago; the ability to demonstrate green production and management processes, recycling of packaging, minimisation of waste, reduced pollution and the ability to use the eco-label will give a competitive advantage to those businesses which have adopted environmentally friendly strategies.
3. The reader will recall that a major benefit of total quality management (TQM) and JIT was minimisation of waste and hence cost-savings. An environmentally friendly policy reinforces this strategy since conservation of scarce non-renewable resources is at the heart of its philosophy, for example through savings on raw materials, less use of energy, and reduced costs of having to treat polluted water (since it is no longer polluted).
4. Most importantly for European business is the need to see an effect on its profitability. The use of disincentives to pollute is one way to impact upon profitability.
5. The growing demand for environmentally friendly production means that growth prospects and opportunities exist for selling green machinery and production methods to other producers across the world
6. There is also an ethical dimension. Businesses are run by people for the ultimate benefit of people even if that is not always immediately obvious. The management and the workforce of any business want to work and live in a clean safe environment and for their children to have the same opportunity. There is therefore an incentive as human beings to develop environmentally sound production and management processes and strategies.

■ How to adopt a green strategy

In Chapter 8 the importance of a business adopting a proactive strategy was discussed. This applies equally to a business adopting an environmentally friendly business strategy. A number of separate points might be considered:

1. By being positive and proactive a business can set its own agenda rather than having to react to environmental production methods and corporate strategies implemented by its competitors. If it lags behind its competitors the danger of loss of market share is real.
2. If a business is not sure how it rates regarding its environmental position it can first undertake an audit or environmental challenge scan. This involves testing itself against a number of criteria including the extent to which recyclable or renewable resources are used as production inputs, the extent to which pollution and waste are minimised in production, the extent of its R&D and investment in new environmentally-friendly processes and plant, and the willingness and capability of staff to adapt to green production methods.
3. Subsequently a business can undertake an in-depth environmental SWOT analysis of the opportunities and threats confronting it externally, and the strengths and weaknesses internally as it seeks to meet these. For example it might have:

Environmental opportunities:
- the option to adopt new more efficient production methods;
- the opportunity to move into new green products;
- the chance to change the image and marketing of the business and its products.

Environmental threats:
- the challenge from competitors already implementing green policies;
- the impending introduction of government anti-pollution legislation;
- the cost of implementing these changes.

Environmental strengths:
- environmentally committed management team;
- desire to reduce production costs/increase productivity makes environmental policies more attractive;
- existence of a TQM system which can be used in environmental management.

Environmental weaknesses:
- organisational structure of the business makes integration of green policies difficult;
- cost and time of educating the workforce regarding their role in operating environmentally friendly policies;
- research and development programmes have not considered environmental aspects in the past – time will be needed to turn these around.

4. The adoption of a green business plan is necessary to implement medium to long-term strategies formulated by the business to make it greener. This will need firstly to consider the corporate personality of the business in terms of adaptability to change. This is indicated above in the SWOT analysis. It will need to include an action plan with specific points identified, who is responsible for their implementation, and by when. To be effective such strategies will need to be a part of all aspects of the business's operations including:

Inputs   using only environmentally friendly/renewable raw materials; where resources are non-renewable these should be used sparingly.

Production   using processes which minimise waste, energy consumption and emissions while offering high health and safety standards for the workforce. Linked to this needs to be an environmental information system, providing information holistically; that is, integrated across the whole business rather than in separate discrete components, which prevent a complete picture.

Output   goods are produced which are neither harmful to use nor will subsequently cause environmental harm when discarded or when their life expires; for example glass bottles which can be recycled rather than plastic bottles which cannot. This applies equally to the packaging into which products are placed, which can be manufactured from recycled materials.

The environmental impact of each product can be monitored by a Product Impact Assessment (PIA) which monitors the social costs and benefits of the product at each stage of its life cycle.

Human resource management   involving workers in the greening of the business at all stages and levels, for example by using the TQM approach of suggestion boxes and environmental quality circles; appointing environmental managers with sole responsibility for implementing the business's environmental policies.

Research and development   of new products which are environmentally sound.

Investment strategies   in best available technology (BAT).

Distribution   using rail rather than road as far as possible, or vehicles with catalytic converters and unleaded fuel.

Marketing   promoting the message of the green conversion through enhanced consumer awareness. This should be extended to the entire marketing mix.

After-sales service   recovering old goods which would cause environmental harm if discarded in rubbish tips, or at least advising consumers how to dispose of them harmlessly.

Monitoring and controlling progress at all stages of the conversion and operation to ensure environmental targets are being met within economic and technological constraints – for example the adoption of green accounting methods to assess the external costs of production as well as the private costs, and also the external benefits of the business's activities. The production of an eco-balance sheet will permit transparency so that people inside and outside the business can see its true costs and benefits.

(Source: ICC, *Business Charter for Sustainable Development Principles*, November 1990)

Most important is the need to be preventative rather than merely to address issues once the pollution has already occurred.

◼ The environmental impact assessment (EIA)

This is an appraisal process or analysis (hence EIA is used for environmental impact analysis or assessment) which enables management to make more informed decisions as to the economic and environmental feasibility of a proposed new investment project. It seeks to identify all the environmental effects of any new investment. To be fully effective it should cover all the stages of a proposed investment project, that is:

1. Development of alternative proposals.
2. Submission of information on the proposals to directors of the business.
3. Appraisal of alternatives.
4. Selection of optimum project.
5. Construction of plant.
6. Operation of production facility.
7. Closure through physical or technological obsolescence.

The European Union's EIA Directive of 1988 required an assessment to be undertaken for all environmentally sensitive investments such as oil refineries and major road programmes. If and when this is extended to all investments undertaken by businesses and by the public sector it will enable a truer picture of the social costs of the project to be obtained and hence a more accurate decision as to whether it should be undertaken; for example costs and means of disposing of extra waste generated by the production process, environmental degradation through destruction of flora and fauna, and so on.

Proposed projects should consider, as part of this, the ecological characteristics of any buildings in terms of energy consumption such as heating, lighting and air conditioning; integration into the surrounding landscape, for example destruction of badger setts to provide a tarmac car park; pleasant working conditions avoiding sick-building syndrome; and avoidance of greenfield site development.

To ensure that the maximum relevant information is obtained, all parties affected in any way by the project must be consulted. This should include pressure groups such as Greenpeace or Friends of the Earth who may oppose a project. The EIA may also include remedies to offset the effects of any environmental impact, for example the erection of noise-reduction barriers along the side of motorways to limit noise for nearby residents. An EIA can be expensive both financially and in terms of time, but it does enable all interested parties to have their say and it does take account of the social costs often neglected in decisions made in the past.

■ The role of TQM and JIT in environmental management

In Chapter 9 it was seen how the adoption of TQM by a business sought high-quality production to reduce costs by preventing faults arising, rather than addressing them after their occurrence. In the same way the JIT method of stock control seeks to minimise holding and opportunities costs by keeping the lowest level of stocks possible. Environmental business management parallels this closely since, by minimising waste, it creates environmentally friendly policies. It builds on existing quality control and quality assurance programmes which are part of the TQM philosophy by giving responsibility for environmental issues to all members of the business.

■ The environmental audit

When a company is operating green policies integrated throughout its operations it needs to monitor closely their efficacy. This may be done through an environmental audit, employing internal staff and/or external consultants to consider both the performance of management and of the plant used; in that sense it is a logical follow on from the EIA discussed above. It is conventional to look at three distinct stages when undertaking an audit, and Figure 11.2 illustrates these.

□ 1 The pre-audit stage

At this stage the audit team meet to consider the remit they face, set objectives and how they might best implement it given time constraints, the need to

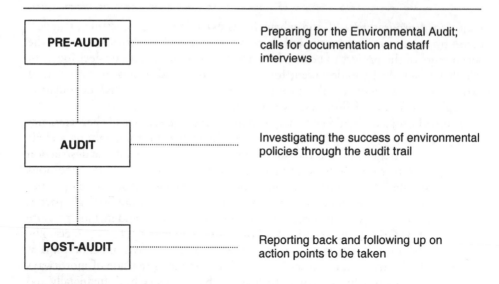

Figure 11.2 The Environmental Audit

interview staff who have ongoing work to do, and so on. In particular their task is to ensure that all key issues are addressed and that an effective assessment of the success or otherwise of the business's environmental strategies is undertaken. At this stage a call for documentation is made and persons to be interviewed are identified across as broad a sweep of the company as possible, that is from directors to workforce.

☐ 2 The audit

The audit team will now consult documentation such as internal policy documents, minutes of committees and so on which clearly identify:

- all stages of the policies to be implemented;
- when and how they were implemented; and
- if problems arise when and how these are addressed, and by whom.

Staff concerned will also be interviewed. The concept of the audit trail is very useful here. The auditors should, if environmental policies are being implemented effectively by the business, be able to pick on any issue – for example the discharge of waste products into the North Sea – and trace it through the documentation from its being a concept to becoming a policy, then its implementation, and then monitoring its effectiveness. This will also include, where a previous audit was undertaken, whether issues identified in that have actually been addressed, and to what effect.

☐ 3 The post-audit stage

The audit team will produce a report which will be read and discussed by relevant parties in the business. Where problems exist the task of the senior management will be to ensure that these are corrected as soon as possible. Strengths need to be identified and built upon. Overall, the effect of the audit should be to provide vital information to senior management and directors as to their success in implementing their environmental strategy so far. Using positive audit feedback can significantly enhance the business's environmental programme.

CASE STUDY   The Growth of Green Audits by UK Companies

The UK's largest companies have been taking environmental reporting increasingly seriously according to a 1997 survey by accountants KPMG. 79 per cent of the companies whose shares are quoted in the FT-SE 100 produce a separate environmental report (compared with 3 per cent in 1993), although only ten companies back their report with an external audit. For British companies overall (as opposed to the FT-SE 100), only 28 per cent were willing to produce separate environmental reports, compared with the US position of 43 per cent of companies.

Within particular industrial sectors, 75 per cent of chemical companies produced individual environmental reports compared with less than 15 per cent for the financial services, food and construction industries. However, KPMG report, only 15 companies set quantifiable targets of environmental standards and only 16 provided the results of previous environmental reports to allow shareholders to assess the progress the companies had made.

Shell, the Anglo-Dutch oil multinational, has opposed requests from some of its shareholders, including the church-based group, the Ecumenical Council for Corporate Responsibility, and Pirc, the pension fund consultancy and ethical lobby, for the identification of who is specifically responsible at board level for environmental issues, arguing that this is part of the chairman's general remit. It has also opposed demands for improving the monitoring of its environmental performance and an external audit of its environmental policies, although BP has an annual environmental audit undertaken by Ernst & Young, while Pirc argues this is best practice within the oil industry.

■ Conclusions

Progress has certainly been made in the greening of European business but there is still a long way to go. Periphery countries such as Spain, Portugal and Greece have made little progress while intermediate countries such as the UK and France have made some progress. The driving force has come from the more prosperous countries of Europe such as Germany and the Scandinavian nations. Not only do they have the wealth to develop new environmental processes and implement them; they have also suffered extensively from cross-border environmental pollution, particularly acid rain and so, more than others, have an incentive to take remedial action.

■ 11.5 The ethical European business

Ethics: Relating to morals, treating of moral questions; morally correct, honourable.

(The Concise Oxford Dictionary, OUP).

Business ethics reflects on the ethical issues and dilemmas for business people setting up transactions in the market place and communicating with government agencies and social interest groups.

(Harvey, van Luijk and Steinmann, 1994)

■ Examples of ethical issues in European business

In recent years the importance of business ethics has grown substantially, both as an area of academic study and as an area of legitimate concern for the stakeholders of businesses, both in the EU and internationally. By stakeholders is meant employees, directors, shareholders, customers, components and raw material suppliers, and so on in other words anyone with a stake in the business being considered. Examples of ethical issues in the marketplace can be clearly seen in many areas, including:

1. Environmental concerns regarding the emission of pollutants with their impact on the ozone layer, the use of non-renewable resources such as oil and coal, and the destruction of the environment through urban sprawl, use of chemical fertilisers and pesticides in farming.
2. The restructuring of industry with the delayering of levels of management, the replacement of assembly-line labour by robots, and the privatisation of industry with its subsequent reductions in labour.
3. Trading with repressive regimes where human rights are violated by the use of secret police and torture of dissidents. South Africa before 1993 is an example of this, and provoked trade, sporting and cultural boycotts by EU and other countries. In the same way the British bank Barclays encountered considerable pressure in the 1970s, and the loss of many accounts, due to opposition to its policy of investment in South Africa. Ethical or social investment is now an important issue.
4. The testing of cosmetics and other non-medical products on animals to assess whether they are harmful for human consumption. Some would argue that medical experimentation on animals to induce cancers, for example, is equally wrong.
5. Favourable treatment of businessmen in Russia enabling them to acquire large quantities of the shares of newly privatised businesses at low cost, in return for the political support they can give.

■ Why do ethical issues matter?

□ 1 Moral freedom

Ethical issues are important because, in a democratic society, we have the free choice to lead our lives as we wish subject to the constraints of laws provided by society, and reinforced by punishment if violated. For example, drink-driving is illegal in all EU countries, although the precise definition of how much one may drink before one's ability to drive becomes impaired will differ from country to country. The reason for drink-driving being illegal is obviously that this action may harm or kill oneself, other people, and/or cause damage to property. The ethical dimension is a person's reasoning that s/he will not drink and drive, not just because of legal penalties if caught, but because it is morally wrong *per se*.

Ethical issues concern us, therefore, because most people want to create and live in a fairer and more just society. As consumers of business outputs, as employees of businesses, as investors in businesses through the purchase of shares, there is an increasing perception of the need for a business to behave in an ethically correct manner. Where it fails to do so then it must answer for its actions – this is normally at annual general meetings of shareholders where pressure groups, owning a few shares, will ask directors to account ethically for their actions. As noted above, the board of directors of the Anglo-Dutch oil conglomerate Shell has been heavily criticised at AGMs for its refusal to allow external verification of its environmental policies.

In turn this means that businesses are now looking increasingly at the ethical dimension and implications of their corporate decisions, since adverse publicity can impact on them severely. This can be in a number of ways including affecting share value and hence willingness of institutional investors to hold their shares, consumer reaction against the products, and, in the worst case, the failure of the business.

□ 2 Corporate governance

Increasing emphasis has been placed in recent years on the concept of corporate governance. By this is meant how companies organise themselves, which covers issues such as the pay executives award each other; the structure of the board of directors, for example recruiting ex-politicians who are paid large sums for little input; violating government arms bans by selling to black-listed countries; and the growing concept of corporate responsibility to stakeholders (including customers and employees) rather than just shareholders.

Recent attention in the UK has focused on the 1995 DTI (Department of Trade and Industry) report into the commercial malpractice of BCGM (Barlow Clowes Gilt Managers) in the period to 1988, the findings of the 1992 Cadbury Committee on Corporate Governance, the 1995 Board of Banking Supervision's report into the Barings collapse, and the 1995 government-backed Greenbury Committee of Inquiry into boardroom pay. All of these have major ethical dimensions.

The Greenbury Committee on boardroom pay has not met with great success as top British companies have refused to comply with its key proposals, although most companies have adopted policies in keeping with the spirit of its recommendations. Greenbury required companies to disclose in their annual reports directors' base salaries in relation to the performance of their company. However, surveys have found that a majority have not done so. Nor have they placed a monetary value on incentives such as share options, while under half have replaced share option plans with other forms of long-term incentives. Also a majority of companies with directors' contracts of more than a year have not shortened them.

Most recently the 1996 Hampel Committee on Governance has extended the work of the Cadbury Committee, seeking to establish a framework within which companies can work for the next 20 years. Its specific remit was to review the implementation of both the Cadbury and Greenbury committees, look at the role of company directors, shareholders and auditors and deal with any other relevant matters. One aspect of this debate on corporate governance has been the problem of trying to balance accountability by the board of directors of a company to their stakeholders, and especially shareholders, with the need to encourage entrepreneurial drive (and hence provide directors with good incentives).

Similarly, Germany belatedly has been trying to address the problems of its opaque accounting system (balance sheets don't present a true financial picture of a company), low standards of company disclosure (until 1 January 1995 German companies only had to disclose shareholdings exceeding 25 per cent, as opposed to 3 per cent in the UK – this is now reduced to 5 per cent), and the outlawing of insider trading (taking advantage of privileged information to gain financial advantage, for example before a proposed takeover). German banks, for example, are now providing data about their financial performance which was never revealed before – such as their hidden reserves, the profitability of regional and divisional activities, and property asset values. Moves to international accounting standards (IAS) place greater attention on shareholder value – including better use of the banks' assets, closer attention to cost control, and an awareness of the need to earn better returns. They also help give shareholders a greater insight into financial performance as well as making it easier to raise money on international capital markets. IAS are also less conservative than the German system which is creditor oriented, and allow better comparison with foreign banks.

There have also been claims that a culture of corruption is flourishing in Germany; this has arisen because small-scale crimes such as tax evasion have become socially acceptable. More probably, however, the assertion that the growth of bribery and fraud are due to legislative laxity are nearer the truth – especially tax laws. As such, bribes are tax-deductible if paid outside Germany (before 1996 it also included bribes paid inside Germany), with German arms manufacturers, for example, allegedly writing off millions of deutschemarks as travel or marketing costs or exceptional items.

In France the 1995 Vienot Report on corporate governance recommended the abolition of cross-holdings where core shareholders held shares in many companies preventing them exercising their corporate functions properly as directors (Crédit Lyonnais is a classic example of this), and the appointment of at least two independent directors per company to improve corporate governance.

☐ 3 Government and EU responsibility

Additionally, national governments and European institutions also have an obligation to act ethically. Issues such as the 1995 French government resumption of nuclear weapons testing in the Pacific Ocean and its 1985 sinking of Greenpeace ship *Rainbow Warrior* with the death of a crew member, Norwegian killing of whales for allegedly 'scientific' purposes, Spanish overfishing in the seas around Europe with the use of illegal nets, and Turkish attacks on their Kurdish population are all decisions by European or near-European governments which have ethical dimensions as well as economic and/or political ones.

In the same way the massive defrauding of EU revenue through fraudulent claims, including under the Common Agricultural Policy, is an area for which the Commission has moral responsibility even though it (and the bulk of EU taxpayers) are the victims not the culprits.

■ 11.6 Models to be used to make ethical judgements

Since the legal system does not always cover ethical issues, then other frameworks for decision-making need to be used, the theoretical underpinning of which is usually philosophical. A number of alternative models are briefly reviewed here:

1. **The profit maximising model**   This model was advanced at the beginning of this text as the working hypothesis of the European business, that is to maximise profits. American economists, in particular Milton Friedman, have argued that increased profitability is the only responsibility of a business, including its social implications. This is perhaps not so surprising as the US is where capitalist principles are embodied more fully than almost anywhere else.
2. **The stakeholder model**   The stakeholder model of corporate social responsibility is the starting point advocated by many authors for businesses; that is, managers are responsible for considering the relative importance of different stakeholders' interests and balancing these against each other. The implication of this for corporate governance is that the business can no longer be seen just as a unit to generate profits and benefit shareholders; rather it impacts on many different people with whom it comes into contact, that is its stakeholders, and it has an obligation to these. The stakeholder model of ethical decision-making therefore takes into account the interests of all stakeholders when the ethical implications of business decisions are considered.

    How one attaches different weights or relative importance to each stakeholder's interests is a major problem, however. The model is also criticised on the grounds of lacking an ethical underpinning – that is, why the business should behave in a certain way.
3. **The Religious Model**   Some organisations have a religious underpinning which enables them to make ethical decisions. Islamic banks operating a policy of no interest charges on the grounds that this is usury is one example – instead lenders are entitled to a share of the profits or losses made by the borrower. Similarly, speculation and investment in businesses producing or distributing alcohol are banned. Although these

banks are mainly located in the Middle East, there are some in Europe, mainly in London. Businesses based in Salt Lake City, USA, and run by the Mormons are motivated by the Mormon faith. In the UK in the last century in Birmingham, a philanthropist named Joseph Rowntree built factories and a village where his workers could live, inspired by Christian principles. In Europe today the influence of the Catholic church, although not always explicitly stated, underpins the behaviour of some entrepreneurs in Italy, Spain, France and so on. In addition there is a Vatican bank. The main problems of this model is that different religions, of course, have different ethical frameworks as reference points, which other religions will not accept.

4. **Sternberg's ethical decision model**   Sternberg (1994) argues against the underlying premise of the stakeholder model. She says that it is not the responsibility of the business merely to balance competing claims of rival stakeholders – its function is 'to hold stakeholders to their proper corporate purposes' and to promote competitiveness in relation to other companies. Because business is a very narrow and precise activity, she argues that its aim is to maximise its financial value to its owners by the sale of its output over time. This is distinct from profits by its long-term nature, compared with the short-term nature of profits. The responsibility of stakeholders is to work to that objective. As can be seen, the Sternberg model is quite different to the stakeholders' model.

She advances a number of steps that may be distinguished in the form of a decision model enabling ethical issues to be addressed. This is by marshalling evidence and identifying which ethical principles apply to it. She argues that these steps are:

(i)   clarify the question;
(ii) determine its relevance for the business;
(iii) identify the peculiar constraints of the situation; and
(iv) assess the available options.

The option which most contributes to 'long-term owner value' and which satisfies 'distributive justice and ordinary decency' is the one to choose. The reader who wishes to pursue this further is recommended to the relevant text.

■ How might European businesses incorporate an ethical dimension into their strategy?

If a business intends genuinely to take account of the ethical dimension of its activities then it will need to incorporate this into its business plan. This means considering the ethical implications of any strategic, tactical or operational decision which it undertakes.

For example, moving a plant from high-cost Western Germany to lower-cost Poland has implications for Germans forced to relocate or who are made redundant, especially if the area where the plant is located is largely dependent on it as the main source of employment. The introduction of European works councils or equal treatment for part-time staff has ethical implications through the assumption that workers have the right to be informed of decisions made by businesses which affect their future, as well as a legal requirement. Similarly, the disposal of toxic waste in rivers, lakes and oceans has a moral dimension which polluting firms, by acting unethically, choose to ignore. The fact that they may able to pollute undetected is irrelevant.

If the stakeholder model is applied to the last case this means that the polluting firms must consider not just cost savings arising from illegal waste disposal, and hence greater profits for shareholders. It must also consider the implications for drinking water, the risk of greater incidence of cancers in this and the next generation, death of wildlife, and so on. After all, both current and future generations of humans are stakeholders in the business. If new ways to treat pollution impose higher costs on the business, resulting in job losses, then this aspect of the ethical problem must also be weighed. Of course, most importantly in this example, legal constraints on the business should prevent such pollution and hence prevent the ethical issue from arising in the first place.

CASE STUDY   Undertaking a Social Audit

Debate in the late 1990s has focused on the idea of businesses undertaking a social or stakeholder audit (comparable to the environmental audit discussed previously). Its purpose is to create voluntary standards for the acceptable and responsible social behaviour of businesses. Where businesses deviate from this standard the theory is that media will draw attention to them, generating pressure on such firms to improve their behaviour. It is also argued that businesses can benefit from social audits through achieving lower costs and improving future productivity. For example, this may be identifying future remedies and hence the resultant costs to combat pollution, or distinguishing poor treatment of local communities, or the working conditions and remuneration of employees in less-developed countries.

There are practical problems with a business conducting a social or stakeholder audit. These include narrowing the problem sufficiently to gain meaningful data, since it can be argued that a business affects every aspect of life. Also, in giving a company a rating there is a debate as to whether it should be on some absolute scale such as a percentage – say with anything over 80 being excellent; 60–80 good, and so on. Alternatives are to benchmark a business against some defined best practice; or against some average conduct by comparable companies producing similar products or services; or against its own defined corporate objectives. There is also a debate over whether the audit should be internal or external, or both. There is an argument that an internal audit provides the detailed knowledge which an external audit will not have, while the external audit provides a neutral unbiased dimension and an ability to compare with other organisations. The reader will recall that with the environmental audit Shell would not accept external verifiers. The UK business Body Shop International has undertaken several social audits of its activities, and has focused mainly on interviews with stakeholders to determine their perception of Body Shop's social behaviour.

Before social audits become widespread, however, there has to be agreement on the measures of social performance or the social impact of companies.

The problem in the first example is that of balancing the good of creating more jobs in Poland through the new factory against the loss of jobs in Western Germany, the impact on component suppliers, transport costs and attendant pollution if by road and so on. This is where the stakeholder model fails, since the relative importance of the benefits of the Polish gain against the losses for Germany cannot easily be determined.

Using the Sternberg ethical-decision model does facilitate decisions since if long-term owner-value would be increased by the relocation to Poland then this should, ethically, be the preferred path of action. The constraint of distributive justice is met since the new Polish employees are rewarded for their cheaper labour compared with Germany, while ordinary decency is not affected by a decision to relocate.

The interested reader may care also to consider the Donaldson (1989) social-contract model of ethical decision-making to compare it against the other two models outlined above.

■ Conclusions

Currently the ethical implications of European business is not a major item on the agenda of the EU. It has received much more attention in the US and, to a lesser extent, the UK, especially through the issue of corporate governance. Quite clearly, however, it is likely to play a much more significant role in future debate for two reasons: firstly, the increasing importance of environmental issues as discussed previously. Secondly, as privatisation is implemented more and more in different EU states, and as the completion of the single market gives more scope for firms to grow, these will raise ethical issues because of the changing nature of European business.

■ Review questions

1. Discuss why the European Union is seeking to adopt a more comprehensive environmental policy.
2. How might European businesses best respond to such initiatives?
3. Discuss critically the advantages and disadvantages to a European business of conducting an environmental audit.
4. Why should a European business take account of the ethical aspects of its strategy?
5. Using one of the ethical-judgement models discussed in this chapter argue for or against the payment of large bonuses and share options to senior management and directors of European businesses.

■ Bibliography

Commission of the European Communities, *The Week in Europe*, June 1992–August 1995, London.

Commission of the European Communities, *Protecting our Environment* (Luxembourg: Office for Official Publications of the European Communities, 1993).

Donaldson, T., *The Ethics of International Business* (New York: Oxford University Press, 1989).

Harvey, B. (ed.), *Business Ethics: A European Approach* (Hemel Hempstead: Prentice Hall, 1994).

Harvey, B., van Luijk, H. and Steinmann H., *European Casebook on Business Ethics* (Hemel Hempstead: Prentice Hall, 1994).

Hopfenbeck, W., *The Green Management Revolution: Lessons in Environmental Excellence* (Hemel Hempstead: Prentice Hall, 1993).

International Chamber of Commerce (ICC), *Business Charter for Sustainable Development Principles* (London: ICC, November 1990).

Jackson, P. M. and Price, C. M. (eds), *Privatisation and Regulation: A Review of the Issues* (Harlow: Longman, 1994).

Ledgerwood, G., Street, E. and Therivel, R., *The Environmental Audit and Business Strategy* (London: Financial Times/Pitman Publishing, 1993).

Mahoney, J., 'How to be Ethical: Ethics Resource Management', in Harvey, Brian (ed.) (1994), *op. cit.*

Moiran, M. and Prosser, T., *Privatisation and Regulatory Change in Europe* (Oxford: Oxford University Press, 1994).

North, K., *Environmental Business Management: An Introduction* (Geneva: International Labour Office, 1992).

Sternberg, E., *Just Business: Business Ethics* (London: Warner Books, 1994).

Also:

The Economist
The European
The Financial Times
The Independent
The Times
The European Environment Agency website: http://www.eea.eu.int

Index